From Scarcity to Visibility

Gender Differences in the Careers of Doctoral Scientists and Engineers

J. Scott Long, *Editor*

Committee on Women in Science and Engineering

Panel for the Study of Gender Differences in the Career Outcomes of Science and Engineering Ph.D.s

Policy and Global Affairs
National Research Council

NATIONAL ACADEMY PRESS
Washington, D.C.

NATIONAL ACADEMY PRESS 2101 Constitution Avenue, N.W. Washington, D.C. 20418

NOTICE: The project that is the subject of this report was approved by the Governing Board of the National Research Council, whose members are drawn from the councils of the National Academy of Sciences, the National Academy of Engineering, and the Institute of Medicine. The members of the committee responsible for the report were chosen for their special competences and with regard for appropriate balance.

This study was supported by a grant between the National Academy of Sciences, the Andrew W. Mellon Foundation, and the National Institutes of Health (Contract No. DHHS P.O. 263-MD-423043). Any opinions, findings, conclusions, or recommendations expressed in this publication are those of the author(s) and do not necessarily reflect the views of the organizations or agencies that provided support for the project.

International Standard Book Number 0-309-05580-6
Library of Congress Catalog Card Number 2001086800

Additional copies of this report are available from National Academy Press, 2101 Constitution Avenue, N.W., Lockbox 285, Washington, D.C. 20055; (800) 624-6242 or (202) 334-3313 (in the Washington metropolitan area); Internet, http://www.nap.edu

Printed in the United States of America

THE NATIONAL ACADEMIES

National Academy of Sciences
National Academy of Engineering
Institute of Medicine
National Research Council

The **National Academy of Sciences** is a private, nonprofit, self-perpetuating society of distinguished scholars engaged in scientific and engineering research, dedicated to the furtherance of science and technology and to their use for the general welfare. Upon the authority of the charter granted to it by the Congress in 1863, the Academy has a mandate that requires it to advise the federal government on scientific and technical matters. Dr. Bruce M. Alberts is president of the National Academy of Sciences.

The **National Academy of Engineering** was established in 1964, under the charter of the National Academy of Sciences, as a parallel organization of outstanding engineers. It is autonomous in its administration and in the selection of its members, sharing with the National Academy of Sciences the responsibility for advising the federal government. The National Academy of Engineering also sponsors engineering programs aimed at meeting national needs, encourages education and research, and recognizes the superior achievements of engineers. Dr. Wm. A. Wulf is president of the National Academy of Engineering.

The **Institute of Medicine** was established in 1970 by the National Academy of Sciences to secure the services of eminent members of appropriate professions in the examination of policy matters pertaining to the health of the public. The Institute acts under the responsibility given to the National Academy of Sciences by its congressional charter to be an adviser to the federal government and, upon its own initiative, to identify issues of medical care, research, and education. Dr. Kenneth I. Shine is president of the Institute of Medicine.

The **National Research Council** was organized by the National Academy of Sciences in 1916 to associate the broad community of science and technology with the Academy's purposes of furthering knowledge and advising the federal government. Functioning in accordance with general policies determined by the Academy, the Council has become the principal operating agency of both the National Academy of Sciences and the National Academy of Engineering in providing services to the government, the public, and the scientific and engineering communities. The Council is administered jointly by both Academies and the Institute of Medicine. Dr. Bruce M. Alberts and Dr. Wm. A. Wulf are chairman and vice chairman, respectively, of the National Research Council.

PANEL FOR THE STUDY OF GENDER DIFFERENCES IN THE CAREER OUTCOMES OF SCIENCE AND ENGINEERING PH.D.S

J. Scott Long, *Chair*
Chancellors' Professor
Department of Sociology
Indiana University

Lilli S. Hornig
1 Little Pond Cove Road
Little Compton, RI 02837

Georgine M. Pion
Associate Professor
Vanderbilt Institute for Public Policy Studies
Vanderbilt University

Anne E. Preston
Professor
Department of Economics
Haverford College

Lee B. Sechrest
Professor
Department of Psychology
University of Arizona

OFFICE OF SCIENTIFIC AND ENGINEERING PERSONNEL ADVISORY COMMITTEE (through January 2001)

Claudia I. Mitchell-Kernan
Vice Chancellor of Academic Affairs and
Dean University of California

Michael T. Nettles
Professor of Education
University of Michigan

Debra W. Stewart
Vice Chancellor and Dean of the Graduate School
North Carolina State University

Tadataka Yamada
Chairman, Research and Development
SmithKline Beecham Pharmaceuticals

A. Thomas Young
Former President and Chief Operating Officer
Martin Marietta Corporation

Ex-officio Member

Robert C. Richardson
F. R. Newman Professor
Department of Physics
Cornell University

NRC Staff

Charlotte Kuh
Executive Director

Marilyn J. Baker
Associate Executive Director

COMMITTEE ON WOMEN IN SCIENCE AND ENGINEERING

Lilian Shiao-Yen Wu, *Chair*
Consultant to Corporate Technical Strategy Development
Thomas J. Watson Research Center, IBM Corporation

Uma Chowdry
Director, Business Planning and Technology
E.I. duPont de Nemours & Company

Ralph Cicerone
Chancellor
University of California, Irvine

Alice S. Huang
Senior Councilor for External Relations
California Institute of Technology

Kathryn O. Johnson
Owner/Principal
Johnson Environmental Concepts, Matrix Consulting Group

Willie Pearson
Professor of Sociology
Wake Forest University

William Phillips
Fellow, Atomic Physics Division
National Institute of Standards and Technology (NIST)

Darryll J. Pines
Associate Professor, Department of Aerospace Engineering
University of Maryland

Sue V. Rosser
Dean, Ivan Allen College
Georgia Institute of Technology

Sally Shaywitz
Professor of Pediatrics, School of Medicine
Yale University

Julia Weertman
Walter P. Murphy Professor Emerita,
Department of Materials Science and Engineering
Northwestern University

NRC Staff

Linda D. Skidmore
Director (to November 1997)

Jong-on Hahm
Director (April 1998-Present)

Preface and Acknowledgments

Issues of gender differences in science and engineering careers continue to merit discussion. In many fields of science and engineering, especially in the life and social sciences, the number of women receiving bachelor's degrees equals or exceeds the number of men. Yet it continues to be the case that women are underrepresented as professors and elsewhere in the upper echelons of science and engineering. Outside the life and social sciences, the proportions of women shrink, being smallest in engineering. A careful statistical study of these differences has not been conducted for almost twenty years, and many barriers to women in science and engineering have been lowered in that time. This study documents the changes that have occurred, both in the representation of women in science and engineering and in the characteristics of women scientists and engineers.

This report is the result of the labor of many hands in addition to the deliberations of the panel. The tireless efforts of Jim Voytuk were greatly appreciated. Charlotte Kuh served as a member of the Panel until she moved to the National Research Council. Her efforts, both administrative and substantive, were critical to the successful completion of this report. Early drafts were improved by the comments of Mary Frank Fox who served as a consultant to the Panel, and by the comments of Lowell Hargens, Patricia McManus, Sharon Harlan, Ed Hackett and Barbara Reskin. The panel is also grateful to the following members of the NRC staff who helped on this project as it moved from building useful data sets from the raw NSF data to completed analyses: Rink van der Have, Stephane Baldi, and Ramal Moonesinghe. Linda Skidmore served as the initial project officer.

This study would not have been possible without funding from the Andrew W. Mellon Foundation, National Institutes of Health, and the National Research Council.

The report has been reviewed in draft form by individuals chosen for their diverse perspectives and technical expertise, in accordance with procedures approved by the NRC's Report Review Committee. The purpose of this independent review is to provide candid and critical comments that will assist the institution in making its published reports as sound as possible and to ensure that the report meets institutional standards for objectivity, evidence, and responsiveness to the study charge. The review comments and draft manuscript remain confidential to protect the integrity of the deliberative process. We wish to thank the following individuals for their review of this report: Margaret Burbidge, University of California, San Diego; Uma Chowdhry, DuPont; Jonathan Cole, Columbia University; Daniel Hamermesh, University of Texas, Austin; Derek Neal, University of Wisconsin, Madison, and Gerhard Sonnert, Harvard University.

Although the reviewers listed above have provided many constructive comments and suggestions, they were not asked to endorse the conclusions or recommendations, nor did they see the final draft of the report before its release. The review of this report was overseen by Judith Liebman, University of Illinois Champaign. Appointed by the National Research Council, she was responsible for making certain that the independent examination of this report was carried out in accordance with institutional procedures and that all review comments were carefully considered. Responsibility for the final content of this report rest entirely with the authoring committee and the institution.

Finally, the panel would like to dedicate this report to the memory of Mary Ellen Jones, Betty Vetter and Robert McGinnis. Mary Ellen served as a helpful member of the Panel until her death. Betty's tireless work with the Scientific Manpower Commission (later renamed the Commission on Professionals in Science and Technology) kept a constant statistical eye on the status of women in science and engineering. Robert McGinnis was a pioneer in the sociology of science and scientific careers and an inspiration for scholars in the field.

J. Scott Long

Contents

List of Tables and Figures

FIGURES

TABLES

Executive Summary

Twenty-five years ago, women were barely represented among doctoral scientists and engineers. Tens of new women Ph.D.s graduated each year in fields such as engineering, physics, chemistry and mathematics, as compared to hundreds of men. Female undergraduates in science and engineering stood a very small chance of ever encountering a woman professor of any description. A similar scarcity existed in industry.

All that has changed. In 1995, women were 32 percent of new science and engineering Ph.D.s and over 30 percent of faculty in many fields. Although they are nowhere close to half of doctoral scientists in most fields, they are a visible presence in the science and engineering workforce. This report traces the change from scarcity to visible presence.

The world did not sit still as women increased their presence in science and engineering. The structure of a scientific career changed, and continues to change, even as women's presence has grown. The share of academic employment, once the predominant destination for new Ph.D.s, shrunk to less than half in most fields. As research funding grew in universities, so, too, did off-tenure track employment, a traditional employer for women in academia. Thus, although the representation of women expanded in all science and engineering fields, traditional measures of status, such as becoming a full professor in a research university, did not expand proportionately.

This report documents many dimensions of the changing representation of women in science and engineering. Using data from two NSF data bases—the Survey of Earned Doctorates for new Ph.D.s and the Survey of Doctoral Recipients for the S&E doctoral workforce—it brings together data on the educational background and demographic characteristics of three decades of new Ph.D.s and then examines their careers as described by the data.

Although the report refers to explanations for the observed changes that are found in the literature, the focus is on the analysis of a very rich data set, not on establishing the root causes that give rise to the observed outcomes. It is the hope of the committee that this report will provide a common basis for decisionmakers in academia, industry and government to discuss whether the differences in career outcomes for women scientists and engineers are a matter for concern. It can identify areas where differences are greatest or most intractable, but it is left to policymakers to discuss what steps should be taken to narrow differences further.

FINDINGS

Degree Attainment and Educational Background

1. From 1970 to 1995, there were significant advances in the entry of women into science and engineering. In the five broad fields considered (engineering, physical sciences, mathematical sciences, life sciences, and social/behavioral sciences) there were 350 percent more women among new Ph.D.s in 1995 than in 1973. In the social and behavioral sciences, women were just over half of the Ph.Ds in 1995 and in the life sciences they reached over 40 percent.

2. Despite these strides toward equal representation in science and engineering, women are not anywhere close to being equally represented in all science and engineering fields. In 1995 they were 18 percent of bachelor's degrees and 12 percent of Ph.D.s in engineering, compared to 50 percent and 40 percent , respectively, in the biological sciences.

3. The move toward equal representation in doctorate achievement in science and engineering has been accompanied by growing similarities among men and women in background characteristics, such as parental educational background, type of baccalaureate institution, ranking of Ph.D. program, time to degree, and type of funding of graduate education. However, women are still less likely to obtain undergraduate degrees from Ph.D. granting institutions and more likely to take longer from time of baccalaureate to Ph.D.

4. Differences remain in the ways that men and women fund their education making it more likely that men are launched into research careers. Men are more likely to receive funding through research assistantships. Women are more likely than men to fund their graduate work by holding teaching assistantships in the physical sciences, mathematical sciences, and engineering—fields in which they are least well represented.

5. Although the gender difference is narrowing, men are more likely than women to be married and to have children at the time they receive their Ph.D. Female Ph.D.s have children later in their career than do men.

The increasing similarity of men's and women's educational background and demographic characteristics point to eventually narrowing career outcomes. Women, however, are systematically different from men in labor force participation, full time status, and the effect of children on labor force participation. These differences have an effect on career outcomes.

Labor Force Outcomes

1. The share of women in the S&E Ph.D. labor force has grown steadily between 1973 (9 percent) and 1995 (21 percent). Comparable figures for full-time scientists and engineers are 6.5 percent and 20 percent, respectively.

2. There are broad differences in full time labor force representation across fields. Women made up almost a third of the social and behavioral science workforce in 1995. In engineering, they were only 5 percent. Their share was 10 percent and 11 percent in the physical sciences and mathematics, respectively. In the life sciences, women made up 26 percent of the doctoral workforce.

3. The age distribution of women in the workforce differs significantly from that of men. Almost 50 percent of women had less than 10 years of experience, as compared to 30 percent of men. This reflects the recent growth in female Ph.D.s, but it also means that men are more likely to have the years of experience that go along with high status in their field.

4. Doctoral women are less likely than men to be working full time in science or engineering. This difference has three components: full time work outside of S&E, part time work, and unemployment. Women are slightly more likely than men to work outside of science (2 percentage points) and considerably more likely to work part time (11 percent vs. 4 percent). Rates of unemployment have been low and declining over time for women in S&E, but the percentage of women who were unemployed and not seeking work rose from 3 percent to 4.6 percent between 1989 and

1995. For men, this rate was 0.3 percent and 1.0 percent for the two survey years. Taken together, these sources led to 17 percent of women who were not employed full time in S&E in 1995 compared to 6 percent for men, despite a marked decline in women's underemployment since 1973.

5. Marriage and family are the most important factors differentiating the labor force participation of male and female scientists and engineers. Single men and single women participate equally in the workforce. Marriage and children are associated with increased rates of full-time employment for men, but declining rates for women. The negative effect of marriage and young children has declined for women over time. As predicted by a statistical model, single women were over 30 percentage points more likely to be working full time compared to women with small children (91 percent vs. 61 percent). By 1995, this predicted rate for women with young children had increased to 71 percent and the gap had narrowed to 22 percentage points.

6. The impact of lower rates of labor force participation for women is that, at any point in her career, a woman on average has fewer years of work experience than a man who received his doctorate at the same time. The gap shrunk from 1979 to 1989, yet with 12 years of experience, the average woman had one year less of work experience than the average man (compared to 1.5 years less in 1979). The difference in work experience matters for career outcomes.

Sector of Employment and Primary Work Activity

1. Differences in the distribution of male and female scientists and engineers across sectors of employment shrunk between 1973 and 1995. In 1973, 8 percent of female scientists and engineers were employed in industry, while 26 percent of men were. In 1995, these percentages had risen to 26 and 37, respectively. The growth in the industry share came largely at the expense of academia, which employed 68 percent of women in 1973 and only 51 percent by 1995. For all fields, gender differences in distribution across sectors of employment narrowed or stayed essentially constant. By 1995, the largest differences in employment sector were in engineering, where 11 percent more men than women were employed in industry, and in the life sciences, where the gap was 7.5 percent.

2. Primary work activity varies by employment sector. In academia, teaching and research are the primary activities. In industry, management and applied research are. Both men and women in academia report a shift to research as a primary work activity over the 1973-95 period. In the physical and life sciences, proportionately more women were engaged in teaching. Social/behavioral science was the only broad field where men reported teaching as their primary activity in higher proportion than

women. In business, there has been a steady decline in the percent reporting management as their primary work activity, but men are more likely than women to be engaged in management in all fields. Women predominate in professional services in the social/behavioral sciences (probably as counseling psychologists) and in applied research in the physical sciences and engineering.

Regrettably, far less detailed data are collected about career paths in industry than in academia. We do know, however, that both men and women doctoral scientists and engineers have been shifting into jobs in industry rather than in academia and that there has been a narrowing in gender differences in sector of employment. Management is rarely a starting position for scientists and engineers in industry, so the continued dominance of men in management may reflect their greater seniority. Data do not permit us to learn if there is gender stratification within the general category of applied research. We do know far more about gradations in academia, and these findings are discussed below.

Academic Careers

The academic sector has a special importance in understanding differences in career outcomes for men and women in science and engineering. It is the sector where all Ph.D.s receive their initial training and, in most fields, it still employs the largest share of Ph.D.s. We look at the presence of women in academic science and engineering generally and then at differences among fields and types of institutions. Differences in career outcomes in what are called Research I Universities in the 1993 Carnegie classification of institutions of higher education are especially important in their dual role of employers and producers. Here we focus on their role as employers.

1. Women are a growing presence in academic employment in all fields. Between 1973 and 1995, their representation almost tripled from 8 percent to 23 percent of full-time academic employment, even as the share of the academic sector in Ph.D. employment shrank.

2. There is wide variation in the representation of women across fields. The life sciences and the social/behavioral sciences, which have shown the greatest increase of women among new Ph.D.s, have also seen the greatest increase in women's representation in academic positions. This creates a difficulty, however, because academia has experienced very little overall growth in recent years and it may be more difficult for women to attain senior faculty positions than it was for men in the 1970s and 1980s when academic positions were growing.

3. Men and women have become increasingly similar in their distribution among types of institutions. In 1973, the percentage of men in Research I institutions exceeded that of women by 11 percentage points. By 1995, this difference had shrunk to 5 points. Earlier, women were more concentrated in master's only and in baccalaureate institutions.

4. Although women are found in research universities in increasing numbers, those numbers are still low in the physical sciences and engineering. In 1995, they made up only 6 percent of the Research I academic workforce in engineering and only 11-12 percent in mathematics and the physical sciences. To the extent that increasing the numbers of the women in these fields requires women as role models, it will be far more difficult than in the life sciences and social/behavioral sciences, where women make up 26 percent and 37 percent, respectively.

5. When we look more closely at the types of academic positions women hold, the semblance of growing equality fades. Men continued to hold a 14 percentage point advantage over women in tenure track positions at a time when these positions were declining as a percentage of academic jobs. Through a logit analysis, we find that much of this difference is due to the lower career age of women, suggesting that women are quite likely to be increasingly well represented in these positions with the passage of time.

6. Career interruptions matter to the chance that a person will achieve tenure track status. Women with interruptions before receiving the Ph.D. are *more* likely to become faculty, while this variable has the opposite effect for men. Being married with young children had a large and negative effect for women in 1979, but that effect had disappeared by 1995. For men, the effect was positive and greater in 1995 than it had been in earlier survey years.

7. A close analysis of achieving tenure yields similar findings to the analysis of tenure track status. Adjusting for differences in the age structure for men and women, men are still more likely to be tenured than women at any professional age. Although these differences have declined over time, they persist, especially in research universities.

8. Some of the difference in women's status in academia can be explained by lower productivity, as measured by publications. It seems clear, however, that differences in the positions held by women are likely the cause of lesser productivity, rather than the other way around.

9. Finally, in all academic ranks and measures of status, women are least represented in Research I institutions. Both Research I and other institutions have increased the representation of women. Comparatively, however, the increases have been greater in non-Research I institutions.

Salary

To the extent that salary is a characteristic of rank and status, we would expect average salaries for female science and engineering Ph.D.s, who are on average younger and of lower rank than men, to be lower. Here, however, we control for a large number of differing characteristics of men and women, such as years of experience and field. Gender differences, although declining over time, persist even in the face of such adjustment. Specifically,

1. Overall, male doctoral scientists and engineers had about a 20 percent salary advantage over women, and this difference persisted between 1973 and 1995. Although sizeable, this gap is smaller than the gender gap in salaries for professionals and in the labor force generally.
2. Women's salaries reach a plateau when they achieve 20 years of experience, while men's continue to rise. This was the case in years preceding 1995, but does not necessarily predict what will happen to recent Ph.D.s as they gain experience. In fact, there is evidence that the salary gap had narrowed somewhat for recent cohorts as they entered mid-career.
3. There are significant salary differentials across fields, with salaries in engineering and mathematics being greater than those in the life and behavioral/social sciences—fields in which there are relatively more women. The same holds true for sector of employment: women are relatively more concentrated in academia, where the median salary is lower, than in industry, where more men are employed.
4. Regression analysis permits all the factors described above to be controlled for simultaneously. Doing so cuts the gender gap in salaries in 1995 from 21 percent to 6 percent with the biggest effects resulting from career age and field. The effect of these controls varies by survey year and is smallest in the early survey years, suggesting a greater degree of gender discrimination then.
5. Generally speaking, the more restricted the population, the smaller the gender gap in salaries. That is, the gap for all full professors (11 percent) is smaller than the gap for all tenure track faculty (20 percent) and even smaller when the comparison is made within field. It appears to be the case, however, that there are larger within-rank within-field gaps in Research I Universities.

CONCLUSION

This report presents an exhaustive analysis of the available data on men and women Ph.D. scientists and engineers from 1979 to 1995. During that period, the numbers of women grew in all fields, sectors of employment and faculty ranks. Regression analysis was used to identify statistically the independent effects of educational background, field choice, career and family experience on a variety of career outcomes for men and women. Disparities in those outcomes have narrowed over time, but they remain.

What the report has not done is to get behind the numbers. It has not systematically investigated the web of decisionmaking by those who have the power to influence careers. Both men and women encounter such guidance and gatekeeping at all stages of their careers in science. Equally important, it has not delved into the decisionmaking of the men and women themselves. It has not examined the complex calculus that men and women must conduct as they balance the pursuit of a scientific career with the often competing demands of marriage, children, and geographical location. We have observed only the outcomes. So far, these outcomes indicate that women, although they have made great progress toward equality in science and engineering in the past 25 years, are still more likely than their male counterparts to be in positions of lower status and lower pay. It is the hope of the Committee that the careful documentation of progress and stasis provided in this report will be of help to those who wish to see more equal use of talented women scientists and engineers to the benefit of science and engineering generally.

1

Introduction and Overview

Women in Science 1973-1995

Thus, within just a few years, starting in 1968 and essentially complete by 1972, there was a legal revolution in women's education and employment rights. It promised, even seemed to guarantee, broad ramifications for women's careers in science and engineering, but its full implementation would require many battles in the years ahead. One era had ended and a new, more equitable one was beginning.

— Margaret W. Rossiter, *Women Scientists in America,* 1995[1]

INTRODUCTION

By the early 1970s, significant changes had occurred in federal civil rights laws governing the treatment of women in higher education. Title IX of the Education Amendments of 1972 required institutions of higher education that received federal funding to treat women and men equally in admissions, funding, residency, and sports, thus eliminating overt discrimination. The Equal Employment Opportunity Act of 1972 specified that educational institutions must abide by equal employment opportunity laws, such as Title VII. The revolution in the laws governing women's education and employment rights grew out of the resurgence of the women's movement in the late 1960s and dramatic changes in our society's view of the role of women at home and in the workplace. The effects of these dramatic societal changes are reflected in the rapid and remarkable changes in the participation of women in higher education, with women accounting for a growing proportion of the enrollment in science and engineering programs.

[1]Rossiter (1995: 382).

Overall, since 1973 there have been impressive and promising changes in the entry into and participation of women in science and engineering. Many of these changes are documented in the pages that follow. *But while women have clearly made enormous gains in their participation in science and engineering, it is also clear that these advances represent neither unconditional success in overcoming gender inequalities nor assurance of continuing progress in the future.*

HISTORY OF THE REPORT

The National Research Council (NRC) has a long and distinguished record of involvement in activities designed to increase the participation of women in scientific and engineering careers. In 1981 the NRC's Committee on the Education and Employment of Women in Science and Education (CEEWISE) undertook a major study and published *Career Outcomes in a Matched Sample of Men and Women Ph.D.s: An Analytical Study* (Ahern and Scott 1981). The Ahern and Scott study, as the report came to be known, examined gender differences in the career paths of primarily academic scientists, engineers, and humanists employed between 1973 and 1979. As a portrait of women in science during the 1970s, the study provided definitive answers to several important questions. First, it found that women suffered disadvantages in career outcomes even after controlling for factors in the background of male and female scientists (e.g., prestige of the doctoral department, years of professional experience, and marital status) that might have caused the differences. Second, differences in career outcomes for several cohorts of scientists showed that gender inequalities were not all due to women being younger and thus more likely to be junior faculty rather than in senior positions. Finally, substantial variations across fields in how female scientists fared in academia were documented. The overall conclusion of the Ahern and Scott report confirmed the findings of many earlier studies (Ahern and Scott 1981: iv-v):

> . . . with male and female scientists and humanists closely matched by education, experience, type of employment, and even subfield in many cases, none of the differences we have previously noted in career progress disappear and few diminish. Women remain less likely to be employed although seeking employment, their careers are apt not to develop as fully, and they remain significantly less well paid.

In partial response to the Ahern and Scott report, the NRC's Office of Scientific and Engineering Personnel (OSEP) held a workshop in 1986 to examine the causes of the underrepresentation and career differentials of women at all levels of science and engineering (Dix 1987a). Following this workshop, the NRC's Committee on Women in Science and Engineering (CWSE) concluded that it was essential to monitor how women are faring in science and engineering in order to ensure that an appropriate share of the best and the brightest people, regardless of gender, choose careers in science. This, in turn, led to interest from the policy community and agencies that support scientific education and research in updating the Ahern and Scott study. As a result, CWSE and OSEP proposed the current study to the NRC's Governing Board.

In 1994, following the approval by the Governing Board, the NRC appointed the Panel for the Study of Gender Differences in the Career Outcomes of Science and Engineering Ph.D. Recipients under the auspices of the Committee on Women in Science and Engineering. The Panel's mandate was to gain a better understanding of the ways in which the careers of men and women in science and engineering differ, the ways in which they are similar, and the changes that have occurred since 1973. To this end, the Panel extended the path breaking work of the Ahern and Scott study with more recent data and a different methodological approach. Key enhancements include:

- A richer characterization of the demographic, educational, and career characteristics of male and female scientists and engineers.
- An examination of nonacademic sectors of employment and gender differences in types of work within each sector, thus taking into account the shifting balance of employment opportunities among sectors of employment and the movement of scientists and engineers into industry during the 1980s and 1990s.
- A focus on the distinction between tenure-track faculty and off-track faculty, including adjuncts, part-time faculty, postdoctoral fellows, and research associates.
- The use of statistical methods rather than the matching strategy of the Ahern and Scott study, allowing more flexible comparisons among cohorts of Ph.D.s.

These changes in focus and methods of analysis, discussed fully in Chapter 2, provide new and useful information about the careers of men and women in science and engineering. But the answers are still incomplete. Indeed, this was a constant source of frustration for the Panel. In pursuing our mandate to provide a broad overview of the change and lack of change in the last 20 years, we could not pursue each topic in the detail that it deserved. As discussed in our conclusions, there is much more that needs to be learned about the opportunities and obstacles faced by women in science and engineering. The Panel hopes that future researchers will use our report as a starting point for this additional research.

STRUCTURE OF THE REPORT

Differences in career outcomes in science and engineering are the result of complex processes that constitute the scientific and engineering career. The educational process leading to the Ph.D. has been described as a *pipeline,* in which a large flow of children enter the pipe with many "leaks" as students flow towards the doctorate (Berryman 1983; U.S. Congress, Office of Technology Assessment 1988: 11-12). Upon receipt of the degree, the participation of women in science is the result of "successive filtering" (Zuckerman and Cole 1975:83). Accordingly, the presence and participation of women in science and engineering can best be understood as a series of processes with the outcomes at each step affecting the choices and opportunities at the next level. For example, there is roughly a 30 percent difference in salaries between men and women who have doctorates in science and engineering. Much of this advantage for men can be "eliminated" by controlling for gender differences in types of work and years of experience. While this does not change the fact that women overall have less well paying jobs, it does help us understand what leads to the observed difference in salary and can guide the development of policies to further improve the status of women in science.

With this in mind, the substantive chapters of the report trace the career through the various filters that affect career outcomes.

- Chapter 3 describes trends in the number of male and female Ph.D.s in science and engineering. The preparation of women for careers in science and engineering is discussed in terms of overall enrollment trends, the number of degrees earned by women, and how the degrees received by women compare to those received by men.
- Chapter 4 considers the labor force participation of those with Ph.D.s. We focus on factors that affect who succeeds in moving from the certification of the doctorate to a full-time career in science and engineering. To understand the lesser participation of women, careful consideration is given to the effects of marriage and family.
- Chapter 5 focuses on gender differences in sector of employment and work activity within each sector. A key focus is on the growth of industry relative to the academic sector.
- Chapter 6 focuses exclusively on the academic sector for which we have detailed information on the type of institution and work activity. The lower academic rank and slower advancement of women in academia are documented and we assess the results of previous studies that attempt to explain gender differences in academia.

• Chapter 7 examines salaries across all sectors and shows the degree to which differences in salary can be explained by differences in work activity. We conclude by discussing the effects of cumulative disadvantage and the way in which "successive filtering" affects the careers of women in science and engineering.

The report begins with Chapter 2, which describes the data sets and variables used and explains our methodology. To fully understand the results of later chapters, it is important to understand the basic information presented in this chapter. Finally, Chapter 8 summarizes key findings and presents the Panel's recommendations.

MINORITY SCIENTISTS

Before proceeding with our report on the status of women in science and engineering, it is important to note that we have not considered the problems and prospects for minority scientists and engineers. Our failure to examine the careers of minorities is not based on a lack of interest or concern about the obstacles faced by many minority groups in science and engineering. As documented in the 1986 workshop on the underrepresentation and career differentials of minorities at all levels of science and engineering (Dix 1987b), the substantial underrepresentation of African Americans, Hispanics, and Native Americans is a national concern.

The small numbers of minority scientists and engineers are a major obstacle for studying their career outcomes. In many cases there are simply too few minorities in science and engineering to support the types of analyses presented in later chapters. This is shown in Figure 1-1, which presents the percent of new Ph.D.s in 1979, 1989, and 1995 by minority status. While the percent of Ph.D.s who are white has declined in all fields since 1979, the increases among other groups are almost entirely for Asian Americans. The numbers of African Americans remains small with only slight increases in engineering and the life sciences. While the percent of Hispanics has increased slightly, as a group Hispanics remain greatly underrepresented. Native Americans are almost entirely absent among new Ph.D.s. *The most important issue involving minorities in science and engineering involves increasing their numbers.* Unfortunately, the Panel did not have the time or resources to adequately study the complex issues facing underrepresented minorities in science and engineering. Hopefully, this important issue will be the focus of a future study.

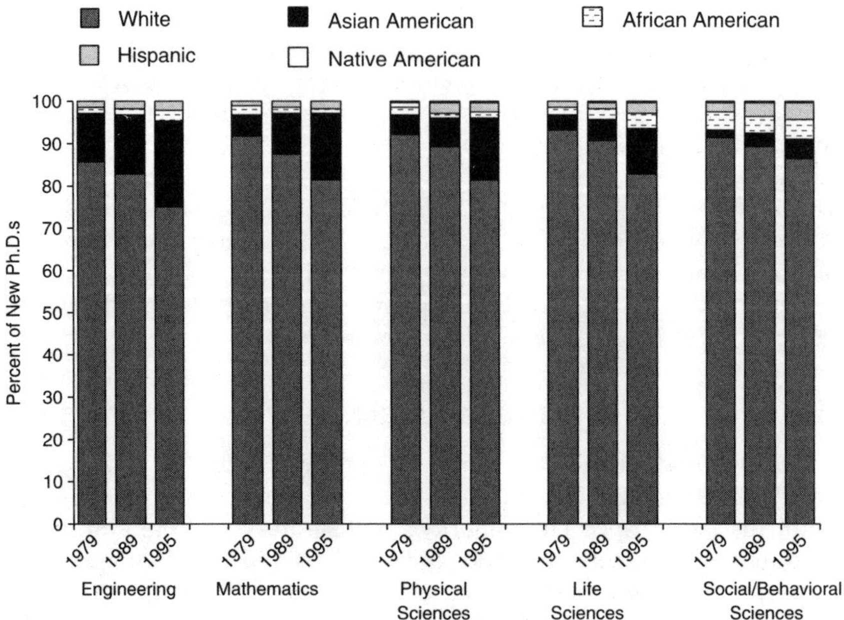

FIGURE 1-1 Percent of Ph.D.s by minority status, field, and year of Ph.D. SOURCE: NSF (2000b).

2

Data and Methods

This chapter describes the data sets, variables, and methodology used for the analyses in the next five chapters. While the substantive chapters are largely self-contained, there is some critical information that was too detailed to include within each chapter. Accordingly, we encourage all readers to at least quickly review the information presented in this chapter.

FIELDS

The Ahern and Scott study examined career differences for women and men in mathematics, physics, chemistry, the biological sciences, psychology, the social sciences, languages and literature, and other humanities. Since the current study panel was charged with examining career outcomes for Ph.D.s only in science and engineering, we examined five broad fields:

- *Mathematical Sciences*: Mathematics, computer science, probability and statistics (including biometrics and biostatistics, psychometrics, econometrics, and social statistics), and other fields of mathematics.

- *Physical Sciences*: Astronomy, physics, chemistry, oceanography, and geosciences.
- *Engineering*: Biomedical engineering, chemical engineering, electrical engineering, industrial engineering, material sciences, and other fields of engineering.
- *Life Sciences*: Agriculture, biological sciences, and medical sciences.
- *Social and Behavioral Sciences*: Anthropology, economics, geography, political science, psychology, sociology, and other social and behavioral sciences.

Further details on these fields are given in Chapter 3 on Ph.D. production.

While our study examines both science and engineering, for simplicity we sometimes use the shorter term "science" rather than "science and engineering" to refer to the fields combined. Similarly, the term "scientists" is sometimes used as shorthand for "scientists and engineers," and "scientist" for "scientist or engineer."

DATA SOURCES

Analyses are based on scientists and engineers who participated in the 1973, 1979, 1989, or 1995 *Survey of Doctorate Recipients* (NSF 1973-1995). In this section we describe this survey, referred to as the SDR, along with other data sources that were used to supplement this key data source.

Survey of Doctorate Recipients (SDR)

The scientists and engineers studied in our report were respondents to the *Survey of Doctorate Recipients* (NSF 1973-1995). Since 1973, with support from the National Science Foundation and other federal sponsors, the National Research Council (NRC) has conducted a biennial survey of doctoral scientists, engineers, and humanists who completed the *Survey of Earned Doctorates* (discussed on page 17). The sample for the SDR is stratified by year and broad field of Ph.D., gender, and other demographic variables. Responses to the survey are weighted to represent the science and engineering doctoral population. Sample weights are computed as the inverse of the probability of a case being selected from the population with adjustments based on the response rate from that stratum. Currently the SDR samples about 10 percent of the doctorates from U.S. universities who remain in the United States after they receive their degree. In earlier years of the survey, the sample was larger and included some individuals with doctorates from foreign institutions. In 1995 computer assisted telephone interviews (CATI) were used to increase the response rate and two weights were computed to account for differences from earlier survey procedures. In our study the CATI weights were used. For technical details on the SDR, see NSF (1997).

For a given year, the SDR provides demographic characteristics and the current employment status of those with doctoral degrees awarded between 1930 and the present. Our analyses are based on data from four years of the SDR: 1973, 1979, 1989, and 1995. The 1973 survey was selected since it was the first year that data were available. The 1979 survey was used since this year was the primary data for the Ahern and Scott study. The 1989 survey provided information on changes in the decade since the 1979 survey. And, the 1995 survey was the most recent available when our analyses began.[1]

Survey of Earned Doctorates (SED)

The sample used for the SDR is based on the *Survey of Earned Doctorates* (NSF 1920-1995),[2] referred to as the SED. The SED is an annual survey that provides a nearly complete roster of recipients of doctoral degrees from American universities. For each respondent there is information on the year, field, and institution of bachelor's, master's, and doctoral degrees; elapsed and enrolled time from the bachelor's to the doctorate; graduate support; plans for postgraduate employment; and the level of education of the respondent's mother and father. The data from the SED become part of the Doctorate Records File (DRF), which is a virtually complete database on doctorate recipients from 1920 to the present. Since some of the information from the SED was not included in the SDR, data from the SED was merged with the SDR.

Publication and Citation Data

For the 1979 and 1989 panels of the SDR, data on publications were obtained by merging the SDR data with publication data from 1982 through 1992 from the Institute for Scientific Information (ISI). The ISI data covers over 16,000 international journals, books, and proceedings in the sciences, social sciences, and arts and humanities. In 1995, the SDR asked respondents to provide the number of publications they had since 1990. For the 1973 SDR, no data on publications were available.

---

[1]Data from the 1997 SDR are now available, but were not used in our report.

[2]Data from the 1996 through 1998 SED are now available, but were not used in our report.

NRC's Assessments of Research-Doctorate Programs

Information on the quality of a scientist's Ph.D. program was obtained by matching the SDR data to the NRC's 1982 and 1995 studies of research-doctorate programs in engineering, humanities, life sciences, mathematics, physical sciences, and social/behavioral sciences in the United States (Goldberger, Maher, and Flattau 1995; Jones, Lindzey, and Coggeshall 1982). The scholarly quality of program faculty, also known as "reputational rating," was used to measure the quality of the program from which the doctorate was received and the quality of the employing program in academia. This measure is the mean response to the survey after dropping the two highest and two lowest scores. The resulting means were converted to a scale from 0 to 5, with 0 denoting "Not sufficient for doctoral education" and 5 denoting "Distinguished." The 1982 quality ratings for both the Ph.D. and employing program were matched with the 1973, 1979, and 1989 SDR data; the 1995 quality ratings were used for the 1995 employing program and for individuals who received their Ph.D.s between 1989 and 1994.

YEAR OF SURVEY, YEAR OF PH.D., CAREER YEAR, AND SYNTHETIC COHORTS

For each year of the SDR, data were analyzed for those with degrees from 1949 until the year of the survey. Those with degrees before 1949 were excluded due to the small number of cases. Table 2-1 is helpful for explaining the type of information provided by this research design. The left column indicates the year in which the SDR survey was conducted. The year of a respondent's Ph.D. is listed at the top of the table; for simplicity the table only lists every fifth year. The body of the table contains the year since the Ph.D., referred to as the *career year*. The career year

TABLE 2-1 Years Since the Ph.D. as Determined by the Year of the Ph.D. and the Year of the SDR Survey

Year of the SDR Survey	Year of Respondent's Ph.D.									
	1949	1954	1959	1964	1969	1974	1979	1984	1989	1994
1995	46	41	36	31	26	21	16	11	6	1
1989	40	35	30	25	20	15	10	5	—	—
1979	30	25	20	15	10	5	—	—	—	—
1973	24	19	14	9	4	—	—	—	—	—

NOTE: — indicates that the year of the survey was before the year of the Ph.D.

is simply the year of the SDR survey minus the year in which a scientist received her Ph.D. For example, consider those with degrees in 1959 (the values have been underlined). For this cohort, we have information on their careers at four different times: when they were 14 years from the Ph.D. in 1973 (i.e., 1973 – 1959 = 14); 20 years from the degree in 1979; 30 years in 1989; and 36 years in 1995. Thinking of years since the Ph.D. as a scientist's professional age (thus excluding any work activities before the Ph.D.), those with degrees in 1969 would have an age of 4 in 1973, 10 in 1979, 20 in 1989, and 26 in 1995.

We used this information to examine both changes that occur as a scientist ages through the career and changes in the climate of science over time.[3] To illustrate the issues involved in using this type of panel data, consider a hypothetical analysis of promotion to the rank of full professor. By tracing the same cohort at different career stages, we can examine changes as a scientist ages. Consider scientists who received their degrees in 1959:

- Using the 1973 SDR, we can compute the percent who were full professors 14 years into their career; using the 1979 SDR we can compute the percent of this cohort who are full professors 20 years into the career; using the 1989 SDR, 30 years; and using the 1995 SDR, the percent 36 years after the Ph.D.

While the same scientists do *not* respond to each survey, the sample weights for those in each year's sample are adjusted to represent the population as a whole. Accordingly, we interpret the sample data as if we are observing the same group of scientists as they age.

This design also allows us to compare the career outcomes of individuals who had the same career ages in different calendar years. For example:

- Table 2-1 shows that the 1959 cohort was 20 years from their Ph.D. in 1979, while the 1969 cohort was 20 years from the degree in 1989. By comparing the two groups, we can see the consequences of changes in the climate of science over the ten years from 1979 to 1989.

This example also illustrates the gaps in our data. We do not know the percent of the 1959 cohort who were full professors 15 years into the career since we do not have data collected in 1974. To fill in these gaps, we

[3]Issues related to analyzing this type of data are sometimes referred to as the age, period, and cohort problem. See Riley (1992) and the literature cited therein.

use the method of *synthetic cohorts*. This idea can be explained by extending our example.

- Since we do not have data on the 1959 cohort 15 years after the Ph.D., we use data from the 1958 cohort collected in 1973, corresponding to 15 years after their degree. Data for the 1958 cohort in year 15 of the career are used to "synthesize" what would have happened to the 1959 cohort in their 15th year.

The degree to which a synthetic cohort is a good representation of the aging process depends on how close in time the cohorts are and the degree to which conditions facing scientists have changed. In later chapters, we are careful to qualify the degree to which this approach can be used to approximate changes over the course of the career.

While the same sample of scientists is *not* used for each year of the SDR, by chance some scientists are selected into the SDR sample in more than one year. We can use scientists who respond to two or more waves of the SDR to trace the same individuals at different times. Such analyses are used when there are a sufficient number of individuals responding to the same question in multiple years of the SDR.

VARIABLE DESCRIPTIONS

This section describes the variables used in later chapters. We begin with the career outcomes and then consider the independent, antecedent, and control variables.

Career Outcomes and the Metaphor of the Pipeline

The report is organized around the metaphor of the pipeline (Berryman 1983; U.S. Congress, Office of Technology Assessment 1988:11-12), with Chapters 3 through 6 considering increasingly selective outcomes. Chapter 3 begins with the most general and inclusive outcome, obtaining the Ph.D. Women are less likely to obtain a doctorate, and those women who do *not* obtain a doctorate are necessarily excluded from consideration in Chapter 4, which examines labor force participation. Chapter 4 shows that female doctoral scientists are less likely than men to be in the full-time labor force. Women who are not working full time are excluded from Chapter 5, where gender differences in sector of employment and primary activity are examined. Chapter 6 further limits analyses to those in the academic sector and within the chapter progressively restricts analyses to those with tenure-track positions, those with tenure, and finally those who are full professors. In reading later chapters, it is essential to keep in mind that those scientists who are "filtered out" in earlier chapters, who are more likely to be women, are not considered in the next chapter. The specific outcomes considered in each chapter are as follows:

Chapter 3: Ph.D. Production

- **Doctoral Degree Attainment**. How has the percentage of doctoral degrees received by women changed since 1973?

Chapter 4: Labor Force Participation

For those with doctorates in science and engineering:

- **Employment Status**. Is the Ph.D. scientist employed full time, part time, unemployed, or underemployed?

Chapter 5: Sector and Work Activity

For those in the full-time science and engineering labor force:

- **Employment Sector**. Does the scientist work in academia, business or industry, government, or the nonprofit sector?
- **Primary Work Activity**. Within each sector, is the scientist's primary work activity teaching, basic research, applied research, development, management, or some other activity?

Chapter 6: Outcomes for Academic Scientists

For scientists and engineers working in academia:

- **Type of Institution**. In what type of educational institution does a scientist work?
- **Tenure-Track Positions**. Does the scientist have a tenure-track position or is the scientist working off-track?
- **Tenure**. Is the scientist tenured?
- **Rank**. What is the faculty member's academic rank?
- **Productivity**. How many publications does a scientist have?

Chapter 7: Salary

Considering all full-time doctoral scientists and engineers:

- **Salary**. What is the respondent's 12-month salary?

Control Variables

Male and female scientists and engineers differ in nearly every career outcome. To understand these gender differences, a wide variety of control variables were considered. These variables include:

Basic Control Variables

- **Field.** Is the doctoral degree in engineering, mathematics, physical science, life science, or the social and behavioral sciences? In some analyses, medical science is split out from the broad field of the life sciences.
- **Year of Survey, Year of Ph.D. and Career Year.** As noted above, each of these measures of time is essential for understanding the changes in the status of women and men in science and engineering. *Career year* or career age is defined as years since the Ph.D., where employment prior to the Ph.D. is not counted.

Demographic Variables

- **Race/Ethnicity.** Is the respondent white, African American, Hispanic, or Asian?
- **Citizenship.** Is the respondent a U.S. citizen?
- **Level of Parents' Education.** What is the highest level of education of the respondent's mother and father?
- **Marital Status.** Is the respondent married?
- **Children.** Does the respondent have young children living at home?

Baccalaureate Education

- **Type of Baccalaureate Institution**. From what type of baccalaureate institution did the respondent obtain an undergraduate degree?
- **HBCU**. Did the respondent receive a baccalaureate degree from a Historically Black College or University (HBCU)?
- **Women's College**. Did the respondent receive a baccalaureate degree from an institution belonging to the Women's College Coalition?

Doctoral Education

- **Time to Doctorate**. How long did it take a scientist to complete the Ph.D.? Both time enrolled in graduate study and elapsed time from the undergraduate degree to the doctorate are considered.
- **Type of Doctoral Institution.** What is the Carnegie type of the

institution from which a respondent received her/his degree? Details on the Carnegie Classification are given below.

• **Quality of Doctoral Department**. What was the prestige of the doctoral department? This is measured on a scale ranging from 0 to 5, with 0 denoting "Not sufficient for doctoral education" and 5 denoting "Distinguished." Further details are given below.

• **Sources of Financial Support**. What types of financial support did the respondent receive during graduate school? Did the respondent receive a research assistantship and/or teaching assistantship? How much debt was incurred during graduate school?

Carnegie Type

There is immense variation among the over 3,000 colleges and universities in the United States. To distinguish among these universities, we have used the well-known Carnegie Classification of Higher Education (Carnegie Commission on Higher Education1973, 1976, 1987, 1994). The 1994 Carnegie Classification includes all colleges and universities in the United States that are degree-granting and accredited by an agency recognized by the U.S. Secretary of Education. For purposes of analysis, we simplified the classification to the following categories (the full classification is given in Appendix A).

• *Research I* institutions offer a full range of baccalaureate programs, are committed to graduate education through the doctorate degree, give high priority to research, and receive substantial federal support.

• *Research II* institutions are similar to Research I institutions, but receive a smaller amount of research support.

• *Doctoral* institutions include baccalaureate, master's, and doctoral programs, but produce a smaller number of doctoral degrees in a more limited number of areas than Research I and II schools.

• *Master's* institutions (also referred to as Comprehensive institutions) offer baccalaureate programs and usually have graduate education through the master's degree. More than half of their baccalaureate degrees are awarded in two or more occupational or professional disciplines.

• *Baccalaureate* institutions (also known as Liberal Arts institutions) are primarily undergraduate colleges with a majority of degrees in arts and science fields.

• *Medical* institutions include medical and health related universities. We consider medical institutions to be Research I institutions except for some analyses of the life sciences.

• *Engineering* institutions include schools of engineering. We have classified these schools as Research I institutions.

• In addition, there are a variety of other types of institutions that include theological seminaries, bible colleges, law schools, business and management schools, schools of art, music, and design, teachers colleges, and corporate-sponsored institutions. Since these institutions employ only around 1 percent of our sample, divided proportionately between men and women, they have been excluded from the following analyses.

The Carnegie classifications are neither absolute nor invariant over time. First, within a given class there is substantial variation. For example, a university that barely meets the requirements to be a Research I university may be very similar to institutions at the upper range of Research II universities. Second, the Carnegie classifications was revised in 1976, 1987, and 1994 (Carnegie Foundation for the Advancement of Teaching 1973, 1976, 1987, 1994), leading to different classifications for the same institution over time. This could occur both because the institution changed, but also because of changes in the classification scheme. For example, a school that did not quite meet the criteria to be Research I in 1987 might satisfy those criteria in 1994 or may have grown into the new category. To avoid artifacts caused by institutions changing classifications, we used the classification of institutions from the 1994 report for all years of the SDR.

Prestige of Doctoral Programs

Data on the quality of the Ph.D. institution and the employing institution of the doctorates were obtained from the 1982 and 1995 NRC studies of research doctorate programs (Goldberger, Maher and Flattau 1995; Jones, Lindzey and Coggeshall 1982). Thirty-two fields were studied in 1982 and 41 fields in 1995. Programs within each field were evaluated on a range of objective and subjective measures. In our analyses, we used the rating for the "Quality of the Program Faculty." On these ratings, scores less than 2 are classified as *adequate* programs; those from 2 through 2.99 as *good* programs; from 3 through 3.99 as *strong*; and those above 4 as *distinguished*.

The measure of quality used for the doctoral department depended on the year in which the degree was received. For degrees before 1988, ratings from the 1982 study were used. For those with degrees from 1989 to 1994, ratings were taken from the 1995 study. To assign quality measures to the Ph.D. program, a crosswalk was developed between the fields in the research-doctorate study and the Ph.D. fields in the DRF taxonomy. Data on the quality of the employing institution was based on the study that would most nearly represent the 1979, 1989, and 1995 employment data. For 1979 and 1989, the same crosswalk was used for employment as for the Ph.D. field since the SDR for those years used the same taxonomy for field of employment as for Ph.D. field. For the 1995 SDR, field of employment was not collected, so we assumed that individuals worked in the field of their Ph.D. and assigned the quality rating of the Ph.D. program at their employing institution.

STATISTICAL METHODS

Matching versus Statistical Controls

The Ahern and Scott (1981: Appendix B) study was based on a matched sample. This involved constructing triads of two men and one woman that matched as nearly as possible on selected background characteristics, such as education and years of experience. Matching was designed to control for the differences in characteristics between male and female Ph.D.s in the population. Comparisons of men to women from the matched sample allowed an assessment of the difference in outcomes after controlling (through matching) for key differences in background characteristics. For example, in comparing the academic rank of women to men, it was possible to show gender differences after controlling for those characteristics that were used to match the samples. The advantage of this approach was that once the matching was done, comparisons were simple since descriptive statistics and cross-tabulations could be used.

There are two limitations of matching that justify an alternative strategy. First, men and women can only be matched on a few characteristics due to limitations in the number of cases that are available. For example, in comparing rank it is not possible to control through matching for the productivity of the scientist or the quality of the employing department. Second, to the degree that men and women in the population of scientists and engineers differ on the variables used to match, matching resulted in a sample that was *not* representative of the population. Since male and female scientists differ on the characteristics used for matching, statistics based on the matched sample should *not* be used to represent the distribution of characteristics in the population. We note, however, that some readers of the Ahern and Scott report appear to have incorrectly used the study's results to generalize to the populations responding to the 1973 and 1979 SDRs.

In response to these concerns, we used statistical analyses of all cases in selected years of the SDR, rather than a matched subsample. Consequently, the descriptive statistics reported can be taken as being representative of the population of scientists (to the extent that the SDR is representative, of course). Moreover, this approach allowed us to introduce a larger number of controls as independent variables in regression models. The greatest cost of this strategy is that the analyses and interpretation of results were more complicated than those required for the earlier study. These methods are discussed below.

The regressions are not used as causal models; rather they are sophisticated descriptions of the association between background characteristics and career outcomes. For example, if women with children are more likely to leave science, this is not conclusive evidence that the *cause* of these women leaving science is having children. Drawing such conclusions requires far more detailed analyses based on complete career histories and the measurement of variables that were not available. Further, the panel recognized that: 1) we did not have a simple random sample; 2) response rates to the surveys varied from 79 percent of those contacted in 1973, to 71 percent in 1979, to 63 percent in 1989, and 85 in 1995; 3) not all variables that we wanted were available; and 4) missing data were a problem for some variables (especially race and ethnic origin). Still, we firmly believe that our analyses provide useful and accurate information about differences in the careers of male and female scientists.

Regression Methods and Statistical Controls

Loglinear regression was used to analyze salaries, while logit analysis was used for binary and nominal outcomes. These methods are now described.

Loglinear Regression

Salary was treated as a continuous variable, which allowed the use of multiple regression. Data from 1973, 1979, and 1989 were converted to 1995 dollars using adjustment factors for inflation from the U.S. Census Bureau (1999). Given the skewed nature of the salary distribution, we used the standard practice of taking the natural log before estimating the regression. To explain the model used, we assume only three independent variables, although many more were included in the actual regressions. Let y indicate salary and let x_1 through x_3 be the independent variables, which can be either binary or continuous. The effects of the independent variables were allowed to vary by sex. Consequently, the estimated model was:

$$\ln(y) = \beta_{0,W} + \beta_{1,W}x_1 + \beta_{2,W}x_2 + \beta_{3,W}x_3 + \varepsilon \qquad \text{for women.}$$

$$\ln(y) = \beta_{0,M} + \beta_{1,M}x_1 + \beta_{2,M}x_2 + \beta_{3,M}x_3 + \varepsilon \qquad \text{for men.}$$

Given the loglinear specification, the effects of variables can be interpreted by transforming the β coefficients. Consider the effect of x_1 for women. The transformation $\exp(\beta_{1,W})$ is the factor change in the expected value of y for a unit increase in x_1, holding all other variables constant. Or, $100[\exp(\beta_{1,W}) - 1]$ can be interpreted as the percentage change in salary y for a unit increase in x_1, holding all other variables constant. For example, if the coefficient for the quality of the doctoral program was 0.049, then $100[\exp(.049) - 1] = 5.02$ indicates that for every unit increase in the prestige of the doctoral department, salary is expected to increase by 5 percent, controlling for all other variables.

We also compared men and women by computing predicted salaries under various conditions. Since the model is loglinear regression, we could *not* compute the expected value as:

$$E(y) = \exp(\beta_{0,W} + \beta_{1,W}x_1 + \beta_{2,W}x_2 + \beta_{3,W}x_3)$$

Rather, we needed to estimate:

$$E(y) = E[\exp(\beta_{0,W} + \beta_{1,W}x_1 + \beta_{2,W}x_2 + \beta_{3,W}x_3 + \varepsilon)]$$

To compute this quantity, Duan (1983) proposed a nonparametric smearing estimator which he described as "a low-premium insurance policy against departures" from the usual assumption regarding the distribution of the errors. If e_i is the ordinary least squares residual, then define:

$$s = \frac{1}{N}\sum_i \exp(e_i)$$

The smearing estimate, which is a consistent estimator of the expected outcome, was used for computing predicted salaries:

$$E^*(y) = s \times \exp(\hat{\beta}_0 + \hat{\beta}_1 x_1 + \hat{\beta}_2 x_2 + \hat{\beta}_3 x_3)$$

Logit Analysis

For binary and nominal outcomes, the logit model was used. The logit model specifies a nonlinear relationship between the probability that some event occurs and a set of independent variables. To interpret the effect of an independent variable, we compute the change in the predicted probability of some outcome when one of the independent variables changes by a given amount. The levels of all other variables are held constant at their mean or at some level that is substantively interesting. To explain this method, we consider the case of a binary outcome. Further details and generalization to nominal outcomes can be found in Long (1997).

Let y be a dummy variable equal to 1 if an event occurred and 0 if not. For example, $y = 1$ if a scientist has tenure and $y = 0$ if not. Let x_1 through x_3 be the independent variables, which can be either binary or continuous. The logit model uses the x's to predict the probability that $y = 1$ according to the equation:

$$\Pr(y=1 \mid x_1,x_2,x_3)=\frac{\exp(\beta_{0,M}+\beta_{1,M}x_1+\beta_{2,M}x_2+\beta_{3,M}x_3)}{1+\exp(\beta_{0,M}+\beta_{1,M}x_1+\beta_{2,M}x_2+\beta_{3,M}x_3)} \text{ for men.}$$

$$\Pr(y=1 \mid x_1,x_2,x_3)=\frac{\exp(\beta_{0,W}+\beta_{1,W}x_1+\beta_{2,W}x_2+\beta_{3,W}x_3)}{1+\exp(\beta_{0,W}+\beta_{1,W}x_1+\beta_{2,W}x_2+\beta_{3,W}x_3)} \text{ for women.}$$

These equations describe a nonlinear relationship between the x's and the outcome probabilities. The problem in presenting results from the logit model is that the expected change in the probability for a unit change in a variable differs depending on the current level of all variables in the model.

To summarize the effect of a variable, we examined how a unit change in a variable affected the outcome probability when all variables were held constant, usually at their mean. For a continuous variable x_c, we computed:

$$\Delta p_c = \Pr(y=1 \mid x_c=\bar{x}_c+.5)-\Pr(y=1 \mid x_c=\bar{x}_c-.5)$$

This is simply the difference in the predicted probability when x_c moves from .5 below its mean to .5 above its mean, holding all other variables at their means. In the text, we interpreted this as: when x_c changes by one unit, the probability of the event changes by Δp_c. For binary independent variables, we computed the effect of a change from 0 to 1:

$$\Delta p_d = \Pr(y=1 \mid x_d=1)-\Pr(y=1 \mid x_d=0)$$

In some cases we focused on predicted probabilities and changes in predicted probabilities at levels of the variables other than the mean. For example, in Chapter 6 we were interested in the predicted probability of being a full professor. Given that promotion to full professor rarely occurs early in the career, we computed the predicted probability holding years of experience constant at 15 years while other variables were held constant at their mean.

3

Entry into Science

Ph.D. Production and Individual Characteristics

The reason for opening science to women is not that they will do it differently and better but that good scientists are hard to find and it seems perversely absurd to place social impediments before half the human race when that half could, person for person, do the job as well as the half granted access.

—Stephan Jay Gould, *New York Times Book Review,* 1984[1]

But a scientist without a Ph.D. (or a medical degree) is like a lay brother in a Cistercian monastery. Generally he has to labor in the fields while others sing in the choir.

—Spencer Klaw, *The New Brahmins,* 1968[2]

INTRODUCTION

The Ph.D. is the *sine qua non* of a scientific career. Without this certification, active participation in science and engineering beyond the level of a technician is an increasingly rare exception. Accordingly, it is appropriate that we begin our study of the careers of women and men in science and engineering (S&E) by examining the number and proportion of women who receive advanced degrees in S&E fields. While more women than men continue to be lost through attrition during the training to become a scientist or engineer, from 1973 to 1995 there was substantial growth in the representation of women in *all* broad fields of science and engineering. Still, women continue to be significantly underrepresented in the fields of mathematics, engineering, and the physical sciences.

We next consider gender differences in the characteristics of scientists and engineers at the time they receive their doctorate. Understanding

[1]Gould (1984).

[2]Klaw (1968: 15).

differences in backgrounds is necessary, but not sufficient, for understanding differences in career outcomes that are the focus of later chapters. We begin by examining the educational background of a scientist's parents. We then turn to characteristics of a scientist's own education, including the type of baccalaureate institution attended, the prestige of the doctoral program, time from the baccalaureate to the Ph.D., and the types of financial support received during graduate study. While there has been a reduction in gender differences in background characteristics, some differences remain that may lead to disadvantages for women in their postdoctoral careers. We end the chapter by examining differences between male and female scientists and engineers in marriage and having children. Later chapters show that the effects of marriage and family on career outcomes are very different for men and women.

While our focus is on quantifying gender differences in individual backgrounds, it is important to keep in mind that gender differences in entry into science and engineering can arise both from differences in the socioeconomic backgrounds of individuals and from differences in access to education. Differences in background can also interact with opportunities in complex ways. For example, a young woman who believes that her chances for a rewarding future in science are not as good as a male classmate's might choose, on that basis alone, to enter a different profession. Similarly, a woman who believes (whether that belief is correct or not) that she must meet higher standards for admission than a man might decide not to enter the competition on such an uneven basis. If women make different decisions about their education than do men, as they often do, the reasons could have less to do with interest and ability than with the perception of unfairness.

While differences in personal background characteristics are easy to document with the types of survey data that we have, the evidence on past discrimination against women is often circumstantial. Nonetheless, until the advent of Title IX of the 1972 Higher Education Amendments, discrimination against women was widely practiced throughout higher education, especially in research universities. The practice of requiring higher grades and test scores for the admission of women was ubiquitous in universities and professional schools, resulting in the exclusion of thousands of women whose abilities matched those of admitted men. Low quotas for the admission of women to certain undergraduate curricula, especially schools and colleges of science, were common. For example, at Cornell University, despite its founding as a coeducational institution, housing for women (but not for men) was limited, resulting in a system of assigning only small numbers of "female beds" to those departments deemed unsuitable for women (Conable 1977:110-117). Following passage of the GI Bill in 1944, most universities reduced female enrollments deliberately in order to accommodate veterans. At the University of Michigan, for example, women's admissions were suddenly reduced by almost one-third (McGuigan 1970:112).[3] The consequence was that women were forced into the newly developing state colleges, formerly normal schools, where opportunities for undergraduate preparation in sciences and engineering were often inadequate or nonexistent. The effect of such practices was exacerbated by discriminatory financial aid practices, at least until passage of the Equal Credit Act of 1974. In sum, all of these factors, while difficult to quantify on a national scale, combined to make it far more difficult for women to study sciences as undergraduates and to pursue professional careers in these fields. While a complete review of the historical evidence on the treatment of women in the pursuit of the doctorate is beyond the scope of our report, Solomon (1985) and Rossiter (1982, 1995) are excellent histories of women in higher education.

THE PIPELINE TO THE PH.D.

The educational process leading to the Ph.D. has been described as a *pipeline*, where a large flow of children enter the pipe with many "leaks" as students flow towards the Ph.D. (Berryman 1983; U.S. Congress 1988:11-12). While only a small proportion of either men or women make it to the end of the educational pipeline, *substantially* more women than men are lost through attrition. In her presidential address to the American Association for the Advancement of Science, Sheila Widnall (1988) described the pipeline as shown in Figure 3-1: out of a cohort of 2,000 girls and 2,000 boys in the ninth grade, 280 boys and 220 girls complete work in high school that prepares them for science in college; of those 500 students, 140 men and 44 women concentrate in science in college, with only 46 men and 20 women receiving a bachelor's degree in science; of these 66 students, just five men and one woman earn a doctorate in science or engineering. The greater loss of women than men on the way to a Ph.D. results in women comprising a smaller proportion of those with advanced S&E degrees. For a discussion of factors affecting the differential achievement of boys and girls prior to entrance into college, see Catsambis (1994) and Kahle and Matyas (1987).

---

[3]The title of this history by McGuigan, *A Dangerous Experiment: 100 Years of Women at the University of Michigan*, is derived from a phrase that appears in the Regents' Report on the Admission of Females in 1858.

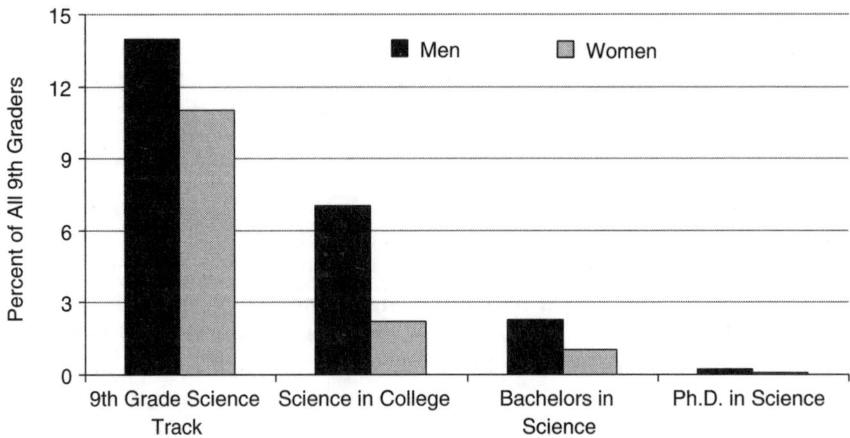

FIGURE 3-1 Summary of the pipeline to the Ph.D. SOURCE: Widnall (1988).

BACCALAUREATE DEGREES

If the college woman is a mistake, Nature will eliminate her.
—David Starr Jordon, President of Stanford University, 1906[4]

Is it time for affirmative action for men?
—Ben Gose, *The Chronicle of Higher Education*, 1997[5]

A bachelor's degree, and usually one in science or engineering, is the normal prerequisite for pursuing a Ph.D. in S&E. Consequently, the dramatic changes in the enrollment of women for undergraduate degrees set the stage for women increasing their representation among Ph.D. scientists. In 1847, Lucy Stone was the first woman to receive a baccalaureate degree in the United States (Solomon 1985:43). Since then, as shown in Figure 3-2, there have been dramatic changes in the presence of women among those enrolled in colleges and universities. From 11,000 women in 1870, to 601,000 in 1940, to nearly 7 million in 1995, the number of women enrolled in baccalaureate programs has increased every year (shown by the dashed line), with explosive growth beginning in 1960. However, the representation of women as a *proportion* of all students has shown periods of increasing success and reversals along the way. The largest decline in

[4]Solomon (1985:207).
[5]Gose (1997: A35).

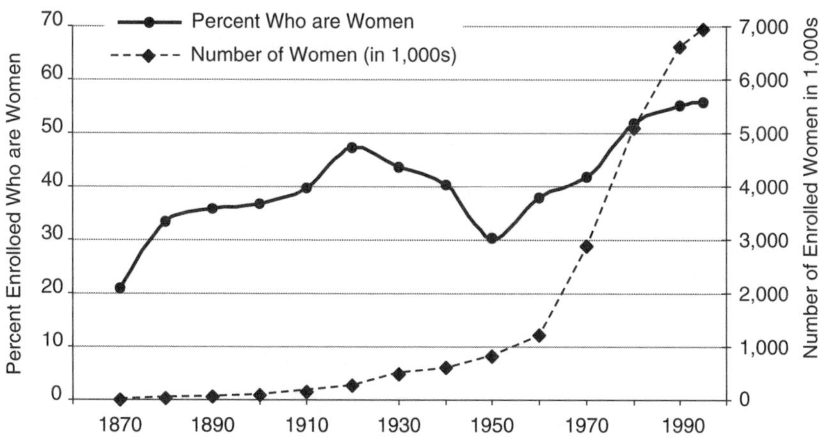

FIGURE 3-2 Percent of those enrolled in college who are women. SOURCES: Solomon 1985:63; NSB 1998:A-53.

representation occurred after World War II as a result of the huge increase in the number of men whose education was funded by the GI Bill. The history of the struggle of women to become full participants in higher education is documented in Barbara Miller Solomon's (1985) fascinating book, *In the Company of Educated Women*.

Beginning in 1950, the proportion of women has grown steadily. By the early 1980s, women were a majority of those enrolled in undergraduate education, with their share approaching 60 percent in 1995. The greater representation of women occurred as the number of women increased and the number of men stayed nearly constant. From 1975 to 1995, the total number of baccalaureate degrees awarded increased by 26 percent, from 931,663 in 1975 to 1,174,436 in 1995.[6] Degrees to women increased by 52 percent, while degrees awarded to men increased by only 4 percent. During this same period, baccalaureate degrees in S&E grew by only 21 percent, from 313,555 to 378,148. The entire growth in the number of S&E degrees was the result of an increase of 71 percent in the number of women, while the number of men *decreased* by 4 percent. The net result of these changes is that men became less likely to choose a degree in science and engineering, down from 41 percent of all degrees to men in 1975 to 38 percent in 1995. In comparison, the percent of women in S&E fields rose

[6]Data in this section are from NSB (1998).

from 24 percent to 27 percent. This increase by women in the pursuit of baccalaureate degrees in S&E is also seen in data on transition rates from high school. Barber (1995) notes that in 1970 only 5 percent of women graduating from high school went on to earn a bachelor's degree in S&E compared to 14 percent of the male high school graduates. By 1989, the difference narrowed with 9 percent of the women compared to an unchanged 14 percent of the men obtaining S&E degrees.

DOCTORAL DEGREES IN SCIENCE AND ENGINEERING

The growth in the number of women with baccalaureate degrees in science and engineering was essential for the growth in doctorates earned by women during this period. But the completion of the baccalaureate does not necessarily lead to an advanced degree. The evidence suggests that a greater proportion of women than men end their education with a bachelor's degree (Hornig 1987:108). Accordingly, women represent an even smaller proportion of those with Ph.D.s and even fewer of those with Ph.D.s in science and engineering fields. The study *Climbing the Ladder* (CEEWISE 1983:1.12) estimated that in 1970 women with bachelor's degrees in the physical sciences were 61 percent less likely than men to obtain a Ph.D.; 49 percent less likely in the biological sciences; and 40 percent less likely in psychology. By 1980, there was substantial movement towards parity, with rates 25 percent lower in the physical sciences, 6 percent in the biological sciences, and 3 percent in psychology.[7] In S&E fields, Barber (1995) calculated that the number of women who earned doctorates each year represented from 5 percent to 7 percent of the women earning baccalaureate degrees in S&E eight years earlier. While the propensity for men to pursue Ph.D.s is much higher than for women, especially in certain fields of S&E, the likelihood for men with bachelor's degrees to pursue a Ph.D. dropped drastically in the 1970s and early 1980s (Barber 1995; Lomperis 1990; CEEWISE 1983). For example, Barber (1995) estimates that from 1970 to 1990 the percent of men with S&E undergraduate degrees who obtained Ph.D.s in S&E 8 years later dropped from 15 percent to 8 percent. The net result of these changes is that women have steadily increased their proportion among new Ph.D.s in science and engineering.

In her history of the education of women, Solomon (1985:134) reports that the first doctoral degree in America was to a man at Yale in 1862. Fifteen years later, the first woman received a doctorate from Boston

[7]Data from the original report included information for mathematics. However, the sample size was too small to be reliable.

University, while most universities continued to exclude women from graduate programs. By the end of the 19th century, 9 percent of all Ph.D.s had been awarded to women, with 228 women and 2,372 men receiving degrees. While women continue to lag behind men in attaining the doctorate, Figure 3-3 shows that since 1960 there has been a steady increase in the percentage of degrees received by women in the natural and social sciences. From the 1920s until the Depression of the 1930s, degrees to women fluctuated between 10 percent and 15 percent in the physical sciences, and between 15 percent and 20 percent in the social sciences. The drop during the Depression was followed by a rapid increase in degrees to women during World War II, reversed by a sharp decline as GIs returned to school. The difficult position of women in graduate programs after the war is reflected in Keller's (1991:230) account of a committee formed at M.I.T. during this period to decide whether the school should continue to admit female students. Remarkably, the percentage of degrees awarded to women did not match the levels of the 1920s again until the mid-1970s.

The dramatic growth in the number of new Ph.D.s in science and engineering from 1963 to 1970, shown by the dashed line in Figure 3-4, was fueled by huge increases in federal support to graduate programs that followed the launch of Sputnik in 1957. During this period, degrees to women, shown by the thick black line, grew a modest 0.3 percentage points each year. The growth for women was limited by competition with veterans from the Korean Conflict returning to school using the GI Bill,

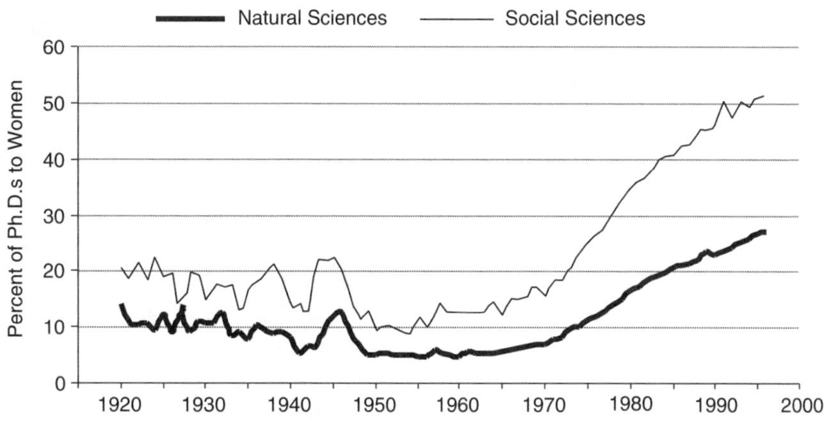

FIGURGE 3-3 Percent of doctoral degrees awarded to women in the natural and social sciences from 1920 to 1996. SOURCES: Harmon, Doctorate Records File (1963).

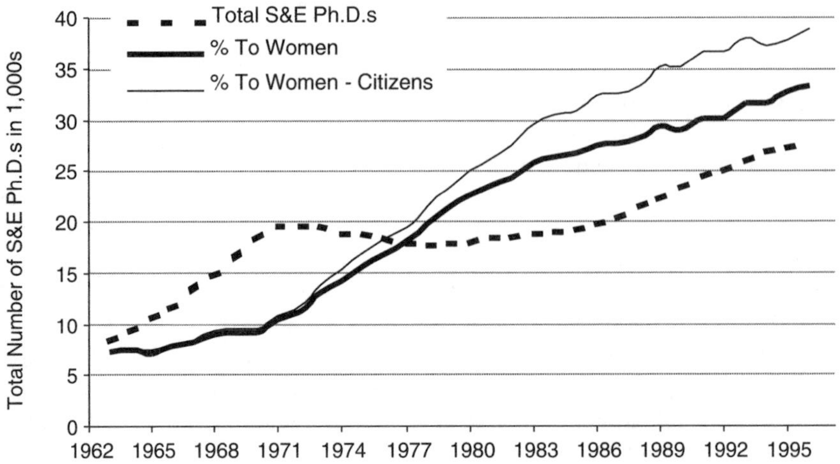

FIGURE 3-4 Total number of S&E doctoral degrees and percent of S&E doctoral degrees awarded to women and percent of S&E doctoral degrees awarded to women among those who are citizens or permanent U.S. residents. SOURCE: Doctorate Records File.

social pressure for early marriage and childbearing, and discrimination against women in admissions and financial aid (CEEWISE 1983:1.13, 2.1). The early 1970s ended the long expansion in higher education, as Ph.D. production declined for 6 years in response to federal cutbacks and a poor academic labor market (McPherson 1985; Wilson 1979:49-53, 78-79). But, while the number of men obtaining S&E doctorates declined annually from 1972 until 1988, the number of S&E doctorates granted to women increased every year since 1963. From 1971 to 1983, the percent of S&E Ph.D.s awarded to women increased on average 1.3 points per year. During this period, the capacities of universities were high while the enrollment of men was decreasing, making schools more receptive to accepting women.

Antidiscrimination laws such as Title IX and the feminist movement also contributed to increases in women pursuing the doctorate (Chamberlain 1988:16). This period of rapid growth for women was followed by slower growth of 0.6 points a year from 1984 to 1996. By 1996, women had attained one third of all doctorates, half of the doctorates in the social sciences, and nearly one quarter of the doctorates in the natural sciences. By 1996, there were over 15 times more degrees received by women than in 1963, and 3.6 times more than in 1973.

Women are more highly represented among those who are U.S. citizens and who have permanent resident status. This can be seen by comparing the thin black line indicating the percent of women among citizens and permanent residents to the thick line representing all Ph.D.s regardless of citizenship. The difference emerged in the early 1970s and grew steadily until the present day. By 1996, women made up 33 percent of all S&E Ph.D.s, but 39 percent of the degrees awarded to U.S. citizens and permanent residents.

Field Differences in Ph.D. Production

Each of our five broad fields showed substantial growth in the representation of women, but there are important differences. While the *percent* of degrees to women is clearly important as an indication of the representation of women, the *number* is also critical, especially in smaller fields such as engineering and mathematics. A given field (or university or department) may need at least a minimum number of women before these women attain a *critical mass* whereby they are no longer viewed as an oddity. Having a critical mass can minimize socialization difficulties otherwise encountered in a male-dominated environment (LeBold 1987:86 and the literature cited therein). For example, Dresselhaus (1986) found that women in physics classes were very quiet until the percentage of women in the class grew to 10 percent or 15 percent, at which time their participation equaled that of men. The importance of number is also related to the idea of *tokenism,* in which a small number of a minority group is seen as representing the entire group (Kanter 1977). Thus, female scientists may be viewed by their colleagues primarily as women, rather than as scientists or engineers (Yentsch and Sindermann 1992:213). Once a critical mass is obtained, the presence of women has the potential to affect the social conditions of science, including personal interactions, policy-making, and tenure decisions (Sonnert 1995:11).

Information on the number and percent of women by field and year is summarized in Figures 3-5 and 3-6. The years 1973, 1979, 1989, and 1995 correspond to the years of the *Survey of Doctorate Recipients* (NSF 1973-1995) (hereafter, SDR) that are used throughout our report. Figure 3-5 shows the *percent* of Ph.D.s awarded to women in a given year; Figure 3-6 shows the *number* of new Ph.D.s who are women in the corresponding fields and years. In assessing these graphs, keep in mind that the years of our survey are not evenly spaced. All else being equal, we would expect larger changes from 1979 to 1989 than from 1973 to 1979 or from 1989 to 1995. With this caveat in mind, there are several important differences across fields.

Engineering. Engineering is the most male dominated of all professions (McIlwee and Robinson 1992:2) and the number and percentage of women with Ph.D.s is smallest in engineering. The number of women

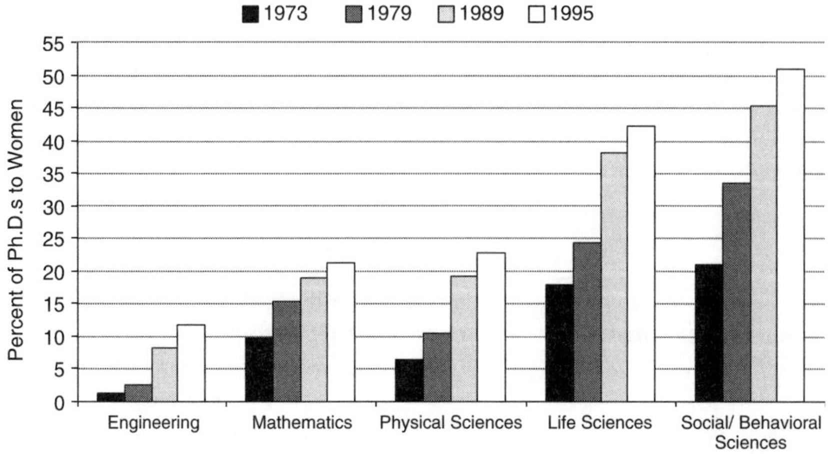

FIGURE 3-5 Percent of Ph.D.s awarded to women, by field and year of survey. SOURCE: Doctorate Records File.

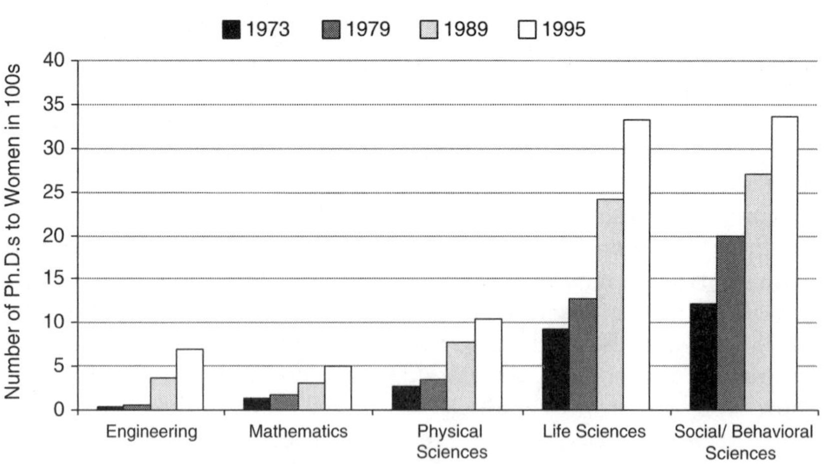

FIGURE 3-6 Number of Ph.D.s awarded to women, by field and year of survey. SOURCE: Doctorate Records File.

grew from a dismal 46 in 1973 to 696 in 1995. Although this represents an increase of over 1,500 percent, in 1995 women still made up less than 12 percent of the Ph.D. recipients. In terms of the percentage of women, the situation in engineering in 1995 was roughly equivalent to the situation in the social/behavioral sciences in 1963, the life sciences in 1966, mathematics in 1976, and the physical sciences in 1980. LeBold (1987) suggested that in engineering a critical mass of women might be particularly important in obtaining the social support necessary to meet the demands of a strict engineering curriculum.

Mathematical Sciences. Mathematics had the slowest growth in the participation of women. While 9 percent of the degrees were given to women in 1973, this increased to only 20 percent by 1995. Given the small total number of degrees awarded in mathematics, this translates into less than 500 degrees to women in 1995.

Physical Sciences. Since 1973, the physical sciences saw a tripling in the number of Ph.D.s given to women, with 1,048 doctoral degrees to women in 1995. However, women still make up less than 25 percent of the total degrees in this field.

Life Sciences. In 1973, 17 percent of the degrees in the life sciences were awarded to women. By 1995, this representation doubled to over 40 percent. In that year, over 3,300 degrees were awarded to women.

Social and Behavioral Sciences. The representation of women is greatest in the social/behavioral sciences. In 1973, women already represented 20 percent of the degrees, and by 1995 the proportion of women was just over 50 percent of the 6,613 degrees granted.

SUMMARY OF DEGREES IN SCIENCE AND ENGINEERING

Figure 3-7 shows the proportion of women among those with high school, baccalaureate, and doctoral degrees since 1960. While half of the high school diplomas have been awarded to women, in 1960 women were substantially less likely to extend their education with a baccalaureate or doctoral degree, especially in S&E fields. Since 1960 there have been steady gains by women in the receipt of all types of advanced degrees, with increasing improvements beginning in 1970, reflecting new civil rights legislation. By 1985, women received half of the bachelor's degrees among all fields and by 1990 they represented 40 percent of undergraduate degrees in S&E. There was similar progress in doctoral degrees, although by 1990 women were still less than 30 percent of the Ph.D.s in science and engineering fields. Overall, even with the significant gains that have been made, women continue to lag behind men, especially in science and engineering fields where the percent of degrees awarded to women remains substantially below 50 percent.

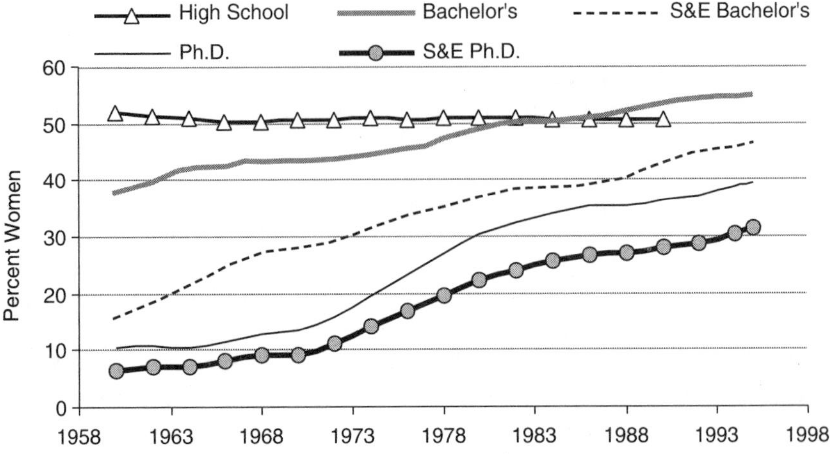

FIGURE 3-7 Percent of degree recipients who are women by year. SOURCES: High school data and years before 1966 (Barber 1995); other data (NSF 2000a).

BACKGROUND CHARACTERISTICS OF SCIENTISTS AND ENGINEERS

In this section, we compare the background characteristics of men and women who receive doctoral degrees in science and engineering. In later chapters, gender differences in background are considered as explanations for differences in career outcomes. We begin by examining the educational characteristics of the parents, as well as the baccalaureate origins of the doctorates themselves. We then consider characteristics of graduate education, including the prestige of Ph.D. department, time from the baccalaureate to the Ph.D., and types of financial support received during graduate education.[8]

Parents' Education

There is both anecdotal and systematic evidence that the educational backgrounds of parents affect the educational outcomes of their children

[8]Given the small number of women in some fields, especially with Ph.D.s in earlier years, we have combined information from the 1973, 1979, 1989 and 1995 samples from the SDR for estimating the distribution of background characteristics at the time of the Ph.D. Since the weights in the SDR are for estimating the labor force population, rather than the Ph.D.s in a given year, we did not use these weights when combining years of the SDR.

and that these influences are greatest for young women. Malcom (1983) found that the most effective pre-college programs for increasing the participation of women in science involved parental input and that the effects of parents were strongest for young women. Solomon (1985:67) concludes that "[t]he influence of mothers extended beyond convincing obdurate fathers to relent," noting that mothers also provide the encouragement and support for a woman to obtain higher education. Sonnert (1995:68) concludes that mothers might be important in imparting to their daughters the value of a scientific career, or at least in not dissuading their daughters from such ambitions. These conclusions are consistent with our data on the education of the mothers and fathers of Ph.D. scientists.

Figures 3-8 and 3-9 show differences between male and female doctorates in the percent of their mothers and fathers with baccalaureate degrees, along with baseline data on the percent of the civilian U.S. population with baccalaureate degrees. While the parents of both male and female Ph.D.s have much higher levels of education than the average man or woman in the United States, there are interesting gender differences. Until recent years, women who received doctorates in S&E were substantially *more likely* than men to have fathers with college degrees, with 47 percent of the fathers of female doctorates graduating from college compared to 29 percent of the fathers of male doctorates.[9] This is seen by comparing the dashed line for women to the thick black line for men in Figure 3-8. As the percentage of fathers with degrees has steadily increased, reflecting trends for higher education in society in general (shown by the thin line with +'s), there is a convergence between male and female doctorates in the percent of fathers graduating from college. By 1994, 59 percent of the women and 57 percent of the men had fathers with baccalaureate degrees.

Figure 3-9 shows that female Ph.D.s are also more likely than men to have mothers who graduated from college, with several key differences from the results for fathers. First, a significantly smaller proportion of the mothers of S&E doctorates, whether men or women, attend college compared to their fathers attending college. This reflects the overall higher education of men than women in society as a whole, as shown by comparing the thin lines with +'s for fathers in Figure 3-8 with the line for mothers in Figure 3-9. Second, differences between women and men in the percent of mothers with college degrees were smaller in 1962 (28 percent versus 16 percent) than the difference in the percentage of fathers (47

[9]In analyses that are not shown, we found similar patterns using other measures of parents' education, such as years of schooling and percent with degrees beyond a baccalaureate.

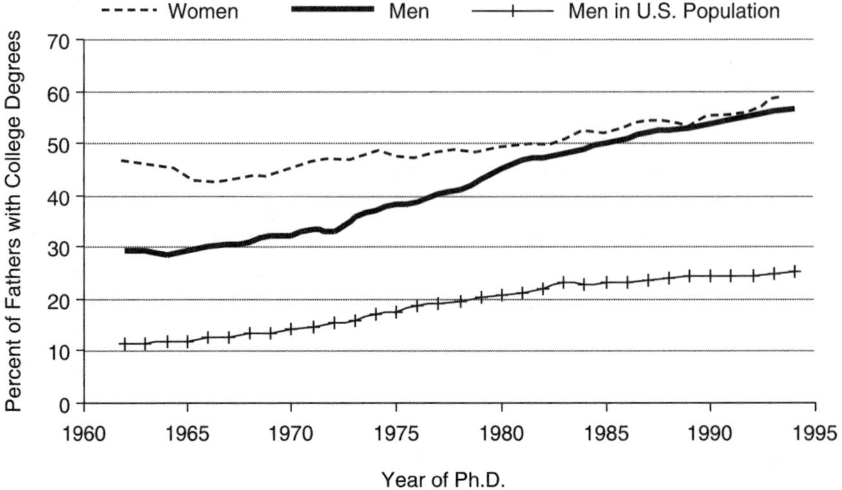

FIGURE 3-8 Percent of the *fathers* of Ph.D. recipients who have college degrees, by sex of Ph.D. scientist and year of survey. SOURCES: U.S. Census (1999); Doctorate Records File.

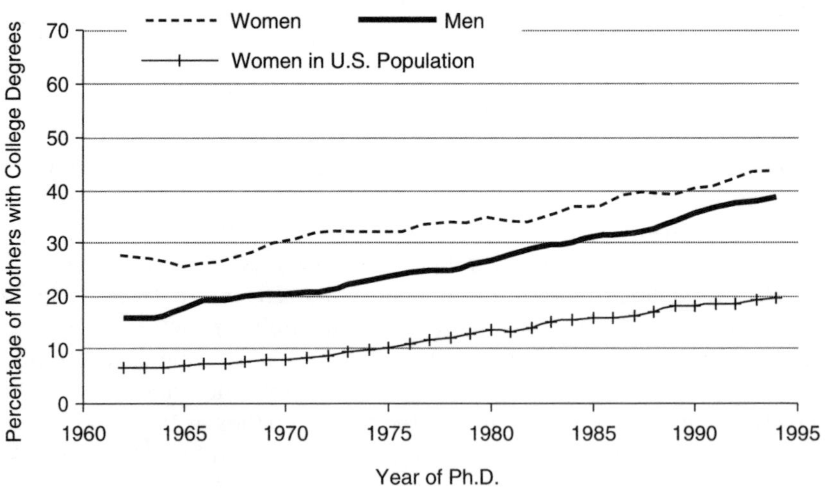

FIGURE 3-9 Percent of the *mothers* of Ph.D. recipients who have college degrees, by sex of Ph.D. scientist and year of survey. SOURCES: U.S. Census (1999); Doctorate Records File.

percent versus 29 percent). But there is less convergence over time for the education of mothers than for fathers. By 1995, 44 percent of the female doctorates had mothers with bachelor's degrees compared to 39 percent of the men, leaving a difference of 5 percentage points.

There are several notable field differences in the percent of fathers and mothers who have college degrees, as shown in Figures 3-10 and 3-11. The parents of engineers are the most highly educated, followed by parents in mathematics and the physical sciences, with lower educational levels of parents for Ph.D.s in the life sciences and the social/behavioral sciences. The more rural backgrounds of those attaining degrees in the life sciences may account for the lower education levels of parents of Ph.D.s in the life sciences (Harmon 1978:41-43).

Overall, the education levels of the families of female doctorates are consistently higher than those of male doctorates. This might reflect the greater importance of parental encouragement for women during a time when female doctorates were rare and societal support for women entering science and engineering was much weaker. The continued difference between men and women in the education levels of their mothers may also reflect the importance to young women of having a same-sex role model and encouragement from another woman. This is especially true in the male dominated field of engineering, with approximately 20 percent

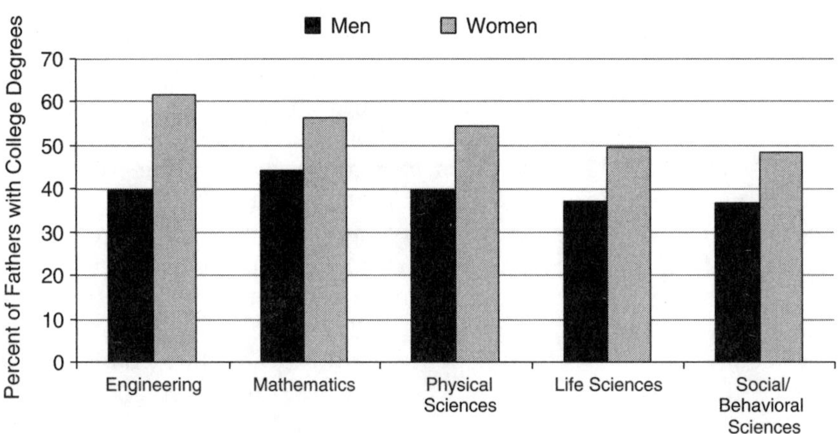

FIGURE 3-10 Percent of *fathers* with college degrees, by field and sex. All Ph.D.s years were combined.

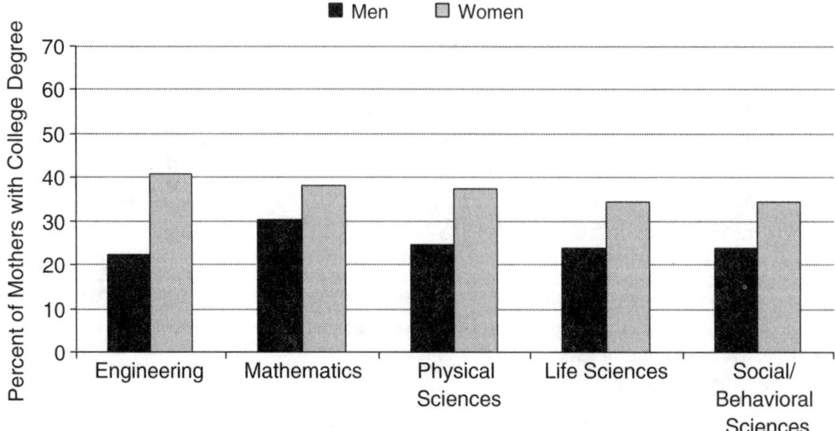

FIGURE 3-11 Percent of *mothers* with college degrees, by field and sex. NOTE: All Ph.D.s years were combined.

more of the parents of female engineers having college degrees. This is consistent with the results of McIlwee and Robinson (1992:29-30) who found that female engineers were more likely to come from professional families than male engineers.

Baccalaureate Origins of Scientists and Engineers

Traditionally, men and women attend different types of institutions for their undergraduate degrees. Women are more likely to attend baccalaureate-only institutions, such as liberal arts or women's colleges, while men are more likely to attend institutions that also grant a doctoral degree. However, Figures 3-12 and 3-13 show that changes in baccalaureate origins since the 1930s have lead to a convergence in the educational backgrounds of male and female doctorates. The most notable change is the steady decline in degrees from baccalaureate-only institutions (shown by the light region at the top of each figure), especially for women. Twenty percent fewer women graduated from baccalaureate-only institutions in the 1990s compared to women in the 1930s, with the largest increases in Master's (9 points), Doctoral (7 points), and Research II (6 points). There has been almost no change, however, in the proportion of degrees to women from Research I institutions. For men, however, the changes in baccalaureate origins have been much smaller, with decreases in degrees from baccalaureate-only institutions of about 10 points, with no other type of institution gaining more than a few points. In general, a large

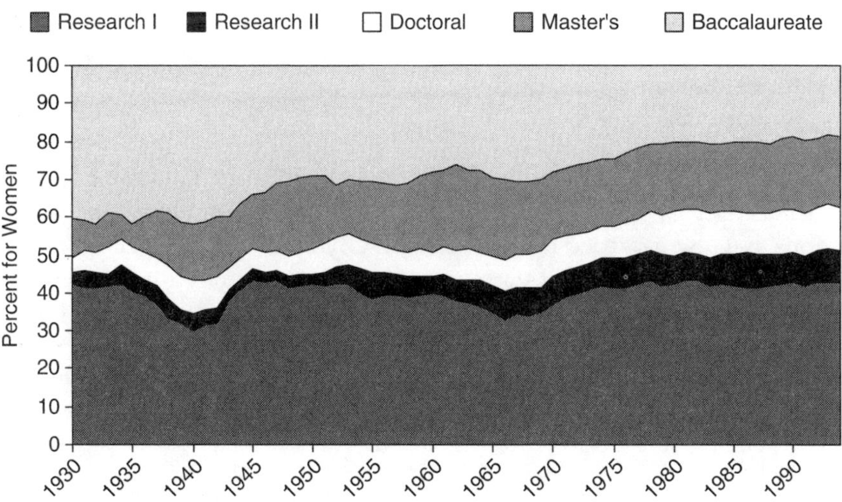

FIGURE 3-12 Carnegie types of baccalaureate degrees for *women*. NOTE: Data for each year are based on 5-year moving averages.

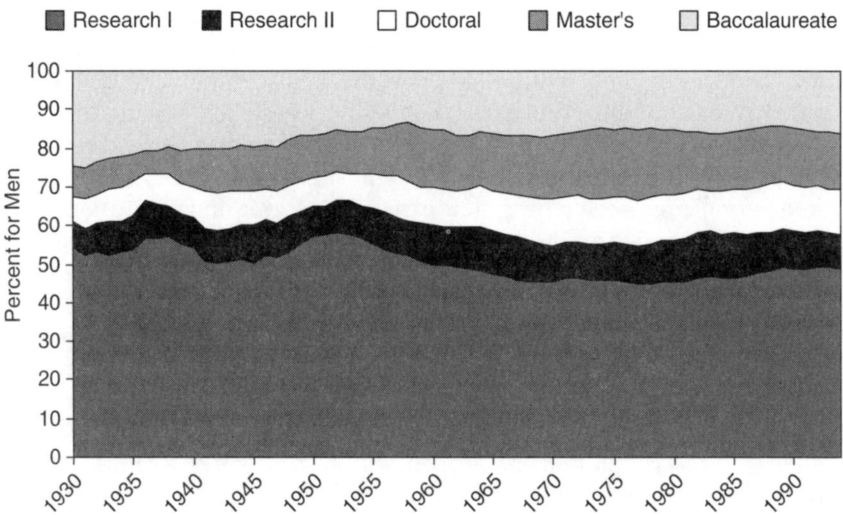

FIGURE 3-13 Carnegie types of baccalaureate degrees for *men*. NOTE: Data for each year are based on 5-year moving averages.

modality of those with Ph.D.s in S&E receive undergraduate degrees from Research I institutions. This is followed by the much smaller categories of Master's, Baccalaureate, Doctoral, and Research II institutions.

The net effect of these changes has been a convergence in the undergraduate origins of men and women. With the exception of a small reversal among those with Ph.D.s from 1965 to 1970, women have become increasingly similar to men in their attendance of undergraduate institutions that also awarded doctoral degrees. By the 1990s, the difference was reduced to 8 percentage points, compared to a difference of 20 points for those with degrees in the 1950s. Still, women are more likely to attend baccalaureate-only or master's-only institutions for their bachelor's degree. The larger proportion of women attending baccalaureate-only colleges tends to put them at a disadvantage in preparation for S&E careers. Except for a few highly selective colleges, most liberal arts colleges lack the sophisticated facilities for modern science study, as well as faculty oriented to or actively engaged in research. Thus, gender differences in baccalaureate origins could give men an advantage by providing them with earlier exposure to graduate level research and a better understanding of what graduate school will be like.

Convergence in baccalaureate origins has occurred in each of the five broad fields. However, there are some differences. First, both male and female doctorates in engineering are far more likely to come from research universities and far less likely to come from baccalaureate-only institutions. For those with degrees in the 1990s, 74 percent of the men and 68 percent of the women had degrees from research universities, with 4 percent of the men and 7 percent of the women with degrees from baccalaureate-only institutions. This almost certainly reflects the lack of predoctoral engineering programs in non-Ph.D. granting institutions. Second, to a lesser degree, both male and female doctorates in mathematics and the life sciences are more likely to come from research universities and less likely to come from baccalaureate-only institutions. By the 1990s in mathematics, 56 percent of the men and 52 percent of the women came from research universities, with 14 percent of men and 17 percent of women coming from baccalaureate institutions. In the life sciences 59 percent of the men and 51 percent of the women came from research universities, with 16 percent of men and 17 percent of women coming from baccalaureate institutions.

Quality of the Ph.D. Department

A scientist's experience in graduate school is essential for learning the craft of science. During graduate school a student develops her or his conception of scientific roles, establishes a style of work, and learns the standards of performance in the field. And, significantly, it is during graduate school that a scientist finds a mentor who helps the student map out a research program, and enter the job market (Zuckerman 1970, 1977; Long and McGinnis 1985). It is not surprising that a substantial body of work (see Long and Fox 1995 for a review of this literature) has found that the quality of a scientist's graduate program has important consequences for the later career, affecting job placement, work activity, and scientific productivity.

Figure 3-14 shows the distribution of the prestige of doctoral origins of scientists and engineers in the 1995 SDR (see Chapter 2 for details on this measure of the quality of the Ph.D. program). Results from other years of the SDR provide similar patterns. The modality of doctorates in all fields except mathematics receive their degrees from strong departments; in mathematics, distinguished programs produce the largest number of doctorates. In engineering, the physical sciences, and life sciences, where expensive laboratories are necessary, there is a smaller proportion of degrees from the least prestigious programs. In the social/behavioral sciences, and to a lesser extent in mathematics, a greater proportion of degrees are produced by lower tier programs.

While the distribution of the prestige of doctoral origins is stable over time, there are some differences between men and women by field. Table 3-1 shows gender differences in the average prestige by field according to the decade in which the Ph.D. was received.[10] The biggest differences are

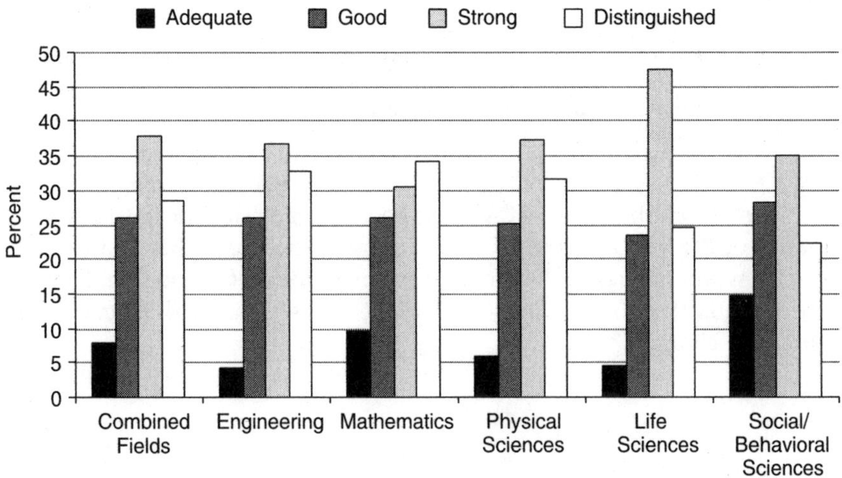

FIGURE 3-14 Distribution of Ph.D.s among programs of differing quality, by field. SOURCE: SDR 1995.

TABLE 3-1 Mean Prestige of Ph.D. Program, by Sex, Field, and Decade of Ph.D.

	Men				Women			
	1960s	1970s	1980s	1990s	1960s	1970s	1980s	1990s
Engineering	3.34	3.31	3.51	3.49	3.42	3.33	3.62	3.50
Mathematical Sciences	3.41	3.29	3.47	3.31	3.43	3.20	3.12	3.02
Physical Sciences	3.33	3.34	3.51	3.51	3.45	3.27	3.44	3.51
Life Sciences	3.32	3.25	3.36	3.28	3.39	3.30	3.32	3.37
Social/ Behavioral Sciences	3.20	3.01	2.98	3.03	3.17	3.11	3.03	2.91

	Difference: Women - Men			
	1960s	1970s	1980s	1990s
Engineering	.08	.02	.11	.01
Mathematical Sciences	.02	–.09	–.35	–.29
Physical Sciences	.12	–.07	–.07	.00
Life Sciences	.08	.05	–.03	.09
Social/ Behavioral Sciences	–.03	.10	.05	–.13

NOTE: Positive values in the "Difference: Women-Men" column indicate that women are from *more* prestigious departments. Prestige scores less than 2 are classified as *adequate* programs; those from 2 through 2.99 as *good* programs; from 3 through 3.99 as *strong;* and those above 4 as *distinguished.*

seen in mathematics, where there has been a steady decline in the average quality of the Ph.D. origin of more recent doctorates. This is especially true for women, resulting in an increase in gender differences in the prestige of the Ph.D. In other fields, differences are smaller with no consistent pattern of change.

[10]Prestige scores are not available for degrees received prior to 1960.

Time Between the Baccalaureate and Doctorate

In examining the time it takes a scientist to complete the doctorate, it is important to distinguish between total time that has *elapsed* between the undergraduate degree and the doctorate (referred to as *total time* to degree) and time during which the student was *registered* in graduate studies (referred to as *registered time* to degree). Panel A of Figure 3-15 shows that from 1970 to the present there has been a steady increase in the mean time between the undergraduate degree and the receipt of the doctorate. This is consistent with the results of Tuckman et al. (1990:7) who noted that this increase reversed the trend toward shorter time to degree that occurred during the 1960s. As shown in Table 3-2, the increase in total time to degree varied across fields, with the smallest increases occurring in engineering and the physical sciences, 8 and 13 percent, respectively, and increases of around 30 percent in all other fields.

Registered time to degree excludes time between the baccalaureate and the doctorate in which the student was not registered as a student. The excluded time would include, for example, time in a job immediately after the baccalaureate and interruptions in schooling to raise a family. Panel B of Figure 3-15 shows that registered time is around 1.7 years shorter in the physical sciences, 3.4 years shorter in the social/behavioral sciences, and around 2.5 years shorter in other fields. But, as shown in Table 3-2, increases in registered time to degree were similar to those for total time to degree.

In mathematics, the life sciences, and the social/behavioral sciences women had substantially longer total times between the baccalaureate and the doctorate than men, as shown in Panel A of Figure 3-16. Until 1990 in engineering, the total time was about .5 years longer for men, with only trivial gender differences in the physical sciences. The longer total time to degree for men in engineering might reflect the greater likelihood of baccalaureate engineers beginning work immediately after the baccalaureate and then returning to graduate study after a period of employment. Gender differences in *registered* time are substantially smaller, as shown in Panel B. That is to say that once they are enrolled, men and women are quite similar in the amount of time taken to complete their graduate education.

With the exception of engineering, women are more likely to have interruptions of a year or more before completion of their doctorate. In engineering men were 10 points more likely to have interruptions for those with degrees from 1970 to 1974, with smaller differences since then. In other fields, women are overall more likely to have interruptions, especially in the life sciences, but there are clear trends (Table 3-3). For the latest cohort, those with degrees in the 1990s, women are about 5 points

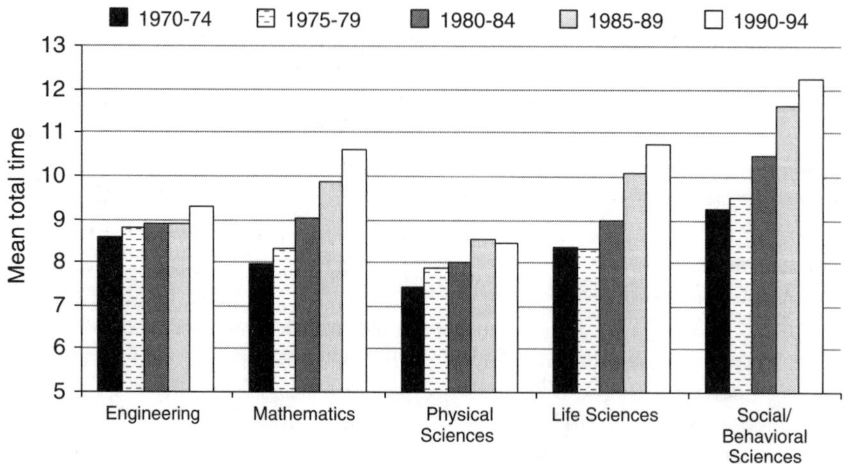

Panel A: Total time to degree

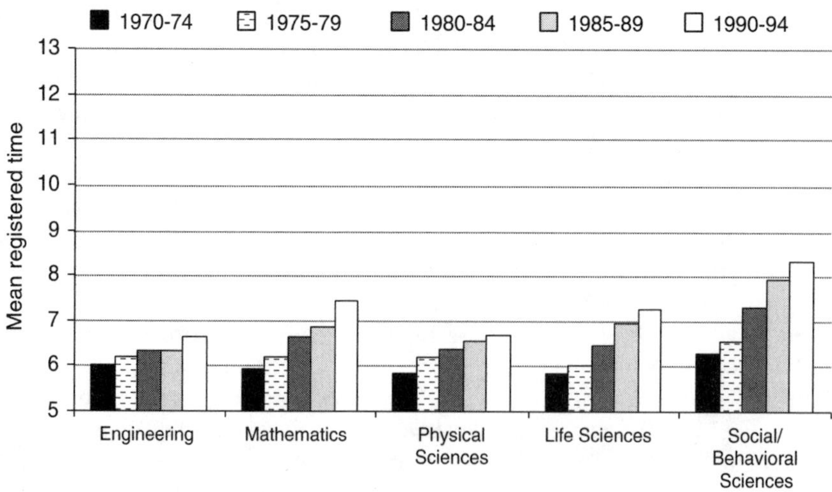

Panel B: Registered time to degree

FIGURE 3-15 Mean time between undergraduate degree and doctorate, by field and 5-year period during which the Ph.D. was received.

TABLE 3-2 Percent Increase in Total Time Between Baccalaureate and Doctorate and Registered Time to Degree Between 1970 and 1994, by Field

	Engineering	Mathematics	Physical Sciences	Life Sciences	Social/ Behavioral Sciences
Total Time	10.5	25.1	14.0	24.0	32.6
Registered Time	8.1	33.2	13.7	28.6	32.3

more likely to have interruptions. These results are consistent with Sonnert (1995:80) who found that women were more likely than men to interrupt their education or to attend school part-time. Recent estimates by Henderson et al. (1996:12, 29) found that gender differences in *registered* time in a doctoral program were smaller than gender differences in *elapsed* time from the baccalaureate to Ph.D. While we do not have information to evaluate the causes of interruptions, it is possible that women postpone their education while raising a family or change institutions when following an older spouse to a job. A second possibility is that interruptions are due to gender differences in support for graduate education, as suggested by Bowen and Rudenstine (1992:12, 192) and Tuckman et al. (1990:51-54). This topic is now considered.

Financial Support during Graduate School

The type of support received in graduate school is likely to affect a student's ability to complete the Ph.D. in a timely fashion and may affect the quality of the research that a graduate student can complete. In the sciences, research assistantships are often considered the ideal form of support, since they allow a student to work with his or her mentor. In the process, the student receives additional training and often is able to pursue research that contributes to the completion of the dissertation (Chamberlain 1988:212). Consistent with this suggestion, Bowen and Rudenstine (1992:179-182, 189) found that students supported with research assistantships were most likely to complete their dissertation. Teaching assistantships, while perhaps superior to student loans, take time away from research and limit contact with the mentor. Since the late 1960s, the SED asked new Ph.D.s to list all sources of funding that were used during graduate education. Their answers reflect the massive change in the funding of graduate education that has occurred since the 1960s and show important gender and field differences. When interpreting these results, keep in mind that a respondent can list multiple sources of support.

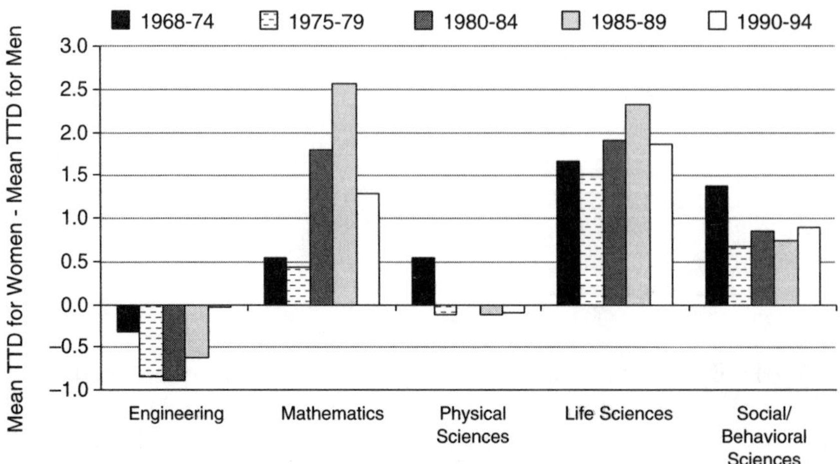

Panel A: Total time to degree (TTD)

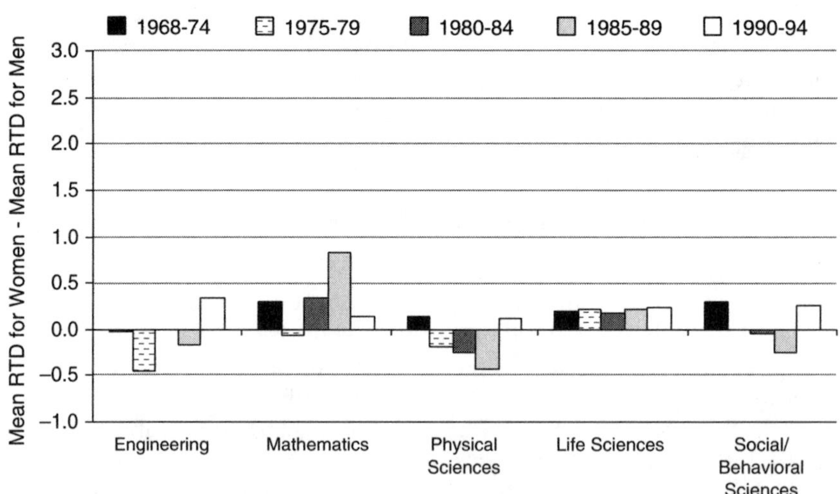

Panel B: Registered time to degree (RTD)

FIGURE 3-16 Gender differences in average time between undergraduate degree and doctorate, by field and 5-year period during which the Ph.D. was received. NOTE: A positive difference indicates that women took longer.

TABLE 3-3 Difference in the Percent of Women and Percent of Men with Interruptions of More Than One Year Between the Baccalaureate and the Doctorate

Year of Doctorate	Engineering	Mathematics	Physical Sciences	Life Sciences	Social/ Behavioral Sciences
1970-74	−10.3	−1.9	−1.6	10.6	6.1
1975-79	−7.5	−0.5	5.2	7.0	1.6
1980-84	−5.7	9.2	1.6	13.0	0.0
1985-89	−7.5	9.8	−2.9	14.1	4.4
1990-94	−2.8	7.0	4.7	4.5	4.5

NOTE: Positive values indicate that women are more likely to have interruptions. For example, 7.0 for mathematics in 1990-1994 means that 7 percentage points more women than men had interruptions.

Figure 3-17 shows the steady increases in the percent of Ph.D.s who use loans to fund their graduate education and the substantial field differences in both the relative frequency and rate of increase in the use of loans. Loans are least likely in mathematics and engineering, and substantially more likely in the social and behavioral sciences, where in the 1990s over 40 percent relied at least partially on loans to support their graduate education. Figure 3-18 shows that in engineering women have been increasingly more likely to use loans, while in other fields men are more likely to report using loans, with decreasing gender differences over time. By the 1990s all gender differences were less than 2 percentage points except in engineering.

During the 1980s, research assistantships (RAs) financed by grants and contracts were the most rapidly growing form of graduate student support (NSB 1993, 1996). This is reflected in Figure 3-19, which shows the increase in funding through research assistantships in all fields. The largest proportions of students with RAs are in the physical sciences and engineering, followed by the life sciences, mathematics, and finally the social/behavioral sciences. Among all sources of funding, the largest gender differences are in the receipt of research positions, as shown in Figure 3-20. In mathematics, men are 4 points more likely to be supported as RAs from 1968-1974, a difference that *increased* to 10 points for 1990-1994. In the life sciences, the differences are also large, decreasing slightly from 9 points in 1968-1974 to 7 points in 1990-1994. Men are slightly more likely to have research funding in the physical sciences and the social/behavioral sciences, although this advantage for men has nearly disappeared by 1994. Even though the activities of RAs are limited by the research agenda

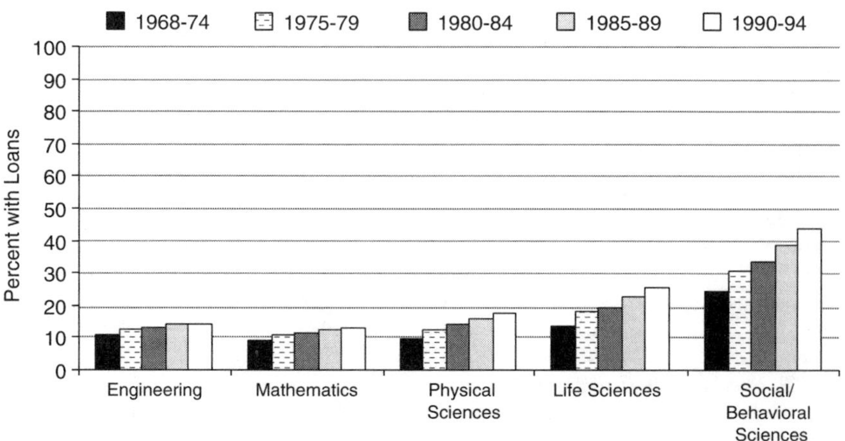

FIGURE 3-17 Percent of doctorates who received funding from loans, by field and year of Ph.D.

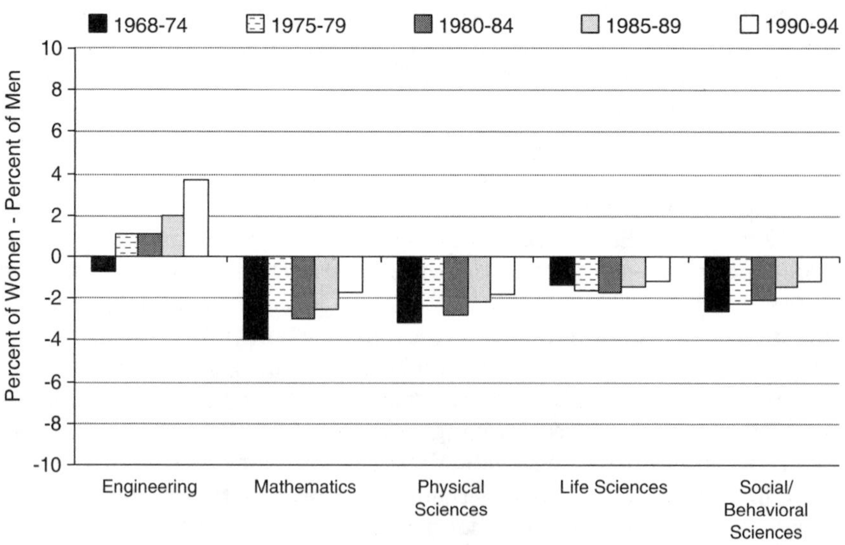

FIGURE 3-18 Differences between percent of women and percent of men who received funding from loans, by field and year of Ph.D. NOTE: Positive values indicate more women than men are supported with loans.

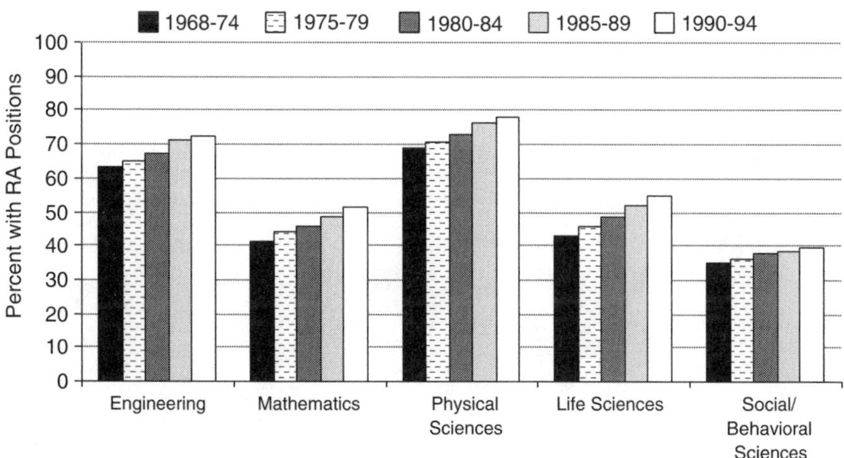

FIGURE 3-19 Percent of doctorates who received funding through research positions, by field and year of Ph.D.

of the principal investigator, research positions are likely to provide holders with opportunities to develop their own research programs. Accordingly, the disproportionate number of men with RA positions may represent a significant disadvantage to women. Finally, it is interesting to note that the physical sciences, with very small gender differences, is the broad field with the most support from the federal government.

Figure 3-21 shows that while there has been relatively little change over time in the percent of students supported by teaching assistantships (TAs), there are large differences across fields. TAs are most common in mathematics, likely resulting from institutional needs to staff a large number of required courses in undergraduate mathematics, followed closely by the physical sciences. They are somewhat less frequent in the social and behavioral sciences, although there has been a steady increase from 1968 to 1994. Women are between 6 and 8 points more likely than men to have teaching positions in engineering. They are also more likely to have TAs in mathematics and the physical sciences. Women are less likely to have teaching positions in the life and social/behavioral sciences, the two fields where research assistantships are least likely. This suggests that women may be given a lower priority for departmental support through teaching assistantships.

There are noticeable differences in sources of funding with clear signs that these differences are decreasing. Except for engineering, women are

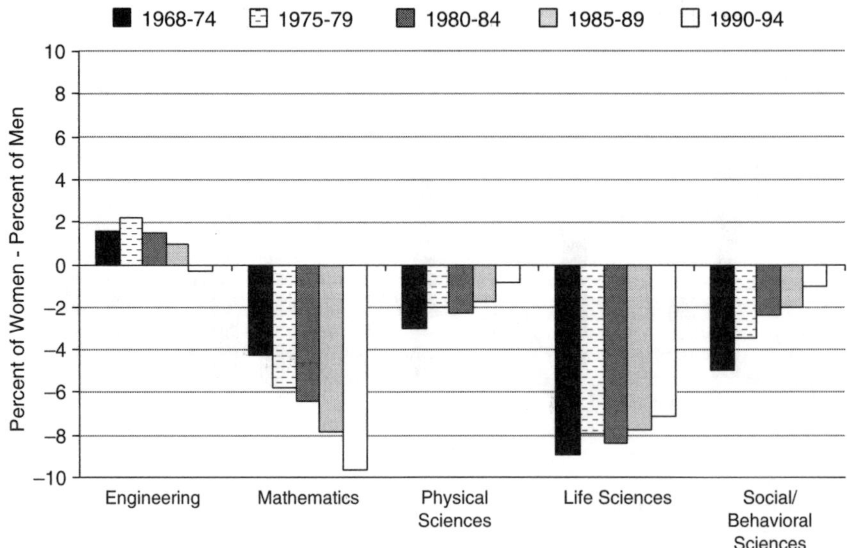

FIGURE 3-20 Differences between percent of women and percent of men who received funding through research positions, by field and year of Ph.D. NOTE: Positive values indicate more women use this type of funding.

more likely to use loans and are less likely to be funded with an RA position. Indeed, gender differences in obtaining RA positions are increasing in the mathematical sciences. Women are more likely to have TA positions in engineering, mathematics, and the physical sciences, with increasing differences in engineering but convergence in the other fields (Figure 3-22). In the life sciences and social/behavioral sciences men are more likely to have teaching positions. While our analyses are too limited to clearly determine the degree to which differences in sources of graduate support either favor or disadvantage women, this is clearly a topic that merits further study.

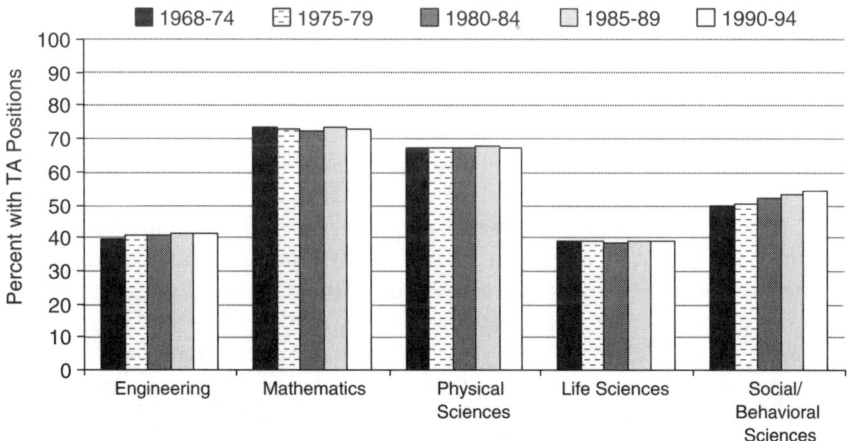

FIGURE 3-21 Percent of doctorates who received funding through teaching assistantship, by field and year of Ph.D.

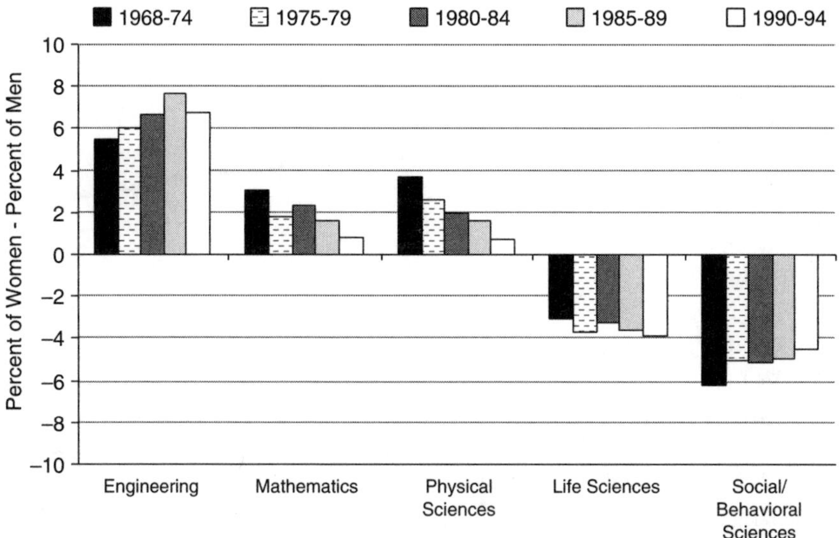

FIGURE 3-22 Differences between percent of women and percent of men who received funding through teaching assistantships, by field and year of Ph.D. NOTE: Positive values indicate more women are supported by this type of funding.

MARRIAGE AND FAMILY

". . . as much as women may want to be good scientists or engineers, we must remember that they want first and foremost to be womanly companions of men and to be mothers."

—Bruno Bettelheim, *Women and the Scientific Professions*, 1965.[11]

Male scientists and engineers are more likely to be married than female scientists and engineers, but this difference has declined significantly in the last 60 years. Figure 3-23 plots the percent of male and female Ph.D.s who are married against the years in which a scientist received his or her Ph.D.[12] Prior to WWII, nearly 95 percent of the men were married, compared to figures increasing from 30 percent to 45 percent for women. After WWII, marriage rates dropped to 90 percent for men, with continuing decreases until 1994. For women, there were steady increases in the percent married until around 1984, when rates began to mirror the gradual decline shown for men. By 1994, the difference between men and women was reduced to 7 percentage points. To understand the declines in the percent married for the most recent Ph.D.s, it is important to keep in mind

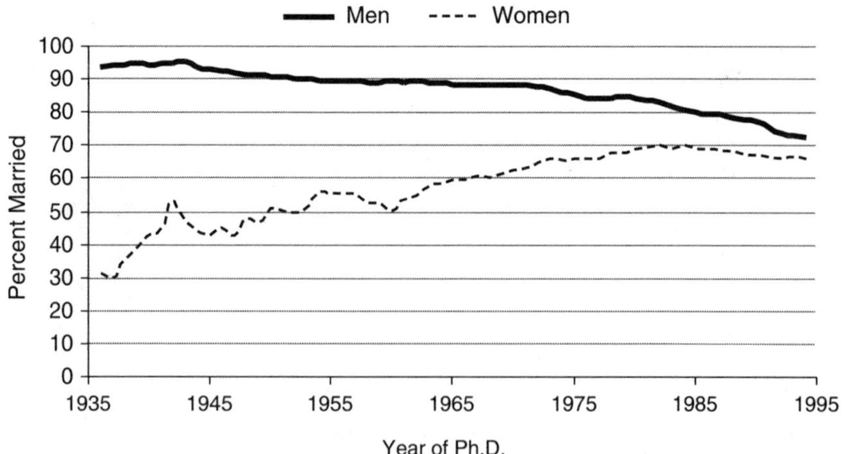

FIGURE 3-23 Percent of men and women who are married, by year of Ph.D.

[11]Bettelheim (1965).

[12]The data for this figure were obtained by merging the 1973, 1979, 1989, and 1995 SDRs. Accordingly, percents for Ph.D. years 1972 and earlier use data from all four surveys; data for Ph.D. years 1973 through 1978 use the last three surveys; and so on.

that Figure 3-23 reflects both general trends for more female and fewer male scientists to marry and also the timing of marriage. For example, marital status for individuals with recent Ph.D.s was obtained from the 1995 SDR and accordingly these scientists were younger; for the 1955 cohort, for example, data were collected in 1973, 1979, 1989, and 1995 when these scientists would have been older. Accordingly, the decline in the percent married since 1985 almost certainly reflects the younger biological age of these individuals at the time of the survey.

Given the demands of a scientific career, and the likelihood that women will undertake more of the responsibilities of raising children, it is not surprising that male scientists are more likely to have children. Figure 3-24 shows the percent of *married* scientists with children age six or younger living at home in 1995, by gender and years since the Ph.D. Immediately after the doctorate, 15 percent more of the married men have young children than married women. With time, gender differences narrow as fewer individuals have young children. Figure 3-25 shows that between 1979 and 1995 married *women* have become more likely to have children. The largest changes occurred between career years 5 and 17, which could reflect societal trends for having children later in life. As a result of these changes, differences in the percentage of men and the

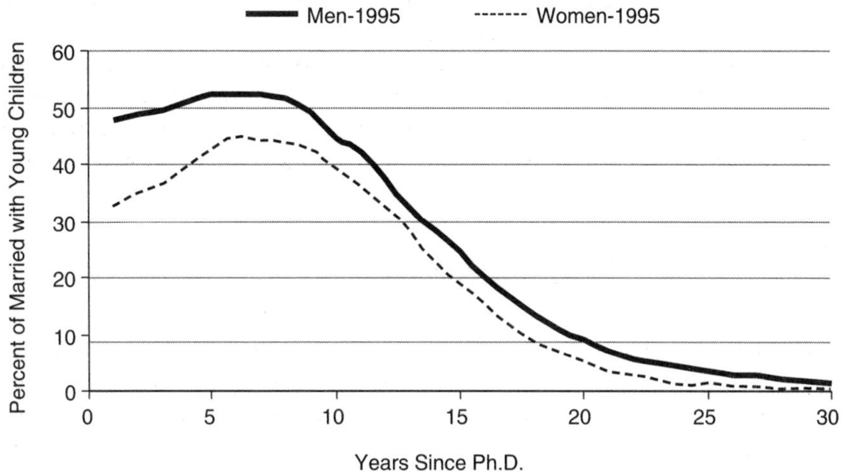

FIGURE 3-24 Percent of married scientists, both men and women, with children six or younger living at home in 1995, by sex and years since the Ph.D.

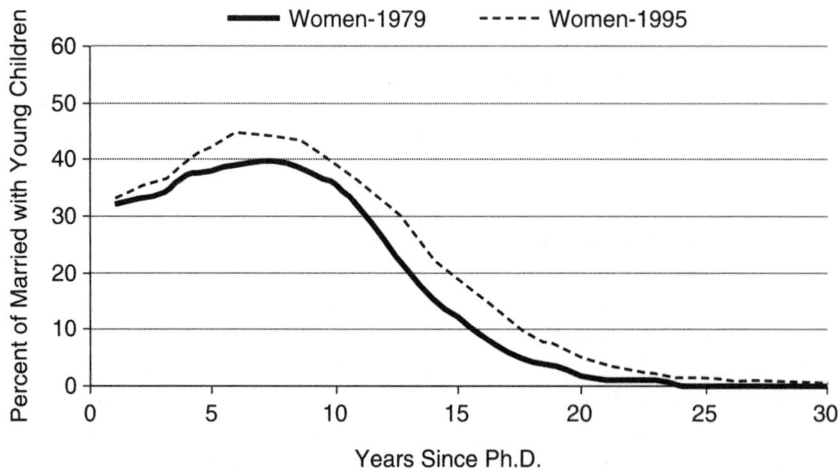

FIGURE 3-25 Percent of married *women* with young children at home, by years since the Ph.D. and year of survey.

percentage of women with young children have decreased substantially since 1979.

Overall, women and men have become increasingly similar in their patterns of marriage and having children. These changes are likely to reflect improvements in child care that help women balance the demands of a demanding career with raising a family. They may also indicate an increasing willingness by men to share the responsibilities of raising children and greater flexibility by employers in accommodating the demands of parenting. Still, the next chapter shows that marriage and family have quite different effects on the careers of men and women in science and engineering.

CONCLUSIONS

From 1970 to 1995, there were significant advances in the entry of women into science and engineering. Combining our five fields, there were 350 percent more women among new Ph.D.s in 1995 than in 1973. In the social and behavioral sciences, women were just over half of the Ph.D.s in 1995 and in the life sciences they reached over 40 percent. The concentration of women's doctoral degrees in psychology and in some of the social and biological sciences suggests that these fields could become female dominated in the future (NSB 1993). The progress toward gender equity in the receipt of science and engineering doctorates seems to have resulted from general social trends in women's advancement in higher education, the enforcement of anti-discrimination laws, falling interest in science and engineering among men, and a more rapid increase for women in degrees in scientific compared to non-scientific fields. Still, as the proportion of doctoral degrees to women in the social/behavioral and life sciences approaches parity, women remain but a small fraction of doctorates in engineering and mathematics.

While the increases are encouraging for attaining the equal representation of women and men in science and engineering, the advances represent neither unconditional success in overcoming gender inequalities nor provide assurance of continuing progress. The trend of greater participation of women in science and engineering may have peaked and the possibility remains of more restricted opportunities for women in years to come. For instance, new data from the American Association of University Women Education Foundation (1992:52) indicate that "the numbers and percents of girls interested in careers in math and science [are] increasing minimally, if at all." Although girls and boys are increasingly taking the same number of science and math credits in high school, many more girls drop out of the pipeline for scientific careers because of a lack of interest and encouragement in scientific fields that are heavily dominated by males.

The greater number of women lost through attrition on the way to the Ph.D. does not reflect a lack of academic ability or potential. For example, a study by Adelman (1991) found that women out-performed men on many dimensions that should positively affect success in science and engineering: high school performance, receipt of awards, rate of completing college, academic performance in college, and positive attitudes toward education. A report of the American Association of University Women Educational Foundation assessed more than 1,300 studies and concluded that (1992): "...girls are not receiving the same quality, or even quantity, of education as their brothers. By stereotyping women's roles, popular culture plays a role in short-changing girls by limiting their horizons and expectations. Unintentionally, schools sometimes follow suit, depriving girls of classroom attention, ignoring the value of cooperative learning, and presenting texts and lessons in which female role models are conspicuously absent."

A great deal of work has been done to understand the different experiences of men and women on the way to the Ph.D. (see Rayman and Brett 1993 for a review of this literature) and to develop initiatives to increase the participation of women (Matyas and Dix 1992). In 1980, Congress passed a law authorizing $30 million to the National Science Foundation (NSF) to be used to increase women's involvement in science at all educational levels and in the workforce. As a result, NSF instituted a number of initiatives, many of which continue to be administered through its Programs for Women and Girls within NSF's Directorate for Human Resources. The lack of funding stability, however, has hampered these programs and some grants have been eliminated. Fox (1998) reviews recent initiatives to support the participation and performance of women in graduate education.

When we examine background characteristics of men and women, we find that while differences persist, they have shrunk considerably. Still, women are less likely to obtain undergraduate degrees from Ph.D. granting institutions, take longer from the time of the baccalaureate to complete the degree, and are less likely to be supported by research positions during graduate education. While these differences are declining, each is likely to have negative effects on career outcomes for women. Finally, men are more likely to be married and to have children. While these differences are much smaller in 1995 than they were in 1973, later chapters will show that women who are married and have small children are less likely to have a full-time career in science and engineering.

4

Labor Force Participation

The Attrition of Women from the S&E Labor Force

. . . receipt of a doctorate in S&E does not imply full participation in these fields.
—J. Scott Long and Mary Frank Fox, *Annual Review of Sociology*, 1995.[1]

INTRODUCTION

Increases in the number of women among new Ph.D.s do not translate directly into increases in the proportion of women in the science and engineering labor force. Each new cohort of Ph.D.s represents only a small fraction of the total number of scientists and engineers. This is shown in Figure 4-1, which compares the growth in the percent of women among new Ph.D.s, to increases in the labor force, and finally among those employed full time in S&E. The proportion of women among new Ph.D.s, shown by the darkest bars, increased by 20 percentage points from 13 percent in 1973 to 33 percent in 1995, while the proportion of women in the labor force increased more slowly from 8 percent in 1973 to 21 percent in 1995. The proportion of women in the S&E labor force must increase slowly as older, predominantly male cohorts retire and are replaced by new cohorts that have a greater proportion of women. Hargens and Long (2000) demonstrate how demographic factors, such as the gender composition of new cohorts and the age distribution of currently employed

[1] Long and Fox (1995).

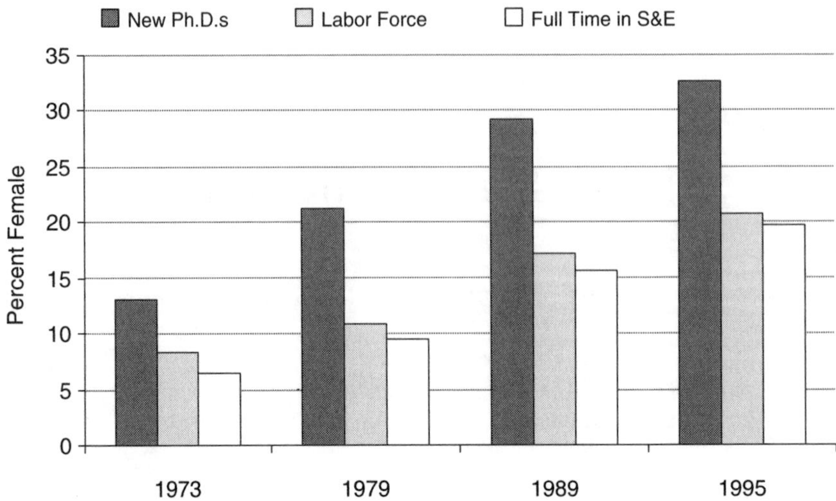

FIGURE 4-1 The percent of women among new Ph.D.s, among all scientists and engineers available to work in science and engineering, and among those working full time, by year of survey. NOTE: Labor force includes those who are not employed or working part time.

scientists, limit the rate of change in the gender composition of the academic labor force. For example, even if women were three-fourths of the new Ph.D.s, it would take decades before gender parity would be achieved in the labor force. Obviously, with women making up far less than half of the new Ph.D.s, changes will be even slower.

Second, after completion of the doctorate, a greater proportion of women than men do not attain full-time careers in science and engineering. While doctoral scientists and engineers have low rates of unemployment compared to the total U.S. labor force, women with doctorates are substantially more likely than men to be unemployed, employed part time, employed outside of S&E, or not be in the labor force. This is reflected by the white bars in Figure 4-1, which show that the percent of *full-time* workers in S&E who are women increased from 6.5 percent to 20 percent. Differences between men and women in labor force participation add up to less accumulated work experience and less valuable experience for women over the course of their careers, a factor that is important for understanding the gender differences in career outcomes that are described in later chapters.

This chapter begins by examining the sex composition of the scientific and engineering labor force in our five broad fields. How do men and women differ in the percent who are working full time in S&E occupations? Of those Ph.D.s who are not working full time in S&E, are they working outside of science, working part time, unemployed and looking for work, or out of the labor force? We find that while there has been improvement since 1973, *female Ph.D.s continue to be substantially less likely than men to be fully employed in scientific and engineering occupations.* Second, we examine the reasons given by scientists and engineers for working part time and look at characteristics of scientists that are associated with less than full employment. We find that *lack of full participation for women is most strongly related to familial status.* Finally, we summarize the effects of the underemployment of women by comparing the average number of years of professional experience for men and women. Overall during the past 20 years, *10 percent of the potential professional work of female doctorates has been lost as a result of women being less likely to be fully employed.*

Before proceeding, it is important to emphasize that participation in the full time scientific and engineering labor force includes a variety of jobs that differ greatly in prestige, security, and remuneration. This chapter considers only the question of *whether* a Ph.D. scientist is working full time in S&E, not the equally important question of *what kind* of work. In later chapters, we consider only those scientists and engineers with full-time employment in S&E and explore differences between men and women in sector of employment, work activity, position, and salary.

A Note on Terminology

Before proceeding, it is helpful to define several terms that are used in this chapter.

- *Labor force* is defined as Ph.D.s in S&E fields who are living in the United States and are under the age of 75. The labor force includes both part time workers and those who are unemployed.
- *Full-time labor force* is defined as members of the labor force who are working full time in some area of science or engineering.
- *Employed outside of S&E* includes doctoral scientists and engineers who are working full time in occupations that are not directly related to S&E as defined by the *Survey of Doctorate Recipients.*
- *Unemployed* includes those without jobs who are seeking work.
- *Out of the labor force* are those who are not working and not seeking work.
- *Underemployment* includes part time workers and the unemployed.

THE FULL-TIME SCIENTIFIC AND ENGINEERING LABOR FORCE[2]

As the growth in the production of new Ph.D.s slowed since 1973, the full labor force of Ph.D. scientists and engineers increased 220 percent from 187,236 in 1973 to 412,497 in 1995. During this period, the entry of increasingly female cohorts gradually changed the gender composition of the full-time labor force, from 6.5 percent female in 1973 to 19.6 percent in 1995 (Figure 4-2). But, as documented in the last chapter, the proportion of female Ph.D.s differs widely by field, which affects the sex composition of the full-time labor force within fields. While there has been substantial movement towards parity, the full-time participation of women in the labor force remains far below 50 percent in all fields.

Engineering: While the number of male Ph.D. engineers working full time doubled from 30,208 in 1973 to 69,013 in 1995, the corresponding number of women increased by a factor of 40, from a mere 82 in 1973 to 3,589 in 1995. Still, by 1995 women were only 5 percent of the full-time labor force. As shown in Table 4-1, in 1995 women were least represented in the largest subfields of electrical and chemical engineering, and were most strongly represented in the smaller fields of industrial engineering with 15 percent women and materials sciences with 10 percent women.

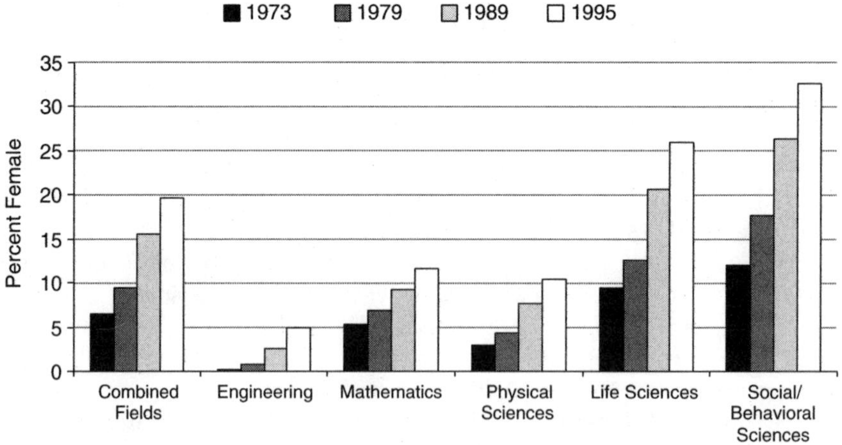

FIGURE 4-2 The percentage of the full-time scientific and engineering labor force that is female, by field and year of survey.

[2]See Appendix Tables B-1 and B-2 for additional data.

Mathematical Sciences: The number of female doctoral mathematicians working full time in S&E grew from 677 in 1973 to 3,728 in 1995. This increase of 450 percent can be compared to a 121 percent increase in male mathematicians from 11,639 in 1973 to 25,711 in 1995. Overall, women represented 5.5 percent of the mathematicians in 1973, which increased to 13 percent in 1995. As shown in Table 4-2, in 1995 women were most strongly represented in statistics and probability with 18 percent of the full-time labor force and in the rapidly growing field of computer science where they were 13 percent.

Physical Sciences. The proportional representation of women in the physical sciences is similar to that in mathematics. In 1973, there were 1,637 women, which corresponded to 3 percent of the total Ph.D.s in the physical sciences working full time in S&E. By 1995 the number of women increased by 480 percent to 9,505 or 10.5 percent of the full-time labor force. During this same period, the number of male physical scientists increased only 50 percent from 52,168 in 1973 to 81,373 in 1995. As shown in Table 4-3, the largest increases overall, as well as for women, were in the large subfields of physics and chemistry, which represented 31 percent and 51 percent of the full time Ph.D.s in 1995, respectively. The largest proportional representation of women is in chemistry, which grew from being 4 percent female in 1973 to 14 percent female in 1995. While the second largest number of women is in physics, with nearly 1,500 women in 1995, the growth was from a mere 1.3 percent of the full-time Ph.D. labor force being female in 1973 to a still small 5 percent in 1995.

Life Sciences: Overall, women have a larger representation in the full-time labor force in the life sciences than the preceding broad fields. In 1973, there were 4,598 women, 9.5 percent of the total, compared to 44,053 men. The proportion of women increased to 26 percent in 1995, as the number of women grew six fold to 29,885, while the number of men only doubled to 85,098. As shown in Table 4-4, women are found most often in the subfield of biological sciences, where they were 49 percent of the full-time labor force in 1995. They were least represented in the agricultural sciences with only 1 percent of the total in 1973, increasing to 12 percent in 1995.

Social and Behavioral Sciences. Women are most highly represented in the social and behavioral sciences. As the number of Ph.D.s working full time increased 150 percent from 43,298 in 1973 to 107,216 in 1995, the representation of women grew from 12 percent to 33 percent. As shown in Table 4-5, women are most highly represented in anthropology with 40 percent of the full-time labor force, followed by 39 percent in the large

TABLE 4-1 Numbers of Engineers Working Full Time in S&E, by Sex, Subfield, and Year of Survey

	1973			1979		
	# Men	# Women	% Women	# Men	# Women	% Women
Biomedical	307	2	0.6	778	10	1.3
Chemical	4,835	13	0.3	6,696	33	0.5
Electrical	7,317	17	0.2	9,578	53	0.6
Industrial	720	4	0.6	1,007	12	1.2
Materials Science	146	0	0.0	599	12	2.0
Other	16,883	46	0.3	23,860	218	0.9
Total	30,208	82	0.3	42,518	338	0.8

TABLE 4-2 Numbers of Mathematicians Working Full Time in S&E, by Sex, Subfield, and Year of Survey

	1973			1979		
	# Men	# Women	% Women	# Men	# Women	% Women
Computer Science	540	30	5.3	1,330	92	6.5
Probability and Statistics	2,233	130	5.5	3,710	318	7.9
Mathematics	8,866	517	5.5	10,871	780	6.7
Total	11,639	677	5.5	15,911	1,190	7.0

TABLE 4-3 Numbers of Physical Scientists Working Full Time in S&E, by Sex, Subfield, and Year of Survey

	1973			1979		
	# Men	# Women	% Women	# Men	# Women	% Women
Astronomy	930	64	6.4	1,531	89	5.5
Physics	16,424	220	1.3	20,603	427	2.0
Chemistry	28,936	1,236	4.1	34,990	2,105	5.7
Oceanography	523	6	1.1	888	37	4.0
Geosciences	5,355	111	2.0	7,287	292	3.9
Total	52,168	1,637	3.0	65,299	2,950	4.3

1989			1995		
# Men	# Women	% Women	# Men	# Women	% Women
1,314	84	6.0	1,729	135	7.2
9,410	257	2.7	9,574	504	5.0
12,595	213	1.7	16,422	601	3.5
901	75	7.7	1,590	279	14.9
1,587	138	8.0	3,304	366	10.0
32,631	791	2.4	36,394	1,704	4.5
58,438	1,558	2.6	69,013	3,589	4.9

1989			1995		
# Men	# Women	% Women	# Men	# Women	% Women
3,670	397	9.8	6,501	933	12.6
5,067	798	13.6	5,165	1,175	18.5
13,610	1,304	8.7	14,045	1,620	10.3
22,347	2,499	10.1	25,711	3,728	12.7

1989			1995		
# Men	# Women	% Women	# Men	# Women	% Women
2,310	175	7.0	2,578	202	7.3
25,577	982	3.7	26,977	1,473	5.2
39,788	4,426	10.0	39,773	6,251	13.6
1,336	132	9.0	1,537	212	12.1
9,857	809	7.6	10,508	1,367	11.5
78,868	6,524	7.6	81,373	9,505	10.5

TABLE 4-4 Numbers of Life Scientists Working Full Time in S&E, by Sex, Subfield, and Year of Survey

	1973			1979		
	# Men	# Women	% Women	# Men	# Women	% Women
Agricultural	8,766	86	1.0	12,093	297	2.4
Medical	30,916	4,131	11.8	41,403	7,218	14.8
Biological	4,371	381	8.0	6,724	1,078	13.8
Total	44,053	4,598	9.5	60,220	8,593	12.5

TABLE 4-5 Numbers of Social and Behavioral Scientists Working Full Time, by Sex, Subfield, and Year of Survey

	1973			1979		
	# Men	# Women	% Women	# Men	# Women	% Women
Psychology	16,048	3,060	16.0	24,690	7,005	22.1
Anthropology	1,226	246	16.7	2,193	756	25.6
Economics	7,359	376	4.9	9,261	781	7.8
Sociology	4,018	753	15.8	5,649	1,592	22.0
Other	9,434	778	7.6	14,058	1,820	11.5
Total	38,085	5,213	12.0	55,851	11,954	17.6

field of psychology and 36 percent in sociology. Women were least represented in the more mathematical field of economics, where they grew from 5 percent of the full-time labor force in 1973 to 15 percent in 1995.

THE AGE STRUCTURE IN SCIENCE AND ENGINEERING

The later entry of women into S&E is reflected in their younger professional age. Professional age is important for understanding career outcomes since years working in the profession affect the positions that scientists and engineers hold. For example, tenure and promotion in academia are related to the time a person has been in rank. If the average female faculty member is younger than the average male, proportionately fewer women would be full professors, all else being equal. Administrative positions and appointment to gatekeeping roles (e.g., editor of a journal) are also associated with age, with older scientists being more likely to

1989			1995		
# Men	# Women	% Women	# Men	# Women	% Women
15,569	1,354	8.0	15,688	2,053	11.6
54,025	14,699	21.4	63,815	22,452	26.0
11,490	4,955	30.1	5,595	5,380	49.0
81,084	21,008	20.6	85,098	29,885	26.0

1989			1995		
# Men	# Women	% Women	# Men	# Women	% Women
34,961	16,818	32.5	36,317	22,833	38.6
2,914	1,441	33.1	3,419	2,283	40.0
11,907	1,654	12.2	11,659	2,063	15.0
6,575	2,717	29.2	6,255	3,536	36.1
18,501	4,251	18.7	14,633	4,218	22.4
74,858	26,881	26.4	72,283	34,933	32.6

hold these influential positions. Zuckerman and Merton (1972) discuss the many ways in which age, aging, and the age structure affect the scientific career.

Age structure is determined by the size of new cohorts of Ph.D.s relative to the size of past cohorts and the rate at which each cohort leaves S&E through retirement, death, and migration to other occupations. If each new cohort were the same size, the age structure would be nearly uniform, with approximately the same number of people at each age until retirement. However, the number of new Ph.D.s grew rapidly after World War II and in response to Sputnik, with slower growth in the 1970s and 1980s. During these periods of slower growth, the proportion of women in each new cohort grew most rapidly. These trends resulted in different age structures for men and women.

Population pyramids are the standard method for examining the age structure in a population. A population pyramid compares the age distri-

TABLE 4-6 Mean Years Since Ph.D., by Field, Sex, and Year of Survey

	Combined Fields		Engineering		Mathematics	
	Men	Women	Men	Women	Men	Women
1973	11.4	10.0	8.8	7.4	9.9	10.3
1979	12.5	9.3	11.3	6.4	11.6	9.6
1989	15.4	10.4	14.9	7.1	15.3	11.7
1995	16.8	11.4	15.1	7.2	15.8	11.6
	Physical Sciences		Life Sciences		Social/Behavioral Sciences	
	Men	Women	Men	Women	Men	Women
1973	13.0	11.4	12.2	10.5	10.8	9.1
1979	14.4	11.4	12.7	10.0	11.4	8.3
1989	16.9	11.5	14.9	10.4	14.8	10.2
1995	18.3	11.3	16.6	11.3	17.2	11.9

butions for two groups by showing the percent of individuals within each group who is a given age. For our purposes, we consider professional age, which is defined as the number of years since the receipt of the doctorate. Panels A and B of Figure 4-3 are population pyramids for male and female scientists and engineers in the S&E labor force in 1973 and 1995. Each figure contains two histograms. The histogram on the left shows the percent of men in each three-year age group; the histogram on the right shows corresponding data for women. Note that the sum of the bars in each histogram will equal 100.

Comparing the plots for men and women in 1973, we see that a greater proportion of women is younger, with a median professional age of seven compared to a median age of nine for men. The shape of the distribution resulted from the proportionately smaller number of women receiving Ph.D.s before 1966 (corresponding to professional age 6), the greater inflow of women after 1965, and the substantial attrition of women who entered S&E before World War II. In 1995, shown in Panel B, the decreasing size of new cohorts of men resulted in an increase in the median professional age of men from 9 to 16. For women, the median age increased only from 7 to 9, since the sizes of new cohorts of women were larger relative to the total number of women in science and engineering. The percent of men at each age 1 through 27 is nearly uniform, while the distribution for women has a triangular shape corresponding to the in-

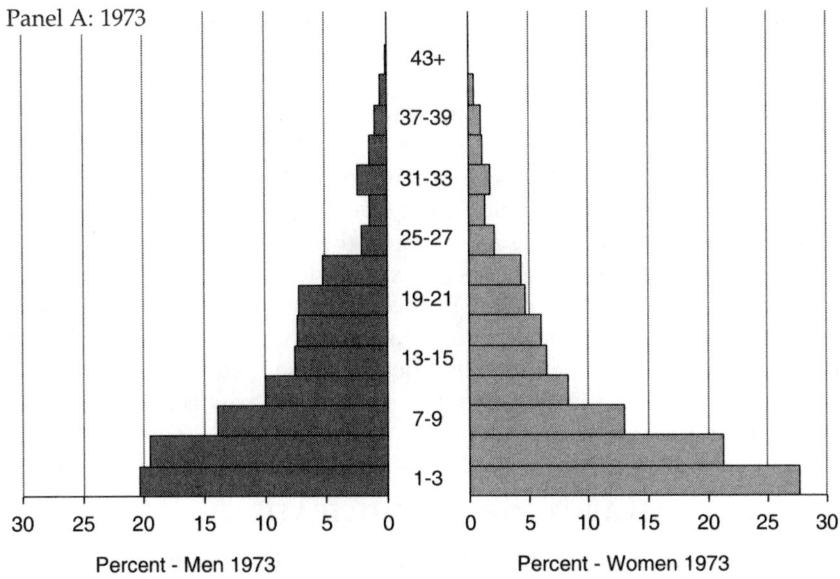

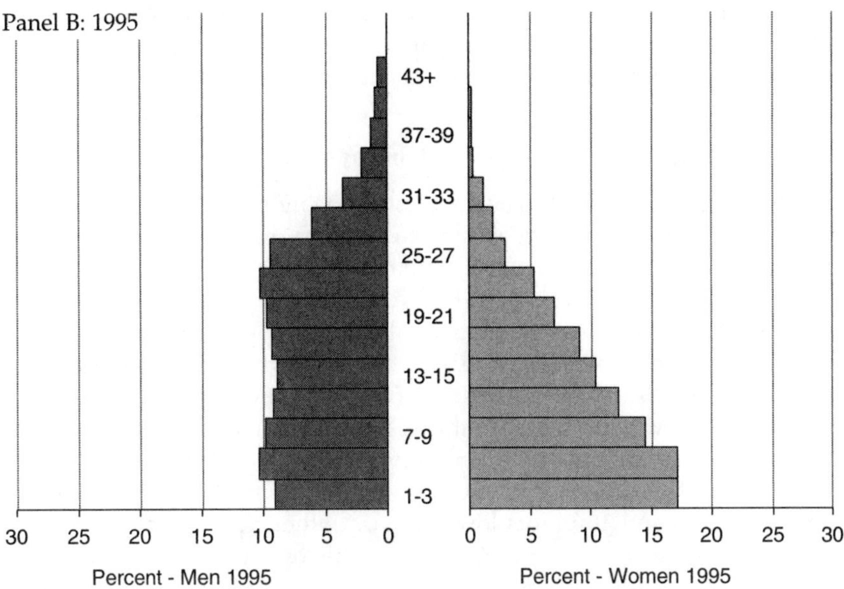

FIGURE 4-3 Distribution of professional ages in the science and engineering labor force, by sex and year. NOTE: Professional age is defined as the number of years since the receipt of the doctorate.

creasing size of newer cohorts. The similarity of the size of age groups 1-3 and 4-6 for women shows that more recent cohorts of Ph.D.s have been more similar in size.

The five fields differ in the rate at which they are growing and in the proportion of women in new cohorts of Ph.D.s. Consequently, the age structures differ among fields, as shown in Table 4-6. While the average age of men increased in all fields, the greatest aging occurred in the more slowly growing fields of engineering and the social/behavioral sciences. The increase in professional age was smallest in the life sciences where growth of the field was greater in recent years. For women, there was very little aging except in the social and behavioral sciences and, to a lesser extent, the life sciences. Historically, these fields had greater proportions of women, and accordingly the impact of new cohorts of Ph.D.s on the age structure has been less.

LABOR FORCE PARTICIPATION[3]

While most doctoral scientists and engineers have full-time employment in science and engineering occupations, women are far less likely than men to be fully employed. The attrition of women from the full-time S&E labor force is the focus of this section. We begin by examining levels of full-time employment, before examining the reasons for less than full-time employment of female scientists and engineers.

Full-Time Employment

In 1973, 91 percent of male scientists and engineers were working full time in occupations that are related to their training, while women were 20 points less likely to have full-time employment in S&E. As shown in Table 4-7, since 1973 levels of full-time employment in S&E for men have decreased in all fields with an overall rate of 85 percent in 1995, while rates for women improved by nearly 10 points. While there is some variation across fields, by 1995 gender differences in all fields had been reduced to around 10 points. Still, this is an important difference, representing 1 out of 10 women with a doctorate in science and engineering.

Rates of full-time employment in the social and behavioral sciences are between 5 and 10 points lower than in other fields. Table 4-8 shows that these lower rates are largely the result of a greater percentage of social and behavioral scientists who are working full time in occupations outside of S&E. Such employment includes positions that are either unre-

[3]See Appendix Tables B-3-B-7 for additional data.

TABLE 4-7 Percent of Doctoral Scientists and Engineers with Full-Time Employment Within Science and Engineering, by Sex, Field, and Year of Survey

		Combined Fields	Engineering	Mathematics
1973	Men	90.9	93.1	94.7
	Women	70.9	—	76.5
	Difference	20.0	—	18.2
1979	Men	89.0	90.9	90.5
	Women	74.1	81.8	78.4
	Difference	14.9	9.1	12.1
1989	Men	88.1	89.7	91.0
	Women	74.4	84.8	80.0
	Difference	13.7	4.9	11.0
1995	Men	85.8	90.6	90.8
	Women	73.5	81.3	79.5
	Difference	12.3	9.3	11.3
		Physical Sciences	Life Sciences	Social and Behavioral Sciences
1973	Men	89.8	93.3	87.0
	Women	64.1	74.4	69.7
	Difference	25.7	18.9	17.3
1979	Men	89.7	92.5	83.2
	Women	73.2	77.9	71.3
	Difference	16.5	14.6	11.9
1989	Men	90.3	91.3	81.0
	Women	79.9	80.3	68.5
	Difference	10.4	11.0	12.5
1995	Men	87.2	85.3	79.6
	Women	77.4	75.9	69.4
	Difference	9.8	9.4	10.2

NOTE: — indicates too few cases to compute statistic. Full-time postdoctoral fellows are considered to be employed full time in S&E.

TABLE 4-8 Percent of Doctoral Scientists with Full-Time Employment Outside of Science and Engineering, by Sex, Field, and Year of Survey

		Combined Fields	Engineering	Mathematics
1973	Men	6.1	4.7	2.9
	Women	6.5	—	4.8
	Difference	–0.4	—	–1.9
1979	Men	7.6	6.0	6.6
	Women	7.7	7.0	6.4
	Difference	–0.1	–1.0	0.2
1989	Men	8.7	7.3	6.8
	Women	9.5	8.0	8.0
	Difference	–0.8	–0.7	–1.2
1995	Men	8.1	4.6	4.2
	Women	9.9	4.3	5.0
	Difference	–1.8	0.3	–0.8
		Physical Sciences	Life Sciences	Social and Behavioral Sciences
1973	Men	6.6	3.9	9.8
	Women	6.9	4.8	8.1
	Difference	-0.3	-0.9	1.7
1979	Men	7.2	4.5	12.5
	Women	7.2	4.4	10.1
	Difference	0.0	0.1	2.4
1989	Men	6.8	6.0	14.4
	Women	7.0	6.7	10.3
	Difference	-0.2	-0.7	4.1
1995	Men	6.3	9.1	13.2
	Women	8.4	11.1	10.3
	Difference	-2.1	-2.0	2.9

NOTE: — indicates too few cases to compute statistic.

lated or indirectly related to a person's doctoral training. For example, a Ph.D. in engineering could work as a sales person for a company manufacturing computers (a related occupation) or could sell insurance (an unrelated occupation). In the social/behavioral sciences, the percentage of Ph.D.s with full-time employment outside of S&E is between 10 percent and 14 percent, with 2 percent fewer women in such positions. The large percentage working outside of S&E is a result of positions such as a social worker being classified as work outside of S&E; these positions could reasonably be classified as being in S&E. In engineering, mathematics, the physical sciences, and the life sciences, between 3 percent and 10 percent of the Ph.D.s have full-time employment outside of S&E, with only small differences in the percentages for men and women. Overall, there is greater employment outside of S&E in the physical sciences and a recent increase in the life sciences where the rate reached 10 percent in 1995.

As a cohort of scientists ages through the career, there are gradual changes in patterns of full-time employment. Figure 4-4 illustrates these changes by examining the cohort of life scientists who received their degrees in the 1970s. The data from the 1979 survey show employment in the early part of the career; 1989 represents the middle of the career, roughly 15 years after the degree; and 1995 shows labor force status about 20 years after the degree. For both men and women, there is a decrease in

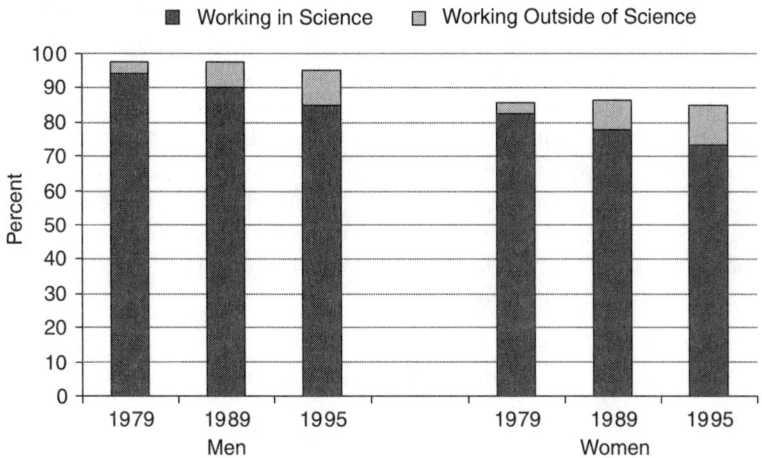

FIGURE 4-4 Change over the career in the percent of life scientists with Ph.D.s from the 1970s who are working full time in science and engineering and outside of science and engineering, by sex, and year of survey.

TABLE 4-9 Percent of Scientists from the 1970 Cohort Who Are Working Full Time in S&E or Outside of S&E, by Sex, Field, and Year of Survey

		1970 Cohort of Men in			1970 Cohort of Women in		
		1979	1989	1995	1979	1989	1995
Engineering	In Science	93.0	88.4	87.4	—	—	—
	Outside	4.7	8.1	6.9	—	—	—
	Total FT	97.7	96.5	94.3	—	—	—
Mathematics	In Science	90.7	91.7	90.0	80.9	80.9	79.4
	Outside	6.1	7.0	5.3	4.3	7.8	3.1
	Total FT	96.8	98.7	95.3	85.2	88.7	82.5
Physical Sciences	In Science	93.2	89.5	87.5	78.0	78.2	70.2
	Outside	4.1	8.1	7.6	7.0	9.7	15.0
	Total FT	97.3	97.6	95.1	85.0	87.9	85.2
Life Sciences	In Science	94.4	90.1	84.8	82.4	77.9	73.3
	Outside	3.2	7.5	7.6	7.0	4.7	10.5
	Total FT	97.6	97.6	92.4	89.4	82.6	83.8
Social and Behavioral Sciences	In Science	84.5	82.3	80.8	72.1	66.1	67.1
	Outside	11.5	14.5	14.0	9.4	15.0	12.5
	Total FT	96.0	96.8	94.8	81.5	81.1	79.6

NOTE: — indicates that there were too few cases to compute this statistic.

full-time employment in S&E as the career progresses, with gradual increases in the percentage who are working outside of S&E. Combining full-time employment both in and out of S&E, there is a slight decrease in full-time employment as the scientists age. Table 4-9 shows that these overall tendencies in full-time employment hold in other fields with the exception of mathematics where there was a slight increase in employment in 1989. These changes in full-time employment occur as scientists move into part-time employment, become unemployed, or leave the labor force. These forms of underemployment, which represent a significant loss of highly trained individuals, are considered following a shorter discussion of postdoctoral fellowships.

Postdoctoral Fellowships

The postdoctoral fellowship is another form of employment that is increasingly common early in the career. The Committee on a Study of Postdoctorals in Science and Engineering in the United States characterized the critical importance of the postdoctoral fellowship as follows (NRC 1981:1):

> For many of the most talented scientists and engineers the postdoctoral appointment has served as an important period of transition between formal education and a career in research. The appointment has provided recent doctorate recipients with a unique opportunity to devote his or her full energies to research without the encumbrance of formal course work or teaching and administrative responsibilities.

While for many scientists, the postdoctoral fellowship is an important first step in launching a promising career, the postdoctoral fellowship can also serve as a "holding tank" until more adequate employment is secured (NRC 1981:60-61).

Since the late 1960s an increasing percent of doctoral scientists and engineers have begun their careers with a postdoctoral fellowship. In the life sciences, the percent of new Ph.D.s who were planning postdoctoral training upon graduation increased from just over 20 percent in 1963 to over 50 percent in 1995 (NRC 1998: 29). While the use of postdoctoral fellowships varies widely by fields, with their most frequent use in the life sciences, followed by the physical sciences, the postdoctoral fellowship is an increasingly important aspect of the career in nearly all fields. Sonnert (1995) provides a detailed study of gender difference among those receiving prestigious postdoctoral fellowships from NSF and NRC. Unfortunately, most other studies of the postdoctoral experience fail to consider gender differences. For example, while the recent NRC (1998) study of the early career in the life sciences (where postdoctoral fellowships are most common) carefully considers the postdoctoral fellowship, it does not provide any comparisons by gender.

Table 4-10 shows the percent of men and women in the first five years: after the Ph.D. who hold postdoctoral fellowships in each of our survey years 1973, 1979, 1989, and 1995. The table highlights several key characteristics of fellowships. First, their use varies widely by field, with substantially more postdoctoral fellowships in the life and physical sciences. Second, since 1973 there has been a steady increase in the percent of scientists and engineers who have fellowships in the period immediately after the Ph.D., perhaps reflecting the relatively weak job market of recent years. Third, in fields where the postdoctoral fellowship is traditional, namely the life and physical sciences, women used to be about 5 percentage points more likely to have a fellowship early in the career. That trend has been reversed.

Unfortunately, our data are too limited to pursue more detailed analyses of gender differences in postdoctoral fellowships. To examine the postdoctoral experience, the focus must be on scientists in the period immediately following the Ph.D. By its design, the SED samples scientists and engineers at all stages of the career. Consequently, there are too few

TABLE 4-10 Percent of Men and Women Within Five Years of the Ph.D. Who have Postdoctoral Fellowships, by Years of Survey and Field

	Men				Women			
	1973	1979	1989	1995	1973	1979	1989	1995
Engineering	1.9	2.0	5.7	8.5	—	2.9	6.9	12.0
Mathematical Sciences	1.4	3.3	5.8	9.4	1.2	2.1	4.1	12.1
Physical Sciences	11.5	13.1	21.1	30.8	15.5	18.9	20.5	22.5
Life Sciences	11.2	23.8	32.7	37.1	18.0	28.8	28.0	37.0
Social/ Behavioral Sciences	1.7	3.2	3.5	5.4	2.9	4.7	4.2	7.0

	Difference: Men – Women			
	1973	1979	1989	1995
Engineering	—	–0.9	–1.2	–3.6
Mathematical Sciences	0.2	1.2	1.7	–2.7
Physical Sciences	–4.0	–5.8	0.6	8.3
Life Sciences	–6.8	–5.0	4.7	0.1
Social/ Behavioral Sciences	–1.2	–1.5	–0.6	–1.6

NOTE: — indicates too few cases to analyze.

scientists, and especially women, within any given field to adequately explore gender differences in the fellowship experience.

Less than Full-Time Employment of Doctoral Scientists and Engineers

Female scientists are much more likely than men to be less than fully employed, as shown by Figure 4-5. The overall height of the bar shows the percent of scientists and engineers who are not working full time, with the divisions within each bar indicating the specific labor force status. Part-time employment is shown with dark gray; being unemployed by light gray; and not seeking work by the white region at the top. In 1973

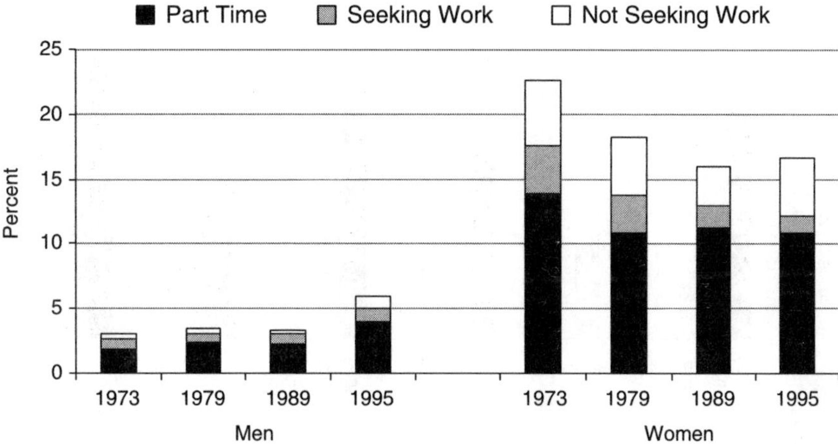

FIGURE 4-5 Employment status of those not working full time for combined fields, by sex, and year of survey.

women were 20 percentage points more likely to be less than fully employed. Since then gender differences have declined somewhat. In 1979 and 1989 there were small decreases for women, while rates were stable for men. In 1995 the rate increased 3 points for men and held steady for women. The net result is that gender differences in being less than fully employed have been reduced to 11 percentage points. Still, 17 percent of the female doctorates do not have full-time employment compared to only 6 percent of the male doctorates. There are also interesting changes in the relative proportion of scientists who are working part time, seeking work, and not seeking work. These issues are now considered.

Part-Time Employment

While women in all fields are much more likely than men to be working part time, Figure 4-6 shows that there are substantial differences across fields and changes over time in the percent of female doctorates who are working part time. Part-time employment for women decreased in all fields between 1973 and 1979, with decreases ranging from a low of 2 points in the life sciences to a high of 5 points in the physical sciences. Since 1979 rates of part-time employment have been highest in the social/behavioral sciences where they have gradually increased. Rates are more similar among other fields, with increases in engineering and mathematics and decreases in the physical and life sciences. For men (figure not shown), rates are between 1 percent and 3 percent in all fields except the

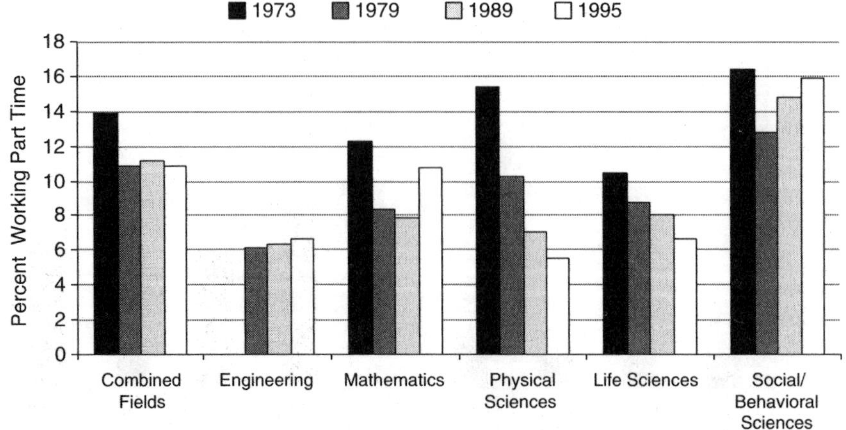

FIGURE 4-6 Percent of *female* Ph.D.s who are working part time, by field, and year of survey. NOTE: There are too few women in engineering in 1973 to estimate the percentage.

social/behavioral sciences, where between 3 percent and 4 percent are working part time. From 1989 to 1995, the rate of part-time employment for men increased by 1 to 2 points in all fields.

Seeking Work and Being Out of the Labor Force

Compared to the rate of unemployment in the United States population, unemployment is extremely rare for doctoral scientists and engineers. The lines in Figure 4-7 show the percent of the U.S. civilian population aged 20 and older who are seeking employment (BLS 1999) in each of our survey years. The dark gray bars show the corresponding percent of scientists and engineers who are unemployed. The percent of men in the United States population who are seeking work is about five times higher than for scientists and engineers whose rates are nearly constant at 1 percent. For female scientists and engineers, the situation is very different. Since 1973, there was a steady decrease in the percent of women who were seeking work, from 4 percent in 1973 to just over 1 percent in 1995. By 1995, the difference between male and female Ph.D.s in the percent *seeking work* was reduced to less than one-half point from a difference of three points in 1973. These low rates of unemployment in 1995 are consistent with what would be expected through the normal circulation of scientists and engineers among jobs.

There are much larger differences between male and female doctor-

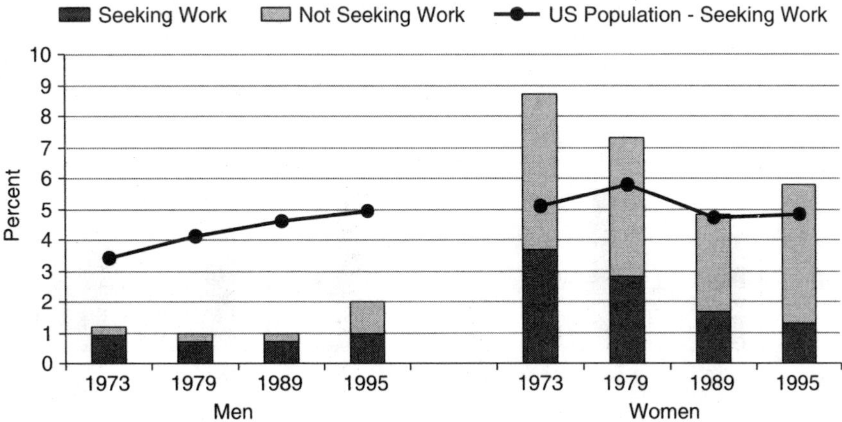

FIGURE 4-7 Rates of unemployment and being out of the labor force (i.e., not seeking work) for combined fields, by sex, and year of survey. NOTE: Rates for the U.S. population are the January rates for the civilian population ages 20 and older.

ates in the percent who are out of the labor force (i.e., not employed and *not seeking work*), represented by the light gray regions. These individuals are fully trained scientists and engineers who have not retired but who are no longer pursuing jobs in their field of training. While these scientists and engineers represent only a small percent of the total, they represent the loss of many years of training. Moreover, this loss occurs primarily to female scientists and engineers. For women, the rate hovers around 4 percent with some variations across fields (considered below). From 1973 to 1989, only three-tenths of 1 percent of the men were no longer seeking employment, a number that grew to 1 percent in 1995. The reasons for the change are unclear, but may correspond to aging of the male S&E labor force with an increasing proportion having accumulated sufficient financial resources to stop working.

Figure 4-8 shows field differences in the percent of female scientists and engineers who are unemployed. There is an overall downward trend in all fields except engineering where there is a spike to 4 percent in 1995. Note, however, that the figures in engineering are based on a small number of women. The largest drop occurred between 1973 and 1979, with smaller changes thereafter. The highest rates are in the physical and life sciences. Since the rates of seeking work for women in these fields do not correspond to higher rates for men, it is unlikely that the female rates reflect labor market conditions in these fields.

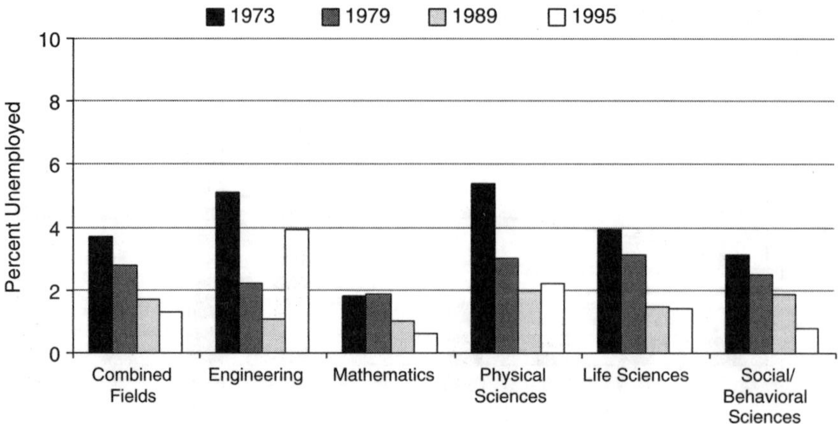

FIGURE 4-8 Percent of women who are unemployed, by field, and year of survey.

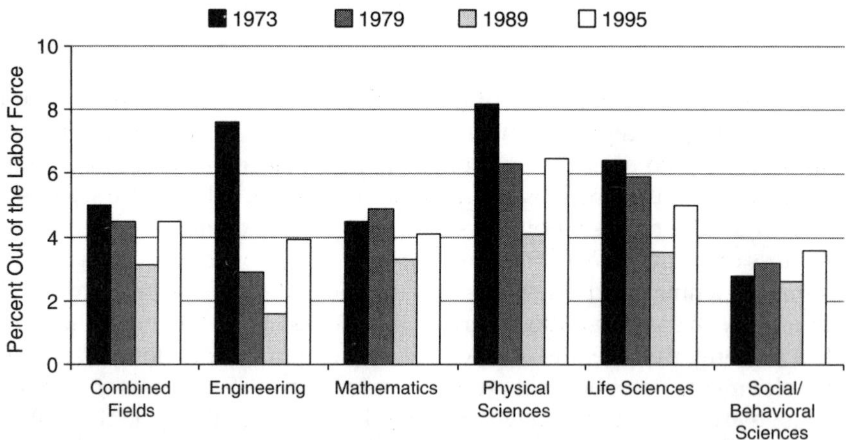

FIGURE 4-9 Percent of women who are not employed and *not seeking work*, by field and year of survey.

Figure 4-9 shows the percent of women who are out of the labor force. That is, they are not employed and not seeking work. The rates for women are substantially higher than for men, with percentages reaching as high as 8 percent in the physical sciences in 1973. While there is a slight decrease between 1973 and 1989, this trend is reversed in 1995. There are also substantial differences across fields, with the highest rates in the physical sciences, followed by the life sciences, mathematics, and then the social/behavioral sciences. Given our findings in later analyses that lack of full-time employment for women is associated with being married and having a family, it is possible that higher rates occur in fields where it is more difficult for women to balance the responsibilities of work and home. Indeed, the higher rates occur in lab sciences where "being tied to the bench" may make it more difficult for a woman to nurture both a research program and a family. These fields are also among the fastest moving, where even a short absence can cause a scientist to quickly cease to be current with the latest research.

Trends over the Career

There are two approaches that can be used to examine how labor force participation changes as scientists and engineers age. First, a cohort of Ph.D.s can be followed as they progress through their career. This was done in Figure 4-4 when we looked at scientists with Ph.D.s from the 1970s using data from the 1979, 1989, and 1995 SDR. While this approach is ideal in many respects, it is limited since we have data only for three years. An alternative approach is to construct a *synthetic cohort* (see Chapter 2 for further details). For example, using data collected in 1995, scientists who obtained their degrees in 1994 are in the first year of the career; scientists with 1993 degrees are in the second year of the career; and so on. These age-defined cohorts can be thought of as a single group of scientists that are aging through the career. But, since each career year is based on a different cohort of scientists with degrees from different years, changes that are observed reflect both the effects of aging and the effects of the historical period (e.g., labor market conditions). Even with these limitations, synthetic cohorts provide valuable information on gender difference in labor force participation.

Figure 4-10 shows the major changes in the labor market behavior of Ph.D. scientists and engineers from 1973 to 1995 and key differences in the career paths of men and women. Consider first the distribution among labor force statuses for men and women in 1973, as shown in Panels A and B.[4] The most striking difference is the much smaller percentage of women who are working full time in S&E at all stages of the career (shown by the smaller dark gray region at the bottom) and the much larger proportion of women who are less than fully employed. For both men and women, there is a decline in full-time employment over the career (shown

[4]The more jagged curves for women are due to the smaller number women with Ph.D.s during this period.

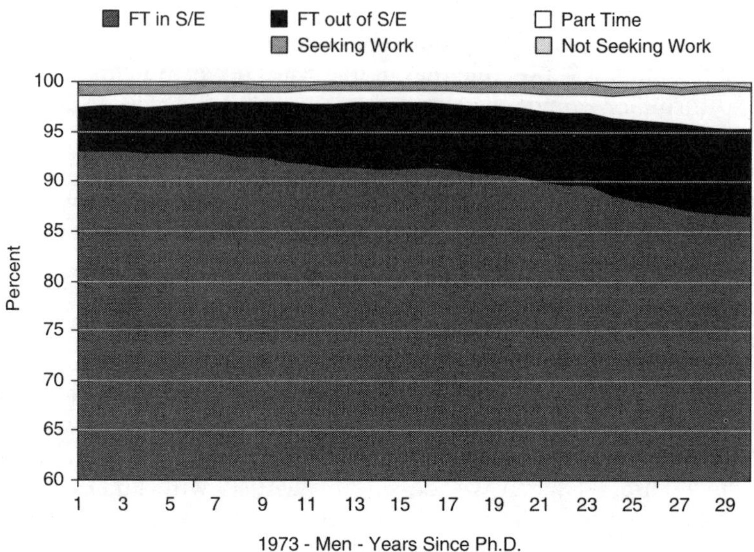

Panel A: Men – 1973

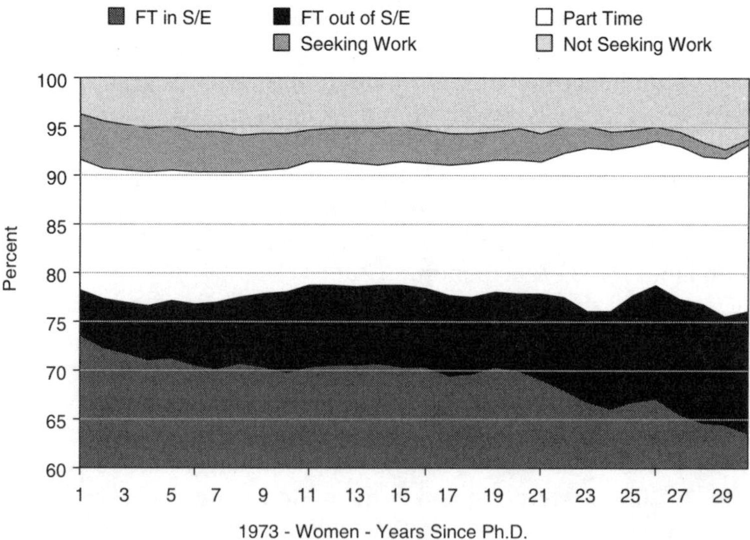

Panel B: Women – 1973

FIGURE 4-10 Distribution of labor force outcomes, by sex and year of survey. NOTE: Percentages at each year since the Ph.D. are based on those scientists with Ph.D.s in the corresponding year. For example, year 1 in 1995 is based on scien-

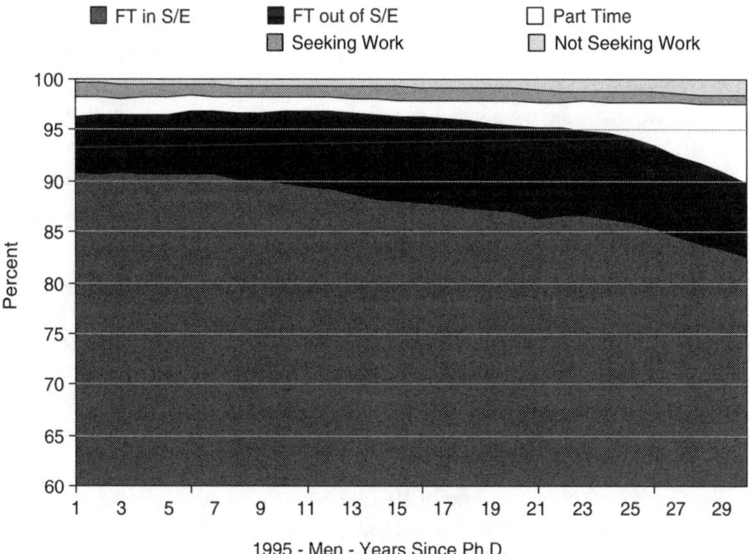

Panel C: Men – 1995

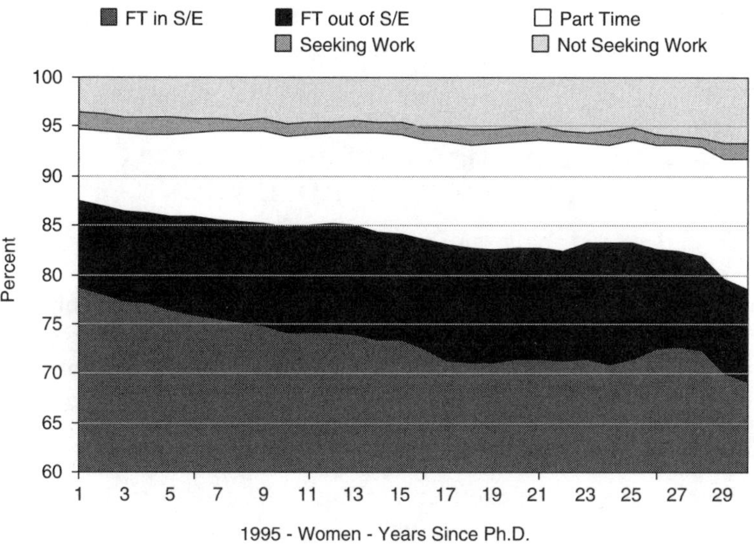

Panel D: Women – 1995

tists with Ph.D.s in 1994. Values are moving averages across five-year periods. Note that the vertical axis begins at 60 percent in order to highlight variation in the categories other than full time work in science and engineering.

by the bottom two regions). For men this is largely the consequence of movement into part-time employment as retirement is approached. For women the change in full-time employment in S&E is due to increases in employment outside of S&E. Our data cannot distinguish the degree to which this change was due to women from earlier Ph.D. cohorts being less successful in obtaining positions in S&E or if female scientists found their S&E employment increasingly unsatisfactory as they aged, perhaps as a result of a lack of opportunity for promotion.

While similar trends are seen in 1995, there are several notable changes since 1973. First, there is a substantial increase in the percent of women working full time in all years. Second, smaller proportions of women are working part time as shown by the narrower white region in the center. Finally, there is a decrease in the percent of women seeking work, particularly at the start of the career.

In assessing these findings, keep in mind that the results are based on synthetic cohorts that reflect both changes as scientists age and differences in the scientific and engineering climate at different historical times. Nonetheless, it is clear that between 1973 and 1995 there has been convergence in the career paths of male and female scientists and engineers. Still, women are far more likely to be less than fully employed, leading to a substantial loss of doctoral women from the active scientific and engineering labor force. We now consider explanations for these gender differences.

EXPLANATIONS FOR DIFFERENCES IN LABOR FORCE PARTICIPATION

To understand the loss of female scientists and engineers from full-time employment, we must explore reasons for the lesser full-time employment of women. In this section, we consider two sources of information. First, we look at responses by scientists and engineers to questions on why they are working part time. Unfortunately, data are not available on reasons for unemployment or being out of the labor force. Second, we estimate statistical models to determine the association between individual characteristics and labor force status. Both sources of information demonstrate the profound effects of familial obligations for the labor force participation of women. It is also the case, however, that the direction of causality in the relationship between factors such as family responsibilities and employment remains unclear. For example, unsatisfactory employment prospects might encourage women to have children and reduce their commitment to work.

Reasons for Part-Time Employment[5]

While female scientists and engineers are less likely to be married (as discussed in Chapter 3), married female scientists and engineers are twice as likely to have a spouse who is working full time compared to married men (NSF 1996: 68). This could have at least two effects on the likelihood of part-time employment for women. First, Marwell, Rosenfeld, and Spilerman (1979) find that geographic constraints imposed by a dual career limit the ability of women to make strategic job changes in the academic marketplace. Such constraints might also increase the necessity of part-time employment as women try to accommodate their spouse's career. Second, women are more likely to have primary responsibility for raising children and part-time employment could be a *relatively* attractive means of raising a family while maintaining links to a professional career.

In 1989 and 1995, the SDR asked scientists and engineers why they were working part time. Respondents chose one or more of the following: there were no jobs available; I had no need to work; and family obligations made part-time work necessary. Figure 4-11 shows that in 1989 nearly half of the women who worked part time cited family obligations and that the percent has increased over time. For men this was the least likely explanation. There are smaller gender differences in other reasons for part-time employment. In 1989, 53 percent of the men who were employed part time reported that they had no need to work full time compared to 31 percent of the women. These percentages were nearly reversed in 1995, when 30 percent of the men and 42 percent of the women indicated no need. A larger percent of men than women said they could not find full-time employment, while the precent of women remained constant at 19 percent.

While the SDR did not ask respondents to indicate the type of family obligation that kept them from full employment, our data suggest that this primarily involves responsibilities in raising children. Figure 4-12 plots the percentages of men and women who cite family reasons for part-time employment against how many years it is since the Ph.D. was obtained. If we assume that the Ph.D. was received at age 30, the horizontal axis corresponds to biological ages from 30 to 56. Immediately after the Ph.D. women cite family obligations 50 percent of the time. This rate increases till it peaks in year 8 for the 1989 survey and year 11 for the 1995 survey. The later peak in 1995 is consistent with recent societal trends for women having children when older. The rates decrease steadily from this point on. For men, the percentages generally stay below 10 percent, with a slight increase occurring from years 5 to 15.

---

[5]See Appendix Tables B-8-B-11 for additional data.

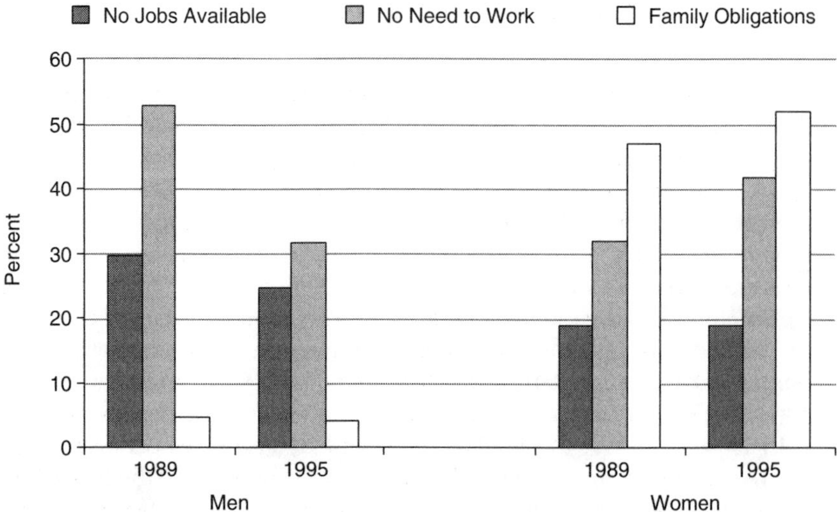

FIGURE 4-11 Reasons for part-time employment, by sex, and year of survey. NOTE: Respondents can choose more than one response.

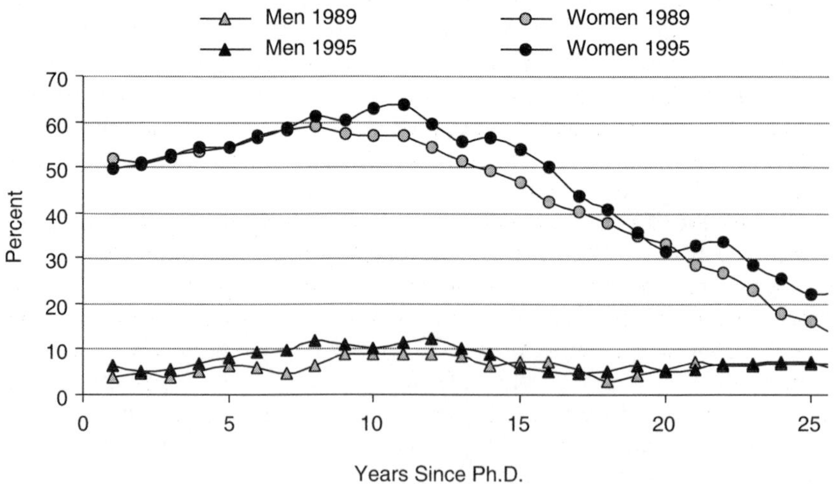

FIGURE 4-12 Percent who cite family reasons for working part time, by sex and year of survey. NOTE: Values are moving averages across 5-year periods.

Factors Associated with Labor Force Participation[6]

Unfortunately, the SDR only asked respondents the reasons for part-time employment. To consider factors affecting other types of less than full employment, we must use statistical models to determine the degree to which characteristics of an individual, such as marital status and Ph.D. origins, are associated with labor force status after controlling for variables such as broad field and Ph.D. cohort. The effects of these control variables are not discussed since they were considered earlier in the chapter.

Marriage and Family

Past research has often found only limited effects of marriage and family on the careers of women in science and engineering. However, most of this research studied only women who were *fully participating* in S&E. But, for example, to say that the success of women who are full professors at research universities is not affected by family obligations does not imply that marriage and family did not affect their chances of staying in the labor force and thus having a chance to become a full professor. Conversely, women who do not become faculty at research universities may have had their career choices limited by familial status. Indeed, our analyses show that there is a strong association between marriage, children, and whether a female doctorate is less than fully employed, while there are only small effects for men. These results are now considered.

Overall, marriage and family are the most important factors differentiating the labor force participation of male and female scientists and engineers. Figure 4-13 plots the percent of male and female scientists and engineers in 1995 who are predicted by our model to work full time either in or out of S&E according to familial status.[7] Four familial statuses are considered: single without children (black bar), married without children (dark gray bar), married with child one or more between the ages of 7 and 18 living at home (light gray bar), and married with one child or more younger than 7 living at home (white bar). Other statuses, such as di-

[6]See Appendix Table B-12 for additional data. Analyses are based on multinomial logit analyses of the five categories: full-time employment in S&E, full-time employment outside of S&E, part-time employment, unemployed and seeking work, and unemployed and not seeking work. Technical details are given in Chapter 2.

[7]Predictions are for an individual who is average on all of the variables in the model. See Chapter 2 for details.

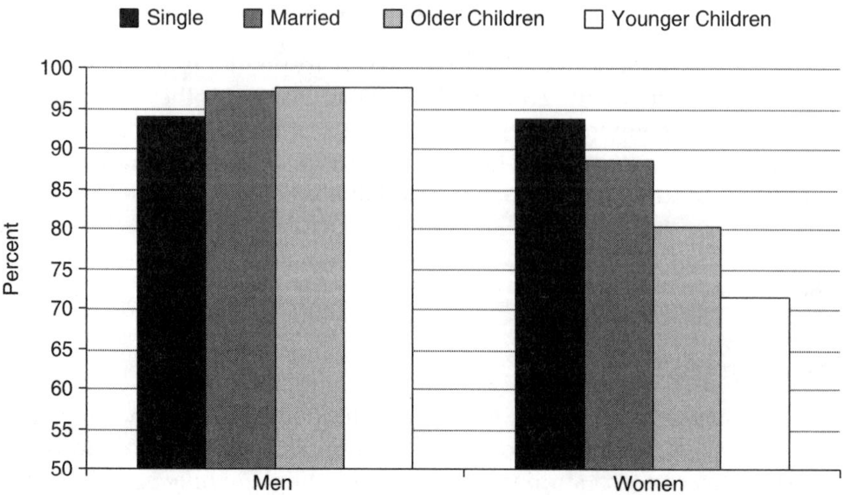

FIGURE 4-13 Predicted percent with full-time employment in 1995, by sex and familial status.

vorced with children, had too few cases to evaluate. Among men, those who are single are least likely to be working full time, with small increases for married men and those with children. In contrast, single women are most likely to be working full time. While being married slightly increases a man's chances of full-time work, being married without children decreases the predicted proportion of women working full time by 5 percentage points. Having older children at home decreases the proportion by 8 more points, while being married with young children decreases the proportion with full-time employment by 22 points. It is interesting to note that as a consequence of the opposite effects of marriage and children for men and women, an identical 94 percent of single men and single women are expected to be working full time. That is, *differences between men and women in labor force participation are eliminated if we compare single men to single women.*

Figure 4-14 shows that for women there were some changes in the effects of marriage and family over time.[8] The percent of women with young children who are predicted to work full-time increased by nearly 10 points between 1979 and 1989, with only a tiny increase in 1995. The predicted percent working among those with older children at home increased by over 3 points between each survey. Figure 4-15, plots differ-

[8]Data on marriage and family are not available for 1973.

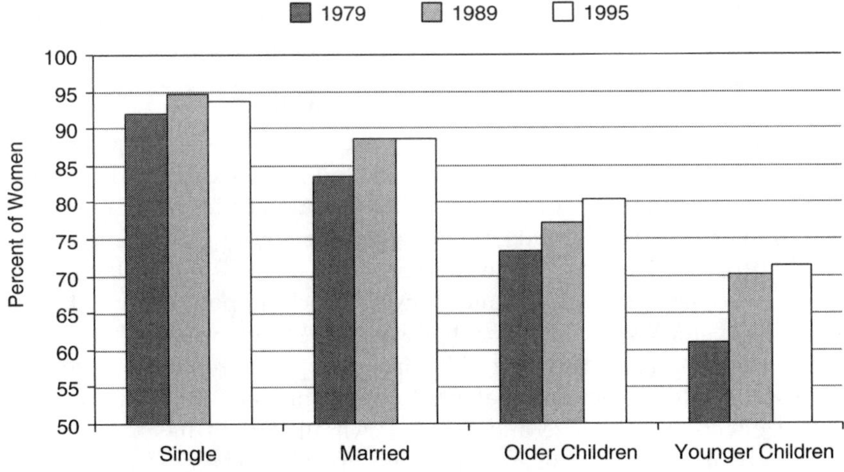

FIGURE 4-14 Predicted percent of women with full employment, by year of survey.

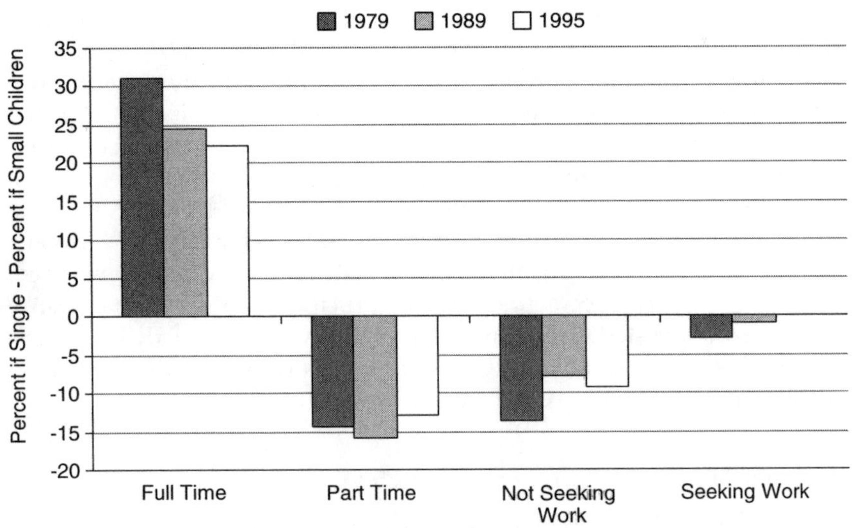

FIGURE 4-15 Differences in predicted labor force status between single women and married women with young children, by year of survey.

ences between single women and married women with small children in the predicted proportion in each category of labor force participation. The biggest difference is in the proportion working full time. In 1979 women with small children were over 30 points less likely to be working full time compared to single women. This difference dropped to 22 points by 1995. The next two categories, part time work and not seeking work, account for the lesser full time work of women with young children. Women with children are nearly 15 points more likely to be working part time, with a slight drop in 1995. The next most likely work status is not seeking work. In 1979 women with young children were nearly 15 points more likely to be in this category, a difference that was reduced to around 10 points by 1995. There is very little effect of having young children for not working and seeking work. Similar analyses for men (not shown) found only the small effects of marriage and family. Overall, family has a significant effect on labor force status, but the effect appears to be gradually declining.

Baccalaureate Origins

The effects of baccalaureate origins on labor force participation were examined by including the Carnegie type of the baccalaureate institution. For men, we found no effect, but for women there was a small, negative association between receiving the bachelor's degree from an exclusively undergraduate institution (e.g., a small liberal arts college) and working full time. Women with degrees from baccalaureate-only institutions were 2 percentage points less likely to be working full time in S&E occupations and roughly 2 points more likely to be working part time, after controlling for other factors. These effects were slightly smaller in 1995. It is possible that this represents differences in critical socialization to the scientific career that would be obtained with an undergraduate degree from an institution with research activities at the graduate level. On the other hand, it may reflect someone with lower career aspirations. We also examined whether receiving an undergraduate degree from a women's college or university affected labor force participation. While some past research has suggested that attending a women's college greatly increased a woman's chances of being highly successful (Tidball and Kistiakowsky 1976), we found no effect on labor force participation.

Elapsed Time from Baccalaureate to Ph.D.

Logit analyses show that the time elapsed between the baccalaureate and the Ph.D. affected the labor force participation of scientists and engineers. Our measure of elapsed time is the difference between the date of the undergraduate degree and the date of the doctorate, thus combining time enrolled in a graduate program and interruptions such as predoctoral employment or raising a family. Past research suggests that individuals with elapsed times of more than 10 years have interrupted their education (Tuckman, Coyle, and Bae 1990). Accordingly, elapsed time was entered into the analyses as a binary variable indicating whether it took more than 10 years to complete the doctorate—that is, indicating whether it is likely that the education was interrupted.

Using data from 1995, Figure 4-16 plots the changes in the proportion of scientists and engineers predicted to be in each labor force status if the education was interrupted. The effects are in the same direction for men and women, but are larger for women. Individuals with interruptions are 5 to 7 percentage points less likely to be working full time in S&E, which is offset by a greater likelihood of working outside of S&E or working part time. Since interruptions between the bachelor's degree and the Ph.D. may involve work outside of S&E (e.g., a social worker who goes back for a Ph.D. in psychology), it is possible that these men and women returned to their original employment after the completion of the degree. It is also possible that those who take longer to complete the degree are either less

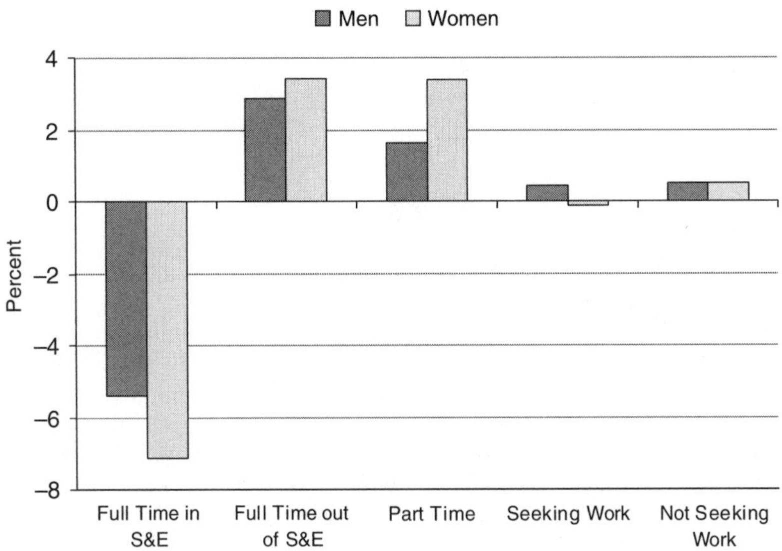

FIGURE 4-16 Changes in labor force status if elapsed time between the baccalaureate and Ph.D. was more than 10 years, by sex for 1995.

committed to their careers or alternatively that they are equally committed but not viewed by employers as being as as committed as their peers who complete the degree more quickly.

YEARS OF WORK EXPERIENCE[9]

The net effects of workforce participation can be summarized by the number of years that a scientist or engineer has spent working since the receipt of the doctorate. The impact of the greater time out of the full-time labor force for women is shown in Figure 4-17 for 1979 and 1989. Comparable data for 1973 and 1995 are not available. The lines plot the difference between the mean years of professional experience for men and women by the number of years since the Ph.D. For example, a value of 1.5 means that an average woman worked 1.5 years less than an average man. In 1979, for every year since the degree the female scientist worked 0.12 years less than an average male scientist; in 1989 this loss was reduced to 0.09, with the largest improvements being noticed between the 9th and 15th years of the career. *Overall, compared to male scientists, nearly 10 percent of the potential work experience of female scientists is being lost.*

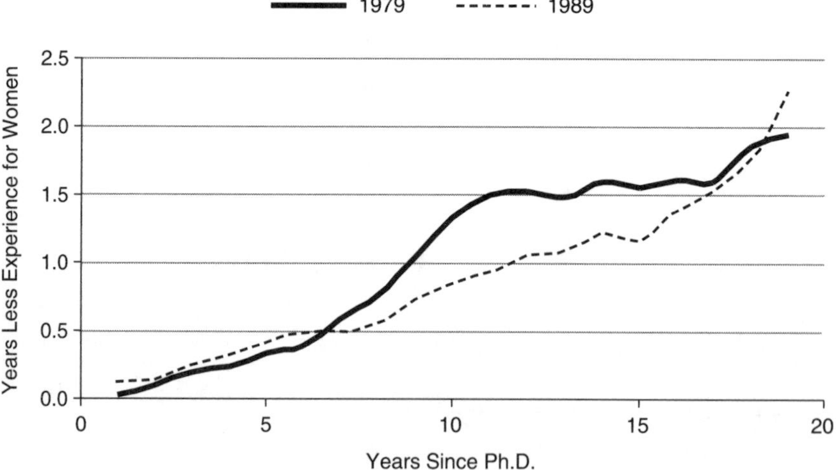

FIGURE 4-17 Difference between men and women in mean years of work experience by years since the receipt of the Ph.D., by year of survey. NOTE: Values are 3-year moving averages.

[9]See Appendix Tables B-13-B-14 for additional data.

A possible explanation for gender differences in professional work experience is that women are taking more time out of the workforce to care for their families. This explanation is consistent with many studies that have shown that within society as a whole women are more likely to be the primary caregivers (e.g., Moen 1985) and consequently to be absent from the paid labor force while they are working as caregivers. While we do not have information on the reasons for interruptions in the career, we do know an individual's familial status at the time of the survey. Panels A and B of Figure 4-18 plot the difference between the mean years of work experience for male and female scientists according to their familial status, with the horizontal axis indicating years since the Ph.D. was received. In 1979, there was no difference in average work experience between single men and single women. For those who were married without children at home, the differences were small with some increase later in the career. But, for those who have children at home, the differences were *much* larger with an average woman with young children losing three-tenths of a year of work compared to men with young children for each year since the doctorate. Panel B shows that there were some decreases in the effects between 1979 and 1989, possibly reflecting increasing trends for women with families to remain in the labor force. Still, for married women and especially for those with young children, there are substantial losses in years of experience.

SUMMARY AND CONCLUSIONS

From 1973 to 1995 there were significant advances in the entry of women into S&E, but their advances did not completely overcome gender inequalities. While the representation of women in the S&E labor force is increasing in all fields, a greater proportion of women than men are not working full time. One way to summarize these differences, as well as to demonstrate the improvements since 1973, is to compare the percent of women working full time to the percent of men. Figure 4-19 plots the ratio of female and male rates of full-time employment. For example, if both 80 percent of men and 80 percent of women were working full time, the ratio would be at .8/.8 = 1. Values less than 1.0 indicate that women are less likely to be working full time. The figure shows that there were large improvements between 1973 and 1979, followed by gradual improvement through 1995. As shown earlier in the chapter, the net effect of the lower labor force participation of women is that as late as 1989 nearly 10 percent of the potential work activity of female scientists and engineers was lost as a result of their less than full employment.

Among the variables we consider, by far the strongest factor that affects a female scientist's labor force participation is familial status. While

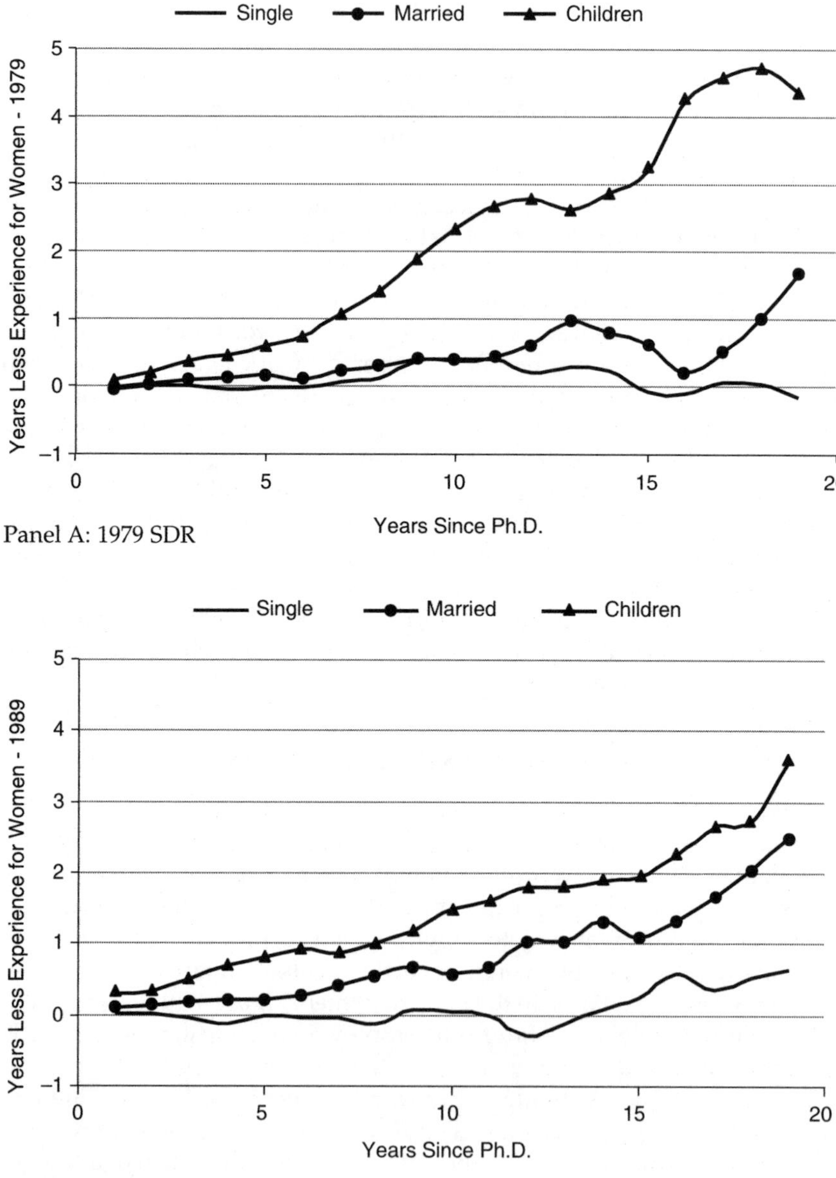

FIGURE 4-18 Difference between mean work experience of men and women, by familial status, years since the Ph.D., and year of survey. NOTE: The vertical axis is the difference in the mean years for women and the mean years of experience for men.

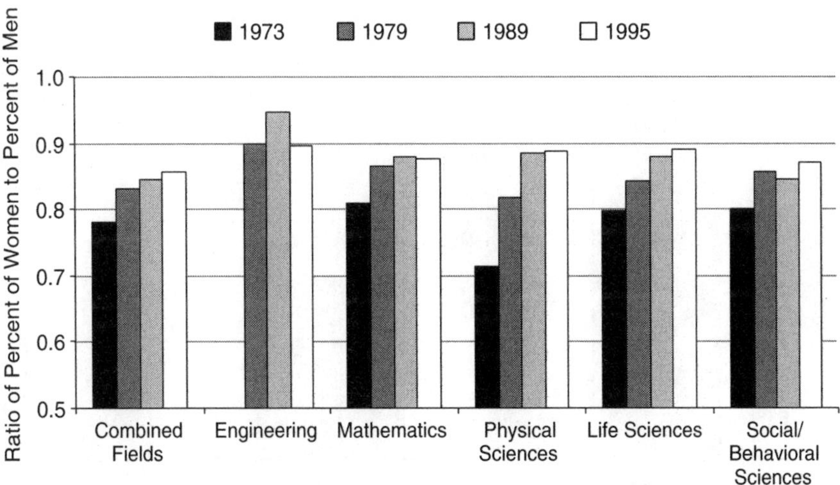

FIGURE 4-19 Ratio of the percent of women who are working full time in S&E to the percent of men who are working full time, by field and year of survey. NOTE: There are too few women in engineering in 1973 to compute statistic.

single women have rates of working full time that are identical to those of single men, being married and having children substantially reduces labor force participation for women but not for men. As summarized in Figure 4-20, married women are less likely to be working full time, women with older children are even less likely, and women with young children at home have rates of only around 70 percent.

Implications for Later Chapters

It is essential to understand the implications of our findings on labor force participation for the analyses of career outcomes in Chapters 5, 6, and 7. Those chapters examine the type of employer and work activity of scientists and engineers who are fully employed. Thus, even if the results in later chapters found no gender differences in career outcomes (which they do *not* find), there would still be important differences between male and female scientists and engineers in their success in moving into full-time employment. The less frequent full-time employment of women that is documented in the current chapter represents a significant loss of highly trained and talented scientific personnel, a loss that is not reflected in later chapters.

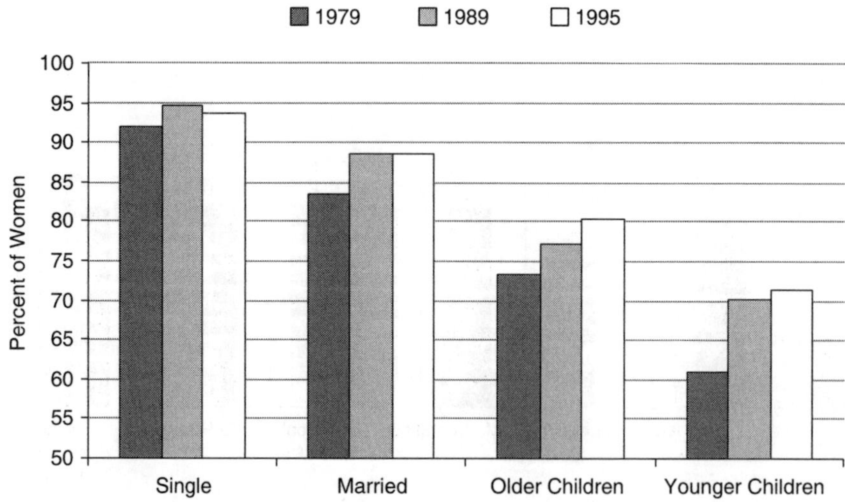

FIGURE 4-20 Predicted percent of *women* with full-time employment, by marital status and year of survey.

5

Sector of Employment and Work Activity

Diverse Careers within Science and Engineering

. . . science is no longer mainly an academic activity carried on in universities. Industry will soon be the largest single employer of scientists.
—Cotgrove and Box, *Science, Industry and Society*, 1970[1]

INTRODUCTION

When viewed within the context of the entire American labor force, scientists and engineers appear as a homogenous and elite group of workers. Studies of social stratification in the larger society, such as Blau and Duncan's classic *The American Occupational Structure* (1967), place all scientists and engineers within the undifferentiated class of professional workers. In popular culture, the common stereotype of a scientist is a professor, white and male, writing at the blackboard in a university with ivy covered buildings. However, as noted by Zuckerman (1970), this seemingly uniform group of scientists is itself highly stratified. Studies of stratification in science focus on the many differences in position and prestige among scientists and engineers.

Most studies of stratification in science focus on the academic career. For example, Cole and Cole's (1973:43) classic study *Social Stratification in Science* only briefly mentions nonacademic employment. Studies of stratification in academic science have generated a huge body of research,

[1]Cotgrove and Box 1970.

which we consider in Chapter 6. The few studies that give greater attention to scientists and engineers in other sectors, such as Kornhauser (1962), Marcson (1960), and Pelz and Andrews (1966), often focus on the conflicts between science as a profession and the contrasting goals of nonacademic employers. There are only a few studies considering factors that affect sector in which a scientist works (Long and McGinnis 1981; Reskin 1979). Yet, sector of employment is a fundamental dimension of the scientific career that affects work experience, opportunities, employment security, and prestige.

In the current climate of science, it is extremely important to consider scientists in nonacademic sectors since the kinds of jobs held by scientists and engineers are changing (Kuh 1996; Tobias, Chubin, and Aylesworth 1995). The foremost indicator of this change is the transition from a primarily academic S&E workforce to one that is more evenly divided between higher education and industry. Changes within academia that have limited the number of jobs occurred simultaneously with the growing presence of women in the academic labor market. The employment shift from education to industry is the result of several economic and political transformations since 1970. While the number of doctoral scientists and engineers in the labor force has continued to grow, the quality of employment deteriorated for those obtaining academic jobs. Between 1976 and 1986, real wages of faculty declined by 4 percent (Touchton and Davis 1991). Compared to other professions requiring postgraduate education in the 1980s, academic salaries fell behind (Magner 1996a). Hackett (1990) and others report growth in the number of off-track positions (e.g., part-time, non-tenure track, postdoctoral positions) in response to reduced opportunities for tenure-track jobs. Academic researchers found it increasingly difficult to secure adequate federal research support while academic employers increased pressure on faculty to obtain externally funded grants (Hackett 1990). During the same period, industry surpassed the federal government as the largest source of research and development (R&D) funding (NSB 1993). Even while corporate downsizing and the defense conversion to civilian R&D displaced science and engineering workers and contributed to their higher unemployment rates, the overall demand in industry for scientists has increased since 1973, as documented below.

This chapter begins by examining differences in the distribution of men and women into the largest sectors of employment: academia, industry, government, and private nonprofit organizations. It is also important to understand the type of employment within sectors. Since the rewards, prestige, and meaning of work activities differ across sectors, we then consider gender differences in work activities within each sector.

Before proceeding to these tasks, and at the risk of repetition, we remind readers that *the analyses in this chapter are necessarily restricted to scientists and engineers in the full time labor force.* While this excludes only about 10 percent of the male Ph.D.s, over 30 percent of the female Ph.D.s are excluded in 1973, decreasing to 19 percent in 1995. Thus, a substantially greater proportion of highly trained women than men fail to enter the full-time scientific labor force. See Chapter 4 for further details.

SECTOR OF EMPLOYMENT

The SDR asks each respondent to provide a brief description of their job (e.g., college professor in electrical engineering) and to choose from a detailed list of job codes and a shorter list of types of employers (e.g., U.S. government, private for-profit company). This information is used to classify scientists and engineers into a sector of employment. While these definitions of sector change across years of the SDR, we were able to construct four major sectors of employment that are consistently defined over all years, plus a small residual category.

1. **Academic.** The academic sector includes colleges and universities that award at least a two-year degree. While this classification blurs the many distinctions among this diverse group of academic institutions, those differences are the focus of Chapter 6. Educational institutions that do not award degrees or award degrees below a two-year associate degree (e.g., a high school diploma) are *not* included in our definition of the academic sector.
2. **Industry.** The industrial sector includes private for-profit companies and businesses. It also includes scientists and engineers who are self-employed. In the following pages, we will refer to this sector simply as "industry," rather than the more cumbersome title of "business and industry."
3. **Government.** Within the government sector most scientists are employed by the federal government (78 percent of total), but this sector also includes those with scientific and engineering occupations in state and local governments.
4. **Private Nonprofit (PNP)**. This sector includes nonprofit, tax-exempt, or charitable organizations, including hospitals.
5. **Other**. A small residual category includes a variety of other organizational contexts, with the largest single employer being educational institutions below the level of a two-year college, primarily teaching at levels K through 12.

The Academic/Industrial Shift

The most dramatic change in sector of employment is the convergence in size of the industrial and academic sectors as employers of scientists and engineers. From 1973 to 1995 the percent of the full time doctoral labor force employed in academia decreased steadily from 57 percent to 46 percent, with a corresponding 11 point increase from 24 percent to 35 percent in the industrial sector. As shown in Figure 5-1, women (marked by circles) were more likely than men (marked by triangles) to work in academia (black markers) than in industry (gray markers). During this period of growth in industry relative to academia, the employment patterns for men and women converged. In the academic sector, the 12 point greater representation of women than men in 1973 declined to 6 points in 1995. In industry, the 18 point "excess" of men in 1973 dropped to 11 points in 1995. Overall, the growth in industrial science and engineering in the 1970s (Cotgrove and Box 1970) has continued to the present.

Table 5-1 shows that women are a smaller minority of scientists and engineers employed in industry than they are in any other employment sector, but that their growth in industry has exceeded that of men in the past 20 years. One explanation for women's underrepresentation in industry is their perception that the working conditions there are inhospitable. This is consistent with Preston's (1993) finding that the attrition rate

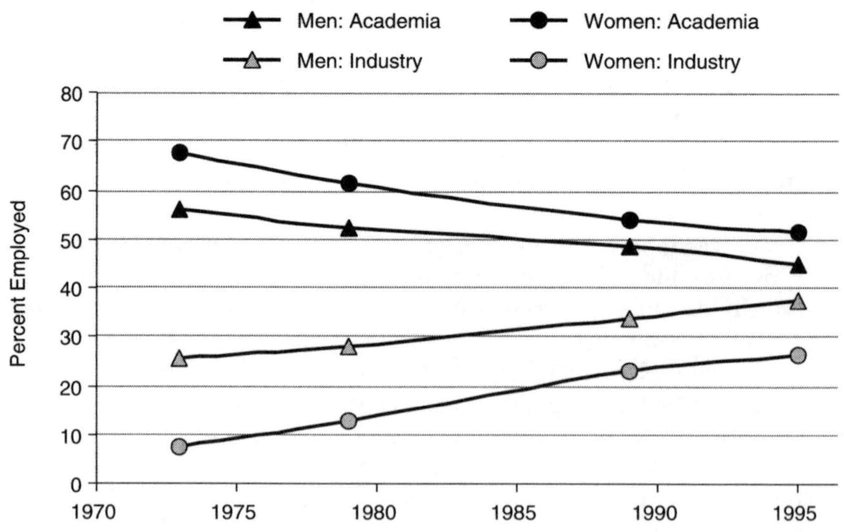

FIGURE 5-1 Employment of full-time scientists and engineers in the academic and industrial sectors, by year of survey and gender.

TABLE 5-1 Percent Employed in each Sector, by Gender and Year of Survey

	Men				Women			
	1973	1979	1989	1995	1973	1979	1989	1995
University	56.0	52.2	48.7	45.0	67.8	61.4	54.0	51.4
Industry	25.6	28.0	33.9	37.3	7.3	12.6	23.2	26.2
Government	11.4	10.8	9.7	10.0	9.9	8.6	8.1	10.0
PNP/Hospitals	5.3	6.4	5.5	4.4	9.6	11.4	10.2	6.3
Other	1.7	2.6	2.3	3.0	5.4	5.9	4.5	6.1

	Difference: Men - Women			
	1973	1979	1989	1995
University	–11.8	–9.2	–5.3	–6.4
Industry	18.3	15.4	10.7	11.1
Government	1.5	2.2	1.6	0.3
PNP/Hospitals	–4.3	–5.0	–4.7	–1.9
Other	–3.7	–3.4	–2.3	–3.0

NOTE: See Appendix Table C-1 for further details.

in industry for female scientists is double the rate for men and higher than that for women in other sectors. In a report of the Federal Glass Ceiling Commission (1996), conference participants reported that they experienced many of the same barriers that hamper all professional women from gaining access to corporate America: recruitment and hiring practices, sexual harassment, different standards for judging women's work, inequitable job assignments, limited promotions, and lower salaries. The table also shows that government employs roughly 10 percent of the full-time doctoral labor force in science and engineering, with relatively small gender differences. Until 1995, women were roughly 5 percentage points more likely to be working in the PNP sector. Finally, women are more likely to be employed in the residual, "other" category. Their greater employment here is largely the result of their work in educational institutions at levels below two-year degree programs, primarily as K through 12 teachers in public schools.

Field Differences in Sector of Employment

To understand more fully the gender differences shown in Table 5-1, it is necessary to consider field differences in sector of employment and the differential growth among sectors since 1973. Figure 5-2 (pages 108 and 109) provides two views of the relative size of each sector by field since 1973. Panel A highlights the substantial differences *across fields* in sector of employment. By comparing the set of bars from 1973 to those for 1995, we see that field differences have gradually decreased. In 1973, 39 percent of the engineers were employed in academia compared to a high of 82 percent of mathematicians, with the physical, life, and social/behavioral sciences falling between these extremes. Engineers and physical scientists have much greater employment in industry, with a much smaller but growing industrial presence in other fields. By 1995 field differences had been reduced, with all fields showing less employment in the academic sector and more in industry. Panel B presents the same data, but highlights changes within fields that explain the greater similarities across fields by 1995. While nonacademic employment grew in each field (shown by the decreasing size of the dark gray bars at the bottom), this occurred at quite different rates across fields. Engineering and the physical sciences experienced small changes in academic employment, 6 and 5 points respectively. Mathematics and the social/behavioral sciences experienced the largest changes, with decreases in academic employment of 21 percentage points. In each field, the decline in academic employment corresponds very closely to the growth of employment in industry.

There has been substantial convergence in the distribution of male and female scientists and engineers among sectors of employment, as shown in Table 5-2 (page 110). The table presents differences between the percent of men and the percent of women working in each sector by the year of the survey. Among all fields combined, the greatest convergence occurred in academia and industry. Still, in 1995 the remaining differences were largest in these sectors. Among broad fields, the greatest gender differences and smallest changes over time occurred in engineering. By 1995, 10 percentage points more female than male engineers were working in colleges and universities, with 11 percentage points more men in industry. There is also a large over-representation of men among mathematicians working in industry. While there were large gender differences in the academic and industrial sectors for the physical sciences in 1973, these were reduced to only 2 points by 1995. The life sciences had the smallest differences in 1973, but there has been little change since then, leaving 6 points more women in academic positions and 8 points fewer in industry. Finally, differences in the social and behavioral sciences were all less than 2.1 points by 1995.

Given the substantial changes in the relative size of employment sectors from 1973 to 1995, it is important to consider the degree to which the changes are due to different hiring patterns for new cohorts as opposed to mobility across sectors by the same scientists over time. Figure 5-3 traces the sector of employment for scientists with degrees from the 1970s at three points in time: 1979, 1989, and 1995. The first three pairs of bars in Panel A show the percent of these cohorts employed in the academic sector; Panel B shows comparable information for the industrial sector. By way of comparison, the figure also includes Ph.D.s from the 1980s as of 1995 (shown on the far right of each panel using gray bars). These results, while limited to a single cohort over time, suggest that there has been mobility across sectors over time and also changes in the pattern of hiring of new cohorts. The overall shift in sector of employment observed for all full-time scientists and engineers also occurred to the 1970 cohort as they aged. Over time, smaller proportions of both men and women in this cohort were employed in academia. While there are some differences between the 1970 cohort and the 1980 cohort, they are quite similar. Overall, it appears that the shifting size of sectors involved both differences in the initial hiring of new scientists and changes in sector of employment over time, with gender differences being reduced through both of these processes.

Summary of Sector of Employment[2]

Since 1973 there have been substantial changes in the relative size of the sectors that employ doctoral scientists and engineers. Accompanying this change has been a convergence in the distribution of men and women among sectors. Still, women remain more likely to be in academia (6 points overall) and less likely to be in industry (11 points overall). While a great deal of the difference in the proportion of men and women working in academia is due to gender differences in the field of the doctorate, the greater likelihood of men working in industry is larger still within some fields. To illustrate both the progress and the remaining challenges, consider the case of female engineers in industry. From 1973 to 1995 the *number* of doctoral women increased by a factor of 56 from 31 to 1,746, while the number of male engineers in industry increased by less than a factor of 3. However, the *percent* of doctorate engineers in industry who are women remains at less than 5 percent as a consequence of the small number of female engineers in the full-time labor force (in large part due to the small number of women with Ph.D.s in engineering). In 1995 in all fields except the social and behavioral sciences, the representation of women in industry lags behind that in academia and generally behind

[2]These figures are based on the weighted estimates from the 1973, 1979, 1989, and 1995 SDR. See Appendix Table C-4 for full data.

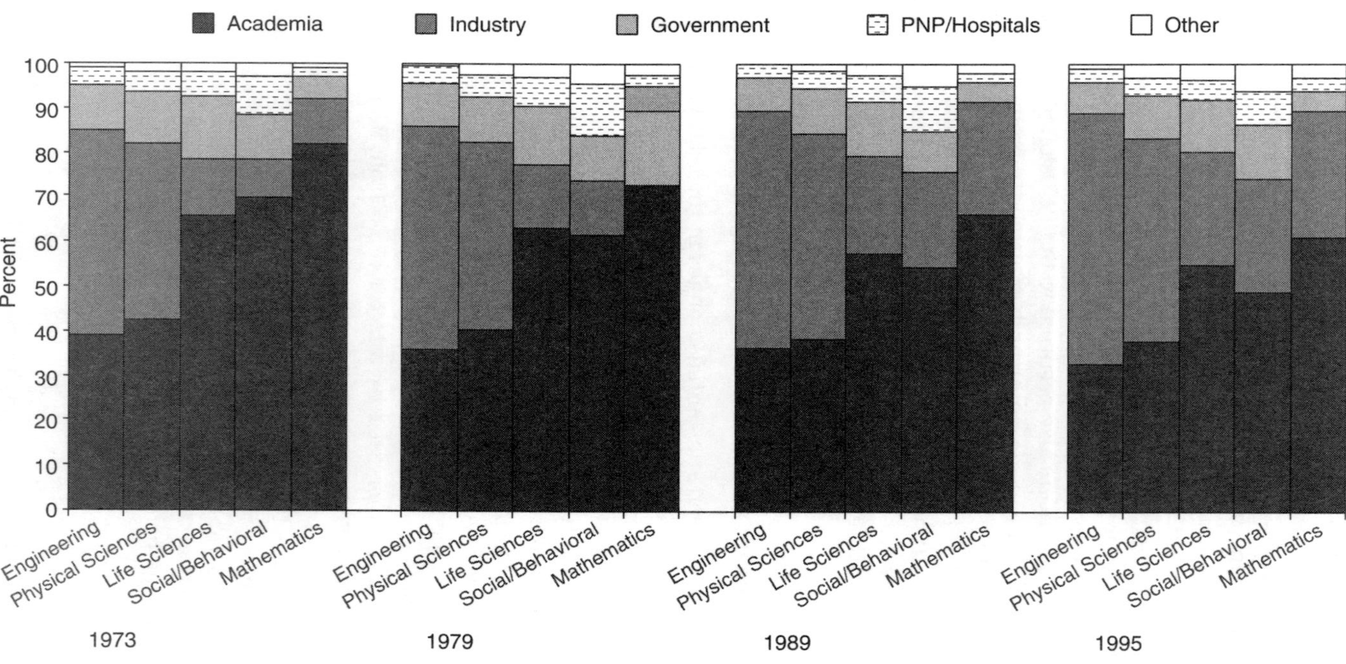

Panel A: Sector of employment organized by field within year of survey.

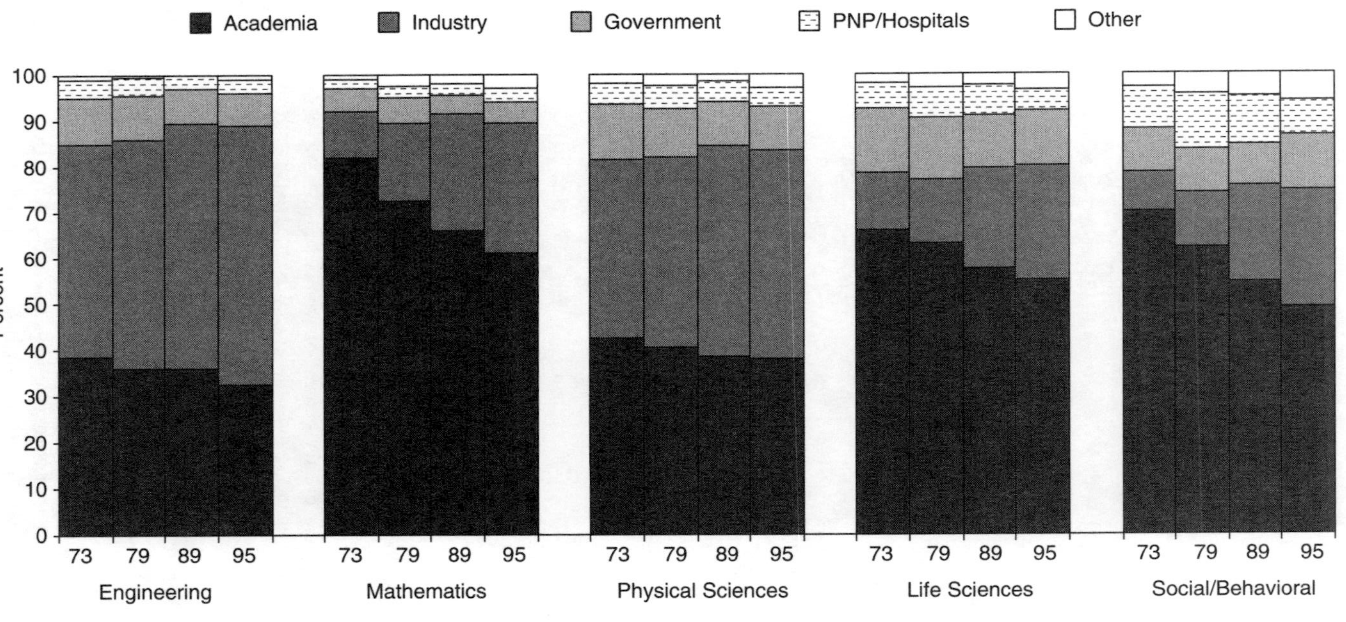

Panel B: Sector of employment organized by year of survey within field

FIGURE 5-2 Sector of employment for full-time scientists and engineers, by field and year of survey.

TABLE 5-2 Difference Between the Percent of Women and the Percent of Men Employed in Each Sector, by Year of Survey and Field

		Year of Survey			
		1973	1979	1989	1995
Combined Fields	*Academia*	—	9.2	5.3	6.4
	Industry	—	–15.4	–10.7	–11.1
	Government	—	–2.2	–1.6	–0.3
	PNP/Hospitals	—	5.0	4.7	1.9
	Other	—	3.4	2.3	3.0
Engineering	*Academia*	8.4	7.1	5.2	10.0
	Industry	–10.5	–5.1	–7.4	–10.8
	Government	–1.2	–0.6	0.8	1.3
	PNP/Hospitals	1.7	–1.2	0.8	–0.7
	Other	1.5	–0.2	0.6	0.2
Mathematics	*Academia*	6.3	0.6	1.6	–0.3
	Industry	–6.7	–2.5	–2.4	–7.7
	Government	–1.8	–2.5	–0.7	1.6
	PNP/Hospitals	–0.2	2.0	–0.1	0.2
	Other	2.4	2.4	1.5	6.2
Physical Sciences	*Academia*	18.7	7.9	0.9	2.2
	Industry	–22.2	–13.3	–5.5	–2.2
	Government	–1.7	–0.9	0.2	–2.1
	PNP/Hospitals	1.9	2.4	1.4	–1.0
	Other	3.2	4.0	3.0	3.1
Life Sciences	*Academia*	4.8	5.8	5.8	6.3
	Industry	–7.5	–7.5	–5.7	–7.5
	Government	–3.9	–4.3	–3.5	–1.9
	PNP/Hospitals	3.7	3.8	2.7	1.1
	Other	3.0	2.2	0.8	1.9
Social/Behavioral	*Academia*	–4.5	–2.5	–4.7	–2.1
	Industry	–3.5	–1.1	1.7	0.4
	Government	0.0	–2.0	–2.5	–2.1
	PNP/Hospitals	3.8	3.1	4.1	1.9
	Other	4.1	2.6	1.3	1.9

NOTES: Positive values indicate a greater percent of women are in a given sector. See Appendix Table C-3 for further details. — indicates too few women to compute difference.

that in government. While this may partially reflect the specific subfields in which women are working, the report of the Committee on Women in Science and Engineering (CWSE 1994) notes that the rate of attrition of female scientists and engineers in industry is more than double that of men and much larger than in other sectors. Clearly, retention, not just training, is essential for increasing the number of women in industry.

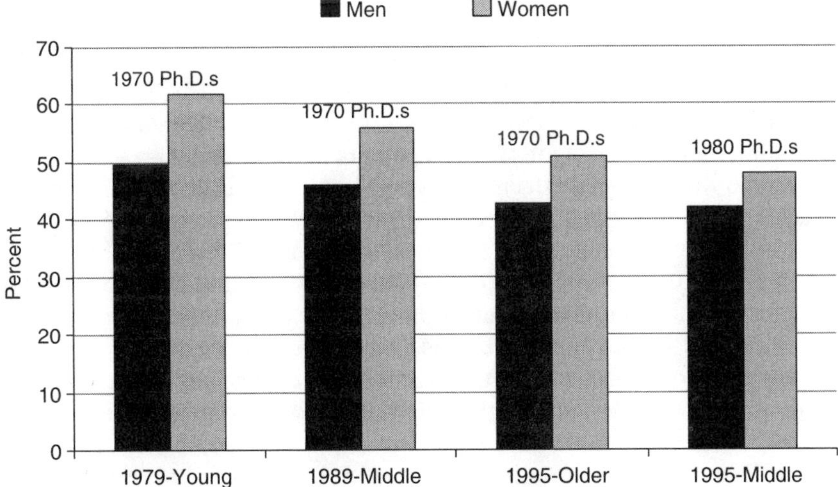

Panel A: Academic sector

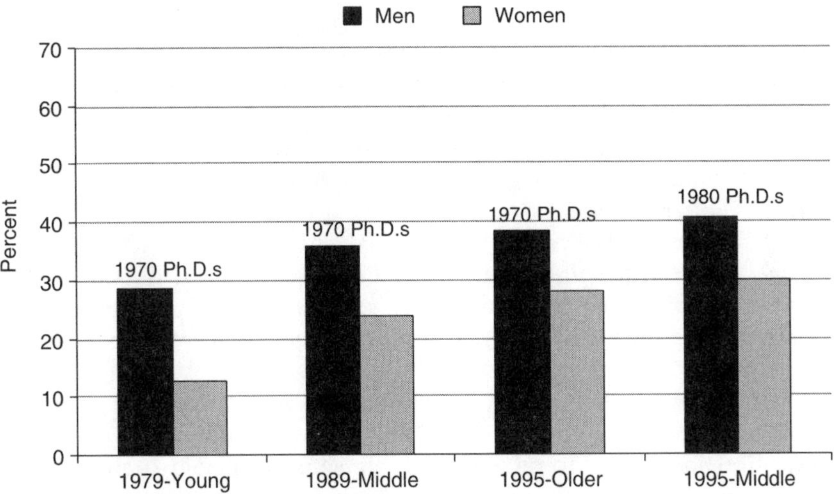

Panel B: Industrial sector

FIGURE 5-3 Percent employed in academia and industry, by gender, cohort, and year of survey. NOTE: The 1970 cohort is traced for years 1979 (young cohort), 1989 (middle cohort), and 1995 (older cohort). For comparison, the middle cohort in 1995 is shown at the right.

PRIMARY WORK ACTIVITY

Even if male and female scientists and engineers were identical in their distribution among sectors of employment, their career experiences would not necessarily be the same. Within each sector there is substantial variation in the types of jobs held by scientists and engineers. A scientist's work activity not only affects the type of work being done, but also the receipt of material and symbolic rewards. In this section we examine gender differences in the type of jobs held within the three largest sectors: academia, industry, and government. There are not enough women in the smaller, private nonprofit sector to allow us to examine their work activity.

The SDR uses job descriptions (e.g., college professor in electrical engineering) and a respondent's selection from a detailed list of job codes to determine primary work activity. We consider six major categories:

1. **Teaching**. Teaching includes faculty in research universities. Faculty in tenure track positions generally indicate teaching as their primary work activity.
2. **Basic Research**. Basic research is study directed toward gaining scientific knowledge primarily for its own sake.
3. **Applied Research**. Applied research involves study directed toward gaining scientific knowledge to meet a recognized need.
4. **Production**. Production work includes the design of equipment or processes, consulting, production, quality control, and sales.
5. **Management**. Management is employment that involves the supervision of other employees.
6. **Professional Services**. Professional services include activities such as health care, financial services, legal services, clinical diagnosis, and psychotherapy. While professional services is a relatively small category, it is retained since there are disproportionately more women with this work activity.

These categories account for all but 6 percent of those employed in education, industry, and government. Men and women are equally likely to be in the excluded category, which includes computer support, those who provided incomplete information on the survey, and a myriad of unclassified activities. For further details on the distribution into other categories, see Appendix Table C-2.

Since the meaning and prevalence of work activities varies by sector, we proceed by considering gender differences in work activity within each sector separately.

Work Activity in Academia

Within academia, teaching has traditionally been the primary work activity of doctoral scientists and engineers. This is changing. As shown in Figure 5-4, from 1973 to 1995 there was a 19 percentage point decrease in those who report teaching as their primary work. By 1989 less than half of the doctoral scientists and engineers reported teaching as their primary activity. Most of this change is accounted for by the 17 point increase in those with research as the main activity. As shown in Table 5-3, which presents work activities by field for 1995 (see Table C-5 for information on other years), there are substantial differences among fields in work activity. Teaching is most common in mathematics (where there is a heavy load of service courses) and the social/behavioral sciences where there is less research funding. While both fields have roughly the same propor-

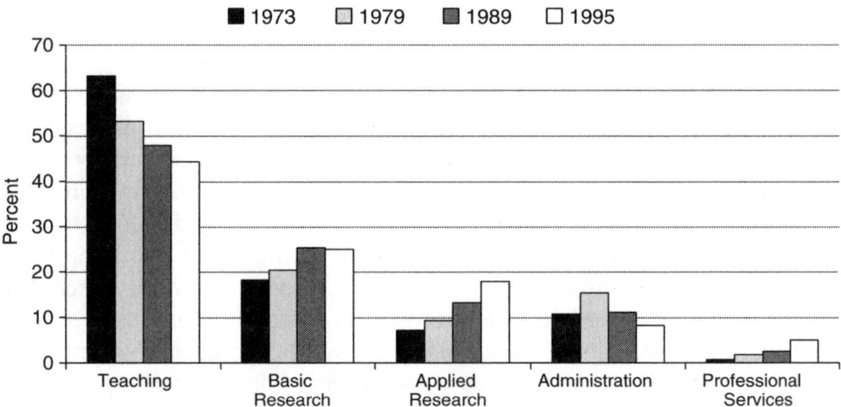

FIGURE 5-4 Percent of academic scientists in each work activity, by year of survey.

TABLE 5-3 Primary Work Activity in Academia by Field, 1995

	Engineering	Mathematics	Physical Sciences	Life Sciences	Social/ Behavioral	Combined Fields
Teaching	48.2	65.4	39.6	29.0	56.7	44.1
Basic Research	11.8	18.4	33.0	37.3	12.9	24.9
Applied Research	30.0	8.9	17.6	18.9	14.3	17.8
Management	8.7	5.9	8.0	7.8	9.3	8.2
Professional Services	1.3	1.5	1.9	7.1	6.8	5.0
N	24,210	16,523	35,409	68,936	59,749	204,827

NOTE: (See Appendix Table C-5 for details.)

tion in research, the social/behavioral sciences have nearly 7 percent working in professional services, a level exceeded only by the life sciences. Teaching is least common in the life sciences where less than one-third teach, while 56 percent are in research. Somewhat larger percentages of academic physical scientists and engineers indicate teaching as their primary work activity.

Since there has been differential growth among fields since 1973 (see Chapter 4), a possible explanation for the decline in teaching as the primary work activity is that fields with less teaching have grown more rapidly. However, teaching has become less common in all fields, although the greatest decline has been in fields where funded research is most common. The following decreases in the percent indicating teaching as their primary work have occurred between 1973 and 1995: 20 percent in engineering, 12 percent in mathematics, 23 percent in the physical sciences, 20 percent in the life sciences, and 15 percent in the social and behavioral sciences.

Table 5-4 presents the difference between the percent of full-time male academics in each work activity and the corresponding percent of women, broken down by field and year. The changing patterns of gender differences in primary work activity within academia are complex, with no clear trend over time. In 1995 across all fields, the largest gender difference in work activity is the 3 point greater representation of women in professional services. As shown in the breakdown by field, this difference is due to the greater proportion of women in the social and behavioral sciences who are employed in clinical psychology. While the percent of men in teaching, research, and administration across fields is very similar (within about 1 percentage point), larger differences are seen within fields. While larger gender differences were observed in engineering in 1989, there was a substantial convergence from 1989 to 1995. Keep in mind, however, that there were only 677 women in 1989 and 1,542 in 1995. In the social and behavioral sciences, the greater proportion of men teaching in recent years reflects the increasing proportion of women in professional services. This may reflect one of two possibilities: either women prefer work in professional services or men are favored in the allocation of non-service jobs when these become scarce. In contrast, within the physical and life sciences women have become less likely than men to teach, and less likely to do research, reversing long term trends. This reversal coincides with increased pressure on research funding in these fields.

The broad classifications of work activity that we are using ignore many critical distinctions among positions in academia. For example, both an endowed professorship at an elite university and an off-track instructorship at a community college are classified as "teaching." These and other important distinctions are the focus of Chapter 6.

TABLE 5-4 Difference in the Percent of Men and the Percent of Women in Academic Work Activities, by Year and Field

		Year of Survey			
	Work Activity	1973	1979	1989	1995
Combined Fields	*Teaching*	–0.5	0.4	1.4	1.1
	Research	–1.4	–2.9	–1.1	0.8
	Administration	3.3	3.4	1.4	0.8
	Professional Services	–1.4	–0.9	–1.7	–2.7
Engineering	*Teaching*	—	—	3.6	–0.8
	Research	—	—	–14.9	1.8
	Administration	—	—	11.5	–1.9
	Professional Services	—	—	–0.1	0.9
Mathematics	*Teaching*	—	–4.9	–8.3	0.5
	Research	—	–1.4	6.8	–4.9
	Administration	—	6.4	1.4	2.8
	Professional Services	—	–0.1	0.1	1.6
Physical Sciences	*Teaching*	3.3	5.7	2.7	–6.3
	Research	–4.7	–9.8	–4.4	3.5
	Administration	2.9	4.6	2.1	2.9
	Professional Services	–1.4	–0.5	–0.4	–0.2
Life Sciences	*Teaching*	0.3	–2.2	–2.2	–4.1
	Research	–4.9	–2.8	–0.3	1.5
	Administration	4.4	3.8	1.7	1.7
	Professional Services	0.2	1.2	0.8	0.9
Social/Behavioral Sciences	*Teaching*	–3.7	3.7	4.9	6.3
	Research	2.8	–4.0	–3.1	–1.5
	Administration	3.1	1.6	0.9	–0.1
	Professional Services	–2.2	–1.4	–2.6	–4.7

NOTE: Positive values indicate that proportionately more men are in that activity.
— indicates too few women to compute percentages.

Work Activity in Industry

Since 1973 the largest change in work activity in industry is the 23 point decrease in the percent who report management as the primary work activity, as shown in Figure 5-5. This decline is made up for with a 10 point increase in those reporting professional service and a 7 point increase in those in production work. The decline in administration occurred in all fields (details in Appendix Table C-6). With the exception of the social and behavioral sciences, this decrease in administration and management corresponds to increases in applied research and production. There are, however, several notable differences among fields in primary work activity, as shown in Table 5-5 for 1995 (for data on other years see Appendix Table C-6). As would be expected, engineering stands out

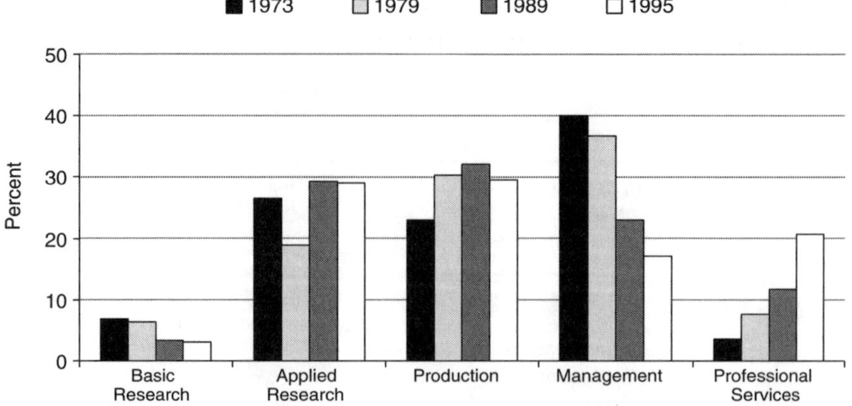

FIGURE 5-5 Percent of scientists in industry in each work activity, by year of survey. NOTE: Teaching, which accounts for less than 0.5 percent of the cases, has been excluded.

TABLE 5-5 Primary Work Activity in Industry, by Field in 1995

	Engineering	Mathematics	Physical Sciences	Life Sciences	Social/ Behavioral	Combined Fields
Basic Research	1.4	4.8	4.3	5.2	0.5	3.0
Applied Research	25.9	36.6	38.4	35.7	12.3	29.0
Production	45.7	32.0	31.6	23.7	12.0	29.5
Management	21.6	19.1	18.8	17.2	9.0	17.1
Professional Services	5.1	6.8	6.5	17.2	65.1	20.7
Total %	99.6	99.4	99.7	99.1	98.9	99.3
N	36,519	4,827	39,228	30,272	29,185	140,031

NOTE: See Appendix Table C-6 for details. Percentages do not add to 100 since teaching has been excluded.

with a large proportion hired for production work, with much smaller percentages in production in the life and social/behavioral sciences. The social/behavioral sciences stand out with nearly two-thirds working in professional services, reflecting the large and increasing number of social scientists in clinical positions.

There are large gender differences in primary work activity when we consider all fields combined, as shown in Table 5-6. In large part these overall differences are due to gender differences in field of employment. For example, while women in all fields combined are 24 percentage points

TABLE 5-6 Difference in the Percent of Men and the Percent of Women in Industrial Work Activities, by Year and Field

		Year of Survey			
		1973	1979	1989	1995
Combined Fields	*Basic Research*	–9.8	–2.5	–0.6	0.3
	Applied Research	–0.6	0.6	4.6	3.1
	Production	7.4	12.6	11.5	12.4
	Management	19.4	16.6	8.7	8.5
	Professional Services	–16.1	–27.3	–24.3	–23.5
Engineering	*Basic Research*	—	—	–2.8	0.2
	Applied Research	—	—	–8.9	–7.4
	Production	—	—	6.7	5.6
	Management	—	—	4.3	4.8
	Professional Services	—	—	0.5	–3.5
Physical Sciences	*Basic Research*	—	–6.7	–2.6	1.7
	Applied Research	—	–5.4	–8.7	–10.5
	Production	—	4.6	3.7	1.2
	Management	—	9.8	8.1	9.9
	Professional Services	—	–2.2	–0.5	–1.9
Life Sciences	*Basic Research*	—	–10.1	–2.7	–1.7
	Applied Research	—	–6.9	–3.6	–1.5
	Production	—	12.0	3.2	0.7
	Management	—	9.5	4.2	4.1
	Professional Services	—	–4.9	–0.7	–1.4
Social and Behavioral Sciences	*Basic Research*	—	0.5	–0.3	–0.2
	Applied Research	—	5.7	–0.1	5.7
	Production	—	12.3	11.4	5.3
	Management	—	10.4	4.4	3.8
	Professional Services	—	–28.5	–15.9	–13.4

NOTE: Positive values indicate that proportionately more men are in that activity. — indicates too few women to compute percentages. There were too few women in mathematics to present results.

more likely to be employed in professional services, 10 points of this "excess" are due to more women being in the social and behavioral sciences where professional services is more common. Within fields, there are several general trends. First, gender differences are decreasing. Second, female scientists are more likely to be in professional services, regardless of field, although this difference has decreased over time. Third, the largest gender differences are seen in engineering and in the physical sciences where women are more likely to be in applied research.

Finally, in all fields and years men are more likely to be in management. Table 5-6 shows that there has been some progress in the percent of women in management in the social/behavioral and life sciences, but that there has been little progress in engineering or the physical sciences. The lack of women in management positions has important implications for the full integration of women into the industry. In a report on female engineers in industry, Mattis and Allyn (1999) report that the lack of women in leadership positions is a key barrier to the recruitment and retention of women. Women in leadership positions serve as role models and mentors, provide critical channels of communication for understanding organizational politics, and establish technical credibility.

Since the representation of women in industry has increased rapidly in recent years, female industrial scientists will be on average younger than men. It is possible that the lower participation of women in management is due to their being younger and hence less likely to be in management. To examine this possibility, Figure 5-6 plots gender differences in the percent in management by years since the Ph.D. The dark line with circles presents results for 1989, while the gray line with squares presents the more recent data from 1995. Over the career, gender differences grow substantially as scientists age. The only major change between 1989 and 1995 occurred during the first five years of the career. In 1995, there were

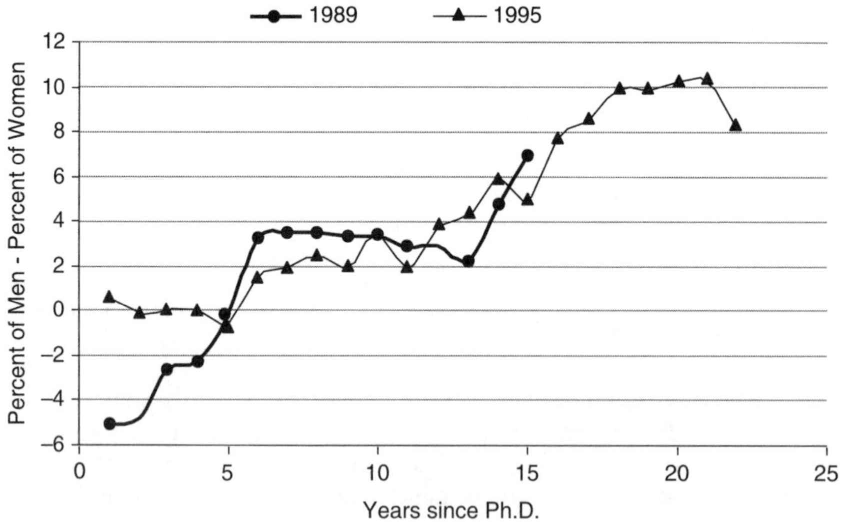

FIGURE 5-6 Difference in the percent of men and the percent of women with management positions in industry, by years since Ph.D. and year of survey. NOTE: Years in which the estimated number of women in industry was less than 500 have been excluded.

no gender differences, while in 1989 women were *more* likely to have management positions. Given their young professional age, it is likely that these positions are at the lowest levels of management. Overall, woman scientists and engineers have been and continue to be under-represented in positions of management.

Work Activity in Government

In several key respects the changes since 1973 in the primary work activity for scientists and engineers in government are similar to those occurring in industry. First, while basic research is more common in government than industry, there has been a steady decline in this activity since 1973. Second, there is a substantial decrease in the proportion of scientists who are in management. And, professional services grew substantially between 1989 and 1995. There are, however, some basic differences between government and industry. As mentioned earlier, basic research is more common in government, while production jobs are relatively rare. With these differences taken into account, field differences among those in government (see Figure 5-7 and Table 5-7) are very much as would be expected given our findings for industry. The major exception is that while social and behavioral scientists rarely hold positions of management in industry, they hold these positions in government at rates similar to those in other fields.

Table 5-8 lists differences in the percent of men and women in government with different work activities. As in industry, women are more

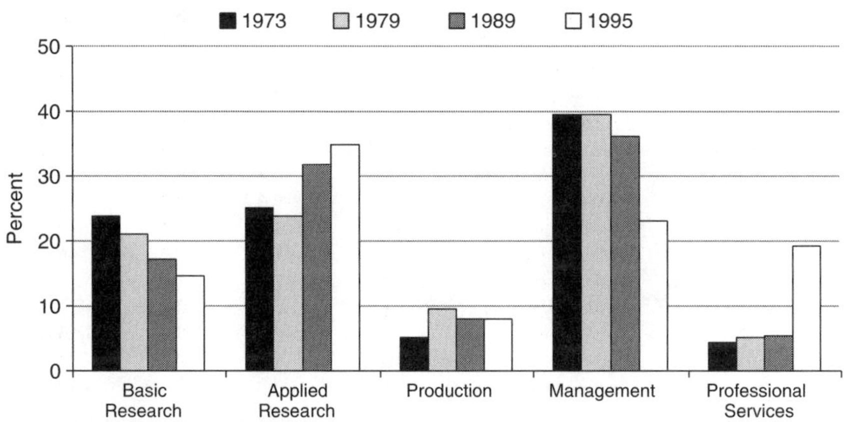

FIGURE 5-7 Percent of scientists in government in each work activity, by year of survey.

TABLE 5-7 Primary Work Activity in Government, by Field in 1995

	Engi-neering	Mathe-matics	Physical Sciences	Life Sciences	Social/ Behavioral	Combined Fields
Basic Research	8.3	15.5	21.2	23.3	3.6	14.5
Applied Research	46.4	41.4	43.2	37.1	23.0	35.0
Production	12.3	14.0	8.5	6.0	7.4	7.9
Management	27.5	23.2	21.8	22.1	23.0	23.0
Professional Services	5.5	5.9	4.9	11.0	42.3	19.2
Total %	99.9	100.0	99.6	99.5	99.3	99.5
N	4,787	859	8,108	13,279	12,980	40,013

NOTE: See Appendix Table C-6 for details.

TABLE 5-8 Difference in the Percent of Men and the Percent of Women in Governmental Work Activities, by Year and Field

		Year of Survey			
		1973	1979	1989	1995
All fields	*Basic Research*	–7.5	–4.7	–2.4	0.8
	Applied Research	8.5	9.8	5.8	9.1
	Production	2.0	–3.1	0.9	2.3
	Management	11.6	3.2	–0.2	2.2
	Professional Services	–13.7	–5.6	–4.8	–14.5
Physical Sciences	*Basic Research*	—	—	–8.9	–16.9
	Applied Research	—	—	4.1	–4.7
	Production	—	—	–3.3	4.7
	Management	—	—	8.6	12.2
	Professional Services	—	—	–0.9	4.3
Life Sciences	*Basic Research*	–22.4	–14.4	–6.8	0.8
	Applied Research	9.9	13.4	8.8	8.4
	Production	–1.2	–5.6	–2.2	–3.1
	Management	13.5	9.9	1.1	–0.2
	Professional Services	0.7	–1.6	–0.3	–6.4
Social/Behavioral Sciences	*Basic Research*	0.4	–1.4	–1.0	0.8
	Applied Research	4.5	4.3	0.1	1.8
	Production	1.5	–2.7	0.3	5.0
	Management	18.0	1.4	–0.1	3.1
	Professional Services	–21.8	–2.7	–3.0	–10.9

NOTE: Positive values indicate that proportionately more men are in that activity. — indicates too few women to compute percentages. There were too few women in engineering and mathematics to present results. The category teaching was excluded.

likely to be in professional services, both across fields and within the social/behavioral and life sciences where professional service is most likely. With respect to management, gender differences are smaller, with the exception of the physical sciences where men are 12 points more likely to hold these positions. In the social/behavioral and life sciences, gender differences in management have decreased substantially since 1973.

SUMMARY

Since 1973 there are increasing similarities between men and women in the sector in which they work and the type of work activity that they pursue. Still, notable differences persist which are summarized in Figure 5-8 using data for 1995. In this figure the height of each pyramid corresponds to the percent of scientists and engineers in the full-time labor force with a given combination of sector and work activity. Several key gender differences are clearly seen. First, women are nearly 5 points more likely to be teaching in academia, shown by the spike in the back, left corner. Second, women are more likely in all sectors to be in professional services, shown by the spikes in the right column in each panel. Last, women are less likely to be managers in industry.

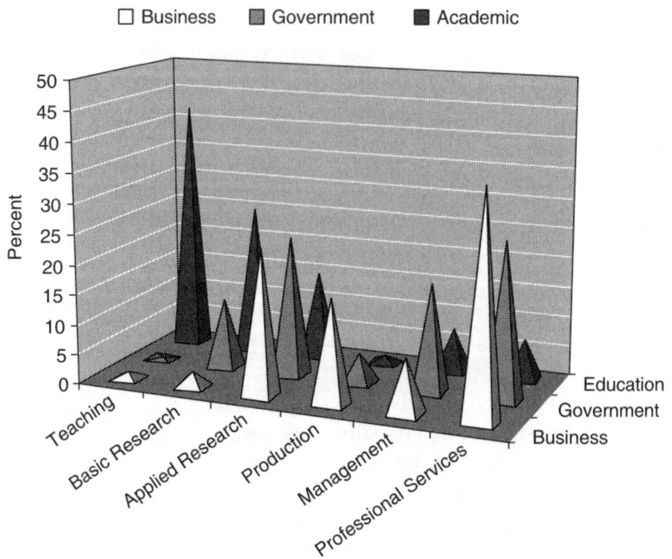

Panel A: Women in 1995

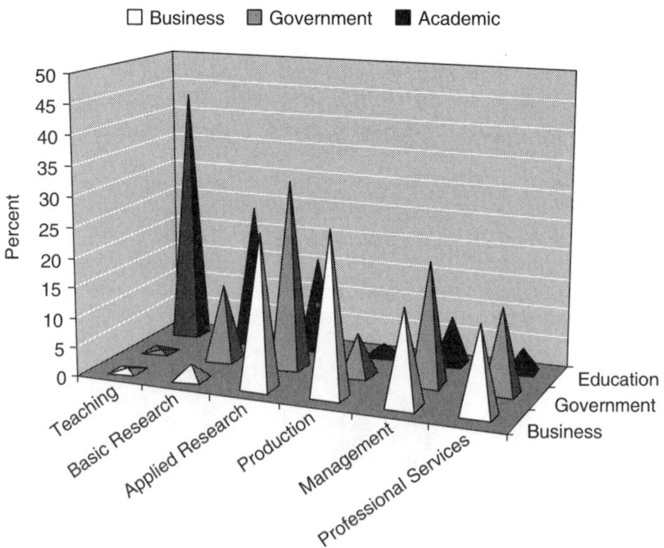

Panel B: Men in 1995

FIGURE 5-8 Combinations of sector and primary work activity in 1995, by gender. NOTE: Data are based on those working full time in the sectors and work activities shown.

6

The Academic Career

Faculty, Unfaculty, and Changes in the Academy

. . . the classic profile of the academic career is cut to the image of the traditional man with his traditional wife.

—Arlie Russell Hochschild, *Inside the Clockwork of Male Careers*, 1975[1]

Academic science is the model for professional science. To rise in this system, one must climb an extraordinarily narrow ladder: from graduate student to post-doctoral fellow to research associate to assistant professor (or principal investigator). The majority of women in science have never completed that rise. They have remained research associates attached to the principal investigator for most or all of their working lives. The cause of arrest is multiple and it has a history.

—Vivian Gornick, *Women in Science*, 1990[2]

INTRODUCTION

In this chapter we examine the careers of doctoral scientists and engineers in academia. Our analysis of the academic sector is far more detailed than those of other sectors for several reasons. First, doctoral scientists and engineers are traditionally trained to work in academia. Although the proportion of scientists and engineers working in academia has been declining since 1970, the academic sector remains the single largest employer of doctoral scientists and engineers. Second, the conduct of basic scientific research in the United States is intertwined with the higher education system. Institutions of higher education traditionally attract the best scientists and provide them with the most resources and rewards (Clark 1995; Wolfle 1972). As documented by Fox (1996), the evolution of science and the evolution of higher education have been reciprocal developments in the United States. In Wolfle's words, academia is "the home of

[1]Hochschild (1975).
[2]Gornick (1990: 81).

science" (Wolfle 1972). Third, indicators of career attainment and rewards are more public and more uniformly defined in academia than in other sectors, allowing researchers to more readily collect detailed data on career outcomes.

The position of women in the academic sector is also critical because it is within academia that future generations of scientists and engineers are trained. Frieze and Hanusa (1984) discuss a variety of reasons why female faculty may be especially important as role models and mentors for female graduate students. The presence of more than a token number of women on the faculty of graduate programs may be important both for recruiting new generations of women to graduate programs and for retaining them once they enroll in graduate education. Accordingly, in the analyses that follow we give special attention to scientists and engineers working in Research I universities and medical schools. Not only do these locations provide the majority of doctoral and postdoctoral training, but they are also the most conducive organizational contexts for a prestigious research career. For women to have an equal standing with men in science and engineering, it is essential that they gain parity within the most prestigious academic locations.

While our focus in this chapter is on scientists and engineers with *full-time employment* in academia, it is important to keep in mind that a greater proportion of women than men are part time employees in academia, as shown in Chapter 4. In the rest of this chapter, unless otherwise noted, we restrict our analysis to the full-time labor force.

FULL-TIME EMPLOYMENT IN ACADEMIA[3]

From 1973 to 1995, the percent of the combined male and female doctoral labor force that worked in academia decreased from 51 percent of all scientists and engineers to 40 percent. In 1973, 5 percentage points *more men* than women were working full time in academia, as shown by the two sets of bars on the left hand side of Figure 6-1. The relative decline in academic employment that occurred after 1973 was more rapid for men than for women, so that by 1995 three percentage points more women than men held full-time academic jobs. While our findings may appear to contradict past research that found women to be over-represented in academia (Zuckerman and Cole 1975 and the literature cited therein), keep in mind that we are considering men and women as a percent of the entire labor force, not as a percent of those working full time. If we consider only those in the *full-time* labor force (i.e., excluding those who are

---

[3]See Appendix Tables D-1-D-2 for further information.

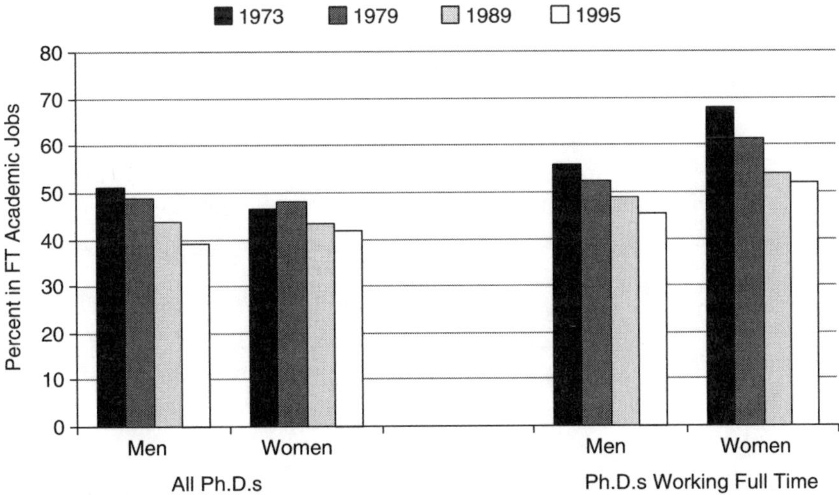

FIGURE 6-1 Percent of the doctoral labor force that is working full time in academia and percent of the *full-time* labor force that is working in academia, by sex and year of survey.

part time, unemployed, retired, or out of the labor force), women are substantially more likely to be in academic positions, as shown by the bar graphs on the right. In 1973, 68 percent of women in the full-time labor force held academic jobs, compared to only 56 percent of the men. By 1995, this 12 point difference decreased to 7 points. Thus, over this 22 year period, full-time employment decreased 18 points for men and 38 points for women.

The net effect of the increasing proportion of Ph.D.s who are women and the greater proportion of women than men in academic jobs is a steady increase in the percent of all full-time academic jobs that are held by women. The gray circles in Figure 6-2 show that 8 percent of all full-time academics were women in 1973, increasing to 23 percent in 1995. While this increase is driven largely by increasing numbers of women in science and engineering, the increase of 15 percentage points exceeded the growth of women as a percent of all Ph.D.s (shown by squares) and as a percent of all scientists and engineers who are working full time (shown by triangles). This reflects a combination of an increasing proportion of women working in academia and the possibility that the attrition of women from academic jobs has decreased.

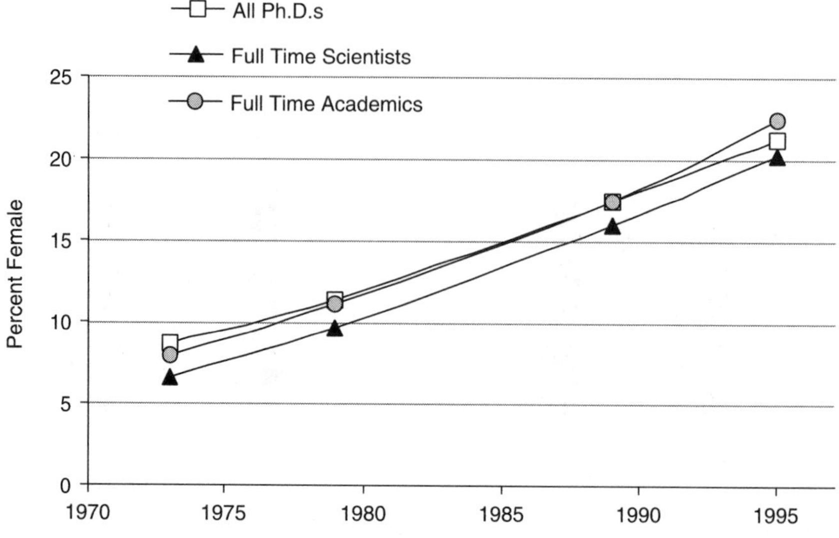

FIGURE 6-2 Women as a percent of all Ph.D.s, as percent of all full-time scientists and engineers, and as percent of all full-time academic scientists and engineers, by year of survey.

Field Differences in Full-Time Academic Employment

Women are proportionally more likely than men to be in academic jobs in all fields except the social and behavioral sciences. This is shown in Figure 6-3, which plots differences between the percent of men with academic jobs Ph.D.s (as a percent of men who are working full time) and the corresponding percent of women. Positive values indicate a greater proportion of full-time women than full-time men are working in academia. In 1973 for all fields combined, 12 percentage points more women than men in the full-time labor force were employed in academia. By 1995 the difference was reduced to 6.5 points. Within fields, we find that even though the largest proportion of female Ph.D.s are found in the social and behavioral sciences, this is the only field with a greater proportion of men than women in academic jobs. Women in engineering and the life sciences are the most likely to be academic, with little change over time. In mathematics and the physical sciences, gender differences in full-time academic employment have nearly disappeared by 1995.

While there is an increasing representation of women in each field, substantial variation exists across fields in the proportions, numbers, and

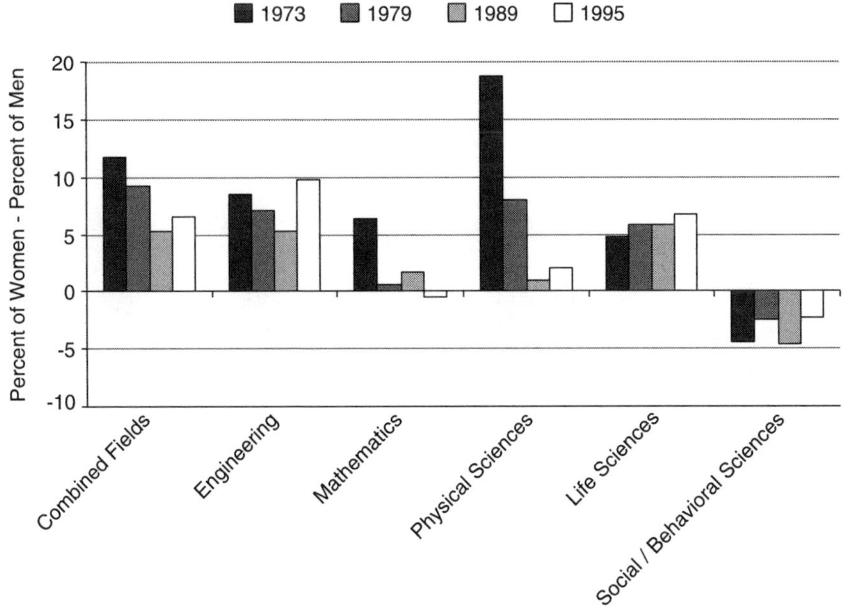

FIGURE 6-3 Gender difference in the percent of Ph.D.s working full time who have academic jobs, by year of survey. NOTE: Positive values indicate women are proportionally more likely to have academic positions.

rates of increase of female academics, as shown by Figures 6-4 and 6-5. In the life and social/behavioral sciences, the percent of full-time academics who are women increased by nearly 20 percentage points from 1973 to 1995. As a result of the greater overall increase in the number of life scientists during this period, by 1995 there were more women in the life sciences than the social and behavioral sciences. In other fields, the increase in the percent of women was only between 6 and 7 points. Even by 1995, women were only 6 percent of the full-time academic work force in engineering, with less than 2,000 full-time female engineers. In mathematics and the physical sciences, women's representation exceeded 10 percent by 1995, but in mathematics the number reached only 2,000 and in the physical sciences just over 4,000. In the life sciences, the percent of women approached 30 percent by 1995.

The rapid change in the percent of academic positions held by women is largely the result of increases in the proportion of new Ph.D.s who are women. The effects of the more recent entry of women are seen by comparing Figure 6-6, which plots the percent women among those who re-

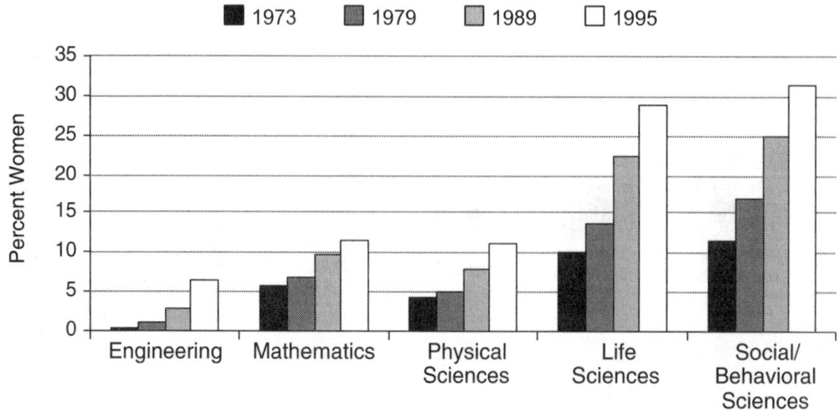

FIGURE 6-4 *Percent* of the full-time academic labor force that is female, by field and year of survey.

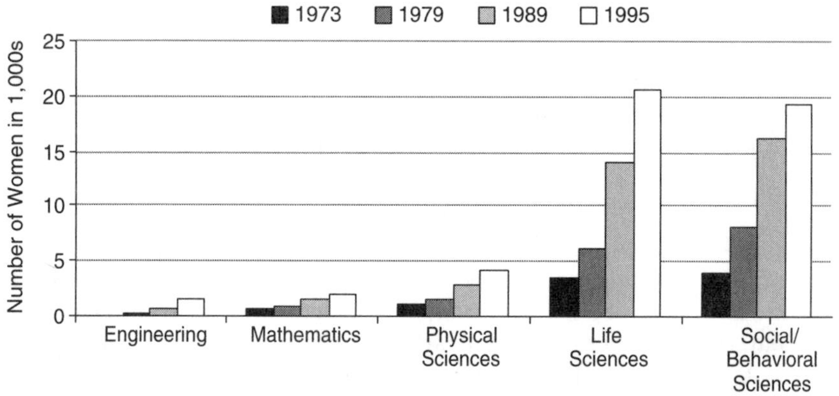

FIGURE 6-5 *Number* of women working full time in academia, by field and year of survey.

ceived their Ph.D.s 11 or more years ago, to Figure 6-7 for those with doctorates within 10 years of the survey. While there were increases in the percent of women among those with older degrees, these changes are substantially smaller than for those with more recent degrees. Among older academics, the presence of women grew most rapidly in the social and behavioral sciences, but in 1995 women still represented less than 25 percent of the total among older social and behavioral scientists. When we consider more recent Ph.D.s, the increases and overall levels are much

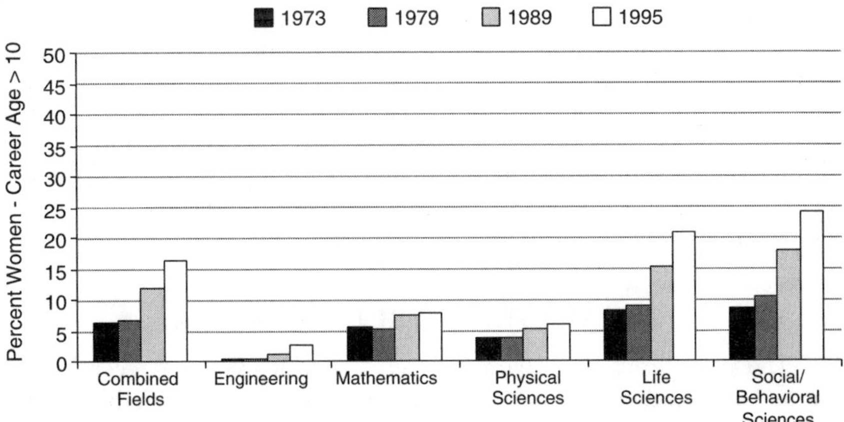

FIGURE 6-6 Percent of the full-time academic labor force that is female for those who received their Ph.D.s more than 10 years ago, by field and year of survey.

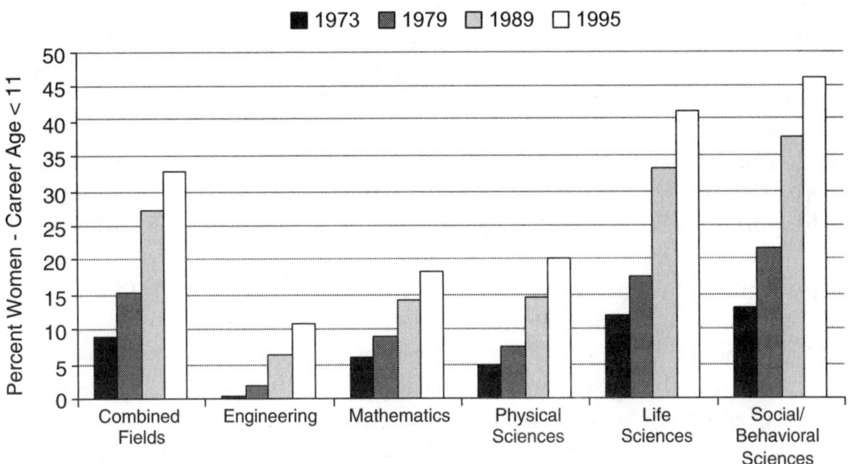

FIGURE 6-7 Percent of the full-time academic labor force that is female for those who received their Ph.D.s in the last 10 years, by field and year of survey.

larger. By 1995, nearly 40 percent of the younger academics in the life and social/behavioral sciences were women. An important implication of the more recent entry of women than men is that women are concentrated among the younger members of the faculty and research staffs. This has important consequences for understanding the presence of women among those who are tenured and have higher ranks, a topic which is discussed in detail below. Consequently, it is useful to consider the age distribution of men and women in academia more thoroughly.

THE AGE STRUCTURE IN ACADEMIA

The average academic woman received her degree more recently than the average academic man. Moreover, the difference between the average career age (i.e., years since the Ph.D. was received) for men and women is increasing. In 1973, the mean career age for women was 9.5 years and 11.1 years for men; in 1979, 8.9 years for women and 12.7 years for men; in 1989, 10.6 years for women and 15.9 years for men; and in 1995, 11.2 years and 17.0 years. The effects of changes in the growth of academia and the entry of women can be seen with a population pyramid (see Shyrock and Siegel 1973: 236-245 for details). A population pyramid is a pair of horizontal histograms, one for men and one for women, with each bar representing the percent in an age group. Typically, the length of the bars corresponds to the percent in a given age-sex group (e.g., women aged between 1 and 3) relative to the size of the *total* population. Alternatively, a *within sex pyramid* can be used in which percentages for men are computed on the basis of the number of men in the population and the percentages for women are based on the number of women. A within sex pyramid is useful when there are large differences in the overall number of men and women, such as in academia. The shape of a pyramid reflects the number of each sex entering the population (e.g., new Ph.D.s) and the number leaving the population through death or retirement. For example, if the same number of new Ph.D.s were hired each year and there was no attrition until the age of retirement, the pyramid would be a rectangle. Or, if the size of new cohorts is increasing with increasing attrition among older members of the population, the pyramid would be triangular.

Figure 6-8 contains *within sex* population pyramids for academic scientists in 1973 and 1995. Consider the age profile for women in 1973 (Panel A). Nearly 30 percent of female academics were within 3 years of their Ph.D. and over half were within 6 years. A substantially smaller number of women were found between ages 7 and 21, with 9 percent more men than women at these ages. The dark half of the pyramid for men has a narrower base and more area at the top, reflecting the greater proportion of men who are older. By 1995 (Panel B), the age structure of

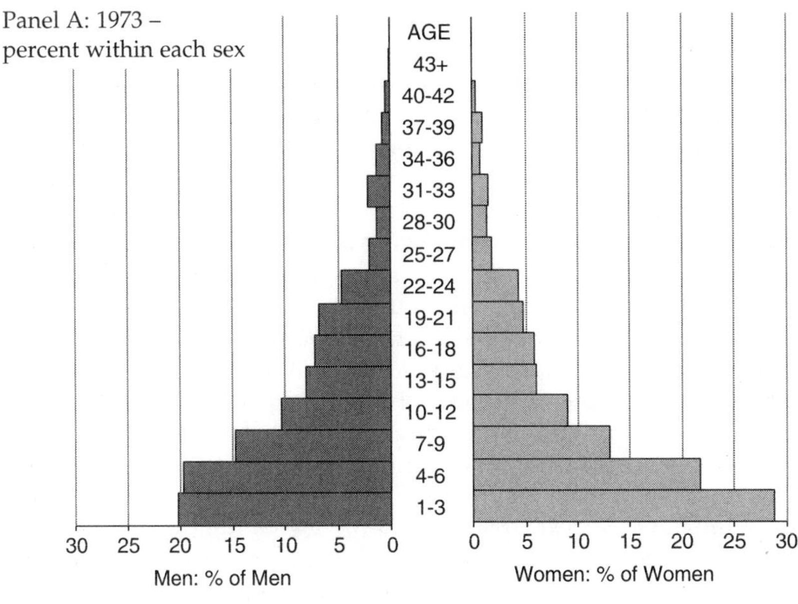

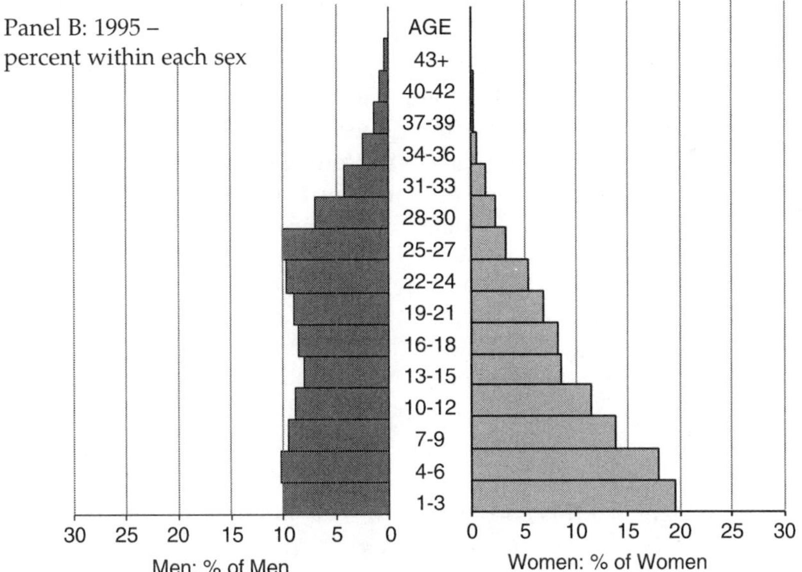

FIGURE 6-8 Sex specific distribution of career ages of scientists in the full-time academic labor force. NOTE: Percentages are sex specific. For example, in 1973, 20 percent of the men were 1-3 years from the Ph.D.

academia had changed dramatically as a result of the rapid entry of women and the end of growth in the size of new cohorts of men. For men, the age pyramid from age 1 to 27 is nearly uniform with roughly 3 percent of the male academics at each year from the Ph.D. The slight narrowing of the pyramid between ages 7 and 22 corresponds to the contraction of the academic labor market between 1973 and 1995. For women, the continuing increase in the entry of women is shown by the triangular shape of the distribution. Given that tenure and rank are time dependent, it is clear that women in 1995 must be found less frequently in advanced ranks, a topic considered below. Finally, it is interesting to note that the age structure for women in 1995 is very similar to the age structure for men in 1973.

Since Figure 6-8 computes percentages within each sex, it does not reflect differences in the relative numbers of men and women. That is, it reflects *rates* of entry and exit from academia, but does not reflect the *number*. Since it is also important to understand how many women are at each age relative to men, Figure 6-9 computes percentages based on the entire population. For example, in Panel A we see that in 1973 women with Ph.D.s within the last 3 years represented 2.5 percent of *all* academic scientists (in Figure 6-8 we saw that these women represented nearly 30 percent of *female* academics). In 1973, the youngest group of men represented nearly 20 percent of all academics, while the youngest group of women represented less than 3 percent. By 1995, new female Ph.D.s grew to 4 percent of academics, while new men dropped to less than 8 percent. Overall, the slowed growth of academia is shown by young Ph.D.s dropping from over 20 percent in 1973 to 12 percent in 1995.

Even with the rapid increase in the percent of women receiving Ph.D.s and entering academia, women are far from being half of the academic labor force, as shown by the much smaller area of the light gray bars compared to the dark gray bars. While new cohorts of Ph.D.s entering the academic marketplace are increasingly female, each new cohort is only a small proportion of those currently employed. Consequently, the move towards parity in the representation of women must occur slowly.

While there has been a substantial increase in women with academic jobs, it remains to be determined whether there is a correspondingly large increase in the presence of women among all types of positions, ranging from full professors at elite research universities to visiting lecturers at two-year colleges. To this end, we begin by examining variations in the types of institutions in which men and women are employed. We then extend these analyses to consider variation in the types of jobs held by men and women in academia.

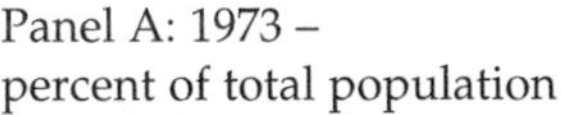
Panel A: 1973 –
percent of total population

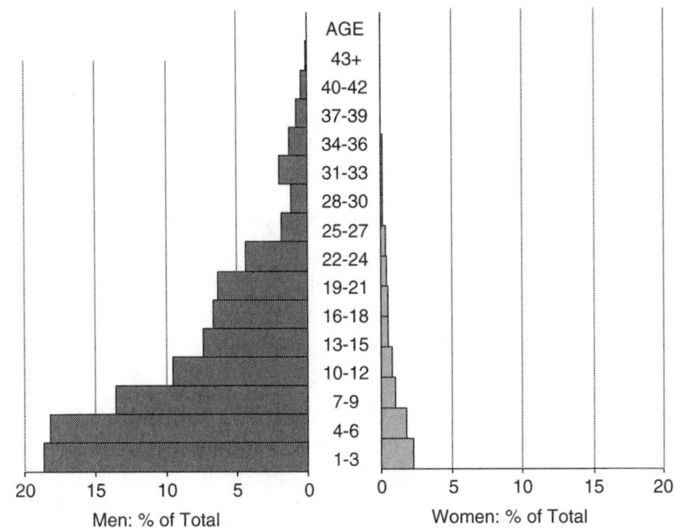

Panel B: 1995 –
percent of total population

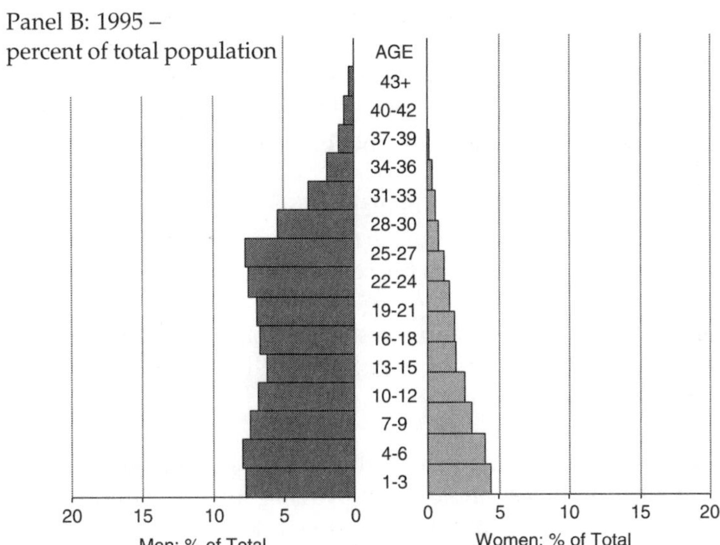

FIGURE 6-9 Distribution of career ages of scientists in the full-time academic labor force. NOTES: Panels A and B show the percent of the total population in a given age/sex category. For example, in 1973 18 percent of *all* scientists were men 1-3 years from the Ph.D.; 2.5 percent of *all* scientists were women 1-3 years from the Ph.D.

TYPES OF ACADEMIC INSTITUTIONS[4]

The over 3,000 institutions of higher education in the United States vary greatly in their prestige, facilities, resources, job expectations, and salaries. The Carnegie Classification is the standard way to classify institutions to reflect these differences (Carnegie Commission on Higher Education 1973, 1976, 1987, 1994). Here we use the simplified classification that was discussed in Chapter 2:

- *Research I* institutions are committed to graduate education through the Ph.D., give high priority to research, and receive substantial federal support. Research I universities along with medical schools are generally considered to be the most prestigious academic locations.
- *Medical* institutions include medical and health related universities. While medical schools may not have graduate programs, they are similar to Research I in their prestige and research orientation, and are important in the life sciences for postdoctoral training.
- *Research II* institutions are similar to Research I institutions, but are smaller, award fewer degrees, and receive less research funding.
- *Doctoral* institutions produce a smaller number of Ph.D.s in fewer areas and receive less funding than Research I and II schools.
- *Master's/Comprehensive* institutions offer baccalaureate programs and usually have graduate education only through the master's degree. We will refer to this combined category as *Master's* institutions. Many of these schools evolved from teachers' colleges and are of low prestige (Clark 1987: 115).
- B*accalaureate* institutions are smaller, primarily undergraduate colleges with a majority of degrees in the arts and sciences. The prestige of these institutions varies greatly with the selectivity of admissions and the quality of the faculty.
- *Research institutions.* In later analyses, we sometimes combine Research I, Research II, and Doctoral institutions with Medical schools and refer to this group as *research institutions.*

Our analyses exclude 4.5 percent of the male academics and 3.5 percent of the female academics who did not provide sufficient information about their employer to determine the Carnegie type. We also exclude those who work in miscellaneous institutions, including theological seminaries, schools of art, and teachers' colleges. These account for less than 1 percent of the sample, and are evenly distributed between men and women.

---

[4]See Appendix Table D-3 for detailed information.

Enrollments in Carnegie Types of Institutions

Comparing the number of students enrolled at different Carnegie types of institutions to the number of full-time doctoral employees at these institutions illustrates the differing missions across the institutions. Figure 6-10 plots the percent of all students who are enrolled in various types of institutions; for a given year, the percentages across types of institutions sum to 100.[5] Figure 6-11 provides corresponding information on the percent of full-time doctoral employees at these institutions. The most dramatic difference is seen by comparing Research I universities to Master's universities. Research I institutions have over twice the doctoral employees relative to the proportion of students, with an increasing difference as the proportion of students in Research I institutions declined while enrollments in Master's schools increased. Master's institutions enroll proportionally twice as many students as they have full-time doctoral employees. These differences reflect the much greater emphasis on research at Research I institutions, where teaching loads are lighter and more scientists and engineers are full-time researchers.

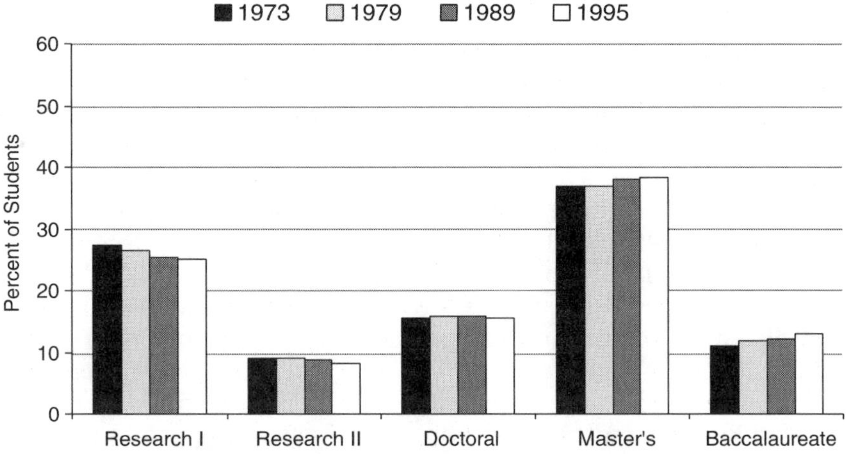

FIGURE 6-10 Student enrollment in higher education, by Carnegie type of institution and year of survey. SOURCE: National Science Board 1998: Appendix Table 2-8.

[5]We excluded those enrolled in 2-year or specialized institutions.

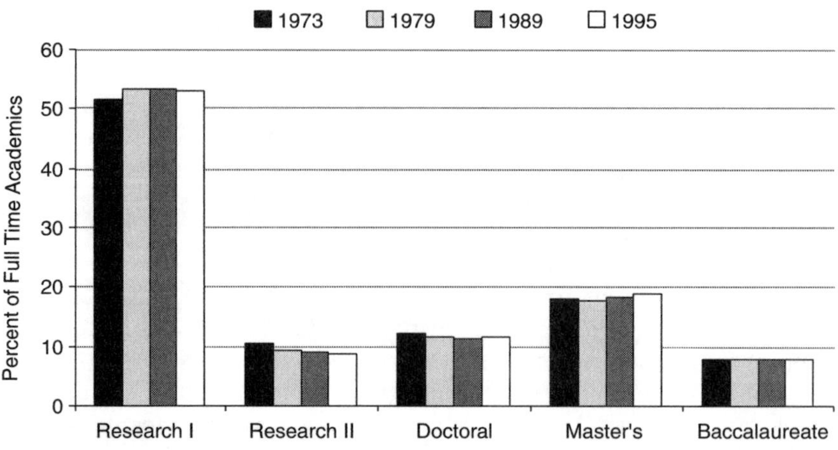

FIGURE 6-11 Employment of full-time academics, by Carnegie type of institution and year of survey.

The Distribution of Academics among Types of Institutions

In their review of the literature on the scientific career, Long and Fox (1995) concluded that the less prestigious the type of institution, the more likely the employment of women and minorities. Our data confirm this generalization, with two qualifications. First, a substantial number of women are working at medical schools, which are generally considered to be prestigious locations. Keep in mind, however, that this does not imply that men and women had the same types of positions within these institutions. This critical issue is discussed below. Second, gender differences in the institutional distribution of employment have declined substantially since 1973, with women being relatively more likely to be in the more prestigious Research and Medical institutions. Table 6-1 presents the distribution of men and women among types of institutions over time. While Research I universities are by far the largest employer, their share of full-time academics has decreased from 1973 to 1995. The percent of men in Research I institutions dropped by 7 percentage points, while the percent of women dropped only 1 point. As a result, the over-representation of men in this important class of institutions has declined from an 11 point differential in 1973 to 5 points in 1995. Women are found proportionally more often in medical schools, which have shown the largest growth in employment since 1973. While the proportion of men employed in other types of institutions has been nearly constant since 1973, for

TABLE 6-1 Distribution of Full-Time Academic Positions Among Carnegie Types of Institutions, by Sex and Year of Survey

		1973	1979	1989	1995	Change from 1973 to 1995
Research I	*Men*	46.8	42.9	41.5	39.6	–7.2
	Women	36.2	36.9	37.4	34.8	–1.4
	Difference	10.6	6.0	4.1	4.9	–5.7
Medical	*Men*	5.1	10.5	11.3	12.6	7.5
	Women	11.1	16.9	18.8	20.4	9.3
	Difference	–6.0	–6.4	–7.6	–7.8	–1.8
Research II	*Men*	10.8	9.7	9.6	9.1	–1.7
	Women	6.3	5.9	7.4	7.0	0.8
	Difference	4.5	3.8	2.2	2.1	–2.4
Doctoral	*Men*	12.4	11.9	11.6	12.1	–0.3
	Women	10.3	11.1	9.6	10.2	–0.1
	Difference	2.1	0.8	2.0	1.9	–0.2
Master's	*Men*	17.5	17.6	18.5	19.0	1.6
	Women	25.0	19.3	18.1	19.0	–6.1
	Difference	–7.6	–1.7	0.4	0.0	7.6
Baccalaureate	*Men*	7.5	7.5	7.6	7.5	0.0
	Women	11.2	10.0	8.8	8.6	–2.5
	Difference	–3.7	–2.5	–1.2	–1.1	2.6
N	*Men*	100,284	123,796	158,800	153,593	
	Women	8,557	15,957	34,267	45,324	

NOTE: For example, 46.8 indicates that 46.8 percent of male academics in 1973 were working at Research I institutions.

women there has been a 6 point decrease in Master's universities and a 3 point decrease in Baccalaureate colleges. The net effect of these changes is that men and women have become increasingly similar in their distribution among types of institutions. And, among Research I and Medical institutions combined, the 5 point over-representation of men in 1973 turned into a 3 point *under-representation* in 1995. Among research institutions,[6] the 11 point advantage for men in 1973 is reduced to a single point advantage in 1995. During this period, there was a corresponding de-

[6]These include Research I, Research II, Doctoral, and Medical institutions.

crease in the over-representation of women in both Master's and Baccalaureate institutions.

There are, however, important differences among fields in the percent who are employed in research institutions. Engineers, who require extensive research funding and sophisticated laboratories to do their research, are much more likely to work at research institutions than are Ph.D.s in other fields. In 1973, 90 percent of all academic engineers worked in research institutions (almost all engineering schools are in research universities), declining only slightly to 86 percent in 1995. Employment in research institutions is next most common in the life sciences, where the percent has increased slightly to just over 80 percent. Employment in research institutions is least common in mathematics and the social/behavioral sciences, fields where research facilities are less critical, where there has been a steady decline to 62 percent in 1995.

While there are differences among fields in the representation of women among research institutions, there are increasing similarities since 1973. The largest changes occurred in the social and behavioral sciences. From 1973 to 1995, women went from being 10 points under-represented to 5 points over-represented in research institutions; in Research I and Medical institutions, the change was from women being 5 points under-represented to 9 points over-represented relative to the rates for men (Table 6-2). In other fields, while the changes generally lead to increased similarities, the convergence was less dramatic. In mathematics, women were significantly under-represented until a sudden decrease in the proportion of men and an increase in the proportion of women in 1995. There was rapid growth in employment in medical schools, with an increase from 13 percent to 28 percent in the proportion of male life scientists working in medical schools. During this same period, the proportion of women in medical schools increased more slowly, from 21 percent in 1973 to 31 percent in 1995. As a consequence, the overrepresentation of women in medical schools decreased from 9 points in 1973 to 3 points in 1995.[7]

The Proportion of Academics Who Are Women

As a result of the increasing proportion of new Ph.D.s who are women and the greater tendency of women to enter academia, the percentage of full-time doctoral employees who are women has increased steadily in all types of institutions, as shown by Figure 6-12. As shown in Table 6-2 by 1995, women were most represented in Medical schools, with a large

[7]Keep in mind that we are only considering scientists in medical schools that have a Ph.D. Those with an M.D. but without a Ph.D. are not included in the SDR or SED.

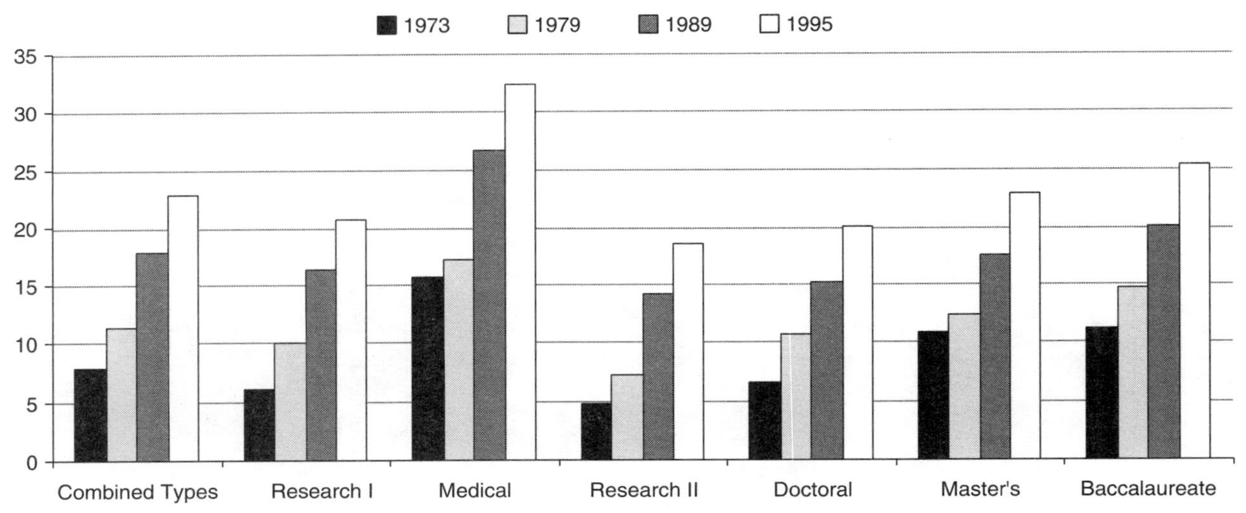

FIGURE 6-12 Percent of full-time academics who are women, by Carnegie type and year of survey.

TABLE 6-2 Gender Difference in Percent of Full-Time Academics in Ph.D. Granting/Medical Institutions and in Research I/Medical Institutions, by Year of Survey

		Ph.D. or Medical Institutions[a]				
		1973	*1979*	*1989*	*1995*	*Change*
Engineering	*Total*	89.9	90.7	89.2	86.2	–3.7
	Men	90.0	90.7	89.4	86.5	–3.5
	Women	—	—	82.2	82.4	0.2
	Difference	—	—	7.2	4.1	–3.1
Mathematics	*Total*	67.2	67.6	64.4	60.9	–6.3
	Men	68.4	68.3	65.6	61	–7.4
	Women	—	57.2	53.6	60.8	3.6
	Difference	—	11.1	12.0	0.2	–10.9
Physical Sciences	*Total*	70.0	69.9	69.1	70.9	0.9
	Men	70.5	70.1	69.0	71.4	0.9
	Women	58.7	66.6	69.9	66.7	8.0
	Difference	11.8	3.5	–0.9	4.7	–7.1
Life Sciences (Research I)	*Total*	80.9	82.2	84.5	82.5	1.6
	Men	81.6	82.8	84.7	83.3	1.7
	Women	75.1	78.7	83.8	80.6	5.5
	Difference	6.5	4.1	0.9	2.7	–3.8
Life Sciences (Medical)	*Total*					
	Men					
	Women					
	Difference					
Social and Behavioral Sciences	*Total*	66.8	66.2	62.8	62.2	–4.6
	Men	68.0	66.1	61.8	60.8	–7.2
	Women	57.6	66.6	65.7	65.3	7.7
	Difference	10.4	–0.5	–3.9	–4.5	–14.9

NOTE: — indicates too few women in category to estimate percentage.
[a]Research institutions include Research I, Research II, Doctoral, and Medical institutions.
[b]For life sciences, Medical and Research I institutions are described separately.

Research I or Medical[b]				
1973	*1979*	*1989*	*1995*	*Change*
59.7	60.6	60.6	58.7	–1.0
59.7	60.6	60.6	58.7	–1.0
—	—	65.7	55.5	–10.2
—	—	–5.1	3.2	8.3
43.7	45.3	41.8	37.7	–6.0
43.7	45.3	41.8	37.7	–6.0
—	37.7	33.2	38.1	0.4
—	7.6	8.6	–0.4	–8.0
47.9	49.5	50.1	50.7	2.8
47.9	49.5	50.1	50.7	2.8
43.4	49.8	53.7	51.4	8.0
4.5	–0.3	–3.6	–0.7	–5.2
46.8	38.5	38.8	35.1	–11.7
47.9	39.1	39.2	36.4	–11.7
37.5	34.8	37.2	31.8	–5.7
10.4	4.3	2.0	4.6	–5.8
13.7	25.1	28	28.9	15.2
12.8	24.6	26.9	28.0	15.2
21.4	28.7	31.5	31.1	9.7
–8.6	–4.1	–4.6	–3.1	5.5
43.0	41.2	39.1	36.9	–6.1
43.0	41.2	39.1	36.9	–6.1
38.1	45.9	46.1	46.0	7.9
4.9	–4.7	–7.0	–9.1	–14.0

TABLE 6-3 Percent of Full-Time Academics Who Are Female, by Carnegie Type of Institution, Field, and Year of Survey

		Research I	Medical	Research II
Engineering	*1973*	0.2		0.1
	1979	1.0		0.4
	1989	3.3		1.6
	1995	5.9		4.7
	Change	5.7		4.6
Mathematics	*1973*	3.8		3.7
	1979	5.8		5.3
	1989	7.9		7.0
	1995	11.7		12.5
	Change	7.9		8.8
Physical Sciences	*1973*	4.0		2.5
	1979	5.6		5.5
	1989	8.9		7.4
	1995	11.4		11.0
	Change	7.4		8.5
Life Sciences	*1973*	8.2	16.0	6.6
	1979	12.2	15.5	6.7
	1989	21.5	25.4	15.7
	1995	26.3	31.2	22.1
	Change	18.1	15.2	15.5
Social/Behavioral Sciences	*1973*	10.2		7.0
	1979	18.6		12.7
	1989	27.8		24.8
	1995	36.5		27.5
	Change	26.3		20.5

increase between 1979 and 1989. Smaller increases were found in Baccalaureate and Master's institutions. The smallest representation of women was the Ph.D. granting institutions: Research I, Research II, and Doctoral institutions.

The increase in the percentage of women occurred in all fields, as shown in Table 6-3, with engineering, mathematics, and the physical sciences showing the least growth. Among these fields, the only increase greater than 10 percentage points in the proportion of women was in the very small number of engineers at Baccalaureate institutions. By 1995, the proportion of women in engineering was just above 5 percent, while women's representation in mathematics and the physical sciences was

Doctoral	Master's	Baccalaureate	Total
0.5	0.6	0.0	0.3
1.1	1.0	1.3	0.9
1.9	5.1	4.7	3.0
7.0	7.3	13.3	6.3
6.5	6.7	13.3	6.0
4.9	8.9	10.4	5.7
6.2	8.9	9.4	6.9
9.6	12.4	13.5	9.8
10.6	10.0	16.5	11.6
5.7	1.1	6.1	5.9
3.4	5.6	6.8	4.4
3.9	5.6	6.9	5.5
7.0	7.4	9.2	8.3
7.2	13.1	12.4	11.3
3.8	7.5	5.6	6.9
8.5	12.7	14.7	10.2
15.7	15.1	19.0	13.6
22.9	23.2	24.3	22.5
32.7	32.4	31.4	28.9
24.2	19.7	16.7	18.7
10.7	14.9	13.6	11.4
15.7	15.8	19.5	17.0
20.4	21.3	25.9	24.6
27.0	27.8	31.6	31.6
16.3	12.9	18.0	20.2

just over 10 percent. The largest increases were in the life and social/ behavioral sciences, where women increased their proportion by nearly 20 points. Within the social and behavioral sciences, the greatest proportions of women are found in Research I and Baccalaureate institutions. In the life sciences, women are working most often in Medical, Doctoral, Master's, and Baccalaureate institutions, where in 1995 they were nearly one-third of the full-time academics. Still, even with the rapid increase, women do not make up 40 percent of the doctoral scientists and engineers in any field or type of institution. The greatest proportion of women is 37 percent, found in Research I universities in the social and behavioral sciences.

THE ACADEMIC LADDER

While the number and proportion of women has increased steadily in all fields and types of institutions, it is also critical that women hold positions of similar status to those of men within these institutions. In this section we examine differences in the types of academic positions held by men and women. Our analytic approach is to explore gender differences at each rung of the academic ladder. First, we examine differences in having tenure-track positions (i.e., faculty) compared to less prestigious and secure off-track positions. For those who are faculty, we consider who has tenure and who does not. Next, we consider advancement to the highest rank, that of full professor. While there is evidence of improvement in the success of women in obtaining positions comparable to those of men, women continue to be less successful in advancing up the ladder of academic success.

Tenure-Track and Off-Track Positions[8]

Female research associates represented a good investment. They were skilled, low cost, and grateful for the work.

—Mary Frank Fox, *The Outer Circle*, 1991[9]

The most fundamental distinction among academic positions is between tenure-track positions and off-track positions. Scientists with tenure-track positions have the possibility of advancing through the faculty ranks from assistant professor to full professor. Accordingly, we refer to those on tenure-track positions as *faculty*. As a result of achievements in teaching, research, and service, faculty can be rewarded with the job security provided by tenure. In comparison, off-track positions have lower pay, fewer resources, and less security. They include temporary teaching positions, research positions funded by soft money, visiting scholars, adjunct faculty without tenure-track appointments elsewhere, postdoctoral fellows, and lower level administrative positions. The second class status of off-track positions is reflected in Kerr's (1963) characterization of these academics as the "unfaculty." Off-track positions greatly benefit the university by providing an elastic, highly trained labor force at a low cost. These marginal positions can be used by the university to respond quickly

[8]The 1973 SDR did not collect information on whether a position was on a tenure track. Accordingly, data in this section are limited to 1979, 1989, and 1995. See Appendix Table D-4 for detailed tables.

[9]Fox (1991).

and cheaply to fluctuations in enrollments, external funding, and faculty leaves (Hornig 1987). Not surprisingly, these positions are less advantageous for the incumbent since they limit access to the resources, such as grants, sabbaticals, secretarial support, and office space, that are needed to establish a successful career (Fox 1996; Hurlbert and Rosenfeld 1992). Consequently, upward mobility from off-track positions to faculty positions is often impossible.

The greater likelihood of women being in off-track positions is well known (Ahern and Scott 1981; Haley-Oliphant 1985; Reskin 1978:1239; Zuckerman 1987:133). Rossiter's (1982, 1995) two volume history of women in science documents the many barriers that women faced in their attempt to obtain full participation through tenure-track positions.[10] In the 1920s and 1930s, the access by women to the academy was often through off-track, research positions, where they were willing to work "harder for lower salaries than were men." With the explosion of research funding in the 1950s and 1960s, women entered research universities in increasing numbers, but as members of the research staff rather than as faculty. The typical experience of female Ph.D.s is aptly summarized by the title of Rossiter's chapter about this period of history of higher education: "Resentful Research Associates: Marriage and Marginality." Since female scientists who are married are often married to other scientists, antinepotism rules kept many faculty wives from becoming faculty (Rossiter 1995; Simon, Clark, and Tifft 1966). While these rules were suspended during World War II, they were often reinstated in the postwar "adjustment." The implications of these changes are painfully illustrated by the case of a woman who was tenured in mathematics, only to find that her contract was not renewed after she married an *untenured* member of the department; his contract, however, was renewed (Rossiter 1995:125). While the blatantly discriminatory antinepotism polices have been outlawed, women continue to be less likely to obtain tenure-track positions.

From 1979 to 1995, the percent of all full-time academic jobs that were on-track decreased from 84 percent to 79 percent, as shown in Figure 6-13. Throughout this decline, men had a steady 14 percentage point advantage over women in obtaining faculty positions. While this suggests that there has been little progress for women in becoming members of the faculty, these overall figures mask broad differences in the availability of faculty positions by field, type of institution, in different historical periods, and at different stages of the career. To see the progress that has been

[10]The information in this section is from Rossiter (1982:203-217; 1995:149-164).

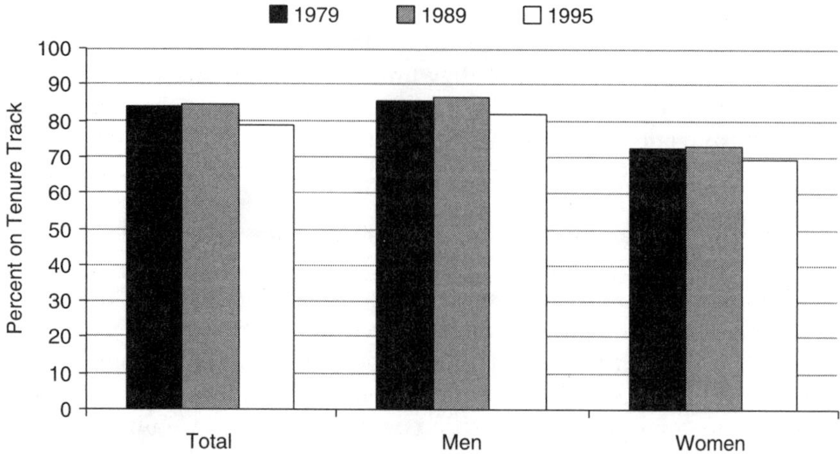

FIGURE 6-13 Percent of all academics, of men, and of women who have tenure-track positions, by year of survey. NOTE: Data were not available in 1973.

made, we must adjust for gender differences in background characteristics and changes over time.

Figures 6-14 and 6-15 show the distribution across fields and types of institutions in the availability of faculty positions. Among fields, employment as a faculty member is least common in the life sciences, especially in medical schools (see also National Research Council 1998, Chapter 3). In medical schools, there was an 11 point drop since 1979 which left only 57 percent of the full-time positions being faculty. Across Carnegie types, tenure-track positions were least common in Medical and Research I institutions, which reflects the large amount of research funding used to hire off-track researchers at these institutions. Research II, Doctoral, and Baccalaureate institutions were the most similar in 1995, with about 85 percent of the jobs on-track. In Master's universities, 90 percent of the full-time doctoral employees were faculty.

Since 1979, the proportion of academic jobs that are tenure track has declined, especially in Medical and Research I institutions. To understand this decrease, it is necessary to consider both the movement of scientists from off-track positions to faculty positions early in their careers and historical decreases in the availability of faculty positions. These two changes are reflected in Figure 6-16. Using data from 1979, the thin line plots the percent of academic scientists who are faculty by how many years have elapsed since the Ph.D. For example, in 1979 those in the first year of the career received their degree in 1978; those in the fifth year in 1974 and so on. Over the first 11 years of the career, there is a steady

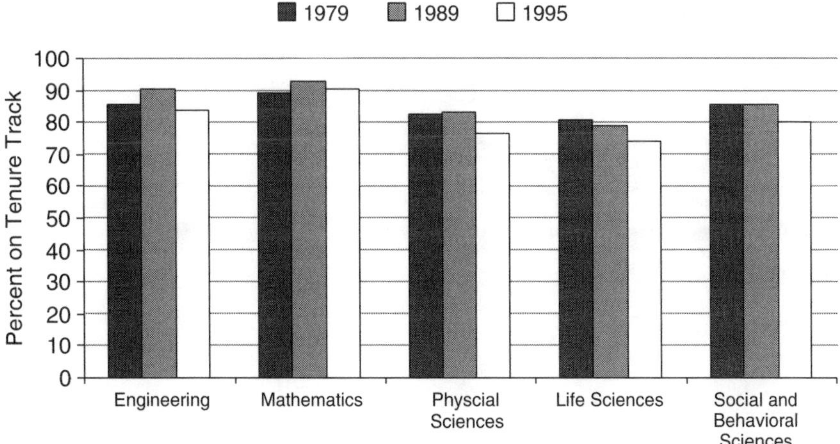

FIGURE 6-14 Percent of full-time academics with faculty positions, by field and year of survey. NOTE: Data were not available in 1973.

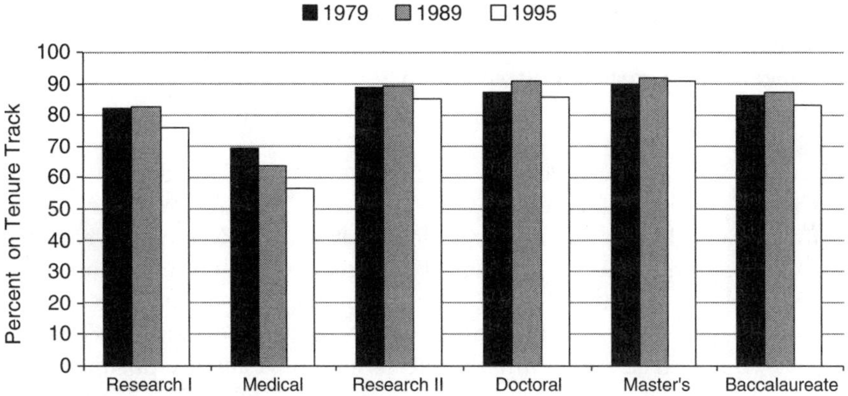

FIGURE 6-15 Percent of full-time academics with faculty positions, by Carnegie type and year of survey. NOTE: Data were not available in 1973.

increase of 2.5 points per year in the percent who are faculty. This is likely to reflect the movement of scientists with postdoctoral fellowships or short-term research positions into full-time positions as faculty. By the eleventh career year (those with degrees in 1968), the proportion levels off around 90 percent.

Data from 1989 are shown by the heavy dark line. For example, in

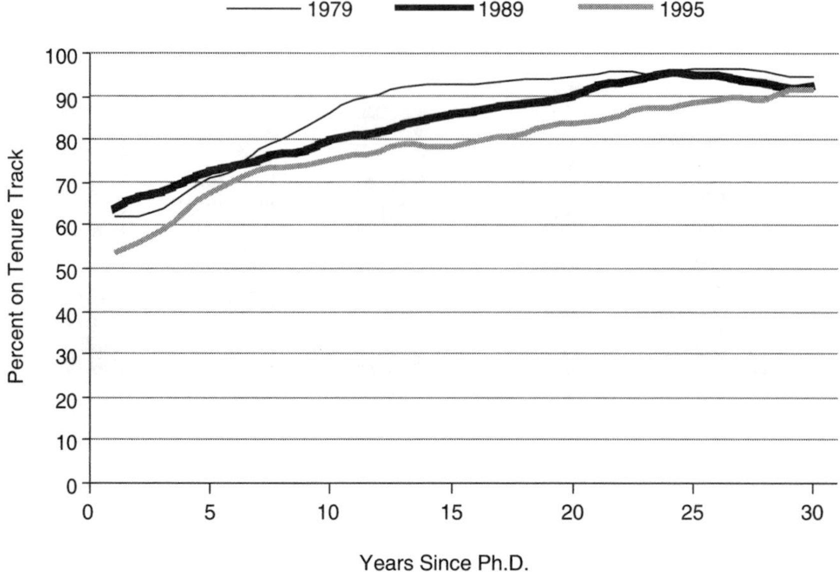

FIGURE 6-16 Percent of academic scientists with faculty positions, by years since the Ph.D. and year of survey. NOTES: Percentages are based on 5-year moving averages. Data were not available in 1973.

1989 those in the first year of the career received their degree in 1988; those in the fifth year in 1984 and so on. The increase over time in the percent with tenure-track jobs is slower, around 1.7 points a year. But, while the trend is more gradual, it continues until the nineteenth year, where it levels off at 90 percent. Comparing the heavy line for 1989 to the thin line for 1979 shows differences over a 10-year period in the proportion of doctoral scientists and engineers who have faculty positions. The biggest change is the decrease in the proportion who have tenure-track faculty positions in years 10 through 20 of the career. In 1979, 93 percent of those 15 years from the Ph.D. were faculty compared to 86 percent in 1989. Similar trends continued in 1995 as shown by the gray line: in all years since the Ph.D., a smaller percent of academics have tenure-track positions. For example, in the fifteenth year, 8 percent fewer academics were on tenure track in 1995 than 1989, and 15 percent fewer than in 1979. Overall, we find a historical decrease in the proportion of scientists who have faculty positions. Over time an increasingly smaller percent of each new cohort find themselves hired as faculty with the possibility of future tenure. Thus, women entered academia in increasing numbers at a time when opportunities for obtaining more permanent and prestigious faculty positions had begun to decline.

Consistent with past research, we find that academically employed men are substantially more likely than women to have faculty positions. Combining fields and types of institutions, men were 14 points more likely to be appointed as faculty in 1979 and 1989, and 13 points more likely in 1995. While these aggregate figures show no overall improvement for women, they correspond to scientists and engineers at all stages in their career. Figure 6-17 plots the percent of men (dark line) and the percent of women (dashed line) with faculty positions in 1995 by the number of years since the Ph.D. During the first 5 years of the career (corresponding to those with degrees from 1991 to 1994), the proportions for men and women are indistinguishable. From year 6 on, men are over 10 points more likely to hold faculty positions. Unfortunately, we cannot tell from these data whether the similarities between men and women among the youngest cohorts will continue as they age or whether the men in these cohorts will become over-represented in faculty positions over time. There is, however, some reason to believe that women have im-

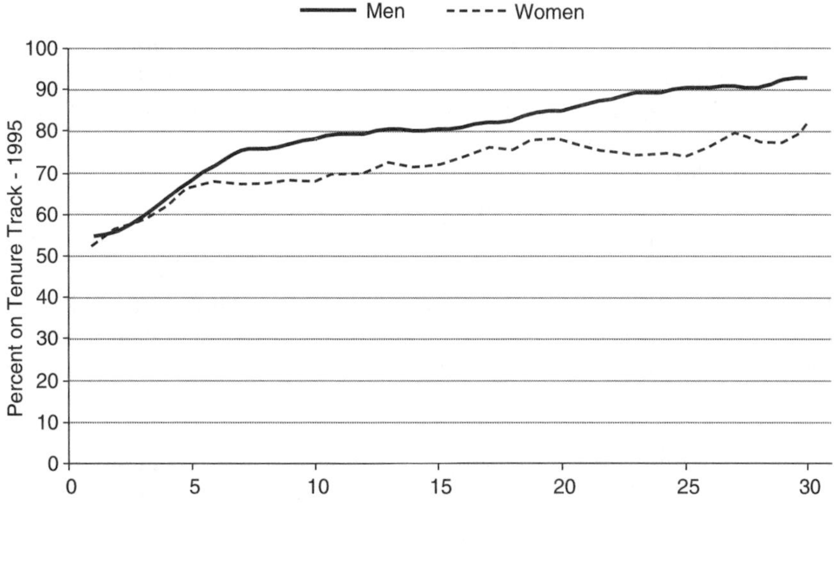

FIGURE 6-17 Percent with tenure-track positions in 1995, by sex and years since the Ph.D.

proved their ability to secure tenure-track positions throughout the career. First, in a similar plot for 1989 (not shown), men were over-represented by about 10 points beginning at the first year of the career and continuing through year 30. Second, the multivariate analyses that we now consider show increasing similarities over time after controlling for background characteristics and, most importantly, professional age.

Logit Analyses of Tenure Track Status[11]

There are too few women in some fields to construct tables that control simultaneously for all of the variables that we believe are important. As an alternative, discussed more fully in Chapter 2, we use logit analysis to predict the proportion of scientists and engineers with tenure-track positions after controlling for characteristics such as field, career year, Ph.D. origin, job type, citizenship status, and family. We refer to the predictions from the logit model as *adjusted* proportions since they are estimates of the proportion of academic scientists and engineers who are faculty after adjusting for (i.e., controlling for) the levels of the variables included in the model. Since the logit model is nonlinear, gender differences in the adjusted proportion with faculty positions depend on the specific values of each control variable. To summarize our findings, we present results for a hypothetical individual in the fifthteenth year of the career.

The dark bars in Figure 6-18 show the *observed* differences in the proportion of men and the proportion of women who have faculty jobs. The unadjusted data show that there was no improvement since 1979 in the over-representation of men. However, these differences do not control for gender differences in scientific age. To adjust for age differences we estimated logit models that predict being in a faculty position after controlling for career age.[12] Separate models were estimated for men and women for each year of the survey. Differences in the adjusted proportions of men and women in their fifthteenth career year are shown by the lighter bars. In 1979, there was only a small decrease from the observed to the adjusted difference. That is, the observed gender difference in the percent with tenure-track positions *cannot* be explained by the younger age of female academics. By 1989, however, the observed difference was substantially reduced by adjusting for age, with a somewhat smaller reduction in 1995. Our results suggest that much, *but not all*, of the differ-

[11]See Appendix Table D-5 for detailed results.

[12]Age is included as the number of years since the Ph.D. and the square of the number of years. The square allows for a decreasing effect of career age over time.

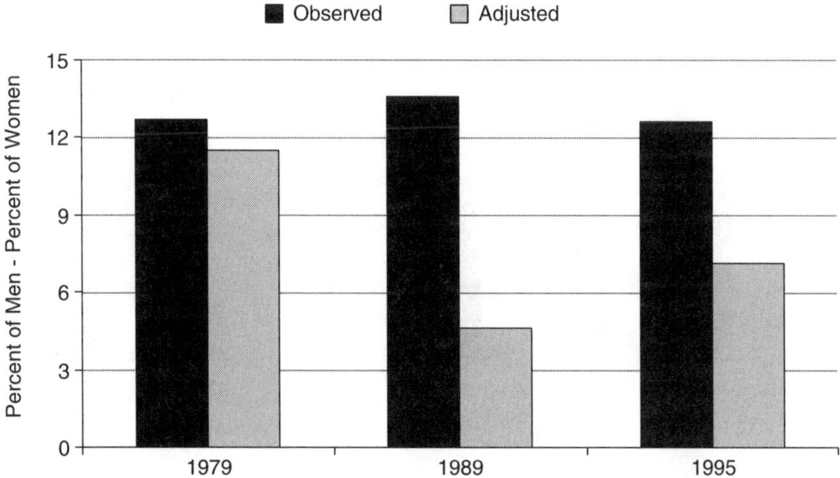

FIGURE 6-18 Difference between men and women in the observed proportions with faculty positions and the adjusted predictions after controlling *only* for years since the Ph.D. NOTES: Predictions are for the fifthteenth year of the career. Data were not available in 1973.

ence between men and women in their success in becoming faculty is due to differences in the stage of the career. The recent entry of women into science and engineering has contributed to the smaller percent of women who are faculty. Accordingly, if current trends in Ph.D. production and the job market for faculty continue, we expect that there will be increases in the percent of women with faculty positions in the next decade.

While the most important factor affecting gender differences in faculty status is the age of a scientist or engineer, there are also important differences related to field, type of institution, and other variables. Figures 6-19 and 6-20 show that the over-representation of men on the faculty differs substantially by type of institution and field, even after adjusting for field differences in age and other variables. Further, these figures demonstrate that women have made significant improvements in becoming faculty in all types of institutions and in most fields. Across institutions, gender differences are largest in Medical, Research I, and Research II institutions, but these institutions also showed the greatest improvement since 1979. By 1995, differences were reduced to 6 points or less in all except Medical institutions. Across fields, the differences were greatest in the life sciences (due to the large number of life scientists in medical schools), but this difference was cut to 8 points by 1995. Differences were

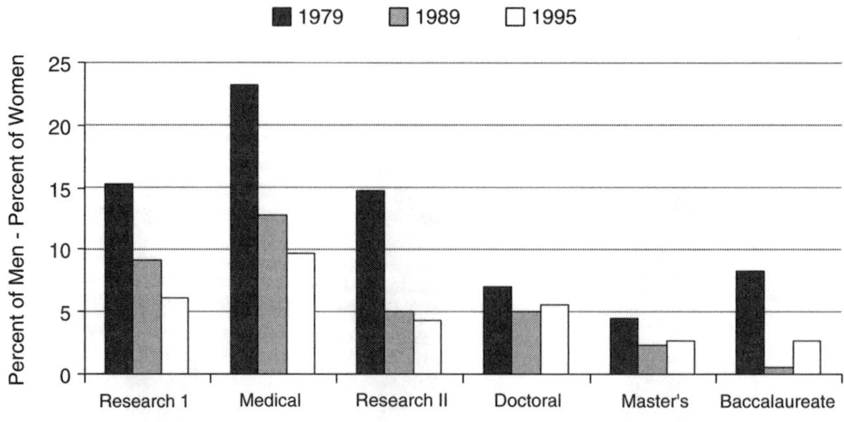

FIGURE 6-19 Gender difference in adjusted proportions with tenure-track positions, by Carnegie type of institution and year of survey. NOTES: Predictions are for career year 15 with other variables held at their means. Data were not available in 1973.

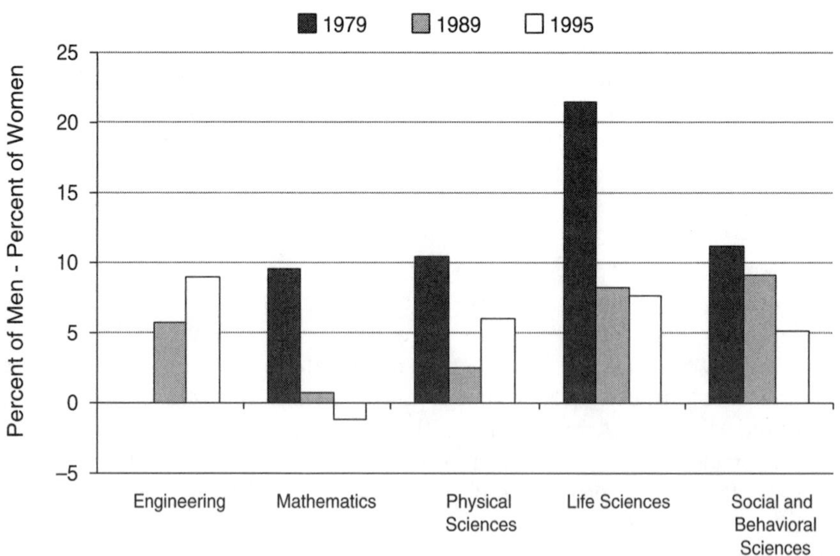

FIGURE 6-20 Gender difference in adjusted proportions with tenure-track positions, by field and year of survey. NOTES: Predictions are for career year 15 with other variables held at their means. There are too few women in engineering in 1979 to estimate the difference. Data were not available in 1973.

TABLE 6-4 Effects of Citizenship, Being at a Private Institution, Prestige of Doctoral Program, and Time from Baccalaureate to Ph.D. on Adjusted Proportions in Tenure-Track Positions, by Sex and Year of Survey

	Women			Men		
	1979	1989	1995	1979	1989	1995
Being a foreign citizen	–8.9	–2.5	–7.4	–5.6	–3.2	–3.2
Working at a private institution	–10.8	–10.1	–7.6	–5.3	–7.3	–9.4
Increase in Ph.D. prestige	1.2	2.8	4.4	0.4	3.0	4.1
More than 10 years from bachelor's to Ph.D.	4.2	0.6	2.1	0.9	–3.3	–6.3

NOTES: Predictions are for career year 15 with other variables held at their means. Data were not available in 1973.

eliminated in mathematics, reduced in the physical and social/behavioral sciences, but showed small increases in engineering.

Other factors are also associated with obtaining a faculty position and some of these factors affect men and women differently. Table 6-4 presents differences in the predicted proportion of academics with faculty positions as we change one variable, holding other variables constant. For example, the value of –8.9 for being a foreign citizen in 1979 for women means that the logit model predicted that 8.9 percentage points fewer women were in faculty positions if they were foreign citizens compared to being an American citizen. The key findings are as follows.

Being a U.S. citizen increases the chances of being a faculty member. There is a larger effect for women and a slight decrease in the effect over time. Being at a private college or university decreases the predicted proportion of scientists with faculty positions by nearly 10 points. This effect decreased for women in 1995, while the effect increased for men since 1979. The proportion of scientists and engineers with faculty positions is slightly higher for those who come from more prestigious doctoral programs. By 1995, the effects were similar for men and women: those from Ph.D. departments that were 1 point more prestigious on a five-point scale were 4 percentage points more likely to be in faculty positions. While Reskin and Hargens (1979) found an insignificant effect of doctoral origins on whether the first job was tenure track, Reskin (1979) found that scientists with postdoctoral fellowships in more prestigious institutions and with more visible mentors were more likely to obtain tenure-track positions.

Recall from our discussion in Chapter 4 that taking longer than 10 years suggests that there was an interruption between the baccalaureate and the Ph.D., perhaps for predoctoral employment or family obligations.

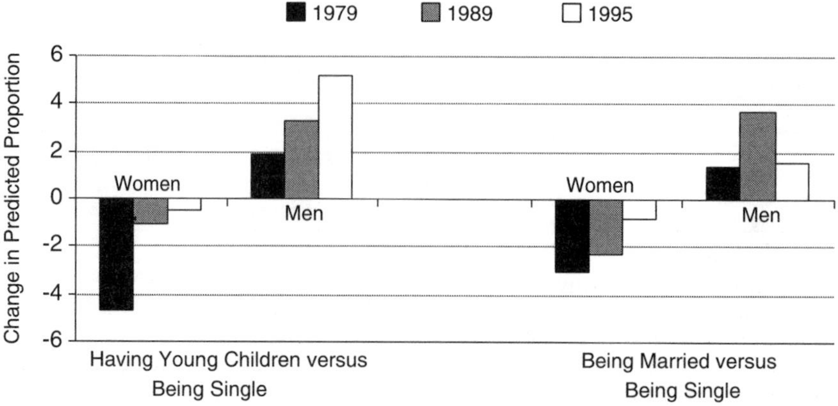

FIGURE 6-21 Differences in the adjusted proportion having tenure-track positions between: a) those with young children and those who are single; and b) those who are married without young children and those who are single, by sex and survey year. NOTES: Predictions are for career year 15 with other variables held at their mean. Data were not available in 1973.

Women with interruptions before receiving the Ph.D. are *more* likely to become faculty, while men who take longer are increasingly *less* likely. While we do not have sufficient information to explain these differences, they could reflect the different reasons that men and women interrupt their education. Women who interrupt their career for family before the doctorate might be less likely to do so after the Ph.D. and consequently would advance more rapidly through the career. This conclusion is consistent with our earlier findings on the effects of marriage and family.

For men, being married with young children compared to being single increases the chances of holding a faculty position (Figure 6-21). The effect is stronger in more recent years. For women, the effects are in the opposite direction, but have largely disappeared by 1995. Given the limitations of our data, it is difficult to interpret the effects of marriage and family on the career, since it is also possible that career outcomes affect familial status. For example, a woman with young children might find it difficult to accept a faculty position, but it is also possible that women who cannot find a suitable faculty position are more likely to start a family. Nonetheless, our findings show that until recently family obligations were important for women in the process of obtaining a faculty positions. This is consistent with Rosenfeld and Jones's (1986:213) interpretation: ". . . departments might assume that all women (single or married) are inhibited by family responsibilities and offer them nontenure-track positions more often than men." Encouragingly, our results suggest that the adverse effects of family for women are declining.

The Representation of Women Among the Faculty and the Unfaculty

The net effect of the increase in women in academia along with the smaller changes in their access to faculty positions are shown in Figure 6-22. This plot shows the percent of *faculty positions* held by women (Panel A) and the percent of *off-track positions* held by women (Panel B). As a point of reference, the set of bars at the far right of each panel shows the percent of all full-time academics who are women, regardless of tenure-track status. The set of bars at the far left of each panel combines academics in all Carnegie types of institutions. Our data show that women account for a larger portion of off-track academics than of faculty, and prior research indicates that this has been true at least since World War II. While there has been a steady increase in the percent of faculty who are women, their rate of increase among off-track scientists and engineers has lessened, resulting in a more even distribution of women across types of positions. Still, in 1995 women made up one-third of those with off-track positions, but only one-fifth of the tenure-track faculty. There is also significant variation across types of institutions. Women are least represented among the faculty at Research I and Research II institutions, which is critical since these institutions train most of the new Ph.D.s. (see Frieze and Hanusa 1984 for further discussion of this issue). If women are not fully represented on the faculty of these schools, their influence in training future generations of women (and men) will be limited. Finally, women are most represented among tenure-track faculty at Baccalaureate and Medical institutions.

Work Activities of Off-Track Academics

Off-track academic scientists and engineers are employed in a variety of jobs, which we break into five categories. *Teaching jobs* are temporary positions, often renewed on a yearly basis, that do not have the security of or potential for tenure. *Research positions* have titles such as lab assistant and research associate, but exclude tenured research positions such as Research Scientists at agricultural schools. *Management* includes lower level positions such as Assistant Dean or Assistant Registrar. *Professional services* includes jobs such as clinical diagnosis and psychotherapy; these positions are normally held by social/behavioral and life scientists in medical schools. Finally, we combine a variety of miscellaneous positions into an *Other* category.

The primary work activities of off-track academics differ greatly by

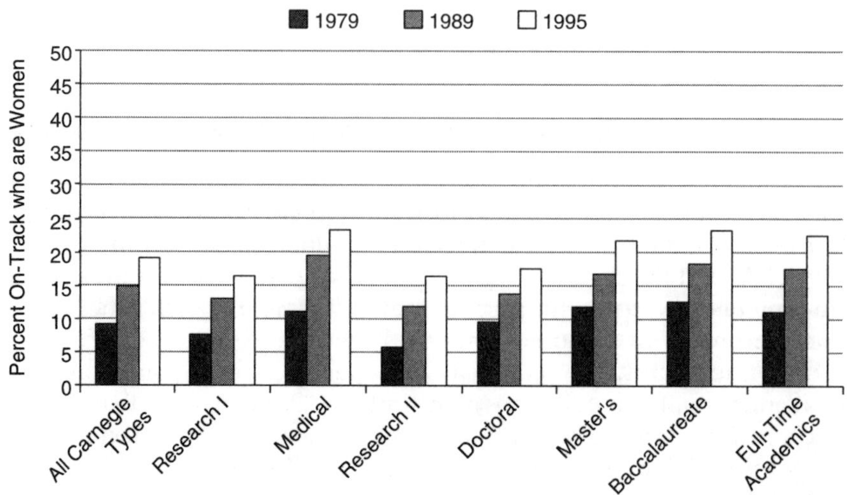

Panel A: The percent of *faculty* who are women

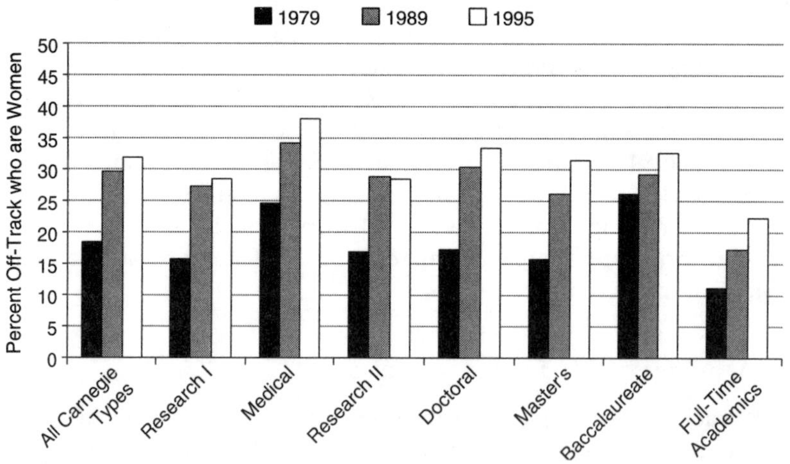

Panel B: The percent of *off-track* academics who are women

FIGURE 6-22 Percent of those in faculty positions and those with off-track positions who are women, by Carnegie type and year of survey. NOTES: The last set of bars is the percent of all full-time academics who are women. Data were not available in 1973.

the type of the institution in which a scientist or engineer is working. There is a gradual shifting of activities as we move along the continuum from Baccalaureate institutions, through Master's, Doctoral, Research II, Research I, and Medical institutions. The four panels of Figure 6-23 show the distribution of jobs for four groups of institutions. The darkest region at the bottom of each bar corresponds to teaching positions that are not on a tenure track.[13] Teaching is the primary activity in Baccalaureate institutions, with steadily falling proportions as we move to Research I and Medical institutions. Correspondingly, there is an increasing proportion of off-track academics who hold research positions. The proportion doing research has decreased slightly over time in Research I and Medical schools, and has increased in other types of institutions. The last notable change is the increasing proportion working in professional services, an area in which women are more likely to work.

Men and women differ in the types of off-track positions that they hold and these differences have changed over time. In 1979, men were 5 to 10 percentage points more likely than women to be teaching in Ph.D. granting and Medical institutions. By 1995 this trend had reversed with women being about 5 points more likely to be teaching in these institutions. Conversely, a greater proportion of women were in research jobs in 1979, changing to a greater proportion of men in these positions by 1995. In Baccalaureate institutions, women were 8 points less likely to be teaching in 1995 and 6 points more likely to be doing research.

Tenure[14]

At its best, tenure is a rigorous test of scholarly achievement that brings great rewards: lifetime job security, better pay and prestige. At its worst, however, tenure is criticized for being a secretive, cabalistic ritual with little accountability for how or why decisions are made.

—Debbie Goldberg, *The Washington Post*, 1997[15]

While the idea of tenure has a long history in the academy (see

---

[13]This does not include part time teaching faculty.

[14]See Appendix Tables D-6 for detailed data. The 1973 SDR did not include the tenure track status of a job, so it was not possible to determine whether a person without tenure held a tenure-track positions without tenure or was not on-track. Accordingly, data from 1973 was not used. We also exclude 0.3 percent of the sample where academic rank was missing.

[15]Goldberg (1997).

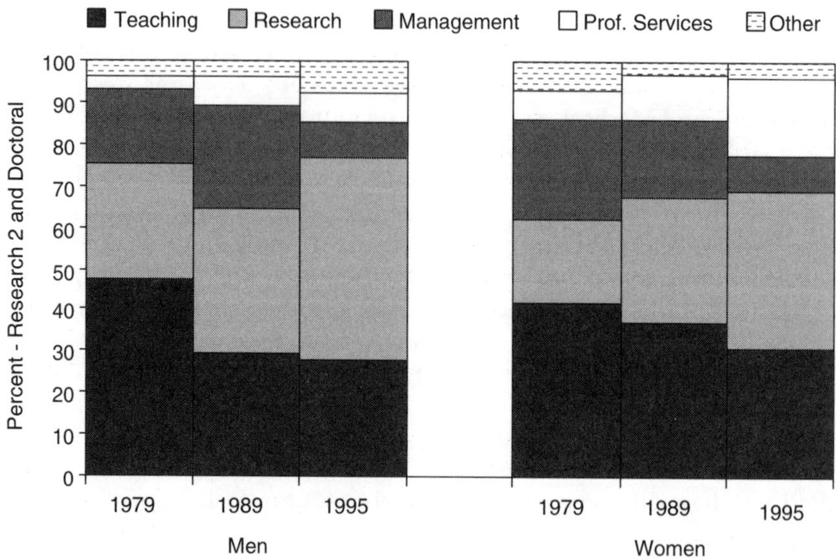

Panel A: Baccalaureate Institutions.

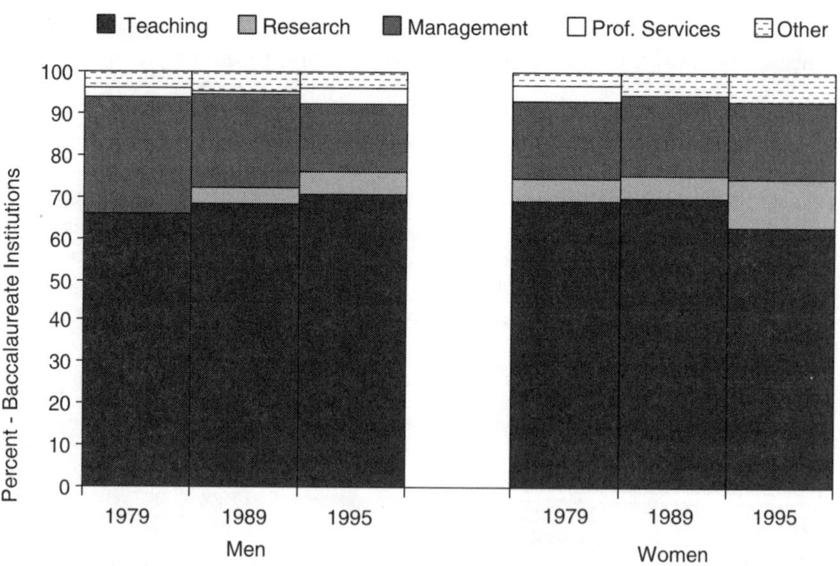

Panel B: Research II and Doctoral Institutions.

FIGURE 6-23 Distribution of non-tenure track academics among work activities, by sex, Carnegie type of institution, and year of survey. (*Continued*)

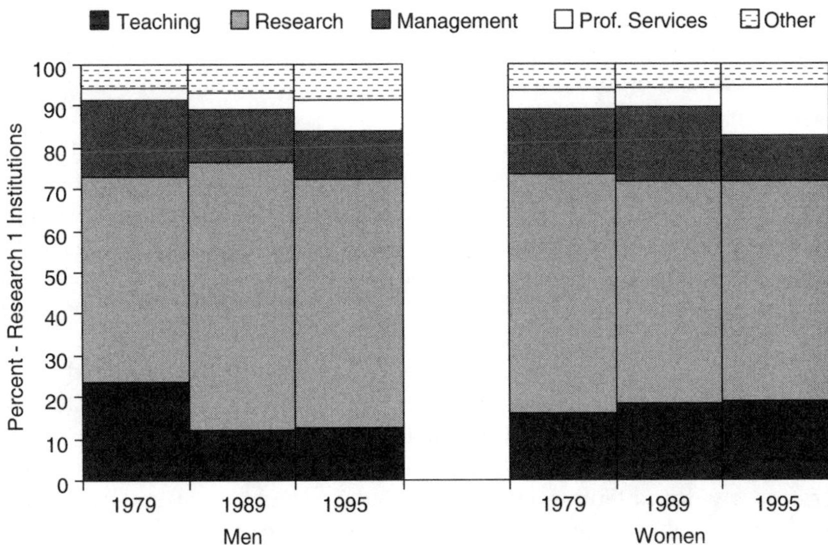

Panel C: Research I Institutions.

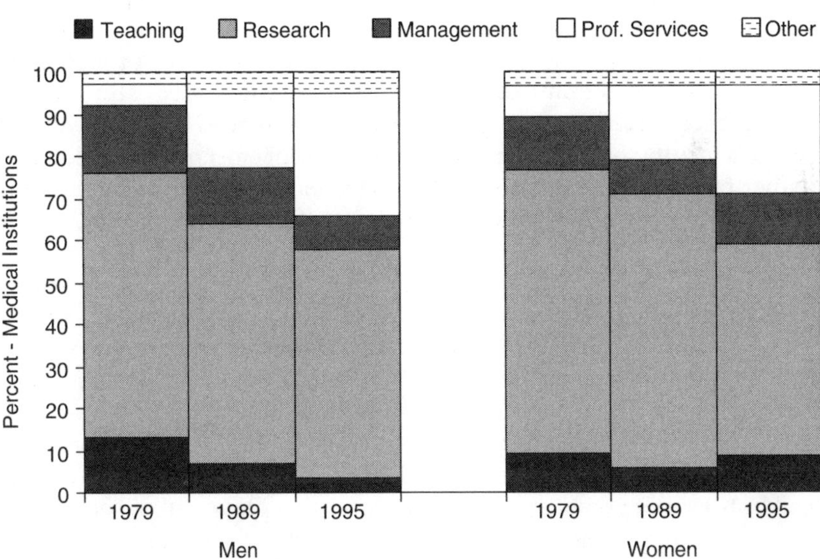

Panel D: Medical Institutions.

FIGURE 6-23 Continued

Metzger 1973 for details), tenure as it is known today has it roots in the 1940 *Statement of Principles of Academic Freedom and Tenure* drafted jointly by the Association of American Colleges and The American Association of University Professors (Commission on Academic Tenure in Higher Education 1973:ix). The essence of this statement is that when a faculty member is granted tenure after meeting requirements of a probationary period, he or she should be terminated "only for adequate cause, except in the case of retirement for age or under extraordinary circumstances because of financial exigencies (Commission on Academic Tenure in Higher Education 1973:3)." By 1970, the principles of this document had been endorsed by nearly every university and college in America.

While the process of granting tenure has varied over time and there are some differences across types of institutions, the granting of tenure normally occurs as follows. A person enters academia upon completion of the doctorate or a postdoctoral fellowship with the initial rank of assistant professor without tenure. During the sixth year as an assistant professor, a faculty member is reviewed for tenure based on criteria established by the college or university. In research universities, research productivity is the main criterion, while in baccalaureate institutions teaching is normally the most important activity. While a tenure review usually occurs in the sixth year (the 1940 statement specified a probationary period of no more than seven years), there is variation among institutions, with private universities and medical schools often having longer probationary periods. If tenure is granted, dismissal occurs only under extraordinary circumstances of financial exigency or personal malfeasance. If tenure is denied, a faculty member is given another year of employment to look for another faculty position at some other (often less prestigious) institution, to accept an off-track position (perhaps at the same institution), or to leave academia entirely.

From 1979 to 1995 there was little change in the percent of tenure-track faculty who had received tenure. For men a nearly constant 80 percent had tenure in each year of the survey, while for women the number increased slightly from 56 percent in 1979 to 62 percent in 1989, dropping to 60 percent in 1995. Throughout this period, a nearly constant 20 percentage points more men than women were tenured. This appearance of a lack of progress for women is due to the shifting age structure for women. In all but cases of exceptional genius, years of employment are critical for receipt of tenure (Ahern and Scott 1981; Hurlbert and Rosenfeld 1992; Long, Allison, and McGinnis 1993). Consequently, when comparing tenure for men and women we must take into account the lower average professional age of women among tenure-track faculty.

The association between professional age and being tenured is shown

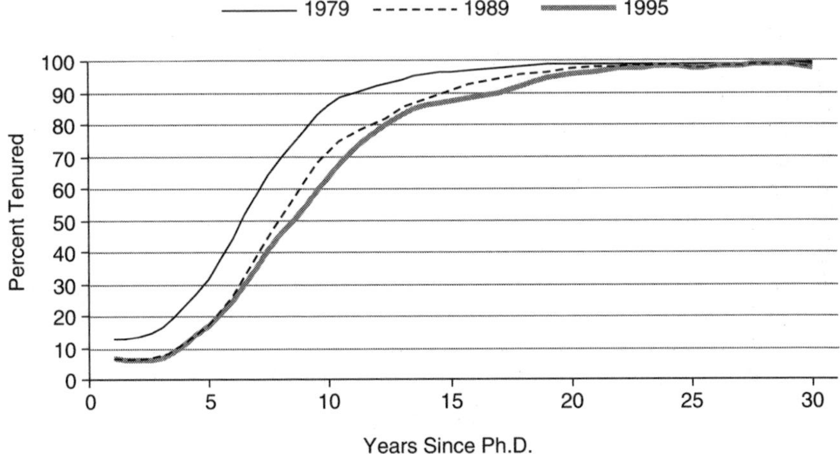

FIGURE 6-24 Percent of tenure-track academic scientists with tenure, by professional age and year of survey. NOTES: Percentages are based on 5-year moving aveages. Data were not available in 1973.

in Figure 6-24 for the survey years 1979, 1989, and 1995.[16] For each year, the proportion of faculty with tenure is quite low immediately after the degree and increases rapidly between years 6 and 10. Keep in mind that while most schools grant tenure after the sixth year in rank, this corresponds to different professional ages for individual faculty depending on the amount of time the person held postdoctoral fellowships or off-track positions before the initial faculty appointment.

Gender differences in age at tenure are show in in Figures 6-25 and 6-26. In 1979, beginning in year 5 male faculty have a 5 point advantage in the percent who are tenured at a given professional age. In 1995, female faculty begin with a 5 point advantage during the first 5 years of the career. This is due to the greater proportion of women with early tenure at Doctoral institutions (5 percent for men; 10 percent for women), Master's institutions (4 percent for men; 21 percent for women), and Baccalaureate institutions (9 percent for men; 16 percent for women). By year 15, a 4 point advantage for men has emerged. Thus, from 1979 to 1995 there is only a small decrease in the *age-adjusted* advantage for men, while at the

[16]For 1979 and 1989 information was collected on the years of work experience. Plots using experience rather than years since the Ph.D. were very similar. The correlation between experience and years since the Ph.D. is .99.

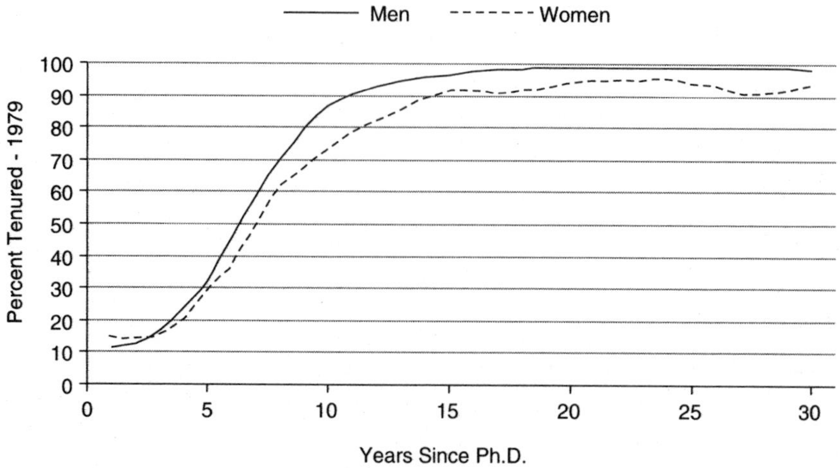

FIGURE 6.25 Percent with tenure in 1979, by gender and year since Ph.D. NOTE: Percentages are based on 5-year moving averages.

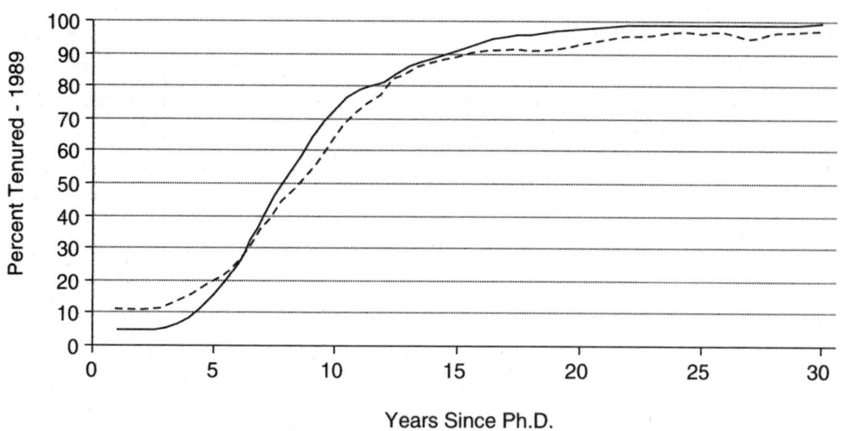

FIGURE 6.26 Percent with tenure in 1995, by gender and year since Ph.D. NOTE: Percentages are based on 5-year moving averages.

same time the percent with tenure at a given stage of the career has decreased.

An important limitation in our analysis of the effects of career age on tenure is that we do not have information on years of experience in off-track positions. For example, we do not know if the average woman in the

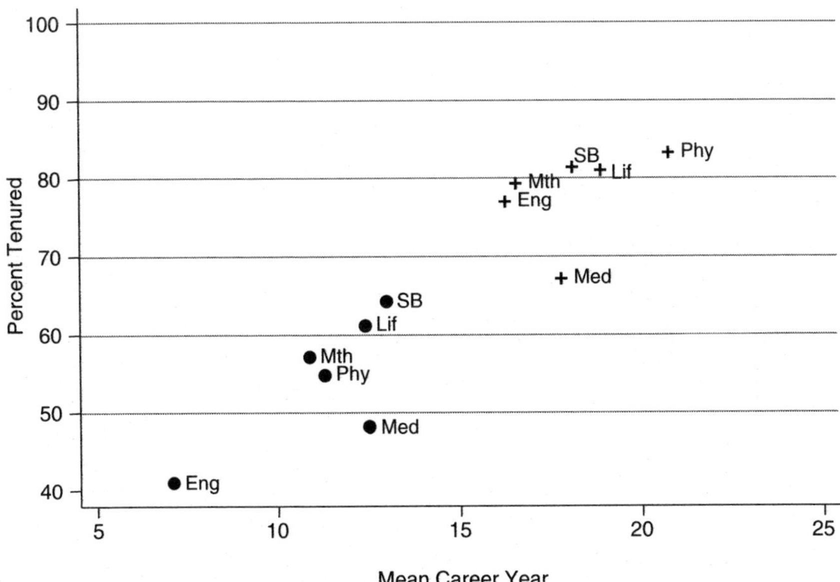

FIGURE 6-27 The percent tenured by mean career age, by field and sex in 1995. KEY: • = Women; + = Men; Eng = Engineering; Mth = Mathematics; Phy = Physical sciences; Lif = Life sciences excluding medical schools; Med = Life sciences in medical schools; SB = Social/behavioral sciences. NOTE: Data points have been adjusted slighlty to avoid overlap in the plotted points.

seventh year of the career has spent more time as an off-track, postdoctoral fellow than the average man. Unfortunately, the SDR provides information on scientists only at a single point in time, namely, the year of the survey. Given the critical importance of tenure for the academic career, further research and more detailed data are clearly called for.[17]

While field differences exist in the percent of faculty who are tenured and in gender differences in rates of tenure, this is largely due to differences in the age structures among fields. Figure 6-27 plots the mean career age in a field by the percent tenured in 1995 for men (shown by +'s) and women (shown by •'s). With the exception of life scientists in medical schools (see +Med and oMed), there is a nearly perfect linear relationship between the percent tenured and the mean age in the field ($r^2 = .96$). The percentage tenured in medical schools, however, is nearly 13 points below what would be expected given the age of those in medical schools.

[17]The curves for each year converge to 100 percent since those who did not receive tenure in earlier years will no longer have tenure-track positions.

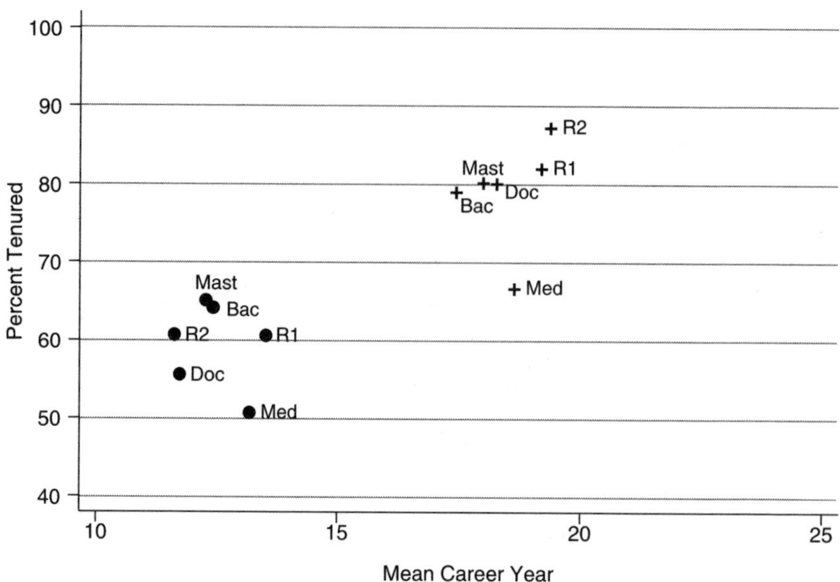

FIGURE 6-28 Percent tenured by mean career age, by sex and Carnegie type in 1995. KEY; • =Women; + = Men; R1 = Research I; R2 = Research II; Med = Medical; Doc = Doctoral; Mast = Master's; Ba c= Baccalaureate. NOTE: Data points have been adjusted slighlty to avoid overlap in the plotted points.

Keep in mind, that for medical schools our sample does *not* include faculty with M.D.s but no doctorate. Further, those in medical schools may require more years after the Ph.D. to obtain tenure in order to meet requirements for residencies and other postdoctoral, off-track activities.

There is a weaker relationship between mean age and the percent tenured across Carnegie types of institutions, as shown in Figure 6-28. This reflects the different career paths (e.g., more or less likelihood of having a postdoctoral fellowship) and policies regarding tenure among different types of institutions (Commission on Academic Tenure in Higher Education 1973:215-226). Tenure is least likely in Medical institutions, followed by Doctoral, Baccalaureate, Research I, Master's, and finally Research II institutions. Since men and women have different proportional representation by Carnegie type of institution, it is important to take this into account when examining gender differences in receiving tenure.

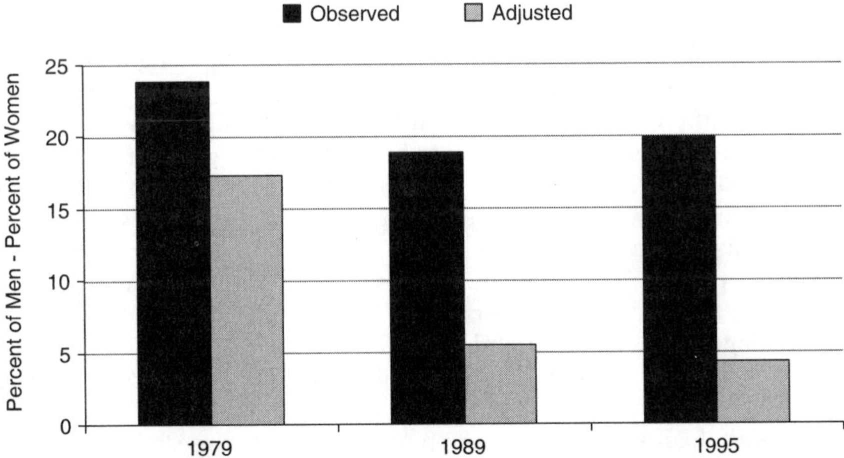

FIGURE 6-29 Difference between men and women in the observed proportion with tenure and the adjusted prediction after controlling for field, career age, and Carnegie type of employer, by year of survey. NOTES: Predictions are for the tenth year after the Ph.D. Data were not available in 1973.

Logit Analyses of Tenure[18]

There was only a 4 percentage point decrease, down from 24 to 20 points, in the observed over-representation of men in tenured positions between 1979 and 1995, as shown by the dark bars in Figure 6-29. However, since male and female faculty differ in average career age and type of institution, it is essential to take these factors into account when comparing the proportion who are tenured. This is done by using logit analysis to predict the proportion of scientists and engineers with tenure after adjusting simultaneously for characteristics such as field, career year, sex, and type of employing institution.[19] To summarize our results, we look at the adjusted proportions of men and women predicted to have tenure in the 10th year after the Ph.D., assuming that all other variables are at the mean. In effect, we are comparing a statistically average male faculty member to a statistically average female faculty member. These controls substantially reduce the differences between men and women in receiving tenure as shown by the gray bars. In 1979, the observed difference was

[18]See Appendix Table D-7 for the complete results.

[19]The model includes years since the Ph.D. and the square of the years since the Ph.D. to allow for the nonlinear effect of career age.

reduced from 24 points to an adjusted difference of 17 points; in 1989 the observed difference of 19 points was reduced to 6 points, dropping to 4 points in 1995. Overall, by 1995 gender differences in being tenured are largely the result of differences in career age and to a lesser extent the result of differences in types of employing institutions. However, even after these controls, men continue to be tenured with greateer likelihood.

To examine the effects of other factors on tenure, we next estimated models that added variables such as prestige of the Ph.D. and marital status. Based on these results, Figures 6-30 and 6-31 plot differences in the adjusted proportion of men and women with tenure according to field, Carnegie type, and year of survey. In 1979, gender differences were 20 percentage points in Research I, Medical, and Baccalaureate institutions. Differences were 10 points smaller in other types of institutions. In 1995, there were large decreases, especially for Medical and Baccalaureate institutions. Still, differences of over 8 points remained in Research I, Research II, and Doctoral institutions even after controlling for professional age and other factors. This important result is explored further in the next section. Among fields, we find that the statistical over-representation of men is eliminated or reversed in the physical sciences and the life sciences. Differences of nearly 10 points remain in engineering, mathematics, and the social/behavioral sciences. Note, however, that the figures for

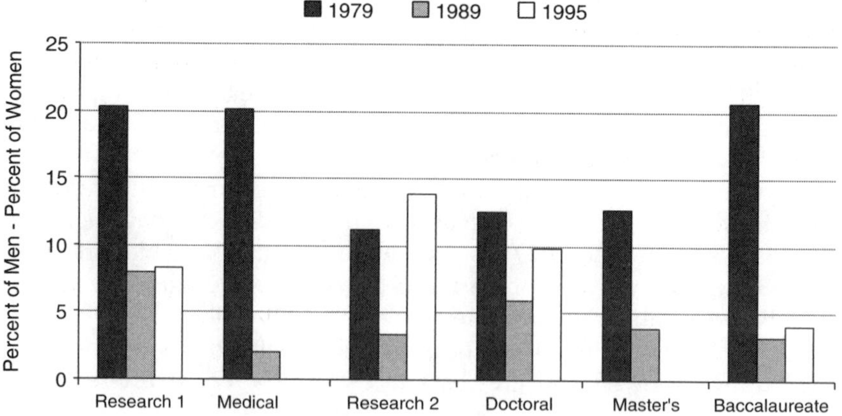

FIGURE 6-30 Difference between men and women in adjusted proportions with tenure, by Carnegie type of institution and year of survey. NOTES: Predictions are for career year 10 with other variables held at their means. The difference is 0 for Medical and Master's institutions in 1995. Data were not available in 1973.

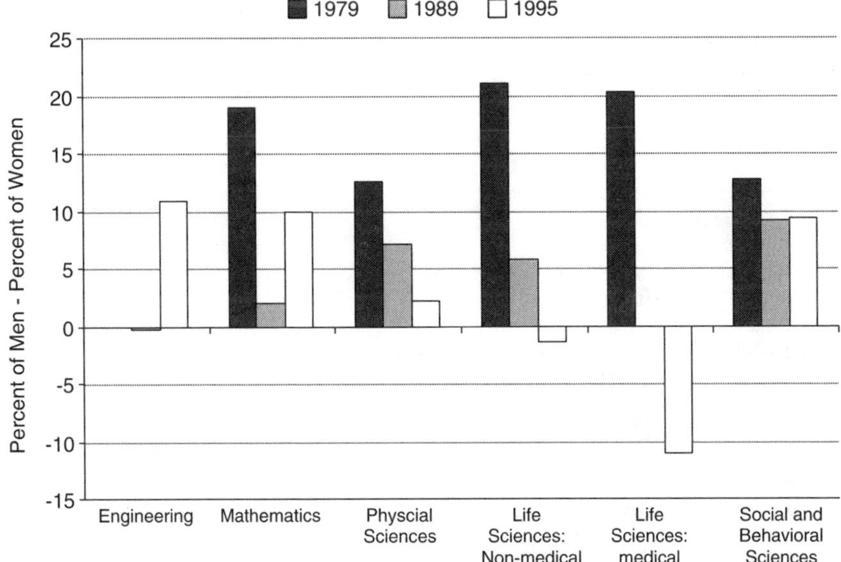

FIGURE 6-31 Difference between men and women in adjusted proportions with tenure, by field and years of survey. NOTES: Predictions are for career year 10 with other variables held at their mean. There are too few women in engineering in 1979 to estimate the difference. Data were not available in 1973.

engineering in 1989 and mathematics in 1979 are based on small sample sizes and may not be reliable estimates.

To assess the effects of other variables, we computed the change in the adjusted proportion with tenure before and after a change in one variable, holding all other variables constant. The results are given in Table 6-5. Both men and women who are foreign citizens are less likely to be tenured, with slightly larger effects for women. Being in a private university or college reduces the proportion with tenure by over 10 points, with increases in more recent years, especially for men. This is consistent with the generally longer probationary periods found in elite, private institutions (e.g., Ivy League schools). Once again, the effects of marriage and children operate in different directions for men and women. Men with young children are more likely to be tenured compared to single men, while for women there is a negative effect in 1979 and no effect in the other years. This result is consistent with findings by Bayer and Astin (1975) and illustrates the recommendation of a female faculty member interviewed by Cole and Zuckerman (1987): "My ideal scenario is to get a tenured position, and then have a child or two." Comparing those who

TABLE 6-5 Effects of Changes in Citizenship, Being at a Private Institution, and Familial Status on Adjusted Proportions with Tenure, by Sex and Year of Survey

	Women			Men		
	1979	1989	1995	1979	1989	1995
Being a foreign citizen	5.8	−10.6	−6.3	1.4	−7.9	−5.3
Working at a private institution	−11.5	−11.8	−12.5	−9.4	−12.6	−17.8
Having Young Children versus Being Single	−5.8	0.3	1.4	0.3	7.9	7.5
Being Married versus Being Single	−6.3	−0.6	3.8	1.7	7.0	9.4

NOTES: Predictions are for career year 10 with other variables held at their means. Data were not available in 1973.

are married to those who are single, married men are more likely to be tenured, while married women were less likely to be tenured in 1979 and 1989, with a smaller positive effect in 1995. We found only a trivial effect of the prestige of the doctoral program, a result that is consistent with prior research (Ahern and Scott 1981; Allison and Long 1987; Hurlbert and Rosenfeld 1992; Long, Allison and McGinnis 1993; Rosenfeld and Jones 1986; Rosenfeld and Jones 1987). Reskin and Hargens (1979), however, found some effect of the prestige of the postdoctoral fellowship; this variable was not available in the SDR.

While there has been dramatic improvement in the percent of women with tenure *after controlling* for age, field, and institution type, it is important to keep in mind the limitations of our data. Specifically, we do not know anything about those who were denied tenure. For example, it is possible that a larger proportion of women than men are denied tenure after their sixth year. These women may show up in our statistics on the proportion of women who *remained* in academia. Among those remaining in tenure-track positions, however, a larger proportion may be tenured. We can gain some insights into this possibility by examining scientists who responded to both the 1979 and 1989 SDR or both the 1989 and 1995 surveys.[20] Using these data, Table 6-6 shows changes from tenure-track positions in 1979 to positions in 1989 and from 1989 to 1995. We restricted

[20]There were 1,640 women and 4,062 men with academic positions in 1979 who were in the 1989 SDR; there were 1,217 women and 4,326 men who were in academia in 1989 who were in the 1995 SDR. The smaller size in 1989 is due to changes in sampling for that year of the SDR and does not necessarily indicate any change in the population.

TABLE 6-6 Mobility Between 5 and 15 Years After the Ph.D. from Tenure-Track Positions to Off-Track, Untenured Faculty, Tenured Faculty, and Nonacademic Positions Between 5 and 15 Years After the Ph.D., by Sex and Year of Survey.

		Percent Moving from Tenure Track to:			
Mobility from Year:		Off-track	Untenured Faculty	Tenured Faculty	Non-Academic
1979 to 1989	Men	3.2	2.8	87.7	6.3
	Women	7.7	2.9	85.9	3.5
1989 to 1995	Men	7.3	9.8	82.6	0.3
	Women	9.4	14.9	75.4	0.3

the sample to those between years 5 and 15 after the Ph.D. in order to keep the average ages of men and women similar and to highlight the period during which most tenure decisions are made.

The mobility data provide some evidence that women are less successful in attaining tenure. During the 10 years between 1979 and 1989, women were 4 points more likely to move from tenure-track faculty positions to off-track positions and 2 points less likely to gain tenure. During the 6 years from 1989 to 1995, women were 2 points more likely to move from faculty positions to off-track positions, and 7 points less likely to gain tenure. Note, however, that in both periods women were slightly younger than men, which may account for some of the observed gender differences. In 1979 the average career age of women was 9.0 and of men was 10.0 years; in 1989 the figures were 10.2 and 9.6, respectively.

Tenure in Research I Universities and Medical Schools

Research I universities employ the largest number of faculty, conduct the most influential research, and train the majority of Ph.D.s. Medical schools have an equally central and prestigious position for research and postdoctoral training in the life sciences. Accordingly, it is important to understand the success of women in obtaining tenure in these locations. The three sets of bars on the left of Figure 6-32 plot the *observed* differences between men and women in the percent who are tenured. In 1979 the largest over-representation of men was over 30 points in Research I institutions, with advantages of about 20 points in both Medical institutions and all other Carnegie types combined. In 1989 there was a 10 point

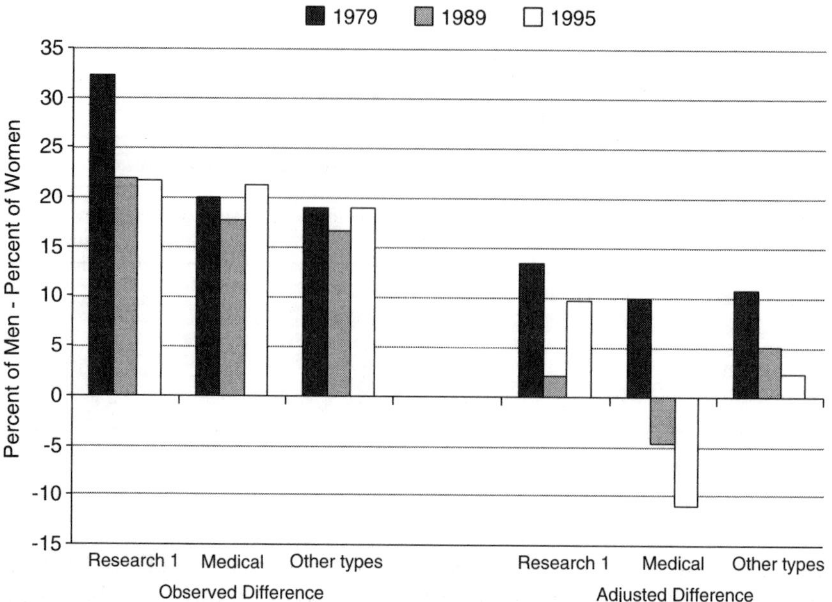

FIGURE 6-32 Differences in the percent of men and the percent of women with tenure, using observed proportions and adjusted proportions, controlling for professional age, field, and type of institution. NOTES: "Other types" combines all Carnegie types except Research I and Medical institutions. Data were not available in 1973.

improvement in Research I schools with only small changes in other types of institutions; there were similar results for 1995. The right hand set of bars show gender differences in *adjusted* proportions after controlling for age and field; the differences for other types of institutions also control for the Carnegie type of institution in which a person was working. The adjusted differences are substantially smaller than the observed differences. In Research I institutions there was a drop from 13 points in 1979 to 3 points in 1989, with an increase to 10 point advantage for men in 1995. In institutions other than Medical and Research I, the difference was nearly eliminated by 1995. In Medical schools an advantage of over 10 points emerged by 1995. Overall, the under-representation of women among the tenured faculty is largest in Research I universities, even after controlling for differences in age and field.

Academic Rank[21]

Gerty Cori was not promoted to a full professorship until the year she received the Nobel prize.

—Harriet Zuckerman and Jonathan R. Cole, *Minerva*, 1975[22]

Progress in the academic career is marked by advancement in rank and it is in this outcome that past research has provided the strongest evidence for the unequal treatment of women in academia. This is a central problem since with rank advancement comes the prestige, resources, and authority that are critical for a successful career in science. In this section we consider the distribution of men and women among academic ranks. Our focus is on the rank of full professor since advancement to associate professor is most often accompanied by the receipt of tenure.[23]

Across fields and types of institutions there are substantial differences between male and female faculty in their academic rank, as shown in Table 6-7. Corresponding to our results for tenure, proportionally more women are assistant professors than are men. In 1979, this difference was 26 points, decreasing to 20 points in 1995. While there is some over-representation of women as associate professors, men are much more likely to be full professors. In 1979 nearly 50 percent of the men but only 22 percent of the women held this rank. Since then, the proportion of full professors increased for men and women as the mean age of the faculty rose. By 1995, 54 percent of the men and 28 percent of the women were full professors, showing a slight improvement from 1979 in the representation of women as full professors.

Before concluding that there has been little progress in rank advancement for women during the past 18 years, it is essential to keep in mind that academic rank, like tenure, is highly dependent upon career age. Controlling for differences in the age structures for male and female faculty shows that there has been limited progress for women in becoming full professors. The strong relationship between professional age and rank is shown in Figure 6-33, which plots the percentage of faculty who are associate and full professors by year of the career. The plot for assistant

[21]See Table D-8 for detailed data. Data from 1973 was not used since information on tenure track status was not collected, making it impossible to distinguish between an adjunct associate professor and a tenured faculty member. For 1989 and 1995, rank was unknown in 0.28 percent of the cases; these were dropped. Less than 1 percent of the cases were instructors; these were combined with the rank of assistant professor.

[22]Zuckerman and Cole (1975).

[23]In our data, 18 percent of those without tenure held the rank of associate professor or full professor.

TABLE 6-7 Percent of Tenure-Track Faculty in Each Rank for Combined Fields and Carnegie Types of Institutions, by Sex and Year of Survey

		1979	1989	1995
Assistant Professors	*Men*	19.5	17.2	17.9
	Women	45.4	37.1	37.9
	Difference	–25.9	–20.0	–20.0
Associate Professors	*Men*	30.8	27.4	27.7
	Women	32.4	35.9	34.6
	Difference	–1.5	–8.5	–6.9
Full Professors	*Men*	49.7	55.4	54.4
	Women	22.3	27.0	27.5
	Difference	27.4	28.5	26.9

NOTE: Data were not available in 1973.

professors is not shown since it provides almost identical information to Figure 6-24 for tenure. In both panels, changes from 1979 (thin line) to 1989 (dashed line) and then to 1995 (gray line) show that there has been a steady increase in the age of promotion to associate professor and then to full professor. For example, in 1979, 30 percent of faculty were full professors in the tenth year, 69 percent in the fifth year, and 85 percent in the twentieth year. By 1995, the corresponding numbers dropped to 11 percent, 42 percent, and 71 percent, with similar changes in the percent who are associate professors. While our data do not allow us to determine the cause of the later dates of promotion, these changes are consistent with our earlier discussion of the changing academic labor market.

Even though much of the greater representation of men in advanced ranks is due to the average female faculty member being younger, Figure 6-34 on pages 174-175 shows that *at any given career age men are more likely to be in a higher rank.*[24] For example, in 1979 (Panel C), 31 percent of the men and only 19 percent of the women were full professors in the tenth year; in the fifthteenth year, the gap increased with 70 percent of the men being full professors and 54 percent of the women; and by the twentieth year, the percentages increased to 67 percent and 86 percent. By 1995 (Panel D), the proportion of full professors is much smaller in a given year of the career. In the tenth year 8 percent of the women and 12 percent of the men were full professors; in the fifthteenth, 33 percent and 45 percent;

[24]The variability in the lines for women is due to the smaller number of women with higher ranks.

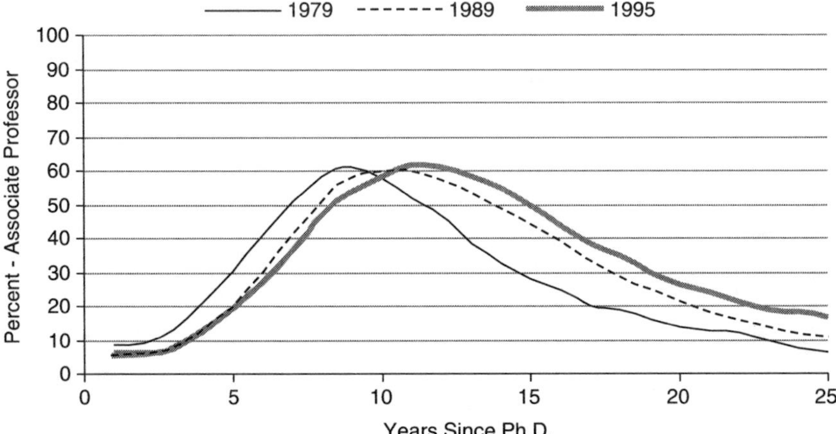

Panel A: Associate professors

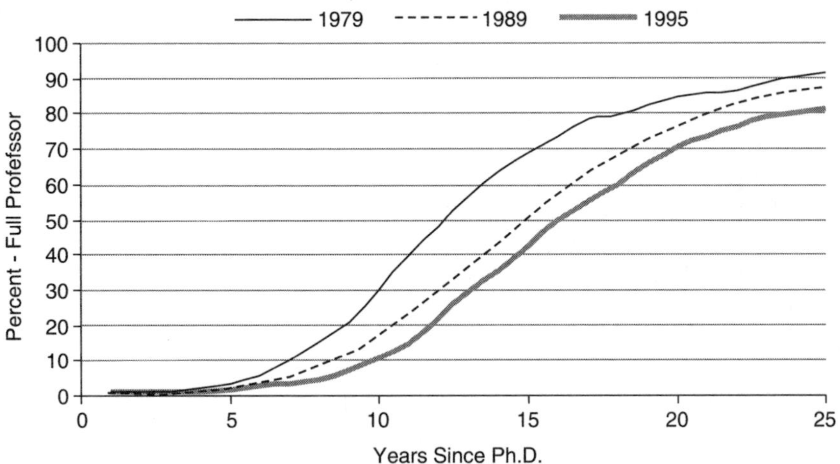

Panel B: Full professors

FIGURE 6-33 Percent of faculty who are associate or full professors, by year since the Ph.D. and year of the survey. NOTES: Estimates are based on 5-year moving averages. Data were not available in 1973.

and in the twentieth year, 64 percent and 73 percent. As the career age for becoming a full professor increased from 1979 to 1995, there was some narrowing in the advantage for men, but some gender differences remained. While there is substantial variation across fields and types of institutions in the percent of faculty at a given rank (see Appendix Tables

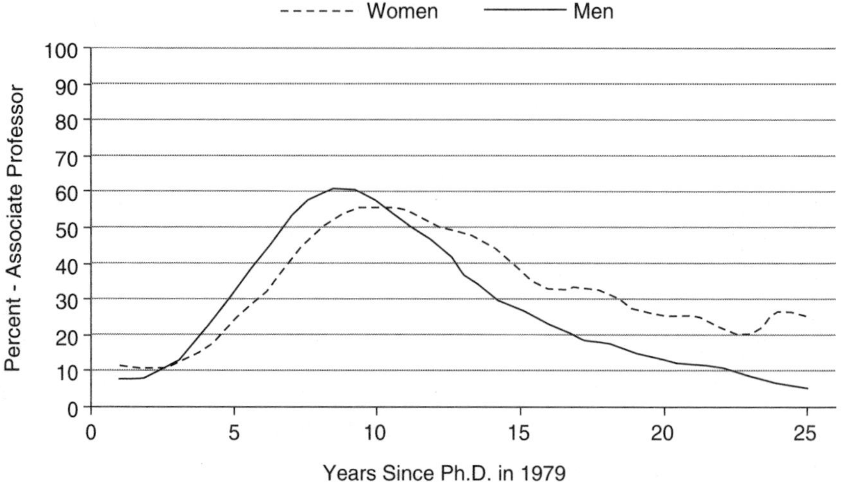

Panel A: Associate professors, 1979

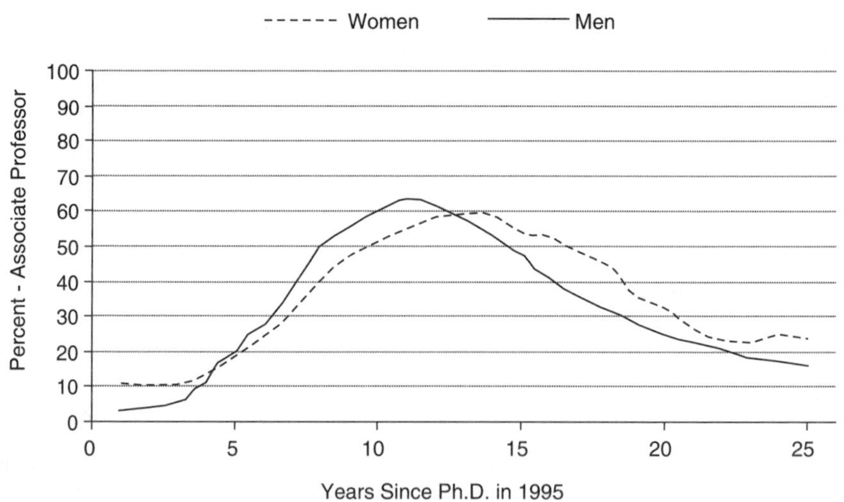

Panel B: Associate professors, 1995

FIGURE 6-34 Percent of faculty with a given rank in 1979 and 1995, by sex and years since the Ph.D. (*Continued*)

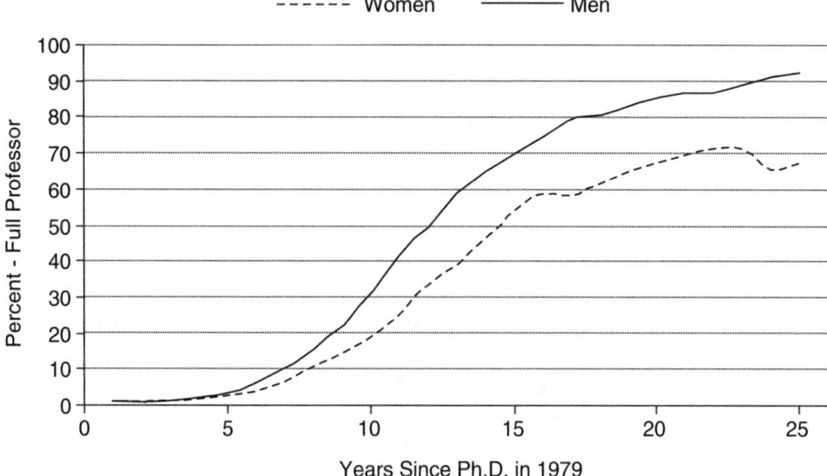

Panel C: Full professors, 1979

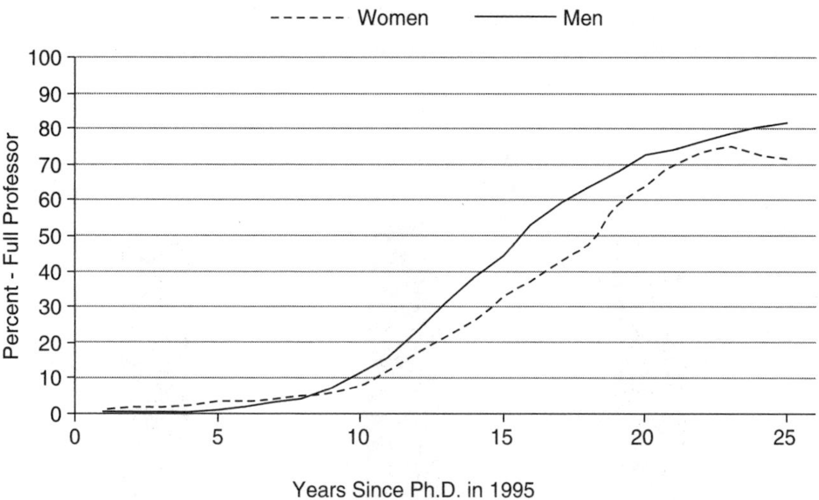

Panel D: Full professors, 1995

FIGURE 6-34 Continued

D-9 and D-10 for detailed information), these differences are largely due to differences in age structures across fields and types of institutions, with a strong correlation between the mean age of a particular group (e.g., women in engineering) and the percent in that group who are full professors.

Logit Analyses of Academic Rank

A multinomial logit was used to predict the proportion of men and women at each rank after adjusting for differences in field, type of institution, and, most importantly, age (Figure 6-35). While the full results of these analyses are given in Appendix Table D-12, our discussion focuses on the proportion of full professors, since results for assistant and associate professors duplicate the information in the section on tenure. As shown by the dark bars in Figure 6-36, there has been little change since 1979 in the observed over-representation of men among full professors. The age-adjusted differences, shown by the gray bars, show a decrease in the over-representation of men from 20 points in 1979 to under 10 points in 1995. Still, even after controlling for gender differences in career age, field of employment, and type of institution, men continue to have an almost 10 percentage point advantage in being full professors.

The improved representation of women occurred in most types of

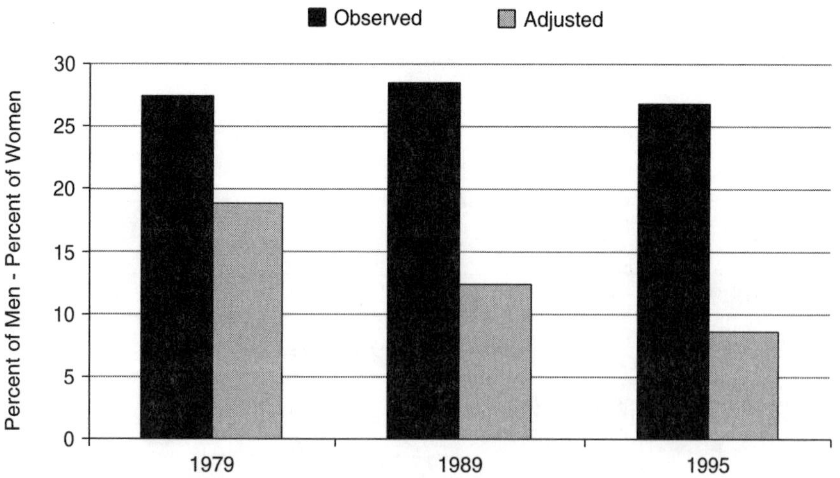

FIGURE 6-35 Difference between men and women in the observed proportion of full professors and the adjusted proportions controlling for field, career age, and Carnegie type of institution, by year of survey. NOTES: Adjusted proportions are for 20 years after the Ph.D. Data were not available in 1973.

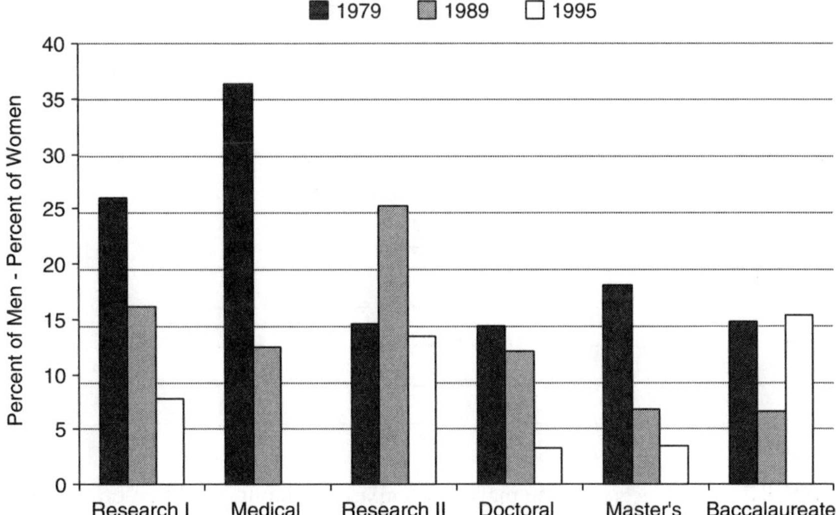

FIGURE 6-36 Differences between men and women in the *adjusted* proportion who are full professors, by Carnegie type of institution and year of survey. NOTES: The difference was 0 in Medical institutions in 1995. Data were not available in 1973.

institutions, as shown in Figure 6-37. Most importantly, because of its implications for training future generations of scientists and engineers, the 25 point over-representation of men among full professors in Research I institutions in 1979 was reduced to 8 points by 1995, and the 35 point advantage in Medical institutions in 1979 was eliminated. Surprisingly, given the historical presence of women in undergraduate institutions, the over-representation of men in Baccalaureate institutions returned to 15 points after dropping in 1989.

To examine the effects of having children, we included a variable indicating whether a scientist had children under the age of 18. The age of 18 was used since delays in promotion may result from the accumulated effects of children over the entire career. Figure 6-37 plots the difference in the adjusted percent of married female faculty who are full professors and the adjusted percent of full professors among those with children. Again we see that the effects of family differ for men and women. In 1979 women with young children were 12 points less likely to be full professors. The effect decreased to 5 points in 1989, where it remained in 1995. The lower probability of being a full professor for women with children may reflect a cost in productivity, delays in beginning their first faculty position, or an assumption on the part of the university or department that women with children are a poor risk. Unfortunately, the SDR does not provide information on when faculty began their current job; while

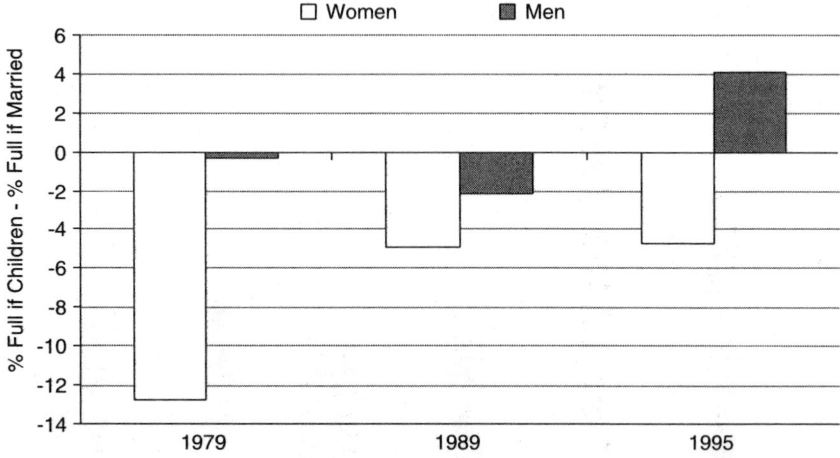

FIGURE 6-37 Effects of being married compared to having children on the probability of being a full professor, by sex and year of survey. NOTES: Negative values indicate children make being a full professor less likely. Data were not available in 1973.

we have information on possible interruptions before the Ph.D., we do not have information on career interruptions after the degree. For men, the small negative effects of having children in 1979 and 1989 became larger and positive in 1995.

Table 6-8 shows that having an interruption between the baccalaureate and the Ph.D. had a large *positive* effect for women, over 10 percentage points, with a smaller effect for men. Without additional information, we can only speculate on why this substantial effect occurs. One possibility is that interruptions for women are due to family obligations and that having these interruptions before the Ph.D. decreases the number of interruptions later in the career. For both men and women, these interruptions may also correspond to predoctoral research experience that makes postdoctoral fellowships less likely, thus speeding up the movement into faculty positions and eventually into more advanced academic ranks. Bayer and Astin (1975) found that career interruptions had a negative effect for women, but these were interruptions after the Ph.D. Zuckerman and Cole (Zuckerman and Cole 1975) suggested that these interruptions are due to familial obligations, which is consistent with our findings on the effect of having children. The table also shows a modest positive effect for both men and women for obtaining a degree from a more prestigious graduate program. While several studies have found that the effects of doctoral origins are insignificant for rank (Cole 1979: 411; Hurlbert and Rosenfeld

TABLE 6-8 Effects of Time from Baccalaureate to Ph.D. and Prestige of Ph.D. on Adjusted Proportion Who Are Full Professors in the Twentieth Year of their Career

	Women			Men		
	1979	1989	1995	1979	1989	1995
More than 10 Years from Bachelor's to Ph.D.	13.2	9.9	13.2	7.1	2.1	5.3
Prestige of Ph.D.	–0.6	3.5	3.7	0.2	2.0	2.0

NOTE: Data were not available in 1973.

1992), Long, Allison, and McGinnis (1993) found a positive effect of doctoral origins on promotion to full professor.

Summary on Academic Rank

Many studies across many fields at different times using a myriad of control variables found evidence of substantial gender differences in academic rank (Ahern and Scott 1981; Astin and Bayer 1979; Cole 1979; Hurlbert and Rosenfeld 1992; Long, Allison and McGinnis 1993; Perrucci, O'Flaherty and Marshall 1983; Rosenfeld and Jones 1986, 1987; Sonnert 1990; Szafran 1984). Our results are consistent with these findings and provide evidence that gender differences in rank are found across fields and types of institutions. While overall percentages that do not control for any variables affecting rank show no improvement since 1979, controlling for age and other factors provides evidence of substantial improvement. However, gender differences still persist in this critical outcome for the academic career.

A possible explanation for the remaining gender differences in rank attainment is that our analyses do not include controls for variables that past research has shown to affect rank. Rosenfeld and her colleagues (Hurlbert and Rosenfeld 1992; Rosenfeld and Jones 1986) found that rank advancement is related to institutional mobility and that women may have more constraints on their opportunities to change institutions. Bayer and Astin (1975) found a negative effect of time devoted to teaching, which is likely to more severely affect women than men. Last, and most importantly, we do not include measures of productivity. The information on productivity that we do have, which is discussed in the next section, is too aggregated over time to be used in predicting promotion.[25]

[25]Since attaining rank leads to resources that enhance productivity, it is essential that publication data be for the period immediately before the decision for promotion or tenure is made.

However, past research suggests that productivity differences do not explain gender differences in promotion. Based on his own results and a review of the literature, J. Cole (Cole 1979:246) concluded: "Historically, productivity patterns simply will not explain the gender differences in academic rank. Other social and economic variables might explain these associations, of course, but in the absence of adequate data to test alternative hypotheses I tentatively conclude that there has been extensive sex discrimination in promotion opportunities over the past 40 years." Later analyses by Long et al. (1993) included detailed, over time data on productivity and found that gender differences persisted after controls for productivity and many other variables. They concluded: "While these differences [in the rates of promotion for men and women] may be due to the exclusion of other variables, it is unclear what these variables might be. We believe that a more reasonable explanation is that women are expected to meet higher standards for promotion."

RESEARCH PRODUCTIVITY

> *More than 50 studies in various fields show that women publish less than men. Moreover, correlations between gender and productivity have been roughly constant since the 1920s. The existence and stability of gender differences in productivity continue to be puzzling.*
>
> —Jonathan R. Cole and Harriet Zuckerman,
> *Advances in Motivation and Achievement*, 1984 [26]

In a review article on gender differences in scientific productivity, Cole and Zuckerman (1984) estimated that men published 40 percent to 50 percent more than women. While our data are inadequate for a full analysis of factors determining gender differences in scientific productivity, we can provide some information that helps us to explain why the overall rate of productivity is greater for men than women. Past research has examined a large number of factors that may be determining the lesser productivity of women. These factors include ability, marriage and family, career interruptions, doctoral and postdoctoral training, the type and prestige of the academic employer, the organizational context of employment, processes of reinforcement, and discrimination. For detailed reviews, see Cole and Zuckerman (1984), Fox (1983), Long (1992), and Xie and Shauman (1998).

The key to understanding the large observed gender differences in productivity is to control for the many differences between men and

[26] Cole and Zuckerman (1984).

women in the types of positions and resources that they have. This approach was taken recently by Xie and Shauman (1998) who analyzed scientific productivity using national surveys from 1969, 1973, 1988, and 1993. Their first conclusion was that gender differences in productivity have declined. Second, they conclude that "gender differences in research productivity stem from gender differences in structural locations and as such respond to the secular improvement of women's position in science." That is, gender differences in productivity reflect differences in positions women have held, rather than differences in abilities or motivation. Given evidence of the larger effect of work context on productivity than of productivity on attaining a given position (see Allison and Long 1990 and the literature cited therein), the increasing entry of women into faculty positions in all types of institutions should lead to future decreases in gender differences in scientific productivity. Still, to the extent that differences in employment persist, differences in productivity can be expected to continue, albeit to a lesser degree.

Figure 6-38 illustrates the degree to which gender differences in scientific productivity are associated with differences in the positions held by male and female scientists and engineers. Each bar indicates the percent more publications by the average male academic than the average female academic. The first bar considers all academic scientists and engineers in 1995 and shows that men have about 30 percent more publications than women. As we move to the right, we increasingly restrict the group of academics to make their characteristics more similar. Among those in Research I institutions, men are just under 25 percent more productive. However, earlier we showed that women were much more likely to have off-track positions which we would expect to be associated with lesser productivity. Restricting our comparison to only faculty we find that men are 13 percent more productive; among tenured faculty in Research I institutions, 8 percent more productive, and when comparing full professors in the life sciences, men are less than 5 percent more productive. Even with the limitations of our data, it seems clear that differences in structural position are a key factor in the lesser productivity of women in science and engineering.

THE PRESENCE OF WOMEN IN ACADEMIC POSITIONS

In prior sections we focused on changes in the relative proportions of men and women who have advanced to more secure and prestigious positions. By comparing the percent of all women who obtained a given status to the corresponding percent of all men, we are able to determine whether men and women have equal success in attaining each type of position. To the degree that such equity occurs, differences in the repre-

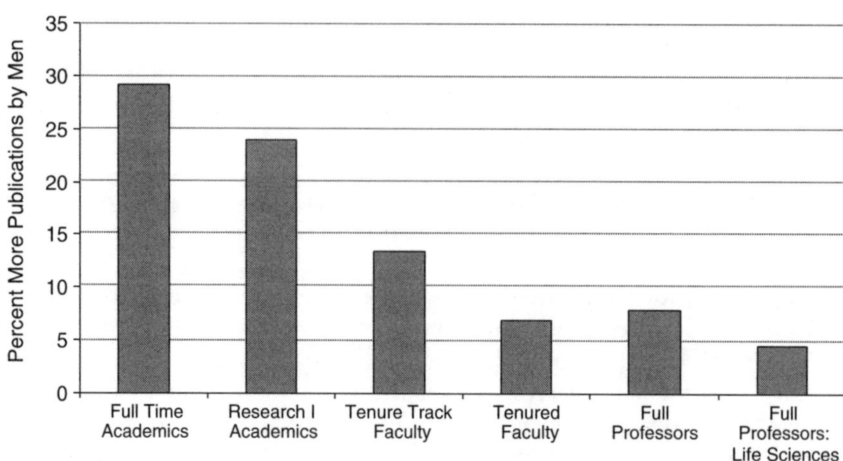

FIGURE 6-38 Percent more publications by the average man compared to the average woman in increasingly similar groups of academic scientists in 1995. NOTES: Moving from left to right, each group is a subset of the prior group. For example, "Tenure-Track Faculty" are full time in Research I institutions.

sentation of men and women are a function of the smaller number of women in academia. As a way to summarize our findings, as well as to show the growing presence of women in the academy, we consider the changing percent of academics who are women. Overall, we find that while there have been dramatic increases in the presence of women in all types of academic positions, women remain well below half of the total in all categories of positions with academia.

Figure 6-39 displays the percent of academic scientists and engineers who are women for various employment statuses within academia. Panel A shows the results for those employed in Research I universities; Panel B presents the results for all non-Research I institutions combined; and Panel C plots the difference in the percent female in non-Research I universities compared to Research I institutions, where positive values indicate a greater presence of women in non-Research institutions. There has been an increase in the percent of women in all categories of academic employment, ranging from off-track positions to being full professors. This trend is driven by the increasing number of women with Ph.D.s and the corresponding increase in the number of women in academia. This is shown by the leftmost set of bars, which gives the percent of all full-time academic scientists and engineers who are women, combining all types of full-time employment. In 1995 women were nearly 20 percent of all academics in Research I universities and nearly 25 percent of those in all other types of

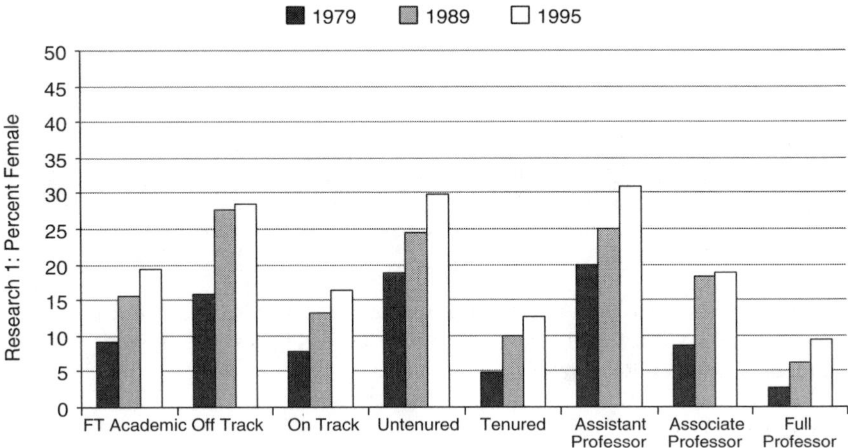

Panel A: Percent women in Research I institutions

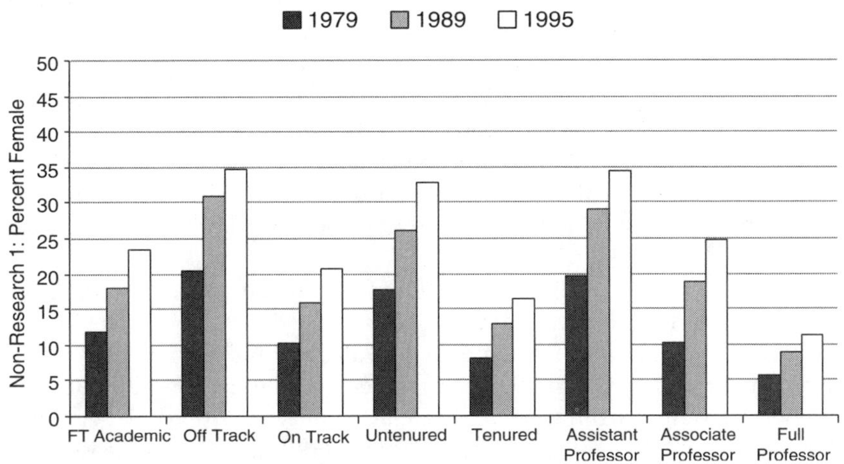

Panel B: Percent women in non-Research I institutions

FIGURE 6-39 Percent of academic scientists who are women, by type of institutions, type of jobs, and year of survey. (*Continued*)

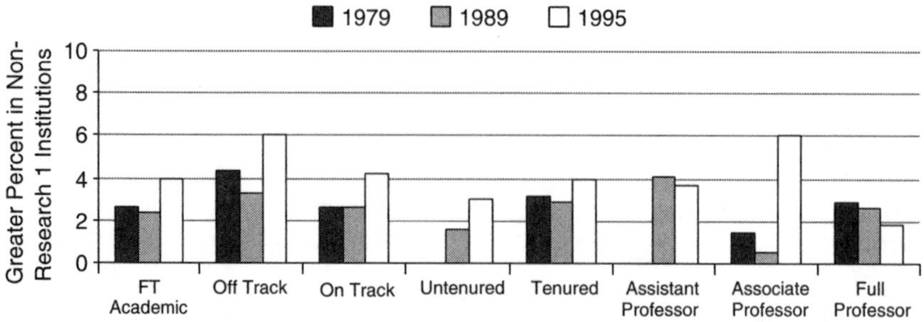

Panel C: Difference between percent women in non-Research I and Research I institutions. NOTE: Positive values indicate a greater presence of women in institutions other than Research I.

FIGURE 6-39 Continued

institutions. As we move to the right, we see that women are found in varying proportions among different types of academic positions. Women are found most often in the least prestigious, least secure, and most poorly paid off-track positions, such as research associates and temporary instructors. Among tenure-track faculty, women are found most often among assistant professors. At the critical rank of full professor, women in 1995 are still less than 10 percent of the full professors in Research I universities and just 12 percent in other types of schools. Panel C shows that the advance in the representation of women in academia has occurred more slowly in Research I universities than in other types of institutions.

The five panels of Figure 6-40 show that women make up very different proportions of the academic labor force in different fields. The first set of bars in each column is the percent of all full time academics who are women. Across fields in 1995, the percent women among all full time academics ranges from 6 percent female in engineering to 31 percent in the social and behavioral sciences. These overall differences across fields are also found when we examine the proportion of women in specific types of positions, such as off-track or tenured positions. In large part, as would be expected, the representation of women within fields of academia is largely dependent on the number of women obtaining degrees in those fields.

Overall, there has been substantial improvement in the presence of women in academia. In all fields, women made up a substantially larger proportion of the academic labor force in 1995 than in 1973. Large field differences persist, with women found least frequently in engineering and most often in the life sciences and the social/behavioral sciences.

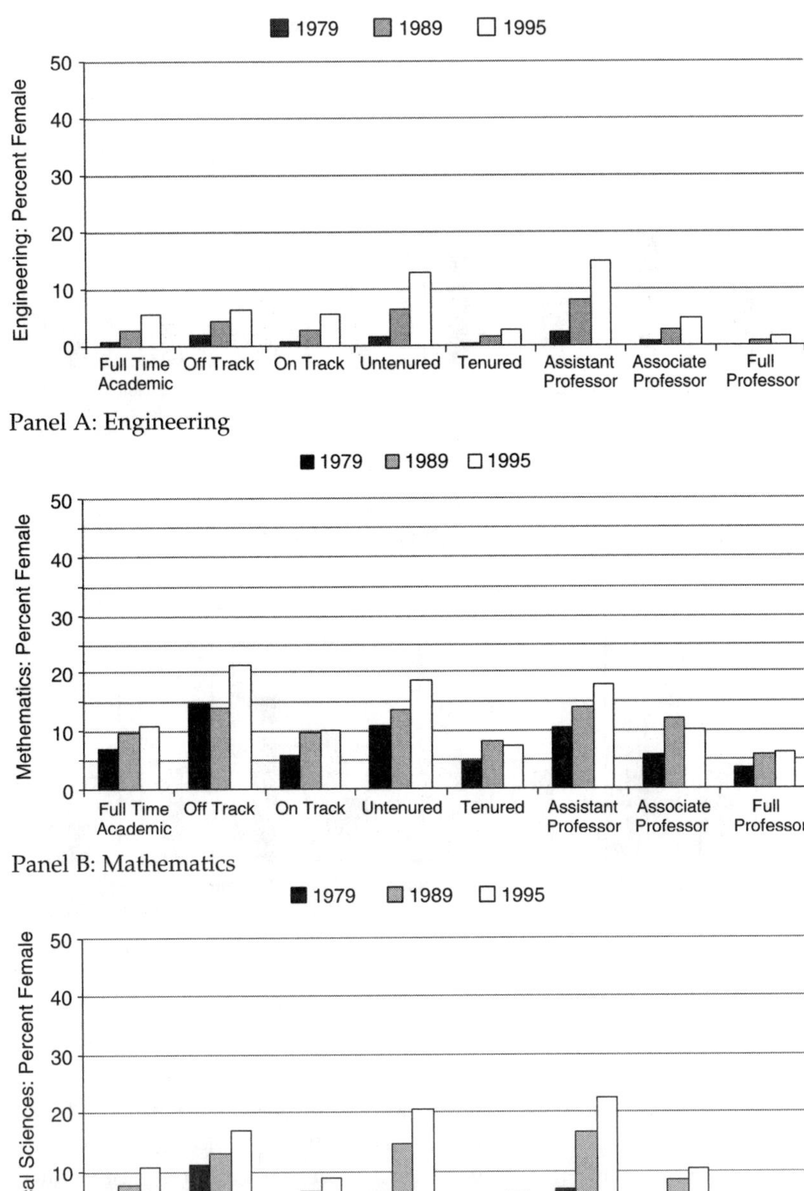

Panel A: Engineering

Panel B: Mathematics

Panel C: Physical sciences

FIGURE 6-40 Percent of scientists in given types of positions who are female, by field and year of survey. NOTE: See Appendix Table D-11 for further details. (*Continued*)

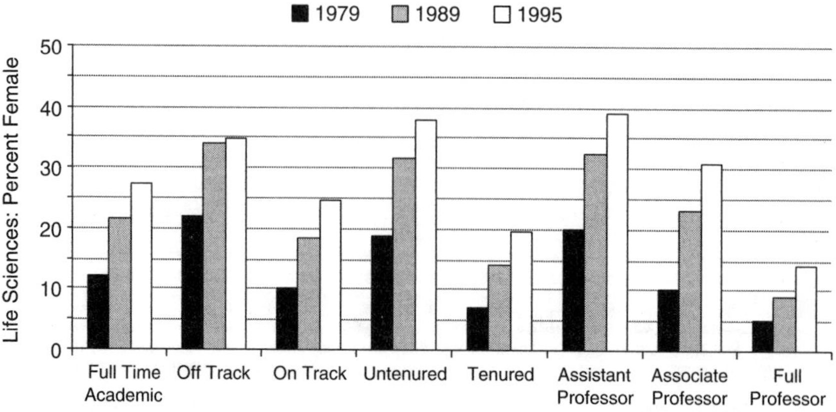

Panel D: Life sciences

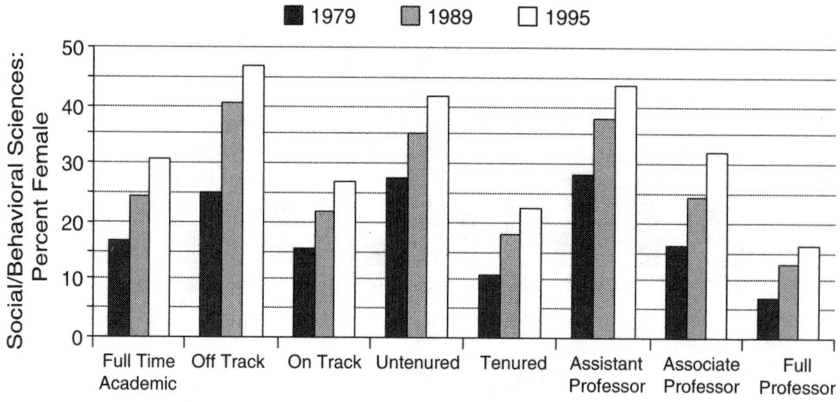

Panel E: Social/behavioral sciences

FIGURE 6-40 Continued

Still, at most, women make up only about 33 percent of the academic labor force in any field. With the proportionally greater entry of women than men into academia in recent years, the average career age of women is less than that of men. This accounts for a substantial amount of the greater representation of men among those with tenure and those with the rank of full professor. However, controls for gender differences in age and field do not eliminate the greater presence of men among those on the tenure track, with tenure, or promoted to full professor. While the presence of women in academia has shown notable improvements, women remain underrepresented in academic science and engineering.

7

Gender Differences in Salary

. . . attitudes have come a long way since F.Y. Edgeworth worried about whether women should receive equal pay for equal work . . .
—Nancy M. Gordon, et al., *American Economic Review*, 1974[1]

INTRODUCTION

Perhaps the most basic way to contrast the differing career outcomes of men and women in science and engineering is by comparing their salaries. Salary reflects both the type of employment obtained and success in meeting the goals associated with the position held. As such, salary is a form of recognition for professional contributions and a measure of worth in the scientific community. Merton (1973 reprinted from 1942) argues that there is a strong presumption in science that recognition, including monetary rewards, should be determined on the basis of universalistic criteria related to scientific achievement. To the extent that female scientists and engineers receive fewer financial rewards than men for *comparable* achievements, their work is undervalued and they are underpaid.

Studies of gender differences in salary for scientists and engineers can be divided into two groups. The first group examines salaries within a

---

[1]Gordon, Morton, and Braden (1974) discussing Edgeworth's presidential address to the British Association in 1922.

single academic institution (see, for example, Becker and Toutkoushian 1995; Ferber 1974; Fox 1981; Gordon, Morton, and Braden 1974; Hoffman 1976; Katz 1973). Single institution studies have the advantage of more detailed data on each individual and are based on a more complete understanding of the nuances of the local context of employment, but they are limited by the unique characteristics of that institution. A second type of study uses a large sample to study differences across fields, and often across sectors of employment. For example, Ferber and Kordick (1978) examined Ph.D.s in all fields with degrees from 1958-63 and 1967-72. Ahern and Scott (1981), the precursor to our study, examined salaries in five broad fields for Ph.D.s from the 1940s through the early 1970s. Many of these studies of salary are restricted to academics, such as Barbezat (1988), Farber (1977), Gregorio, Lewis, and Wanner (1982), Johnson and Stafford (1979), and Tolbert (1986), or a single field such as Hansen, Weisbrod, and Strauss (1978) or Morgan (1998).

While studies of salary differences for men and women in science and engineering differ widely in their samples, focus, and methodology, *each study has found that the average female scientist or engineer earns less than her male counterpart*. There have been several proposed explanations for this gap in earnings:

1. Women earn less because they are less qualified than men. While our analysis in earlier chapters found few gender differences in educational backgrounds, it is still possible that qualifications attained at the completion of formal education may be lower. Due to longer periods out of the labor force, women accumulate fewer years of experience and during periods of absence from S&E their skills may depreciate. Consequently, when women reenter the S&E labor force they will earn a lower salary than at the time of exit and will have foregone the salary increases due to accumulated experience. In anticipation of time out of the labor market, women may choose to invest less in on the job training or employers may invest less in female employees. Lower investment in training early in the career will produce lower future female earnings (Duncan and Hoffman 1979). Or, even with similar education and experience, women may be less productive than men in the scientific workplace. See Cole and Zuckerman (1984), Long (1992), and Xie and Shauman (1998) for a review of the literature on gender differences in productivity.

2. Cumulative advantage, as defined by Merton (1973 reprinted from 1942), suggests that men are the beneficiaries of gender inequities early in the career and that these early advantages are magnified over time. Even if salary is based entirely on productivity, early disadvantages in employment for women may lead to a pay gap that will grow over the course of their careers.

3. There may be crowding of women into certain subfields either because of choice, social norms and mentoring, or entry barriers to other subfields. Because salaries are the result of interactions between supply and demand, increases in supply will put downward pressure on wages in these more female friendly subfields. See Bergman (1974) for a general treatment of this phenomenon.

4. The theory of *comparable worth* (Bellas 1994) posits that fields that employ a higher proportion of women pay lower salaries because women's work is devalued by society (Treiman and Hartmann 1991). According to this theory, the suppressing effects of gender composition occurs after controlling for economic factors that affect salaries.

5. Finally, and perhaps most controversially, female scientists and engineers may receive less pay than men for equal work as a result of subtle or blatant discrimination by employers. This discrimination may take the form of lower wages for women doing the same work as men at all levels of experience. For example, Bellas (1994) and Ahern and Scott (1981) found that the effects of experience on salary were larger for men than women, indicating that men are compensated more than women for any given level of experience. Discrimination may also be reflected in society's tendency to devalue women's work, paying lower salaries in fields where large numbers of women work (see point 4 above). Or, discrimination may come in the form of barriers to entry into certain prestigious subfields or jobs resulting in crowding of women into less prestigious, lower paying alternatives.

In this chapter we use data from four years of the SDR to examine the extent and causes of gender differences in salaries. We begin by describing the gross gender differences in salaries without controls for characteristics of either individuals or their employers. We find that men have had a nearly constant 20 percent advantage in salary during the 23 years from 1973 to 1995. To understand why men receive higher salaries and why there has not been an improvement, we add controls for variables that have been suggested by prior research. This is done initially by simply comparing the median salaries of men and women in, for example, the same fields or with the same year of Ph.D. To control simultaneously for a large number of factors, we estimate a series of multiple regressions. The differing characteristics of men and women, such as in experience and field of study, can explain much of the gross gender difference in salary. However, even with numerous controls, gender differences in salary remain. Reasons for these differences are discussed in the summary.

Methodological Issues

Salary data from 1973, 1979, and 1989 were converted to 1995 dollars using adjustment factors for inflation from the U.S. Census Bureau (1999). Multiple regression was used to estimate salaries for men and women after controlling for a large number of variables simultaneously. The effects of the control variables were allowed to differ by gender. In these regressions, the dependent variable is the natural log of salary in 1995 dollars. Since raises are generally based on a percentage increase, a loglinear model provides a better fit. See Hodson (1985) and Becker and Toutkoushian (1995) for further details. A loglinear model predicts the *log of income* for a given set of characteristics. Since an unbiased estimate of the predicted income (as opposed to the log of income) cannot be computed by simply taking the exponential of the predicted log income, we use Duan's (1983) nonparametric smearing estimator to compute predicted incomes. For additional details, see Chapter 2.

GROSS GENDER DIFFERENCES IN SALARY

Figure 7-1 plots the median salaries of men and women in the full time, year-round U.S. labor force and for our sample of full time scientists and engineers for the years of the SDR used in our report.[2] Doctoral scientists and engineers, whether male or female, are well-paid professionals who earn substantially more than the average worker in the U.S. economy. The median salaries of male scientists and engineers have remained about 100 percent higher than those of full-time men in the general population, while the median income of female scientists and engineers have declined from being 200 percent greater than those of women in the general population in 1973 to around 150 percent greater in later years. This decline for doctoral women corresponds to a rise in income for women overall in the U.S. labor force while the real income of women in S&E declined slightly (Figure 7-2).

Since 1973 the median income of male scientists and engineers has been approximately 20 percent higher than the median salary of female scientists and engineers, as shown by Figure 7-1. While large, the earnings gap between male and female doctoral scientists and engineers is much smaller than the gap in the entire U.S. labor force, which would be

[2]For scientists and engineers, we plot the median salary for those employed full time. Data for the U.S. labor force were compiled by the U.S. Census for people 15 and over beginning with March 1980 and people 14 years and over as of March of the following year for previous years. Between 1974 and 1976, wage and salary income were restricted to civilian workers.

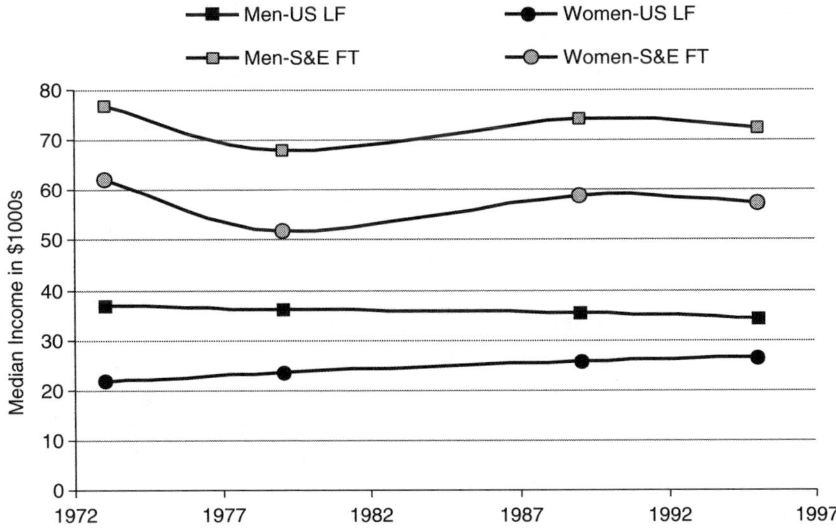

FIGURE 7-1 Median incomes in 1995 dollars for full-time, year-round workers in U.S. labor force and for full-time scientists and engineers, by gender.

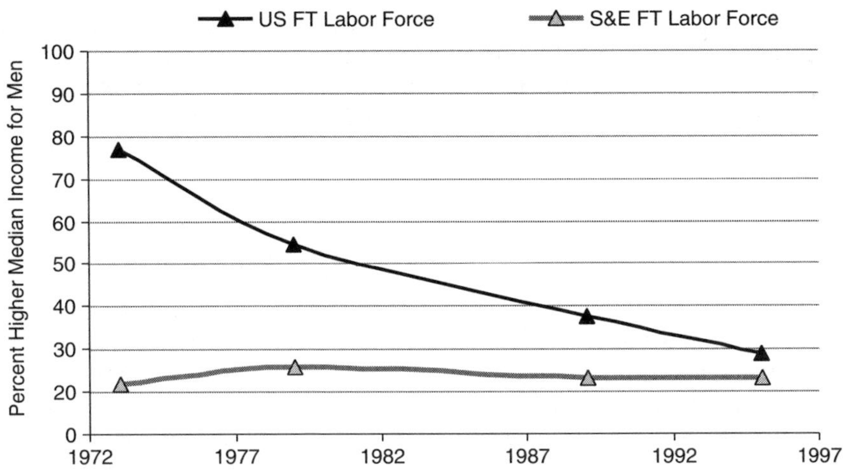

FIGURE 7-2 Percent greater median income for full-time, year-round workers in U.S. labor force and for full-time scientists and engineers.

expected given that male and female scientists and engineers are more homogenous in their characteristics than are men and women in the general population. Further, the gender gap in earnings is smaller than that for other female professionals (e.g., physicians, executives) or for scientific occupations that require less than a doctorate, such as technicians and programmers (U.S. Department of Labor-Women's Bureau 1994). However, there has been no sustained improvement in the salary disadvantage for doctoral women in S&E during the 22 years since 1973, while there has been a steady improvement in salaries for women relative to men among full-time, year-round workers in the U.S. population. According to the National Commission on Pay Equity (1996), the shrinking gap is due to the gains women have made in real wages relative to men as a result of increasing years of work experience, increasing equality of education, improved market skills, and the decreased number of high-paying jobs for men. Men's real wages (in constant dollars adjusted for inflation) drifted downward, while women's real wages increased.

While gross gender differences in salaries for scientists and engineers have not narrowed since 1973, salary is the outcome of a stratification process that involves many steps, each of which is associated with differences in pay. Earlier chapters showed that due to the increasing entry of women in recent years, female scientists and engineers are on average younger than their male counterparts. Accordingly, we would expect the younger women to earn less. Further, there are gender differences in field of study, sector of employment, and primary work activity. Each of these dimensions of the career is associated with differences in salary and we find generally that women are more likely to be in positions associated with lower salaries. In the remainder of this chapter, we decompose the overall gender differences in salaries, attempting to determine the degree to which men and women with similar characteristics are paid differently.

PROFESSIONAL AGE AND DOCTORAL COHORT

While there has been no improvement since 1973 in the pay discrepancy between the average male and female scientist or engineer, we know from Chapters 3 and 4 that the average professional age of women is less than that of men. Since salary is strongly affected by years of experience (Ahern and Scott 1981), even if women were compensated in the same way as men, we would expect the average salary for the younger population of women to be lower than that of men. If, however, men had a slight salary advantage at the start of the career, this small difference in starting salary would multiply over time since raises are often calculated on a percentage basis. Further, if women have more interruptions after the

Ph.D., this loss of experience would lead to increasing gender differences over time. Ferber and Kordick (1978) found such an increase in a study of Ph.D.s from 1958-63 and 1967-72, and found convergence in income after women reentered the labor force.

Panel A of Figure 7-3 plots the median salaries of men and women in 1973 by the number of years since the Ph.D. The median salary in any given year is a 5-year average centered on that year. At the start of the career, men are making 12 percent more than women, compared to the 22 percent gross difference we found when the different age structures for men and women were ignored. The gender difference in salary increases steadily to 20 percent in year 15. For the next 10 years, there is an overall increase, although there are substantial fluctuations due to the small number of women with Ph.D.s from the years prior to 1958. Panel B plots similar data for 1995. The first thing to note is that the salaries for both men and women are lower at all stages of the career compared to those in 1973. Since data in both figures are in 1995 dollars, this documents a decline in real income for scientists and engineers between 1973 and 1995. Second, in 1995 the gender gap begins at 20 percent in year 1. For later years, the differences in salaries are generally smaller than in 1973, but for all career years men earn at least 10 percent more than women of the same career age.

The conclusions that we can draw from Figure 7-3 are limited since we are *not* plotting the salaries of the same group of people as they age over the career. Instead, each year of the career corresponds to a different Ph.D. cohort. For example, in 1973 those in year 5 received degrees in the years around 1969 (recall that we are plotting five-year averages), while those in year 10 received degrees in the years around 1965. Cohorts of Ph.D.s from different years are used to approximate what *might* happen to a cohort from a single year as it progresses through the career. When interpreting results based on these synthetic cohorts, it is impossible to differentiate empirically between alternative explanations of the results. For example, in Panel A it appears that women encounter a "glass ceiling" around year 20 while men's salaries continue to increase. An alternative explanation is that the cohorts of women that received their Ph.D.s more than 20 years earlier faced obstacles earlier in their careers that limited their incomes later in the career. If more recent cohorts do not face these obstacles, their salaries would continue to increase as they age. Using this argument and data for engineering, Morgan (1998) concludes that the "earning penalties to women are more a matter of when they started their careers than of how long they have worked."

Given the limitations of synthetic cohorts and the results of Morgan (1998), it is important to examine what happens to the *same* cohort of Ph.D.s over time. This is done in Figure 7-4, which plots gender differ-

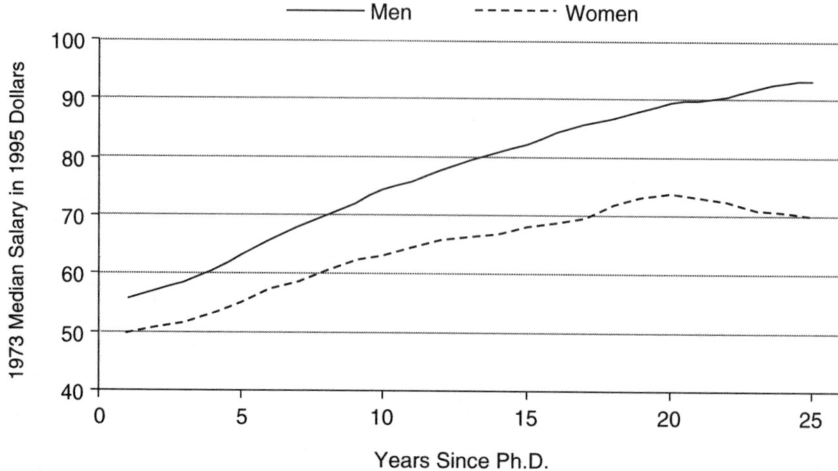

Panel A: 1973

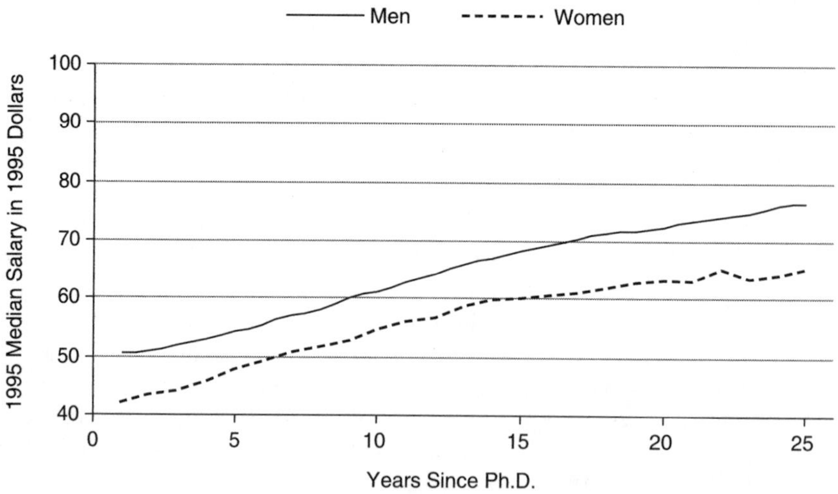

Panel B: 1995

FIGURE 7-3 Median salaries for women and men, by years since the Ph.D. and year of survey. NOTES: Median salary is computed using a 5-year moving average. Salaries have been converted to 1995 dollars.

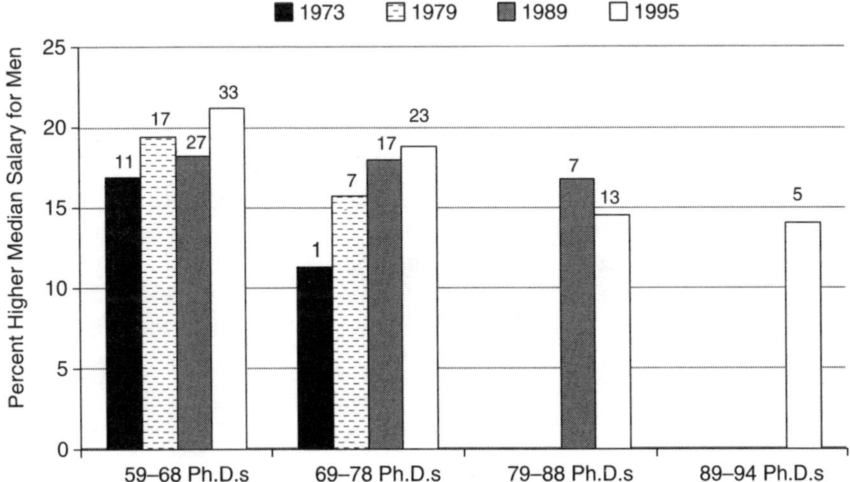

FIGURE 7-4 Percent higher salaries for men, by Ph.D. cohort and year of survey.
NOTES: Numbers at the top of each bar are the average professional age of a given cohort in a given year of the survey. There are no bars for the 1979-88 cohort in 1973 and 1979, or for the 1989-94 cohort in 1995 since they had not yet received their degrees.

ences for four cohorts defined by the Ph.D. year at four years of the SDR. Each bar shows the percent higher median salaries for men at a given number of years since the Ph.D.; the number at the top of each bar is the approximate career age for that cohort in a given survey year. The set of four bars above shows that the salary advantage for men with degrees from 1959-1968 increased from 17 percent at career year 11 to 19 percent by year 17, with a drop in year 27, ending with a difference of 21 percent in year 33. A steady increase in the salary advantage for men is also seen in the 1969-1978 cohort. By comparing those with similar career ages in different cohorts (e.g., age 11 for the 1956-1968 cohort, age 7 for the 1969-1978 and 1979-1988 cohorts, and age 5 for the most recent cohort), we find some evidence of a modest decrease in the salary differences for men and women in more recent years.

While these results demonstrate that some of the overall gender difference in salaries can be explained by gender differences in professional age, substantial differences remain. These results are based on years since the Ph.D. Ideally, we would compare salaries of individuals with the same years of *full-time* professional experience, taking into account interruptions in the career and part time employment. Unfortunately, complete data on years of postdoctoral work experience are not available. Since women are more likely to have interruptions, perhaps due to family obligations, the results given above may over-estimate the age standardized gender differences in salary. For example, career age for women is more likely to over-estimate professional experience than for men. Using data from 1983, Lewis found that career interruptions had equal effects on the salaries of male and female scientists and engineers, but that women were more likely to have interruptions.

The gender differences in salary may also be accounted for by gender differences in other dimensions that affect salary, such as field and type of employment. These dimensions of the career and their effects on salary are now considered.

FIELD DIFFERENCES

The link between a field's sex makeup and its salary level led us to ask whether more female fields pay less partly because *their practitioners are mostly women.*
—Marcia L. Bellas and Barbara F. Reskin, *Academe*, 1994[3]

Fields differ substantially in the median salaries received by Ph.D.s employed in those fields, as shown in Figure 7-5. Engineers have the highest median income, followed by physical scientists, with mathematicians, life scientists, and social/behavioral scientists following. Field differences have been increasing since 1973, confirming the results of Bellas (1997). For example, in 1973 the median salary in engineering was 8 percent greater than in the social and behavioral sciences; by 1995 the difference was over 20 percent.

While Johnson and Stafford (1979) found no discernable pattern of field differences in salary, a series of papers by Bellas and collaborators (Bellas 1993, 1994; Bellas and Reskin 1994) demonstrated that fields employing higher proportions of women pay lower salaries. Her work is based on the concept of *comparable worth* that argues that since women's work is devalued by society (Treiman and Hartmann 1991), occupations that are predominantly female receive lower compensation. A simple labor market supply and demand framework can also explain this phenomenon. With the influx of women into science, certain fields saw more absolute growth of employees than others, possibly due to free choice of entering women or to entry barriers imposed to prevent female entry into other fields. In particular, psychology, life sciences and the social sciences were the destinations for many female entrants. With the large increases

[3]Bellas and Reskin (1994).

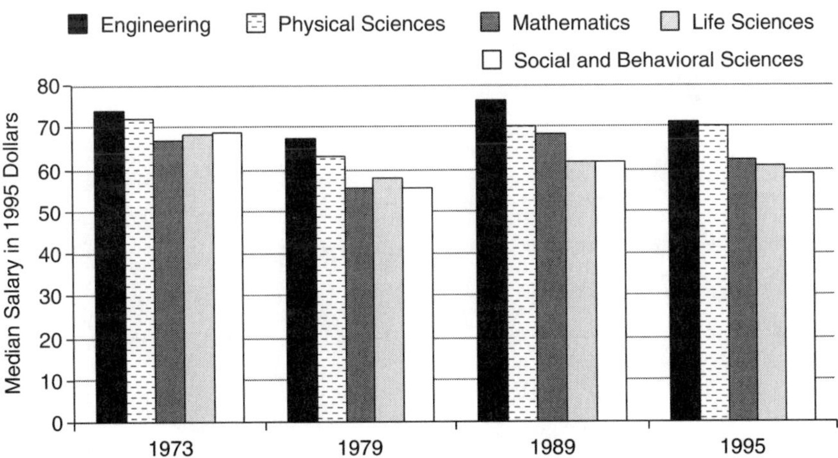

FIGURE 7-5 Median salaries of full-time employees, by field of Ph.D. and year of survey. NOTE: Salaries have been converted to 1995 dollars.

in supply of employees, and without similar increases in demand, wages were depressed in these fields relative to fields without these large supply increases. Studies of comparable worth have, however, included controls for labor market conditions. For example, Bellas (1994) used the 1984 National Survey of Faculty sponsored by the Carnegie Foundation (1984) and found that the negative effects of gender composition persisted after control for individual characteristics and labor market conditions.

For 1989 and 1995, Figure 7-6 shows the negative relationship between the percent of Ph.D.s who are female in the full-time labor force of a field and the median salary for that field. There was a weaker relationship in 1973 and 1979 (not shown) since there was little variation in the percent women among fields. Clearly, women are more frequently found in those fields with the lowest salaries. For example, women are much less likely to get degrees in the more highly paid field of engineering and much more likely to obtain degrees in the social and behavioral sciences. There are also differences in subfields. For example, women are much less likely to obtain a doctorate in economics, where salaries are higher, than in anthropology, where they are lower.

While comparable worth suggests that both men and women, not just women, earn less in those fields where there are proportionally more women, our data suggest that women receive less than men even within lower paying fields. Figure 7-7 shows that men have higher salaries in all fields in each of the years examined. However, with the exception of the social and behavioral sciences, there has been a within field decline in the

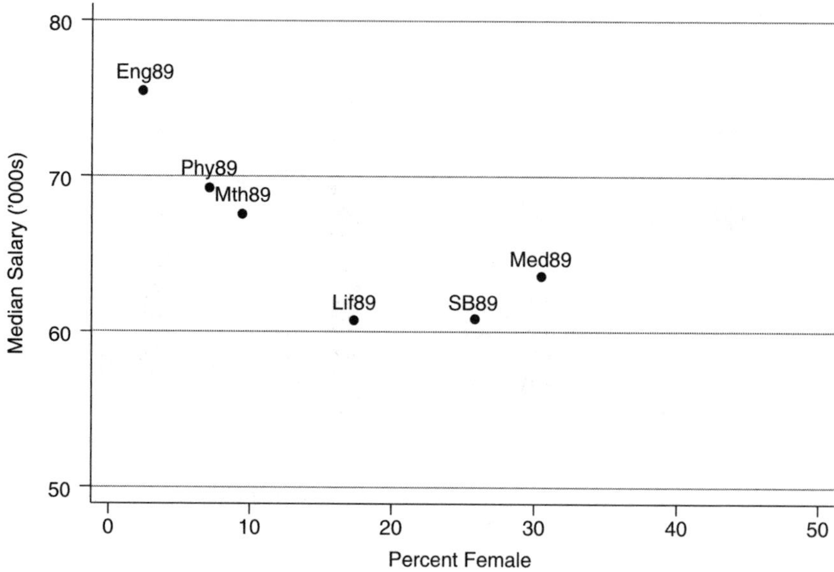

Panel A: 1989

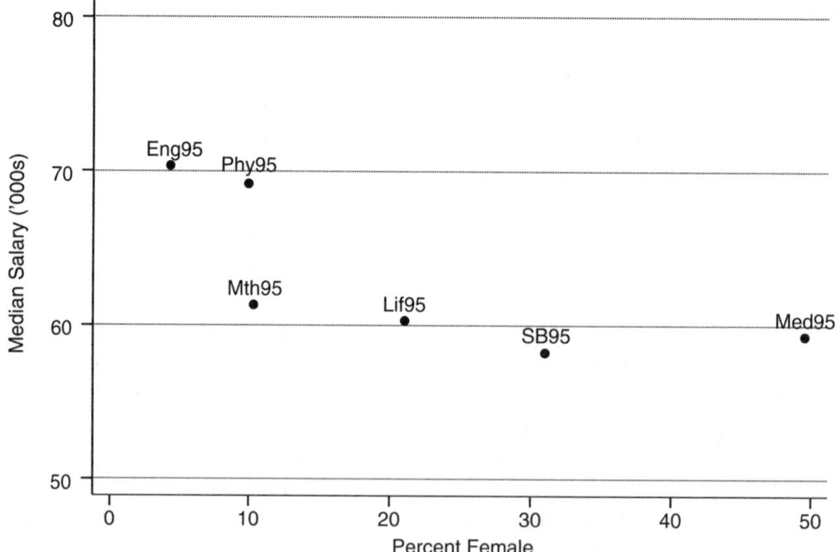

Panel B: 1995

FIGURE 7-6 Relationship between median salary and percent female, by field and year of survey. NOTE: Eng = engineering; Phy = physical sciences; Mth = mathematics; Lif = life sciences; Med = medical sciences; SB = social and behavioral sciences.

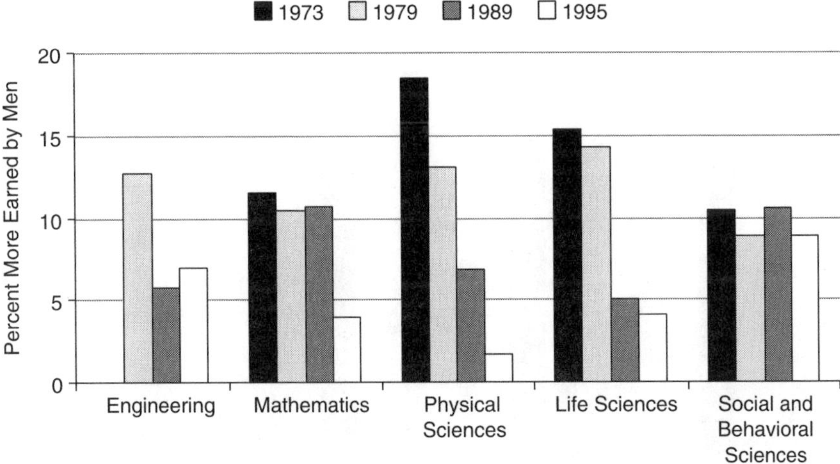

FIGURE 7-7 Percent higher salaries for men, by field and year of Ph.D. NOTE: There were too few women in engineering in 1973 to make an estimate.

salary advantage for men. In the social and behavioral sciences, men have had a nearly constant 10 percent salary advantage. Thus, women are most likely to have degrees in the broad field that pays the least and in which salary advantages for men have persisted longest. Keep in mind, however, that these figures do not control for professional age.

Regardless of the explanation, women are more frequently found in those fields with the lowest salaries. Overall, field differences accounts for a significant proportion of the gross differences in salary that were documented in the last section.

EMPLOYMENT SECTOR AND PRIMARY WORK ACTIVITY

Figures 7-8 and 7-9 plot median salaries by sector of employment and primary work activity. In each year the salaries are highest in industry, which in large part explains the higher overall salaries of engineers. While in 1973 the median salary in government was close to that in industry, since 1973 government salaries for Ph.D.s have dropped significantly relative to those in industry. Salaries are lowest in academia, where women are most likely to work. Even larger salary differences exist among work activities, as shown in Figures 7-10 and 7-11. The highest salaries are in management, due in large part to managers having more work experience than the average Ph.D. Salaries drop steadily as we move from pro-

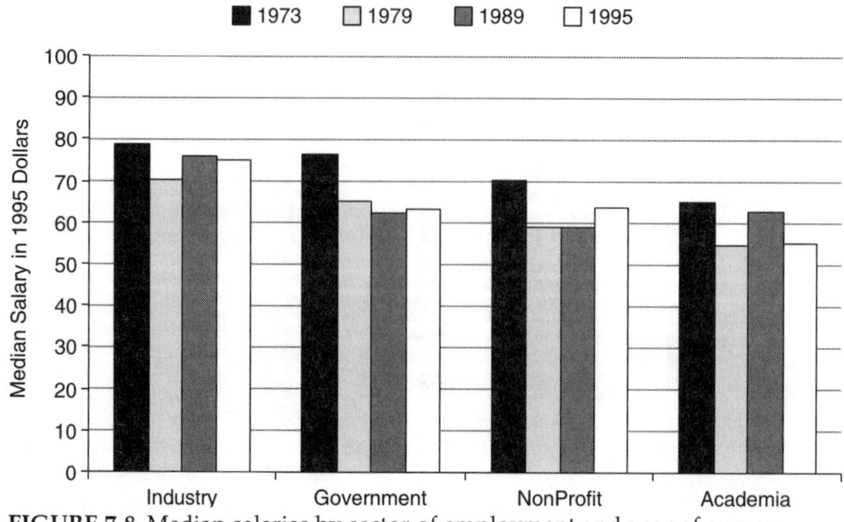

FIGURE 7-8 Median salaries by sector of employment and year of survey.

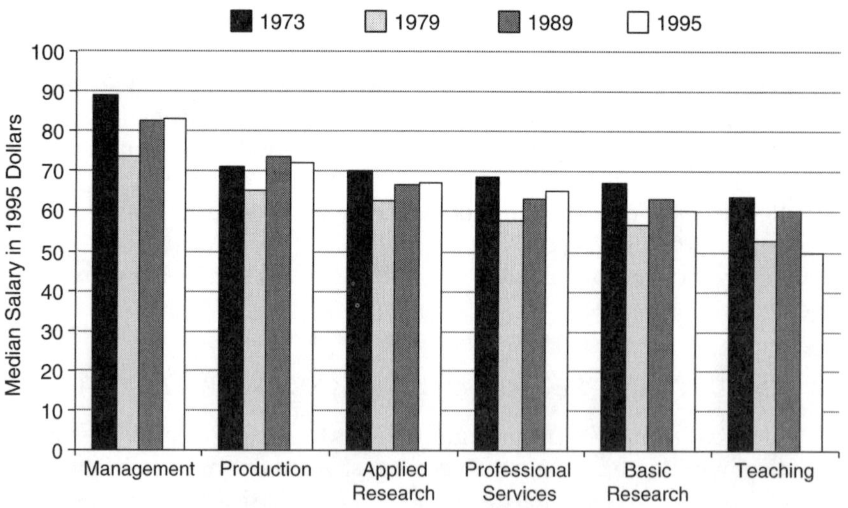

FIGURE 7-9 Median salaries by primary work activity and year of survey.

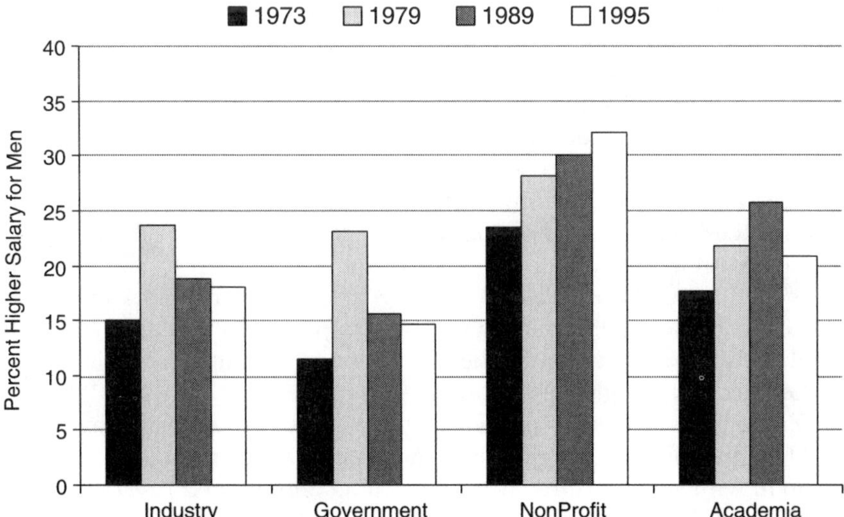

FIGURE 7-10 Percent higher median salaries for male Ph.D.s, by sector of employment and year of survey.

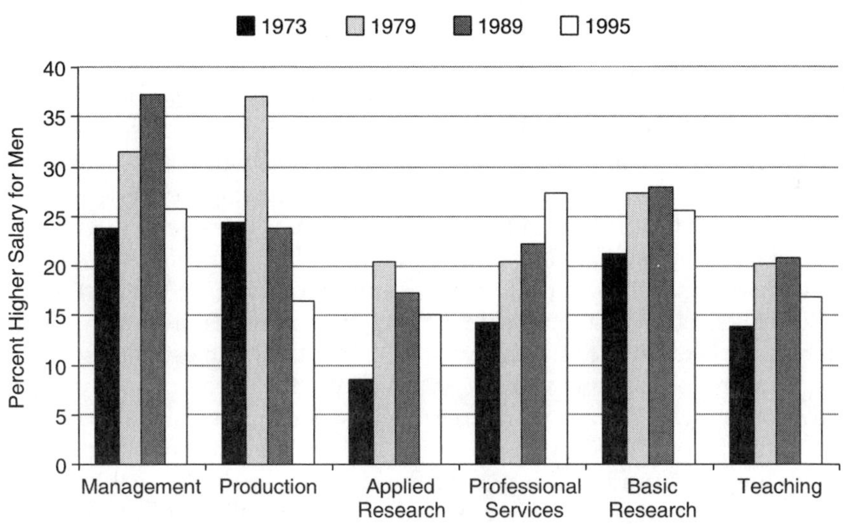

FIGURE 7-11 Percent higher median salaries for male Ph.D.s, by primary work activity and year of survey.

duction work to applied research, and finally to the lowest salaries for those who are teaching. Overall, differences in salaries by sector and activity are important for understanding gender differences in salaries since women are more likely to be employed in those sectors that pay less and in work activities associated with lower salaries.

There are also differences among sectors and work activities in the degree to which men receive higher salaries than women. Figure 7-10 shows that the salary advantages for men are greatest in the nonprofit sector, with a steady increase from 23 percent in 1973 to 32 percent in 1995. Differences are smallest in government, with a small increase between 1973 and 1995, including a spike to nearly 25 percent in 1979. In both industry and academia, there has been an overall increase in gender differences, although there is evidence of a decrease between 1989 and 1995. Gender differences also vary by work activity, as shown by Figure 7-11. Differences are largest in management, production, and basic research, with smaller differences in teaching and applied research. While there is no clear trend over time, it is important to keep in mind that these figures do not control for gender differences in professional age.

REGRESSION RESULTS

The results so far have controlled for only a single factor at a time (e.g., professional age, sector). But, many key dimensions of the career are interrelated. For example, employment in industry is more likely in engineering and less likely in the social and behavioral sciences. And, within some sectors applied research is more likely, while in other sectors basic research is more common. Interpretation is further complicated since there are significant gender differences in years of professional experience with increasing entry of women occurring at different rates across fields and sectors. Accordingly, to more fully understand gender differences in salary it is necessary to control for these simultaneously. In this section we use regression to examine gender differences in salary after controlling for multiple dimensions of the career. Our strategy is to estimate separate regressions for men and women, which allows the effects of each variable to differ by sex. For each pair of regressions, one for men and a second for women, the predicted salaries for men and women are computed for the combined male and female average levels of the control variables in the equation.[4] These predictions are used to compute the percentage differ-

[4]Since the regressions are nonlinear, predicted values are computed using a nonparametric smearing estimator (Duan 1983). The regressions includes scientists and engineers who are working full time in any sector. Professional age is included by adding years since the Ph.D. and the square of years since the Ph.D., allowing a nonlinear effect of professional age.

ence in the salaries of men and women. Additional variables are added to the regressions and the advantage in salary for men is computed after controls for the additional variables. See Chapter 2 for further details.

Figure 7-12 shows changes in the salary advantage for men as additional variables are added cumulatively to the regression. The two panels present the same information organized to highlight different aspects of the results. The first set of bars in Panel A plots the percent higher salaries for men when only the gender of the individual is used to predict salary. As shown earlier, there is no consistent pattern over time, with men earning between 22 percent and 26 percent more than women. For the second set of bars, career age is added to the regression. Gender differences drop only 2 points in 1973, with drops of between 7 and 10 percentage points in later years. By 1995 the percentage advantage for men has decreased to 13 points after controlling for differences in career age. Keep in mind that we had to use career age rather than years of full-time experience due to missing data for the experience variable. Since women have more time lost to interruptions, we expect that gender differences would have been even smaller if controls for experience were used. The third set of bars adds field of doctoral study, reducing the adjusted gender difference by only 1 point in 1973, with decreases of over 5 points in 1989 and 1995. The male salary advantage continues to drop as controls for sector and primary work activity are added.

With all controls added, the advantage for men was cut in half to 14 percent in 1973 and 1979. In 1989, the advantage was reduced an additional two-thirds to slightly below 10 percent and by 1995 the advantage for men was further reduced to slightly above 5 percent, a drop of three-quarters. After adding controls for differences in background and work experience, a steady decrease over time in the salary advantage for men is found.

Bayer and Astin (1975) argued that the explained variation (i.e., R^2 or coefficient of determination) in salary regressions for women should be smaller than for men. Their argument was that the salaries of women are more strongly affected by discrimination and consequently would not be explained by other variables such as field or years of experience. It is also likely that the careers of women are less predictable than those of men due to a greater number of career interruptions. Figure 7-13 shows that this was clearly the case in 1973 and 1979, but that the difference has declined and is nearly eliminated by 1995. There has also been a steady decrease in the amount of variation that can be explained by the structural variables included in our models. This decrease in what can be explained may reflect the changes in the scientific and engineering labor market that have occurred since 1973.

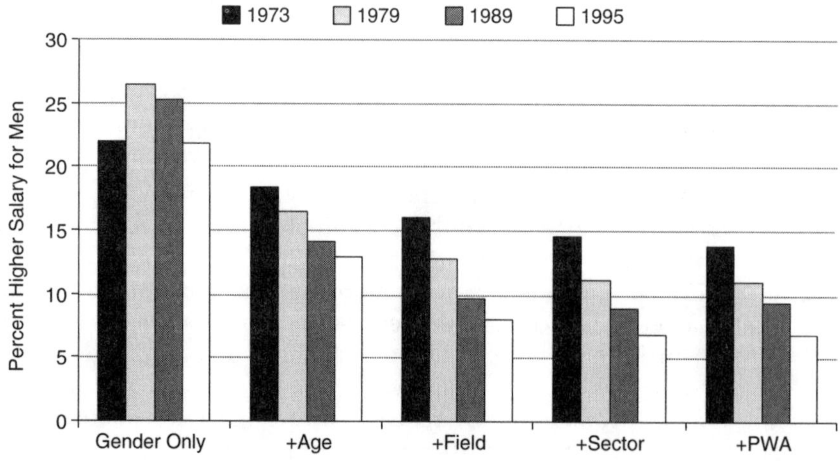

Panel A: Results organized by variable affecting salary

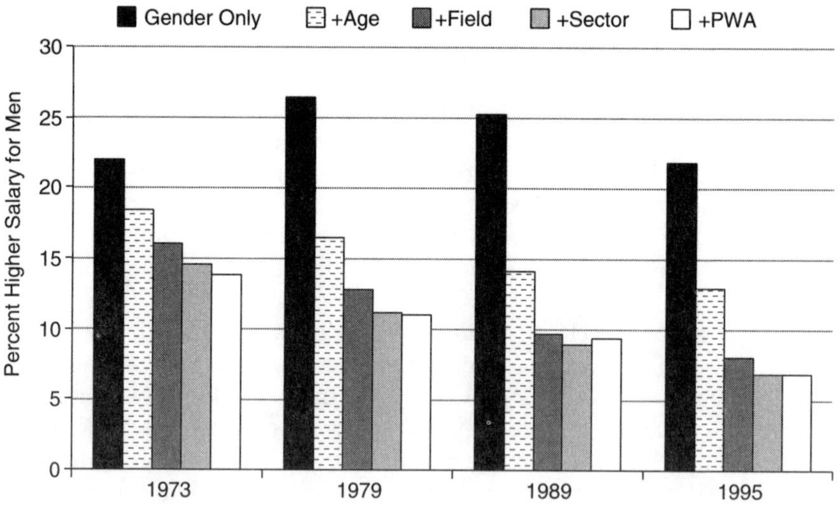

Panel B: Results organized by year of survey

FIGURE 7-12 Effects of age, field, sector, and primary work activity on gender differences in salary. NOTE: Each bar indicates the percent difference between male and female salaries. Gender Only is the percentage difference in mean salaries; +Age adds controls for professional age and age squared; +Field adds dummy variables for the field of Ph.D.; +Sector adds dummy variables for the sector of employment; and +PWA adds controls for primary work activity.

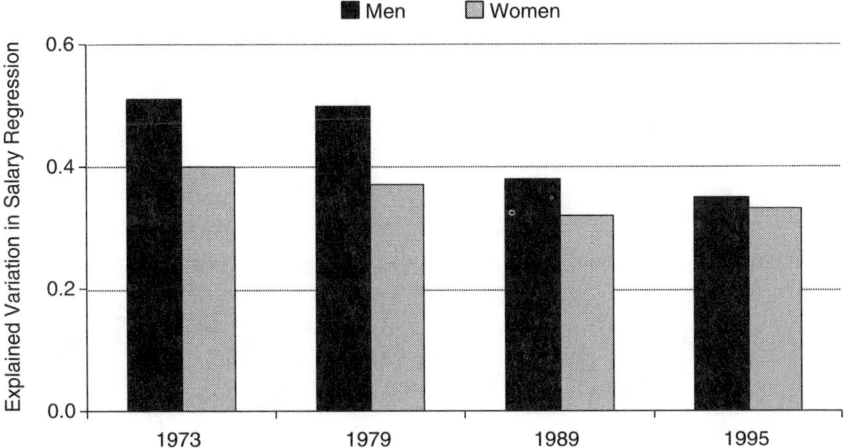

FIGURE 7-13 Explained variation in salary regressions, by sex and year of survey.

SALARIES IN INDUSTRY AND GOVERNMENT

The effects of age, field, and work activity may differ by sector of employment. For example, the salary advantage for men in engineering may be larger in one sector than another. To allow for this possibility, a series of regressions was run for each sector separately for industry, government, and academia; there were too few cases for separate analyses of those working in the nonprofit sector.

Figure 7-14 shows the percentage difference in salaries for men and women in industry after controlling for age, field, and work activity. With all controls, shown by the set of bars labeled "+PWA", the higher salaries for men are reduced from an 18 percent to a 7 percent advantage in 1973; in 1979 the male advantage was over 15 percent even with controls. By 1995 there was a substantial reduction to an adjusted difference of less than 5 percent. These results are consistent with Vetter's (1992) finding that there has been convergence in the salaries of doctoral chemists in industry.

Figure 7-15 presents similar data for those employed in government. Overall, the salary advantage for men is smaller than that in industry, and by 1995 after controlling for age, field, and sector, women are estimated to have marginally higher salaries than men.

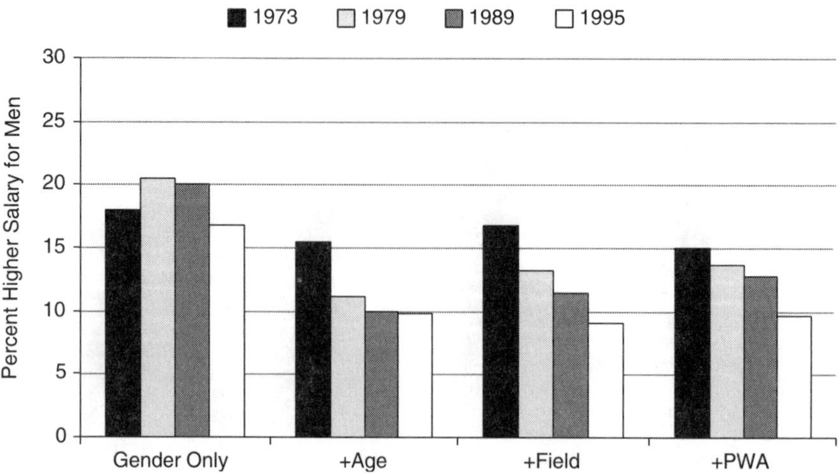

FIGURE 7-14 Gender differences in salary for those with *industrial* jobs, controlling for age, field, and work activity, by year of survey.

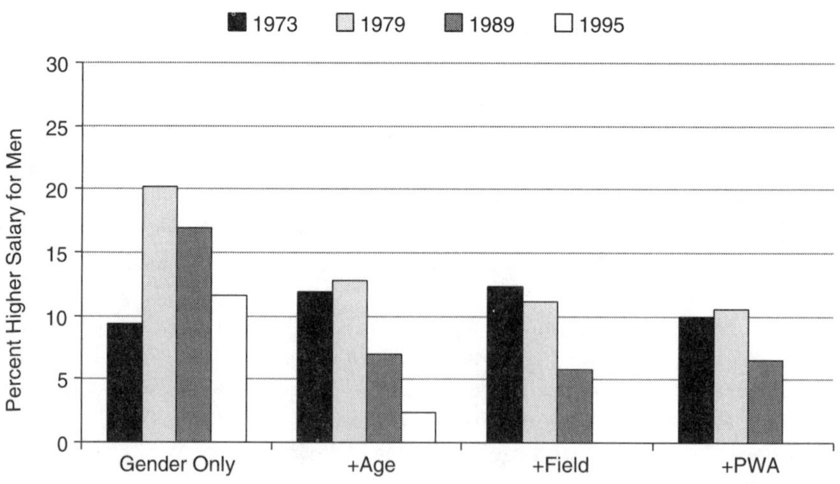

FIGURE 7-15 Gender differences in salary for those with *government* jobs, controlling for age, field, and work activity, by year of survey.

SALARIES IN ACADEMIA

> *. . . [academic] salaries are not of the nature of wages and that there would be a species of moral obliquity in overtly so dealing with the matter.*
>
> —T. Veblen, *Higher Learning in America*, 1918[5]

Despite Veblen's warning of moral delinquency, the majority of studies of the salaries of scientists and engineers are focused on the academic sector, often being further restricted to those with faculty positions. A key advantage to studying the academic sector is that more is known about characteristics of the employing institutions, the work activity, and, to some extent, productivity. These studies include: Bayer and Astin (1968; 1975), Becker and Toutkoushian (1995), Ransom and Megdal (1993), Barbezat (1988), and Toutkoushian (1998). Gray (1993) provides a detailed review of statistical analyses of faculty salaries used in court cases. Overall, these and many other studies have concluded that there has been substantial progress in academia in reducing gender differences in salaries. Barbezat (1988) concluded that "salary discrimination" in the academic market is less than in other sectors of the economy. In this section, we begin by examining gender differences in salaries among all full-time, doctoral academic employees. We then restrict our analysis to the influential group of tenure-track faculty at research universities.

Figure 7-16 plots the percentage salary advantage for academic men after controlling for key dimensions of the academic career. Analyses are based on doctoral scientists and engineers employed full time in academia, regardless of work activity or type of institution. The two panels present the same information organized first by the variables added to the regression and second by the year of the survey. The first column in Panel A shows the overall gender differences in salaries without any controls. The higher salaries for men increase from 18 percent in 1973 to a high of 24 percent in 1989 before dropping back to 20 percent in 1995. The results labeled "+Age" show that the increasing overall differences in academic salaries during this period were due to the younger professional age of women in academia. Controlling for professional age substantially decreases the salary advantage for men, particularly in 1979 and later. By 1995, the advantage for men is reduced to 10 percent. If data on years of experience had been available, these decreases would probably have been even larger. Looking at Panel B, we see that the effects of professional age only became large after 1973 (shown by the large drop from the solid black bar to the adjacent bar). This corresponds to the rapid influx of

[5]From Veblen (1918) page 161, note 1.

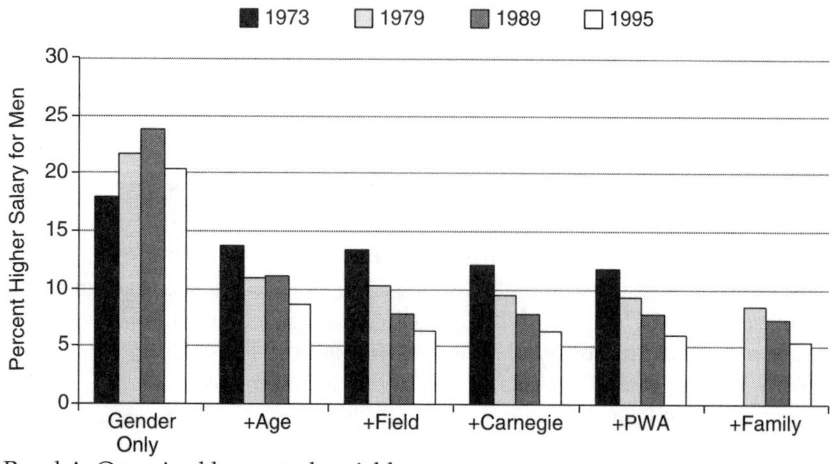

Panel A: Organized by control variable

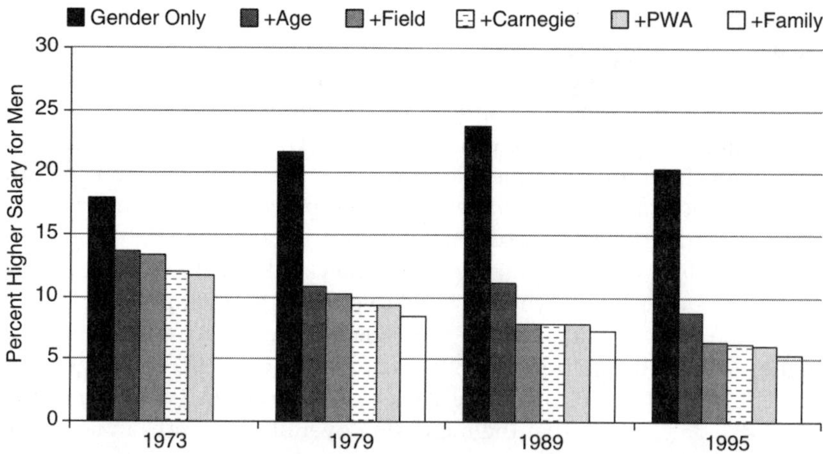

Panel B: Organized by year of survey

FIGURE 7-16 Percentage higher salaries for academic men after controlling for structural variables, by year of survey. NOTE: Gender Only is the percentage difference in mean salaries; +Age adds controls for professional age and age squared; +Field adds dummy variables for the field of Ph.D.; +Carnegie adds dummy variables for Carnegie class of employer; +PWA adds controls for primary work activity; +Family adds controls for married with young children (not available in 1973).

women into academia during this period. Since women are more likely to have interruptions due to family obligations, our measure of experience as years since the Ph.D. is likely to overestimate the professional experience of women. If we had a measure of years of work experience, the reduction in gender differences in salary would likely be even greater. Ferber and Kordick (1978:227), in a study of Ph.D.s from 1958-1963 and 1967-1971, concluded that "the relatively lower earnings of highly educated women can be explained largely by their career interruptions..." She found that once women reentered the labor force on a permanent basis, gender differences in salary were reduced. Unfortunately, more recent data are not available.

In academia, as in other sectors, there are significant salary differences across fields. Feldberg (1984:315) found that in academia, as in science as a whole, faculty in fields where there are proportionately more women receive lower salaries even after controlling for human capital and scientific productivity. Bellas (1994) confirmed this result in several studies that were discussed earlier. Note, however, that women tend to be found least often in those fields in which there is the greatest demand from industry, and accordingly salaries would be expected to be higher. While we confirm the direction of field differences from past research, the magnitudes are small after controlling for differences in years of experience. In 1973 and 1979, controls for broad field resulted in only trivial reductions in gender differences, with somewhat larger reductions of 3 points in 1989 and 2 points in 1995. Since our measure of field is based on the doctoral degree, it is possible that the effects of field of employment would be larger. However, since there is relatively little switching across broad fields, this difference is unlikely to be large.

Different Carnegie types of institutions have substantially different rates of pay. For example, in 1995 academics in the elite Research I universities were making 5 percent more than those in Research II universities, 15 percent more than in Doctoral universities, 20 percent more than in Master's, and 33 percent more than in Baccalaureate institutions. As shown in Chapter 6, women are more likely to be employed in those institutions with lower median salaries. Figure 7-16 shows that adding controls for Carnegie type to the regression containing professional age and field does not substantially reduce the overall gender differences in salary. However, if we examine the gender difference within each type of institution, we find some important differences. Figure 7-17 plots the percentage higher salaries for men by Carnegie type of employer based on the regressions described above. The plot is computed for an academic 15 years from the Ph.D. who is average on other characteristics. The results show that gender differences in salaries have declined since 1973 in all types of institutions, but that the largest changes since 1973 are found in

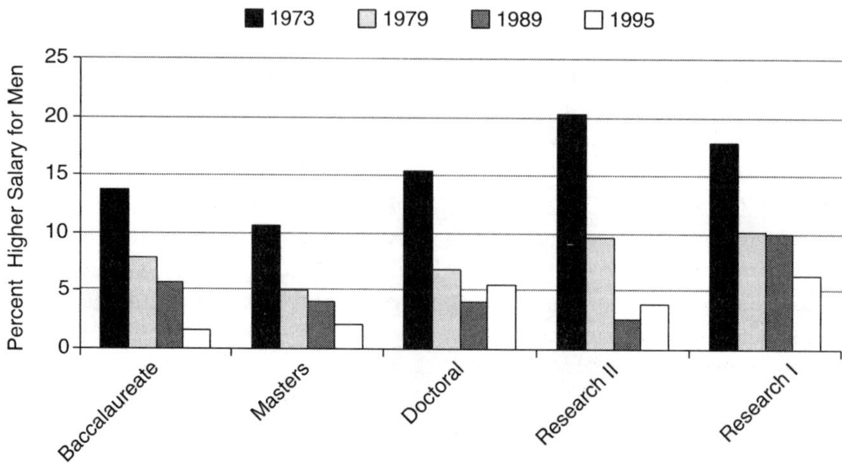

FIGURE 7-17 Gender differences in salaries by Carnegie type of institution and year of survey. NOTE: Predictions are based on regression estimates.

those institutions with doctoral degree programs. This finding is explored further in the next section where we focus on academics located in Research I universities.

Adding controls for the type of work activity further reduces gender differences in salary, but by a relatively small amount. If we further refine work activity to include distinctions among faculty ranks, shown by the last set of bars in Panel A in Figure 7-16, the overall salary differences between men and women are reduced to less than 8 percent in all years and just 5 percent in 1995.

Tenure Track Faculty at Research Universities

Our findings above have shown that a great deal of the overall gender differences in salaries can be accounted for by the differing professional ages of men and women in academia, with smaller reductions introduced by controls for field, type of institution, and work activity. This section provides a more detailed analysis of faculty with tenure-track positions in research universities (i.e., Research I or Research II universities according to the Carnegie classification). We limit our analyses to this group of scientists and engineers for two reasons. First, work environments differ widely among types of academic institutions. Consequently, the effects of variables such as rank and productivity may operate differently at different types of institutions. By restricting our analyses to a more homogenous group of academics, the meaning of our findings should be clearer. Second, tenure-track positions at research universities are often considered to be the most prestigious academic appointments and these faculty train the largest number of Ph.D.s and produce the majority of research in the United States. Accordingly, it is appropriate to give more detailed consideration to this group of academics.

From 1979 to 1995,[6] the overall salary advantage for tenure-track men in research universities dropped slowly from 30 percent in 1979 to 26 percent in 1989 and finally 25 percent in 1995. Note that salary differences in these positions were greater than in the population as a whole. A possible explanation for the slow progress in overall salaries for female faculty in research universities is the greater professional experience of male faculty. Not only is the average male faculty member older, but some research has suggested that the salary advantage for men increases with age. Using data from 1970, Johnson and Stafford (1979) found that the salary disadvantage for women starts small but rises dramatically over time. They conclude (Johnson and Stafford 1979:241): "As time passes, the earnings differential between the sexes grows, and this can be attributed to cumulative effects of discrimination or to the market's reaction to voluntary choices for reduced hours of work and on the job training by women." More recently, faculty salary data from the American Association of University Professors show a salary gap between women and men at each rank and across all academic fields, with the widest gap among full professors who tend to be the oldest Ph.D.s (Magner 1996b).

Our data, shown in Figure 7-18, show a more complicated picture. In 1979 (shown by the solid line), there was an increase in the salary advantage for men during years 1 through 5, a nearly constant 6 percent difference from year 5 till year 15, followed by increasing differences until a decline beginning in year 18 (which is based on a small number of female faculty). In 1995 there are larger differences in most years, with a gap of 14 percent in year 1, dropping to 11 percent in year 5. The remaining years track closely with the results from 1979. An alternative way to examine salary differences over the career is to examine gender differences by academic rank. Figure 7-19 shows the percentage higher salaries for men by academic rank for the years 1979, 1989, and 1995. As with years of experience, after controlling for rank women are increasingly less well paid than men later in the career with no evidence of improvement by 1995. Keep in mind that we have not yet controlled for other variables.

Barbezat (1988) reviews the debate on whether rank should be in-

[6]Data are not available for 1973 since information on tenure track status was not collected that year.

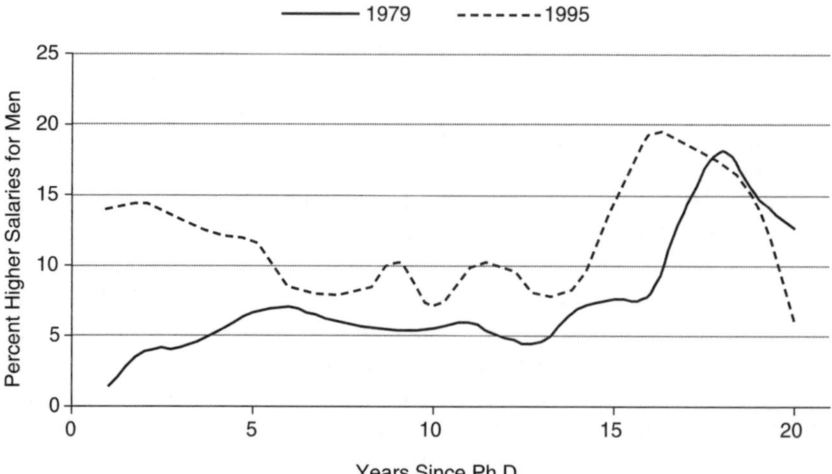

FIGURE 7-18 Percent higher salaries for tenure-track men by years since the Ph.D., by year of survey. NOTE: Each year is computed as a 5-year moving average.

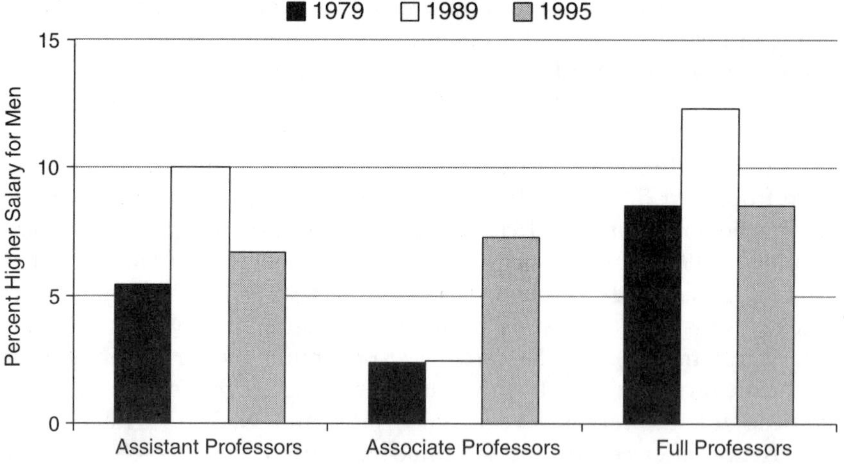

FIGURE 7-19 Percent higher salaries for tenure-track men, by rank and year of survey. NOTE: Data are not available for 1973 since information on tenure-track status was not collected that year.

cluded in regressions predicting salary in academic positions. The argument (Hoffman 1976) is that since women may be discriminated against by slower advancement in rank, estimates of discrimination in salary that include rank may be downwardly biased. Ahern and Scott (1981) found that both academic rank and salary are explained by the same set of individual-level variables and did not use rank to predict salary because "rank itself is influenced by gender." Nonetheless, we believe that there are important reasons to examine salary differences within rank. It is important to know if men and women in the same rank receive comparable salaries. If, in fact, women are promoted more slowly, the allocation of raises on a percentage basis would make their salaries higher than men within a given rank (since women have been in rank longer), thus providing a lower bound for gender differences independent of the process of rank advancement. Accordingly, in the regression results that follow, rank is included as a predictor of salary.

Figure 7-20 summarizes the most important results of our regression analyses of faculty salaries in research universities. The first set of bars for each survey year shows the predicted percent difference in salaries for men and women after controlling for rank and professional age. The results are similar to those presented earlier, showing that controlling for professional age is largely equivalent to controlling for academic rank. The second set of bars for each year adds controls for characteristics of the scientists, including field, prestige of the Ph.D., elapsed time from baccalaureate to Ph.D., whether the employing institution is public or private, the prestige rating of the individual's department, and whether it is a Research I university. Significantly, this substantially *increases* the predicted gender differences in salaries, with predicted differences in salary of 12 percent in 1979, 8 percent in 1989, and 10 percent in 1995. Essentially, these results indicate that men have substantially higher salaries than women with very similar educational backgrounds, institution locations, and experience. We have not, however, included controls for productivity.

As argued by Merton (1973 reprinted from 1942), rewards in science should be based on contributions to the body of scientific knowledge. In academia, unlike many locations in industry and government, these contributions are freely published. Johnson and Stafford (1979) argue that lower salaries may be due to lower productivity. Barbezat (1988), however, questioned whether differences in productivity might also be due to discrimination in publications and found that adding publication variables decreased gender differences in salaries. While there is a huge literature on how to measure scientific productivity (see Long 1992, Gray 1993, and the references cited therein for details), our analysis is limited to simple counts of publications obtained from the Institute for Scientific Information (see Chapter 2 for details). For 1979 we used publications

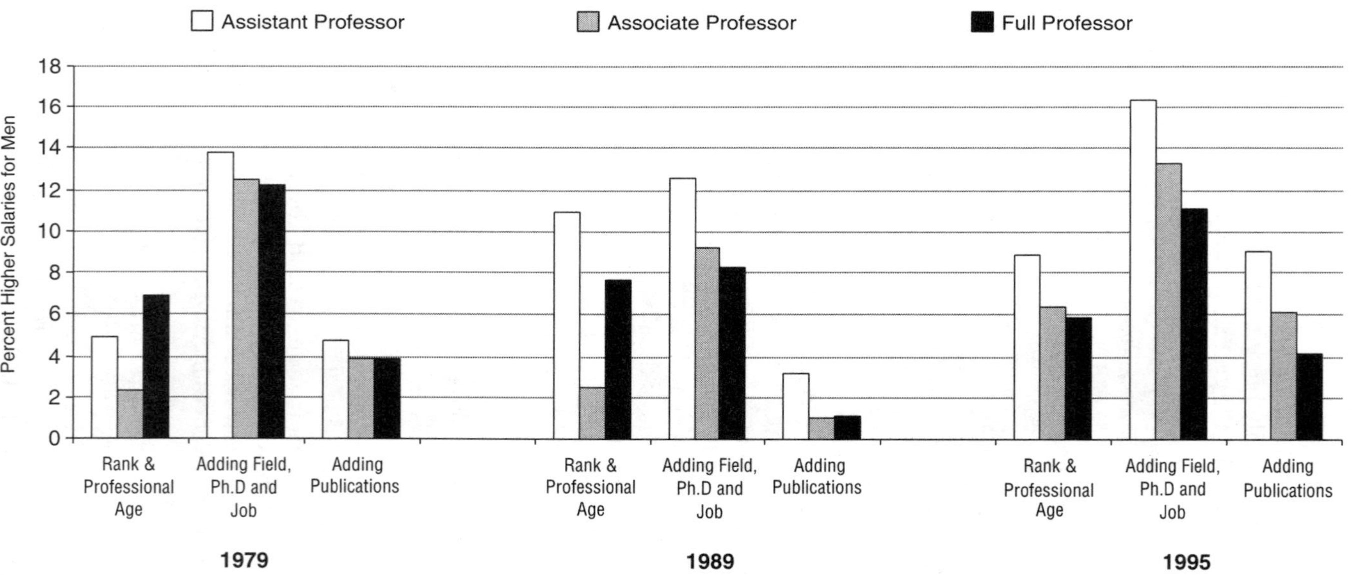

FIGURE 7-20 Percentage higher salaries for men after controlling for different sets of variables, by year of survey. NOTES: "Rank & Professional Age" includes controls for academic rank, years since Ph.D., and years squared. "Adding Field, Ph.D., and Job" adds controls for field, prestige of the Ph.D., elapsed time from baccalaureate to Ph.D., whether the employing institution is public or private, and whether it is a Research I university and the prestige rating of the individual's department. "Adding Publications" adds the number of scientific publications. Estimates at each rank are computed at the mean professional age for that rank: 5.6 for assistant professors, 13.4 for associate professors, and 23.3 for full professors.

from 1981-1986; for 1989, we used publications from 1987-1992; and for 1995, from 1990-1995. We do not have information on productivity for prior periods (e.g., total productivity over the career) or measures of contributions to service, administration, or teaching. Thus, our measure of productivity is crude. Nonetheless, the last column for each year in Figure 7-20 shows that controlling for publications has a major impact. *Controlling for publication substantially reduces the gender differences in salary*, with smaller remaining differences at higher ranks. Still, even with these controls, significant differences in salaries remain: in 1995 female assistant professors were earning 9 percent less than men, female associate professors 6 percent, and female full professors 4 percent. Keep in mind that these differences might be further reduced if we had a better measure of professional experience.

SUMMARY

This chapter presents a lot of detailed information that reflects the complexities of the scientific and engineering labor market. Salary is closely related to the outcomes analyzed in earlier chapters: professional age, sector of employment, and work activity. The more recent entry of women into science and engineering that was documented in Chapters 3 and 4 leads to women in the S&E labor force being younger, which in turn affects their salary. The greater tendency of women to be in the academic sector and in off-track positions, as shown in Chapters 5 and 6, leads to employment in jobs with lower salaries. Yet, adding controls for these dimensions of the career does not eliminate gender differences in salaries.

Figure 7-21 summarizes our findings by comparing gender differences in salaries across increasingly similar groups of men and women. Among all scientists and engineers, regardless of field, sector, professional age or other characteristics, there is a 28 percent salary advantage for men in 1979 that drops to 23 percent in 1995. If we consider only academics, where salaries are more homogeneous than across all sectors, the salary difference drops slightly. Restricting our comparison to faculty in tenure track positions results in an additional small decline. To standardize for age and achievement, we further restrict the comparison to full professors, resulting in a differences of around 10 percent. Since salaries differ across field, the next comparison considers only those in the social and behavioral sciences, where women are more likely to work. In 1979 this leads to few further reductions, but reduces the salary advantage to less than 3 percent in 1995. The last column shows that looking at more similar groups of men and women will not necessarily reduce the salary advantage for men. Among full professors in Research I universi-

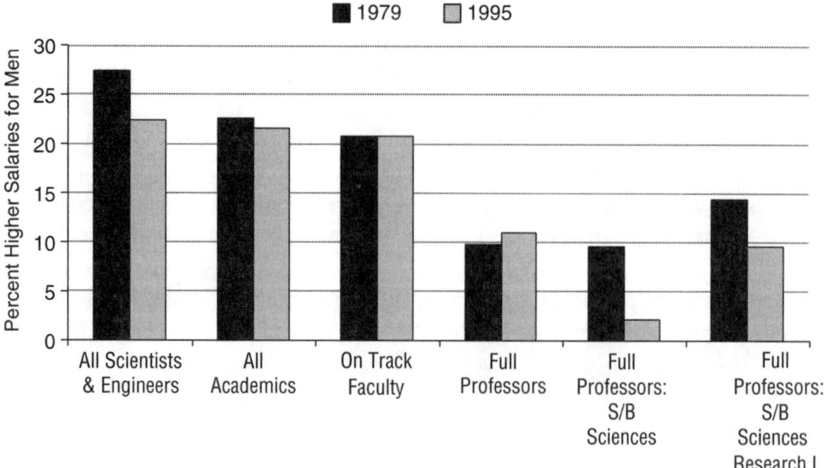

FIGURE 7-21 Ratio of male to female median salaries for increasingly similar groups of scientists and engineeers, 1979 and 1995.

ties in the social and behavioral sciences, men were earning nearly 15 percent more in 1979 reduced to 10 percent in 1995.

While controlling for background differences eliminates much of the gender difference in salary, it does not eliminate it altogether. Why? One possibility is that key variables are missing from the analyses or that others are measured poorly. Indeed, we can suggest many ways in which our analyses could be improved with more and better data. Our results show that at least for those in research-oriented locations, such as Research I universities, controls for productivity are essential and that not having such controls may grossly overestimate gender differences. But we can think of no compelling reason why other variables that we might like to have had, or to have measured better, would account for the remaining differences in salary. Moreover, while comparing men and women who are more similar reduces much of the overall salary difference, this does not change the fact that overall, women have significantly less well paying jobs in sciences. *Discrimination need not come only in the form of differential salaries for equal work, but also through differential access to higher paying jobs.* As Conway and Roberts (1983) put it: "Another type of possible discrimination is placement discrimination, which refers to the 'shunting' or 'steering' of females or minorities into lower job levels than their qualifications warrant." Further, with each progressive stage of the stratification process, it becomes more difficult to distinguish outcomes that are the result of individual differences between women and men from outcomes that are the result of men's cumulative advantage over women in science.

In summary, the male/female earnings gap in science is not fully explained by the individual or contextual factors that have so far been measured. Even analyses that methodically control for measurable differences between women and men and attempt to measure discrimination directly leave a large residual of the wage gap unexplained. While some of the remaining differences may be due to measurement error and it is possible that some control variables are missing, there appear to be differences that remain. Clearly, more research is necessary—not only on faculty salaries but also on gender differences in other employment sectors—in order to assess the effects of discrimination against women at each step in the stratification process.

8

Conclusion and Recommendations[1]

SUMMARY

The last five chapters documented the truly remarkable changes that have occurred in the representation of women in science and engineering. In all aspects of the career, from the receipt of the Ph.D. to entry into the labor force to attaining the rank of full professor, women are an increasing presence, both in absolute number and as a proportion of all scientists and engineers. As positive and encouraging as these changes are, it is equally clear that substantial differences remain. Women as a group remain less well represented and less successful than men in every dimension of the career that we have examined. For example, women remain below 50 percent of new Ph.D.s, are proportionally less likely to enter the full-time scientific and engineering labor force, are less likely to hold more advanced positions in industry or academia, and receive lower salaries even after adjusting for differences in age, field, and type of work.

In seeking to understand why women are less well represented and less successful than men, we labored to avoid making judgments regarding the motivations of those determining the outcome of the scientific career, either of the scientist herself as she moves through the life course, or of the gatekeepers and institutions that control the careers of young

[1]The editor would like to acknowledge his helpful discussions with Edward J. Hackett regarding this chapter.

scientists. For example, given the lesser full-time employment of women, we do not say: "Women *fail to pursue* full-time employment," since this implies an unrestricted choice by the young female scientists to not work. Nor, do we say: "Women *are given fewer opportunities* for full-time employment," since the data we have do not provide information on whether opportunities to work exist. Instead, we say: "Women *are less likely* to attain full-time employment." This reflects the outcome of a process that remains largely hidden in the large scale, quantitative data that we have presented in the report.

Still, we believe that the Panel would be remiss if it did not bring to light some of the evidence for the inequitable treatment of women in science and engineering. This has been done through our citations of historical events and anecdotal accounts. Such information makes it painfully clear that some, and probably many, women faced obstacles that men did not. While stories of overt discrimination against women in science and engineering are increasingly rare and federal legislation has eliminated *blatantly* discriminatory policies for the treatment of women, we believe that despite the massive progress since 1973, the assertion by Harriet Zuckerman and Jonathan R. Cole in 1975 may still be, albeit to a lesser extent, an accurate characterization of the situation facing women in science (Zuckerman and Cole 1975):

> The principle of the triple penalty, as we have observed, asserts that women scientists are triply handicapped . . . first by having to overcome barriers to their entering science, second by the psychic consequences of perceived discrimination—limited aspirations—and third by actual discrimination in the allocation of opportunities and rewards.

RECOMMENDATIONS

The report does not lend itself to conventional recommendations. At least, it does not do so without a significant infusion of thinking that goes beyond the evidence we have provided. The report documents the persistence of inequalities that future programs and policies must address as they seek to improve further the situation for women in science and engineering. Our data highlight where changes have occurred, where parity is being approached, and where major differences remain. While each member of the Panel had ideas regarding the policies and programs that are necessary to maintain and enhance the presence of women in science and engineering, we must leave the issues of program and policy design to others, as the practical, political, and ethical issues are beyond the mandate of our Panel. Still, there are several points that we want to make.

- First, there is evidence that familial obligations affect women differently than men and affect the transition from the Ph.D. to the full-time scientific and engineering labor force. For women the biological demands of childbirth often conflict with the timing of the ideal career. All employers of scientists and engineers would benefit by considering their policies to assist promising careers for employees with young families.

• Second, a key to the full integration of women in science and engineering is the increase in their numbers. To this end, efforts need to be continued to overcome the greater attrition of girls and young women on the path to the Ph.D. and entry into a scientific career. Future studies are needed of the effectiveness of programs to attract and retain girls and women in science and engineering.

THE NEED FOR FUTURE RESEARCH

While our report provides a great deal of new and useful information about the careers of men and women in S&E, our answers and analyses are incomplete. Indeed, it was a constant source of frustration to the study panel that in pursuing our mandate to provide a broad overview of the change and lack of change that has occurred since 1973 we could not pursue each topic in the detail that it deserved. There is much more that needs to be learned about the opportunities and obstacles faced by women in science and engineering. The panel hopes that other researchers will use our report as a starting point for further research. In closing, we suggest that the following topics are of particular importance:

1) A set of key measures and benchmarks should be established for assessing the progress of women in science and engineering. An assessment of progress relative to these benchmarks should be made available shortly after each public release of the *Survey of Earned Doctorates* and the *Survey of Doctoral Recipients.*

2) Detailed studies of several key issues in the scientific career are necessary for understanding key junctions in the career.

a) Entry into the Ph.D.: What accounts for the lower entry of women into some fields? Given the progress made by those women already in science, a clear objective needs to be increasing the number of women entering science and engineering. To fully understand the entry of women into the Ph.D., studies are needed of admissions practices, especially among top institutions. The lower representation of women as undergraduates in Research I institutions also needs to be more fully understood.

b) For those in graduate programs, further information is needed on graduate support and how career interruptions for women affect their options for support.

c) The transition from the Ph.D. to the full-time labor force is a critical point at which relatively, more women than men are lost. To understand this substantial loss of women who have completed their graduate education, requires an examination of postdoctoral fellowships and the effects of marriage and family. Our evidence clearly indicates that having young children is related to the entry of women into the full time labor force.

d) Throughout the career, proportionally more women than men leave science and engineering entirely. More information is need on why these highly trained scientists are lost. Here also constraints imposed by familial obligations, career interruptions, and constraints on mobility need to be considered. To this end, the SDR should be revised to collect additional information particularly relevant to understanding the loss of a disproportionate number of women from the full time S&E labor force. Questions on reasons for part time employment should be expanded and new questions on reasons for not being in the labor force or working outside of S&E should be added.

3) Finally, while women remain underrepresented, most minority groups are even less well represented. Detailed studies of the situation facing minorities are needed. Given the small numbers of minority scientists and engineers, these studies may require the collection of new data.

Bibliography

Adelman, Clifford. 1991. *Women at Thirty Something*. Washington, DC: U.S. Department of Education.

Ahern, Nancy C., and Elizabeth L. Scott. 1981. *Career Outcomes in a Matched Sample of Men and Women Ph.Ds: An Analytical Report*. Washington, DC: National Academy Press.

Allison, Paul D., and J. Scott Long. 1987. Interuniversity mobility of academic scientists. *American Sociological Review* 52:643-652.

Allison, Paul D., and J. Scott Long. 1990. Departmental effects on scientific productivity. *American Sociological Review* 55:469-478.

American Association of University Women Educational Foundation. 1992. *How Schools Shortchange Girls–The AAUW Report*. New York: Marlowe and Co.

Applebome, Peter. 1996. Publishers' squeeze making tenure elusive. Pp. A1, A12 in *The New York Times*. New York.

Astin, Helen S. 1969. *The Woman Doctorate in America: Origins, Career and Family*. New York: Russell Sage Foundation.

Astin, Helen S., and Alan E. Bayer. 1979. Pervasive gender differences in the academic reward system: Scholarship, marriage and what else? Pp. 221-229 in *Academic Rewards in Higher Education*, edited by D.R. Lewis and W.E. Becker. Cambridge, Mass.: Ballinger Publishing Co.

Barber, Leslie A. 1995. U.S. women in science and engineering, 1960-1990: Progress toward equity? *Journal of Higher Education* 66(2):213-234.

Barbezat, Debra. 1988. Gender differences in the academic reward system. Pp. 138-164 in *Academic Labor Markets and Careers*, edited by D.W. Breneman and T.I.K. Youn. New York: Falmer Press.

Bayer, Alan E., and Helen S. Astin. 1968. Sex differences in academic rank and salary among science doctorates in teaching. *Journal of Human Resources* 3:191-201.

Bayer, Alan E., and Helen S. Astin. 1975. Gender differentials in the academic reward system. *Science* 188:796-802.

Becker, William E., and Robert K. Toutkoushian. 1995. The Measurement and cost of removing unexplained gender differences in faculty salaries. *Economics of Education Review* 14:209-220.

Bellas, Marcia L., and Barbara F. Reskin. 1994. On comparable worth. *Academe* September-October:83-85.

Bellas, Marcia L. 1993. Faculty salaries: Still a cost of being female? *Social Science Quarterly* 74:62-75.

Bellas, Marcia L. 1994. Comparable worth in academia: The effects on faculty salaries of the sex Ccomposition and labor-market conditions of academic cisciplines. *American Sociological Review* 59:807-821.

Bellas, Marcia L. 1997. Disciplinary differences in faculty salaries: Does gender bias play a role? *Journal of Higher Education* 68:299-321.

Bergman, Barbara R. 1974. Occupational segregation, wages, and profits when employers discriminate by race or sex. *Eastern Economic Journal* 1:103-110.

Berryman, S.E. 1983. *Who Will Do Science?* New York: Rockefeller Foundation.

Bettelheim, Bruno. 1965. "The commitment required of a woman entering a scientific profession in present day American society. Pp. 3-19 in *Women and the scientific professions: The M.I.T. Symposium on American Women in Science and Engineering,* edited by J.A. Mattfeld, C.G. Van Aken, and Massachusetts Institute of Technology. Association of Women Students. Cambridge: Massachusetts Institute of Technology Press.

Blau, Peter M., and Otis Dudley Duncan. 1967. *The American Occupational Structure.* New York: Wiley.

BLS (Bureau of Labor Statistics). 1999. Information obtained from the Bureau of Labor Statistics Internet site at http: //www.bls.gov/cpihome.htm. Visited March 12, 1999.

Bowen, Howard R., and Jack H. Schuster. 1986. *American Professors: A National Resource Imperiled.* New York: Oxford.

Bowen, William G., and Neil L. Rudenstine. 1992. *In Pursuit of the Ph.D.* Princeton, NJ: Princeton University Press.

Caplow, Theodore, and Reece J. McGee. 1958. *The Academic Marketplace.* New York: Basic Books.

Carnegie Commission on Higher Education. 1973, 1976, 1987, 1994. *A Classification of Institutions of Higher Education: A Technical Report.* Berkeley, CA: The Carnegie Commission.

Carnegie Council on Policy Studies in Higher Education. 1975. *Making Affirmative Action Work in Higher Education: An Analysis of Institutional and Federal Policies with Recommendations.* San Francisco, CA: Jossey-Bass Publishers.

Carnegie Foundation for the Advancement of Teaching. 1994. *Carnegie Foundation National Faculty Surveys.* Princeton, NJ: Opinion Research Corporation.

Cartter, A.M. 1971. Scientific manpower for 1970-1985. *Science* 172:132-140.

Catsambis, Sophia. 1994. The Path to math: Gender and racial-ethnic differences in mathematics participation from middle school to high school. *Sociology of Education* 67:199-215.

CEEWISE (Committee on the Education and Employment of Women in Science and Engineering), National Research Council. 1983. *Climbing the Ladder: An Update on the Status of Doctoral Women Scientists and Engineers.* Washington, DC: National Academy Press.

Centra, John A. 1974. *Women, Men and the Doctorate.* Princeton, NJ: Educational Testing Service.

Chamberlain, Mariam K. (ed.) 1988. *Women in Academe: Progress and Prospects.* New York: Russell Sage Foundation.

Clark, B.R. 1987. *The Academic Life: Small Words, Different Worlds.* Princeton. NJ: Princeton University Press.

Clark, Burton R. 1995. Places of Inquiry: Research and Advanced Education in Modern Universities. Berkeley, CA: University of California Press.

Cole, Jonathan R. 1979. *Fair Science*. New York: Free Press.

Cole, Jonathan R., and Harriet Zuckerman. 1984. The productivity puzzle: Persistence and change in patterns of publication among men and women scientists. Pp. 217-258 in *Advances in Motivation and Achievement*, vol. 2, edited by P. Maehr and M. W. Steinkamp. Greenwich, CT.: JAI Press.

Cole, Jonathan R., and Harriet Zuckerman. 1987. Marriage and motherhood and research performance in science. *Scientific American* 256:119-125.

Cole, Jonathan R., and Stephen Cole. 1973. *Social Stratification in Science*. Chicago: The University of Chicago Press.

Commission on Academic Tenure in Higher Education (edited by W.R. Keast and J.W. Macy). 1973. *Faculty Tenure: A Report and Recommendations*. San Francisco: Jossey-Bass.

Conable, Charlotte Williams. 1977. *Women at Cornell: The Myth of Equal Education*. Ithaca, NY: Cornell University Press.

Conway, Delores A., and Harry V. Roberts. 1983. Reverse regression, fairness, and employment discrimination. *Journal of Business and Economic Statistics* 1:75-85.

Cotgrove, S., and S. Box. 1970. *Science, Industry and Society: Studies in the Sociology of Science*. London: Allen & Unwin.

Crane, Diana. 1965. Scientists at major and minor universities: A study in productivity and recognition. *American Sociological Review* 30:699-714.

Culotta, Elizabeth. 1993. Study: Male scientists publish more, women cited more. *The Scientist* 7(15):14-15.

CWISE (Committee on Women in Science and Engineering-National Research Council). 1994. *Women Scientists and Engineers Employed in Industry: Why So Few?* Washington, DC: National Academy Press.

Dix, Linda Skidmore. 1987a. *Women: Their Underrepresentation and Career Differentials in Science and Engineering*. Washington, DC: National Academy Press.

Dix, Linda Skidmore. 1987b. *Minorities: Their Underrepresentation and Career Differentials in Science and Engineering*. Washington, DC: National Academy Press.

Dresselhaus, M.S. 1986. Women graduate students. *Physics Today* 38:74-75.

Duan, N. 1983. Smearing estimate: A nonparametric retransformation method. *Journal of the American Statistical Association* 78:605-610.

Duncan, Greg J., and Saul Hoffman. 1979. On the job training and earnings differences by race and sex. *Review of Economics and Statistics* 61:594-603.

Edgeworth, F.Y. 1922. "Equal Pay to Men and Women for Equal Work." *Econ. J.* 32:431-457.

Farber, Stephen. 1977. The earnings and promotion of womenfaculty: Comment. *American Economic Review* 67:199-206.

Federal Glass Ceiling Commission. 1996. *Good for Business: Making Full Use of the Nation's Human Capital*. Washington, DC: U.S. Department of Labor.

Feldberg, R. 1984. "Comparable worth: Toward theory and practice in the United States." *Signs* 10:311-328.

Feldman, Saul D. 1974. *Escape from the Doll's House*. New York: McGraw Hill.

Ferber, Marianne A. 1974. "Professors, performance, and rewards." *Industrial Relations* 31:69-77.

Ferber, Marianne A., and Betty Kordick. 1978a. Sex differentials in the earnings of Ph.D.s. *Industrial and Labor Relations Review* 31:227-238.

Ferber, Marianne A., J. Loef, and H. Lowry. 1978b. The economic status of women faculty: A reappraisal. *The Journal of Human Resources* 13:385-401.

Ferber, Marianne, and Joan Huber. 1979. Husbands, wives, and careers. *Journal of Marriage and the Family* 41:315-325.

Fox, Mary Frank, and Catherine A. Faver. 1985. Men, women, and publication productivity. *The Sociological Quarterly* 26:537-549.

Fox, Mary Frank. 1981. Sex, salary, and achievement: Reward-dualism in academia. *Sociology of Education* 54:71-84.

Fox, Mary Frank. 1983. Publication productivity among scientists: A critical review. *Social Studies of Science* 13:285-305.

Fox, Mary Frank. 1989. Women and higher rducation: Gender differences in the status of students and scholars. Pp. 217-235 in *Women: A Feminist Perspective*, edited by J. Freeman. Mountain View, CA: Mayfield Publishing.

Fox, Mary Frank. 1991. Gender, environmental milieu, and productivity in science. in *The Outer Circle: Women in the Scientific Community*, edited by H. Zuckerman, J.R. Cole, and J.T. Bruer. New York: Norton.

Fox, Mary Frank. 1998. Women in science and engineering: Theory, practice, and policy in programs. *Signs* 24:201-223.

Fox, Mary Frank. 1996. Women, academia, and careers in science and engineering. Pp. 265-289 in *The Equity Equation: Fostering the Advancement of Women in the Sciences, Mathematics, and Engineering*, edited by C.S. Davis, A. Ginorio, C. Hollenshead, B. Lazarus, and P. Rayman. San Francisco, CA: Jossey-Bass.

Frieze, Irene Hanson, and Barbara Hartman Hanusa. 1984. Women scientists: Overcoming barriers. Pp. 139-163 in *Advances in Motivation and Achievement*, vol. 2, edited by P. Maehr and M.W. Steinkamp. Greenwich, CT.: JAI Press.

Goldberg, Debbie. 1997. Who makes the cut? Pp. R04 in *The Washington Post*. Washington, DC.

Goldberger, Marvin L., Brendan A. Maher, and Pamela Ebert Flattau. 1995. *Research-Doctorate Programs in the United States: Continuity and Change*. Washington, DC: National Academy Press.

Gordon, G., and Sue Marquis. 1962. Freedom and control in four types of scientific settings. *American Behavioral Scientist* 6.

Gordon, N., T.E. Morton, and I.C. Braden. 1974. Faculty salaries: Is there discrimination by sex, salary, and achievement. *American Economic Review* 64:469-477.

Gornick, Vivian. 1990. *Women in Science*. New York: Simon and Schuster.

Gose, Ben. 1997. Liberal-arts colleges ask: Where have the men gone? *The Chronicle of Higher Education*. June 6, 1997: A35.

Gould, Stephan Jay. 1984. Review of Bleier's *Science and Gender*, *New York Times Book Review*, August 12, 1984.

Gray, Mary W. 1993. Can statistics tell us what we do not want to hear? The case of complex salary structures. *Statistical Sciences* 8:144-179.

Gregorio, David I., Lionel S. Lewis, and Richard A. Wanner. 1982. Assessing merit and need: Distributive justice and salary attainment in academia. *Social Science Quarterly* 63:492-505.

Hackett, Edward J. 1990. Science as a vocation in the 1990s: The changing organizational culture of academic science. *Journal of Higher Education* 61:241-279.

Hagstrom, W.O. 1965. *The Scientific Community*. New York: Basic Books.

Hagstrom, Warren O. 1967. *Competition and Teamwork in Science*. Final Report to the National Science Foundation for Research Grant GS-657.

Haley-Oliphant, Ann E. 1985. International perspectives on the status and role of women in science. In *Women in Science: A Report from the Field*, edited by J.B. Kahle. Philadelphia: Falmer Press.

Hamovitch, William, and Richard D. Morganstern. 1977. Children and the productivity of academic women. *Journal of Higher Education* 48:633-645.

Hansen, W. Lee, Burton A. Weisbrod, and Robert P. Strauss. 1978. Modeling the earnings and research productivity of academic economists. *Journal of Political Economy* 86:729-741.

Hargens, Lowell H., and J. Scott Long. Forthcoming. *Assessing Discrimination in Academia: Demographic Inertia and Women's Representation among Faculty in Higher-Education.*

Hargens, Lowell L., J. McCann, and Barbara F. Reskin. 1978. Productivity and reproductivity: Marital fertility and professional achievement among research scientists. *Social Forces* 52:129-146.

Harmon, Lindsey R. 1963. *Doctorates Production in United States Universities 1920-1962: With Baccalaureate Origins of Doctorates in Sciences, Arts and Professions.* Washington, DC: National Academy Press.

Harmon, Lindsey R. 1978. *A Century of Doctorates: Data Analysis of Growth and Change.* Washington, DC: National Academy Press.

Henderson, P.H., J.E. Clarke, and M.A. Reynolds. 1996. *Summary Report 1995: Doctorate Recipients from United States Universities.* Washington, DC: National Academy Press.

Hochschild, Arlie Russell. 1975. Inside the clockwork of male careers. Pp. 47-80 in *Women and the Power to Change*, edited by F. Howe. New York: McGraw-Hill.

Hodson, Randy. 1985. Some considerations concerning the functional form of earnings. *Social Science Research* 14:374-394.

Hoffman, E.P. 1976. Faculty salaries: Is there discrimination by sex, race, and discipline? *American Economic Review* 66:196-198.

Hornig, Lilli S. 1987. Women graduate students: a literature review and synthesis. in *Women: Their Underrepresentation and Career Differentials in Science and Engineering*, edited by L.S. Dix. Washington, DC: National Academy Press.

Hurlbert, Jeanne, and Rachel A. Rosenfeld. 1992. Getting a good job: Rank and institutional prestige in academic psychologists' careers. *Sociology of Education* 65:188-207.

Johnson, George E., and Frank P. Stafford. 1979. Pecuniary rewards to men and women faculty. Pp. 231-243 in *Academic Rewards in Higher Education*, edited by D.R. Lewis and J. William E. Becker. Cambridge, MA: Ballinger.

Jones, Lyle V., Gardner Lindzey, and Porter E. Coggeshall. 1982. *An Assessment of Research Doctorate Programs in the United States.* Washington, DC: National Academy Press.

Kahle, Jane Butler, and Marsha Lakes Matyas. 1987. Equitable science and mathematics education: A discrepancy model. In *Women: Their Underrepresentation and Career Differentials in Science and Engineering*, edited by L.S. Dix. Washington, DC: National Academy Press.

Kanter, Rosabeth Moss. 1977. *Men and women of the Corporation.* New York: Basic Books.

Katz, D. 1973. Faculty salaries, promotion, and productivity at a large university. *American Economic Review* 63:469-477.

Keller E.F. 1991. The wo/man scientist: Issues of sex and gender in the pursuit of science. In *The Outer Circle: Women in the Scientific Community*, ed. H. Zuckerman, J.R. Cole, J.Y. Bruer, 227-236. New York: W.W. Norton.

Kerr, Clark. 1963. *The Uses of the University.* Cambridge, MA: Harvard University Press.

Klaw, Spencer. 1968. *The New Brahmins: Scientific Life in America.* New York: Morrow.

Kornhauser, W. 1962. *Scientists in Industry.* Berkeley, CA: University of California Press.

Kuh, Charlotte V. 1996. Is there a Ph.D. glut? Is that the right question? in *Presentation to the Higher Education Secretariat on March 6.* Washington, DC.

LeBold, William K. 1987. Women in engineering and science: An undergraduate research perspective. In *Women: Their Underrepresentation and Career Differentials in Science and Engineering.* Linda S. Dix, ed. Washington, DC: National Academy Press.

Lewis, Gwendolyn L. 1986. Career Interruptions and Gender Differences in Salaries of Scientists and Engineers. A Working Paper for the Office of Scientific and Engineering Personnel of the National Research Council. Washington, DC: National Academy Press.

Lomperis, Ana Maria Turner. 1990. Are women changing the nature of the academic profession? *Journal of Higher Education* 61:643-677.

Long J. Scott, and Robert McGinnis. 1985. The effects of the mentor on the academic career. *Scientometrics* 7:255-80.

Long, J. Scott, and Mary Frank Fox. 1995. Scientific careers: Universalism and particularism. *Annual Review of Sociology* 21:45-71.

Long, J. Scott, and Robert McGinnis. 1981. Organizational context and scientific productivity. *American Sociological Review* 46:422-442.

Long, J. Scott, P.D. Allison, and R. McGinnis. 1980. Entrance into the academic career. *American Sociological Review* 44:816-830.

Long, J. Scott, Paul D. Allison, and Robert McGinnis. 1993. Rank advancement in academic careers: Gender differences and the effects of productivity. *American Sociological Review* 58:703-722.

Long, J. Scott. 1978. Productivity and academic position in the scientific career. *American Sociological Review* 43:889-908.

Long, J. Scott. 1992. Measures of gender difference in scientific productivity. *Social Forces* 71:159-178.

Long, J. Scott. 1997. *Regression Models for Categorical and Limited Dependent Variables*. Thousand Oaks, CA: Sage Press.

Magner, Denise K. 1996a. A parlous time for tenure: Minnesota professors are furious over plans they say would erode job security. Pp. A21-A23 in *The Chronicle of Higher Education*.

Magner, Denise K. 1996b. Professors' salaries hit $50,000, edging inflation." Pp. A18-A22 in *The Chronicle of Higher Education*.

Malcom, Shirley M. 1983. *Equity and Excellence: Compatible Goals*. Washington, DC: American Association for the Advancement of Science.

Marcson, Simon. 1960. *The Scientist in American Industry*. Princeton, NJ: Industrial Relations Section, Princeton University.

Marwell, Gerald, Rachel Rosenfeld, and Seymour Spilerman. 1979. Geographic constraints on women's careers in academia. *Science* 205: 1225-31.

Mattis, Mary, and Jennifer Allyn. 1999. Women scientists in industry. *Annals of the New York Academy of Sciences* 869:143-174.

Matyas, Marsha Lakes, and Linda Skidmore Dix (editors). 1992. *Science and Engineering Programs: On Target for Women?* Washington,DC: National Academy Press.

McGuigan, Dorothy Gies. 1970. *A Dangerous Experiment: 100 Years of Women at the University of Michigan*, Ann Arbor, MI: Center for Continuing Education of Women.

McIlwee, Judith Samsom, and J. Gregg Robinson. 1992. *Women in Engineering: Gender, Power, and Workplace Culture*. Albany: State University of New York Press.

McPherson, Michael S. 1985. Numbers and quality: Analyzing the market for university scientists and engineers. Pp. 1-5 in Office of Scientific and Engineering Personnel, *Forecasting Demand for University Scientists and Engineers*. Washington, DC: National Academy Press.

Merton, Robert K. 1973 reprinted from 1942. The normative structure of science. Pp. 267-278 in *The Sociology of Science*. Edited by N. Storer. Chicago: University of Chicago Press.

Metzger, Walter P. 1973. Academic tenure in America: A historical essay. Pp. 93-159 in *Faculty Tenure: A Report and Recommendations*, edited by Commission on Academic Tenure in Higher Education. San Francisco, CA: Jossey-Bass.

Moen, Phyllis. 1985. Continuities and discontinuities in women's labor force activity. Pp. 113-155 in *Life Course Dynamics*, ed. Glenn H. Elder. Ithaca, NY: Cornell University Press.

Morgan, Laurie A. 1998. Glass-ceiling effect or cohort effect? A longitudinal study of the gender gap for engineers, 1982 to 1989. *American Sociological Review* 63:479-483.

NRC (National Research Council). 1981. *Postdoctoral Appointments and Disappointments: A Report of the Committee on a Study of Postdoctorals in Science and Engineering in the United States*. Washington, DC: National Academy Press.

NRC (National Research Council). Committee on Dimensions Causes and Implications of Recent Trends in the Careers of Life Scientists. 1998. *Trends in the Early Careers of Life Scientists*. Washington, DC: National Academy Press.

National Commission on Pay Equity. 1996. The Wage Gap. Hyattsville, MD.

National Science Board. 1998. *Science and Engineering Indicators 1998*. Washington, DC: U.S. Government Printing Office.

NSB (National Science Board). 1993. *Science and Engineering Indicators 1993*. Washington, DC: U.S. Government Printing Office.

NSB (National Science Board). 1996. *Science and Engineering Indicators 1996*. Washington, DC: U.S. Government Printing Office.

NSB (National Science Board). 1999. *Science and Engineering Indicators 1998*. Washington, DC: U.S. Government Printing Office.

NSF (National Science Foundation). 1920-1995. *Survey of Earned Doctorates*. Washington, DC: National Science Foundation.

NSF (National Science Foundation). 1973-1995. *Survey of Doctorate Recipients*. Washington, DC: National Science Foundation.

NSF (National Science Foundation). 1996. *Women and Minorities in Science and Engineering*. Washington, DC: National Science Foundation.

NSF (National Science Foundation). 1997a. *Characteristics of Doctoral Scientists and Engineers in the United States: 1995*. Washington, DC: National Science Foundation, Division of Science Resources Studies.

NSF (National Science Foundation). 1997b. *Who Is Unemployed? Factors Affecting Unemployment Among Individuals with Doctoral Degrees in Science and Engineering*. Washington, DC: National Science Foundation.

NSF (National Science Foundation). 2000a. Tabulations from data from Department of Education, National Center for Education Statistics: Integrated Postsecondary Education Data System Completion Survey; and NSF Survey of Earned Doctorates.

NSF (National Science Foundation). 2000b. Special tabulation, WebCASPAR Database System.

Pelz, D.C., and F.M. Andrews. 1966. *Scientists in Organizations*. New York: Wiley.

Perrucci, Robert, Kathleen O'Flaherty, and Harvey Marshall. 1983. Market conditions, productivity, and promotion among university faculty. *Research in Higher Education* 19:431-449.

Preston, Anne. 1993. A study of occupational departure of employees in the natural sciences and engineering. In *Committee on Women in Science and Engineering Conference on Women Scientists and Engineers Employed in Industry*. Irvine, CA.

Ransom, Michael, and Sharon Megdal. 1993. Sex differences in the academic labor market in the affirmative action era. *Economics of Education Review* 12:21-43.

Rayman, Paula, and Belle Brett. 1993. *Pathways for Women in the Sciences*. Wellesley College: Center for Research on Women.

Reskin, Barbara F. 1977. Scientific productivity and the reward wtructure of science. *American Sociological Review* 42:491-504.

Reskin, Barbara F. 1978. Scientific productivity, sex, and location in the institution of science. *American Journal of Sociology* 83:1235-1243.

Reskin, Barbara F. 1979. Academic sponsorship and scientists' careers. *Sociology of Education* 52:129-146.

Reskin, Barbara F., and Lowell L. Hargens. 1979. Scientific Aadvancement of male and female chemists. Pp. 100-122 in *Discrimination in Organizations*, edited by K.G. Lutterman and A.R. Alvarez. San Francisco: Jossey-Bass.

Riley, Matilda White. 1992. Cohort Analysis. Pp. 231-237 in *Encyclopedia of Sociology*, vol. 1, edited by E. F. Borgatta. New York: Macmillan.

Rosenfeld, Rachel A., and Jo Ann Jones. 1986. Institutional mobility among academics. *Sociology of Education* 59:212-226.

Rosenfeld, Rachel A., and Jo Ann Jones. 1987. Patterns and effects of geographic mobility for academic women and men. *Journal of Higher Education* 58:493-515.

Rosenfeld, Rachel A., and Jo Ann Jones. 1988. Exit and re-entry in higher education. Pp. 74-97 in *Academic Labor Markets*, edited by D.W. Breneman and T.I.K. Youn. New York: Falmer Press.

Rossiter, Margaret W. 1982. *Women Scientists in America: Struggles and Strategies to 1940*. Baltimore, MD: Johns Hopkins Press.

Rossiter, Margaret W. 1995. *Women Scientists in America: Before Affirmative Action 1940-1972*. Baltimore, MD: Johns Hopkins Press.

Shyrock, Henry S., Jacob S. Siegel, and Associates. 1973. *The Methods and Materials of Demography*, vol. 1. Washington, DC: Department of Commerce.

Simon, R.J., Shirley M. Clark, and L.L. Tifft. 1966. Of nepotism, marriage and the pursuit of an academic career. *Sociology of Education* 39:344-358.

Solomon, Barbara Miller. 1985. *In the Company of Educated Women*. New Haven, CT: Yale University Press.

Sonnert, Gerhard and (G. Holton). 1995. *Gender Differences in Science Careers: The Project Access Study*. New Brunswick, NJ: Rutgers University Press.

Sonnert, Gerhard. 1990. Careers of women and men postdoctoral fellows in the sciences. Presented at the *American Sociological Association* meetings.

Szafran, Robert F. 1984. *Universities and Women Faculty: Why Some Organizations Discriminate More Than Others*. New York: Praeger.

Tidball, M. Elizabeth, and Vera Kistiakowsky. 1976. Baccalaureate origins of American scientists and scholars. *Science*, August 20:646-652.

Tobias, Sheila, Daryl E. Chubin, and Kevin Aylesworth. 1995. *Rethinking Science as a Career: Perceptions and Realities in the Physical Sciences*. Research Corporation, Tucson, AZ.

Tolbert, Pamela S. 1986. Organizations and inequality: Sources of earnings differences between male and female faculty. *American Sociological Review* 59:227-235.

Touchton, Judity G., and Lynne Davis. 1991. *Fact Book on Women in Higher Education*. New York: American Council on Education and Macmillan.

Toutkoushian, Robert. 1998. Sex matters less for younger faculty: Evidence of disaggregate pay disparities from the 1988 and 1993 NCES Surveys. *Economics of Education Review* 17:55-77.

Treiman, Donald J., and Heidi I. Hartmann. 1991. *Women, Work, and Wages: Equal Pay for Jobs of Equal Value*. Washington, DC: National Academy Press.

Tuckman, Howard, Susan Coyle, and Yupin Bae. 1990. *On Time to the Doctorate: A Study of the Increased Time to Complete Doctorates in Science and Engineering*. Washington, DC: National Academy Press.

U.S. Census. 1999. Information obtained from the U.S. Census Internet site at http: // www.census.gov/population/socdemo/hhes/income/histinc/p36.html. Visited 9/21/00. Table P-36: Full-Time, Year-Round Workers (All Races) by Median Income and Sex: 1970 to 1997.

U.S. Congress, Office of Technology Assessment. 1988. *Educating Scientists and Engineers: Grade School to Grad School*. Washington, DC: U.S. Government Printing Office.

U.S. Department of Labor-Women's Bureau. 1994. *Handbook on Women Workers: Issues and Trends*. Washington, DC: U.S. Department of Labor.

Veblen, Thorstein. 1918. *The Higher Learning in America*. New York: B.W. Huebsch.

Vetter, Betty M. 1992. What is holding up the glass ceiling? Barriers to women in the science and Eengineering workforce. Occasional Paper 92-3. Publication: Washington, DC: Commission on Professionals in Science and Technology.

Widnall, S.E. 1988. AAAS Presidential lecture: Voices from the pipeline. *Science* 241:1740-1745.

Wilson, Logan. 1979. *American Academics: Then and Now*. New York: Oxford University Press.

Wilson, Robin. 1997. At Harvard, Yale, and Stanford, women lose tenure bids despite backing from departments. Pp. A10-A11 in *The Chronicle of Higher Education*.

Wolfle, D. 1972. *The Home of Science*. New York: McGraw-Hill.

Xie, Yu, and Kimberlee A. Shauman. 1998. Sex differences in research productivity: New evidence about an old puzzle. *American Sociological Review* 63:847-870.

Yentsch, Clarice M., and Carl J. Sindermann. 1992. *The Woman Scientist: Meeting the Challenges for a Successful Career*. New York: Plenum Press.

Zuckerman Harriet. 1970. Stratification in American science. Pp. 235-57 in *Social Stratification*, Edward O. Laumann, ed. Indianapolis: Bobbs-Merrill.

Zuckerman, Harriet. 1977. *Scientific Elite: Nobel Laureates in the United States*. New York: The Free Press.

Zuckerman, Harriet, and Jonathan R. Cole. 1975. Women in American science. *Minerva* 13:82-102.

Zuckerman, Harriet and Robert K. Merton. 1972. Age, aging and age structure in science. Pp. 292-356 in M.W. Riley et al. (eds.), *A Sociology of Age Stratification*, Volume 3 of *Aging and Society*. New York: Russell Sage Foundation.

Zuckerman, Harriet. 1987. Persistence and change in the careers of men and women scientists and engineers. Pp. 127-156 in *Women: Their Underrepresentation and Career Differentials in Science and Engineering*, edited by L.S. Dix. Washington, DC: National Academy Press.

Appendix A

Carnegie Classifications

The complete 1994 Carnegie Classification is:

- Research Universities I: These institutions offer a full range of baccalaureate programs, are committed to graduate education through the doctorate, and give high priority to research. They award 50 or more doctoral degrees each year. In addition, they receive annually $40 million or more in federal support.
- Research Universities II: These institutions offer a full range of baccalaureate programs, are committed to graduate education through the doctorate, and give high priority to research. They award 50 or more doctoral degrees each year. In addition, they receive annually between $15.5 million and $40 million in federal support.
- Doctoral Universities I: These institutions offer a full range of baccalaureate programs and are committed to graduate education through the doctorate. They award at least 40 doctoral degrees annually in five or more disciplines.
- Doctoral Universities II: These institutions offer a full range of baccalaureate programs and are committed to graduate education through the doctorate. They award annually at least ten doctoral degrees in three or more disciplines or 20 or more doctoral degrees in one or more disciplines.
- Master's (Comprehensive) Universities and Colleges I: These institutions offer a full range of baccalaureate programs and are committed to

graduate education through the master's degree. They award 40 or more master's degrees annually in three or more disciplines.

- Master's (Comprehensive) Universities and Colleges II: These institutions offer a full range of baccalaureate programs and are committed to graduate education through the master's degree. They award 20 or more master's degrees annually in one or more disciplines.
- Baccalaureate (Liberal Arts) Colleges I: These institutions are primarily undergraduate colleges with major emphasis on baccalaureate degree programs. They award 40 percent or more of their baccalaureate degrees in liberal arts fields and are restrictive in admissions.
- Baccalaureate (Liberal Arts) Colleges II: These institutions are primarily undergraduate colleges with major emphasis on baccalaureate degree programs. They award less than 40 percent of their baccalaureate degrees in liberal arts fields or are less restrictive in admissions.
- Associate of Arts Colleges: These institutions offer associate of arts certificate or degree programs and, with few exceptions, offer no baccalaureate degrees.
- Specialized Institutions: These institutions offer degrees ranging from the bachelor's to the doctorate. At least 50 percent of the degrees awarded by these institutions are in a single discipline. Specialized institutions include: Theological seminaries, Bible colleges and other institutions offering degrees in religion: This category includes institutions at which the primary purpose is to offer religious instruction or train members of the clergy.
- Medical schools and medical centers: These institutions award most of their professional degrees in medicine. In some instances, their programs include other health professional schools, such as dentistry, pharmacy, or nursing.
- Other separate health profession schools: Institutions in this category award most of their degrees in such fields as chiropractic, nursing, pharmacy, or podiatry.
- Schools of engineering and technology: The institutions in this category award at least a bachelor's degree in programs limited almost exclusively to technical fields of study.
- Schools of business and management: The schools in this category award most of their bachelor's or graduate degrees in business or business-related programs.
- Schools of art, music, and design: Institutions in this category award most of their bachelor's or graduate degrees in art, music, design, architecture, or some combination of such fields.
- Schools of law: The schools included in this category award most of their degrees in law. The list includes only institutions that are listed as separate campuses in the 1994 Higher Education Directory.

• Teachers' colleges: Institutions in this category award most of their bachelor's or graduate degrees in education or education-related fields.

• Other specialized institutions: Institutions in this category include graduate centers, maritime academies, military institutes, and institutions that do not fit any other classification category.

• Tribal colleges and universities: These colleges are, with few exceptions, tribally controlled and located on reservations. They are all members of the American Indian Higher Education Consortium.

Notes on Definitions of the Carnegie Classifications

1. Doctoral degrees include Doctor of Education, Doctor of Juridical Science, Doctor of Public Health, and the Ph.D. in any field.

2. Total federal obligation figures are available from the National Science Foundation's annual report called *Federal Support to Universities, Colleges, and Nonprofit Institutions*. The years used in averaging total federal obligations are 1989, 1990, and 1991.

3. Distinct disciplines are determined by the U.S. Department of Education's Classification of Instructional Programs 4-digit series.

4. The liberal arts disciplines include English language and literature, foreign languages, letters, liberal and general studies, life sciences, mathematics, philosophy and religion, physical sciences, psychology, social sciences, the visual and performing arts, area and ethnic studies, and multi- and interdisciplinary studies. The occupational and technical disciplines include agriculture, allied health, architecture, business and management, communications, conservation and natural resources, education, engineering, health sciences, home economics, law and legal studies, library and archival sciences, marketing and distribution, military sciences, protective services, public administration and services, and theology.

Appendix B

Tables

TABLE B-1 Total Number of Ph.D.s in the Labor Force, by Sex, Field, and Year of Survey

	1973		1979		1989		1995	
Engineering	*Men*	*Women*	*Men*	*Women*	*Men*	*Women*	*Men*	*Women*
Biomedical	317	5	870	10	1373	94	1913	205
Chemical	5427	19	7497	43	11004	322	11879	714
Electrical	7962	21	10375	68	14438	249	19513	704
Industrial	815	5	1312	18	1304	107	2110	307
Materials Science	178	0	691	14	1768	153	3558	521
Other	18743	77	26584	269	38595	927	43552	1996
Total	33442	127	47329	422	68482	1852	82525	4447
Mathematical Sciences	*Men*	*Women*	*Men*	*Women*	*Men*	*Women*	*Men*	*Women*
Computer Science	571	33	1428	104	3950	484	6942	1133
Probability & Statistics	2399	191	4003	434	5655	1066	6525	1479
Mathematics	9883	766	12661	1079	15995	1698	17100	2204
Total	12853	90	18092	1617	25600	3248	30567	4816
Physical Sciences	*Men*	*Women*	*Men*	*Women*	*Men*	*Women*	*Men*	*Women*
Astronomy	1023	99	1627	127	2478	240	2866	224
Physics	18944	395	23792	628	30319	1236	33781	2058
Chemistry	34784	2198	41278	3058	49102	5814	52841	8478
Oceanography	583	10	922	46	1516	167	1724	310
Geosciences	6024	162	8259	376	11981	1083	13288	1790
Total	61358	2864	75878	4235	95396	8540	104500	12860

Life Sciences	*Men*	*Women*	*Men*	*Women*	*Men*	*Women*	*Men*	*Women*
Agricultural	10009	163	13750	399	19273	1704	21059	2906
Medical	35416	6356	47014	9979	64361	19499	80407	29511
Biological	5013	600	7369	1395	13121	6295	8345	8570
Total	50438	7119	68133	11773	96755	27498	109811	40987
Social/Behavioral Sciences	*Men*	*Women*	*Men*	*Women*	*Men*	*Women*	*Men*	*Women*
Psychology	18964	4942	28766	9975	43169	24400	47473	34677
Anthropology	1378	343	2528	1026	4101	2374	4727	3305
Economics	9755	603	12175	1102	16782	2185	16809	2737
Sociology	4910	1134	7177	2222	9254	4330	8745	5024
Other	12289	1385	19156	3133	26474	7479	21270	6243
Total	47296	8407	69802	17458	99780	40768	99024	51986

TABLE B-2 Number of Full-Time Scientists and Engineers, by Sex, Field, and Year of Survey

	1973		1979		1989		1995	
Engineering	*Men*	*Women*	*Men*	*Women*	*Men*	*Women*	*Men*	*Women*
Biomedical	307	2	778	10	1314	84	1729	135
Chemical	4835	13	6696	33	9410	257	9574	504
Electrical	7317	17	9578	53	12595	213	16422	601
Industrial	720	4	1007	12	901	75	1590	279
Materials Science	146	0	599	12	1587	138	3304	366
Other	16883	46	23860	218	32631	791	36394	1704
Total	30208	82	42518	338	58438	1558	69013	3589
Mathematical Sciences	*Men*	*Women*	*Men*	*Women*	*Men*	*Women*	*Men*	*Women*
Computer Science	540	30	1330	92	3670	397	6501	933
Probability & Statistics	2233	130	3710	318	5067	798	5165	1175
Mathematics	8866	517	10871	780	13610	1304	14045	1620
Total	11639	677	15911	1190	22347	2499	25711	3728
Physical Sciences	*Men*	*Women*	*Men*	*Women*	*Men*	*Women*	*Men*	*Women*
Astronomy	930	64	1531	89	2310	175	2578	202
Physics	16424	220	20603	427	25577	982	26977	1473
Chemistry	28936	1236	34990	2105	39788	4426	39773	6251
Oceanography	523	6	888	37	1336	132	1537	212
Geosciences	5355	111	7287	292	9857	809	10508	1367
Total	52168	1637	65299	2950	78868	6524	81373	9505

Life Sciences	*Men*	*Women*	*Men*	*Women*	*Men*	*Women*	*Men*	*Women*
Agricultural	8766	86	12093	297	15569	1354	15688	2053
Medical	30916	4131	41403	7218	54025	14699	63815	22452
Biological	4371	381	6724	1078	11490	4955	5595	5380
Total	44053	4598	60220	8593	81084	21008	85098	29885
Social/Behavioral Sciences	*Men*	*Women*	*Men*	*Women*	*Men*	*Women*	*Men*	*Women*
Psychology	16048	3060	24690	7005	34961	16818	36317	22833
Anthropology	1226	246	2193	756	2914	1441	3419	2283
Economics	7359	376	9261	781	11907	1654	11659	2063
Sociology	4018	753	5649	1592	6575	2717	6255	3536
Other	9434	778	14058	1820	18501	4251	14633	4218
Total	38085	5213	55851	11954	74858	26881	72283	34933

TABLE B-3 Labor Force Participation Status by Sex, Field, and Year of Survey

	1973		1979		1989		1995	
Engineering	*Men*	*Women*	*Men*	*Women*	*Men*	*Women*	*Men*	*Women*
Full Time in Science	.931	.695	.909	.818	.897	.848	.906	.813
Full Time out of Science	.047	.042	.060	.070	.073	.061	.046	.043
Part Time	.012	.136	.021	.061	.021	.063	.029	.066
Seeking Work	.008	.051	.005	.022	.006	.011	.011	.039
Not Seeking Work	.003	.076	.005	.029	.002	.016	.009	.039
n	32443	118	46765	413	65149	1838	76200	4416
Mathematical Sciences	*Men*	*Women*	*Men*	*Women*	*Men*	*Women*	*Men*	*Women*
Full Time in Science	.947	.765	.905	.784	.910	.800	.908	.795
Full Time out of Science	.029	.048	.066	.064	.068	.080	.042	.050
Part Time	.008	.123	.021	.083	.016	.078	.030	.108
Seeking Work	.013	.018	.003	.019	.003	.010	.009	.006
Not Seeking Work	.003	.045	.005	.049	.002	.033	.012	.041
n	11191	771	15684	1335	22038	2580	26137	3891
Physical Sciences	*Men*	*Women*	*Men*	*Women*	*Men*	*Women*	*Men*	*Women*
Full Time in Science	.898	.641	.897	.732	.903	.799	.872	.774
Full Time out of Science	.066	.069	.070	.072	.068	.070	.063	.084
Part Time	.018	.154	.023	.103	.020	.070	.041	.055
Seeking Work	.014	.054	.008	.030	.006	.020	.012	.022
Not Seeking Work	.004	.082	.002	.063	.003	.041	.012	.065
n	58068	2554	72808	4029	87354	8164	93274	12285

Life Sciences	*Men*	*Women*	*Men*	*Women*	*Men*	*Women*	*Men*	*Women*
Full Time in Science	.933	.744	.925	.779	.913	.803	.853	.759
Full Time out of Science	.039	.048	.045	.044	.060	.067	.091	.111
Part Time	.019	.105	.020	.087	.017	.080	.032	.066
Seeking Work	.006	.039	.008	.031	.007	.015	.012	.014
Not Seeking Work	.003	.064	.003	.059	.003	.035	.011	.050
n	47218	6176	65137	11027	88785	26152	99706	39379
Social/Behavioral Sciences	*Men*	*Women*	*Men*	*Women*	*Men*	*Women*	*Men*	*Women*
Full Time in Science	.870	.697	.832	.713	.810	.685	.796	.694
Full Time out of Science	.098	.081	.125	.101	.144	.122	.132	.103
Part Time	.024	.164	.030	.128	.036	.148	.059	.159
Seeking Work	.007	.031	.008	.025	.008	.019	.006	.008
Not Seeking Work	.002	.028	.004	.032	.002	.026	.008	.036
n	43793	7480	67100	16761	92385	39230	90829	50313

TABLE B-4 1973 Labor Force Participation Status, by Sex, Field, and Cohort

	1940 Ph.D.s		1950 Ph.D.s		1960 Ph.D.s		Total	
Engineering	*Men*	*Women*	*Men*	*Women*	*Men*	*Women*	*Men*	*Women*
Full Time in Science	.889	.667	.919	.444	.942	.745	.934	.695
Full Time out of Science	.072	.000	.063	.222	.039	.011	.047	.042
Part Time	.028	.000	.009	.222	.009	.128	.010	.136
Seeking Work	.008	.000	.008	.111	.007	.043	.008	.051
Not Seeking Work	.003	.333	.001	.000	.002	.074	.002	.076
n	2174	6	6667	18	23032	94	31873	118
Mathematical Sciences	*Men*	*Women*	*Men*	*Women*	*Men*	*Women*	*Men*	*Women*
Full Time in Science	.963	.732	.966	.817	.948	.761	.953	.768
Full Time out of Science	.023	.070	.028	.063	.028	.042	.028	.049
Part Time	.007	.127	.000	.079	.005	.122	.004	.115
Seeking Work	.007	.014	.006	.000	.015	.025	.012	.019
Not Seeking Work	.000	.056	.000	.040	.004	.050	.003	.049
n	828	71	2326	126	7487	523	10641	720
Physical Sciences	*Men*	*Women*	*Men*	*Women*	*Men*	*Women*	*Men*	*Women*
Full Time in Science	.871	.596	.911	.662	.915	.656	.907	.649
Full Time out of Science	.093	.135	.067	.089	.053	.048	.064	.07
Part Time	.016	.175	.007	.132	.014	.149	.012	.149
Seeking Work	.015	.023	.014	.043	.014	.070	.014	.057
Not Seeking Work	.005	.070	.001	.075	.004	.077	.003	.075
n	8579	342	15409	562	29534	1509	53522	2413

Life Sciences	*Men*	*Women*	*Men*	*Women*	*Men*	*Women*	*Men*	*Women*
Full Time in Science	.905	.719	.932	.737	.953	.759	.941	.75
Full Time out of Science	.054	.091	.048	.062	.028	.036	.037	.047
Part Time	.030	.099	.013	.094	.010	.107	.013	.103
Seeking Work	.008	.029	.003	.036	.006	.044	.006	.041
Not Seeking Work	.003	.062	.003	.072	.002	.054	.003	.059
n	5580	615	13076	1280	25263	3939	43919	5834
Social/Behavioral Sciences	*Men*	*Women*	*Men*	*Women*	*Men*	*Women*	*Men*	*Women*
Full Time in Science	.815	.708	.861	.677	.894	.709	.876	.702
Full Time out of Science	.144	.101	.111	.093	.079	.073	.095	.079
Part Time	.034	.174	.021	.178	.017	.156	.020	.162
Seeking Work	.005	.009	.005	.031	.009	.034	.007	.031
Not Seeking Work	.003	.009	.003	.021	.001	.028	.002	.025
n	4274	576	12433	1536	25439	5130	42146	7242

TABLE B-5 1979 Labor Force Participation Status, by Sex, Field, and Cohort

	1950 Ph.D.s		1960 Ph.D.s		1970 Ph.D.s		Total	
Engineering	*Men*	*Women*	*Men*	*Women*	*Men*	*Women*	*Men*	*Women*
Full Time in Science	.868	.769	.902	.625	.930	.857	.914	.822
Full Time out of Science	.079	.000	.071	.089	.047	.070	.058	.071
Part Time	.032	.231	.023	.143	.013	.041	.018	.061
Seeking Work	.003	.000	.002	.071	.007	.015	.005	.022
Not Seeking Work	.018	.000	.002	.071	.003	.018	.004	.024
n	4971	13	15127	56	25880	342	45978	411
Mathematical Sciences	*Men*	*Women*	*Men*	*Women*	*Men*	*Women*	*Men*	*Women*
Full Time in Science	.884	.762	.918	.765	.907	.809	.908	.796
Full Time out of Science	.084	.143	.068	.088	.061	.043	.066	.060
Part Time	.027	.060	.008	.078	.023	.081	.019	.079
Seeking Work	.000	.012	.000	.000	.005	.028	.003	.020
Not Seeking Work	.005	.024	.006	.068	.004	.04	.005	.045
n	1504	84	5055	294	8533	906	15092	1284
Physical Sciences	*Men*	*Women*	*Men*	*Women*	*Men*	*Women*	*Men*	*Women*
Full Time in Science	.865	.687	.902	.683	.932	.780	.909	.744
Full Time out of Science	.103	.118	.070	.101	.047	.051	.066	.072
Part Time	.024	.089	.017	.126	.010	.078	.015	.091
Seeking Work	.005	.016	.010	.034	.008	.034	.008	.032
Not Seeking Work	.003	.091	.001	.056	.003	.057	.002	.061
n	12911	451	23403	968	31363	2402	67677	3821

Life Sciences	*Men*	*Women*	*Men*	*Women*	*Men*	*Women*	*Men*	*Women*
Full Time in Science	.900	.668	.928	.742	.944	.824	.932	.791
Full Time out of Science	.068	.104	.051	.043	.032	.033	.044	.042
Part Time	.018	.076	.013	.141	.012	.060	.013	.080
Seeking Work	.010	.061	.007	.023	.008	.031	.008	.032
Not Seeking Work	.004	.091	.000	.050	.004	.051	.003	.054
n	10777	953	18451	2446	33295	7210	62523	10609
Social/Behavioral Sciences	*Men*	*Women*	*Men*	*Women*	*Men*	*Women*	*Men*	*Women*
Full Time in Science	.797	.682	.835	.720	.845	.721	.835	.719
Full Time out of Science	.151	.134	.130	.113	.115	.094	.124	.100
Part Time	.046	.140	.024	.117	.026	.126	.028	.125
Seeking Work	.001	.016	.008	.018	.011	.028	.008	.025
Not Seeking Work	.005	.028	.003	.031	.004	.030	.004	.030
n	9775	900	17372	2955	38455	12507	65602	16362

TABLE B-6 1989 Labor Force Participation Status, by Sex, Field, and Cohort

	1960 Ph.D.s		1970 Ph.D.s		1980 Ph.D.s		Total	
Engineering	*Men*	*Women*	*Men*	*Women*	*Men*	*Women*	*Men*	*Women*
Full Time in Science	.870	.714	.884	.796	.943	.867	.902	.848
Full Time out of Science	.107	.125	.081	.097	.044	.050	.074	.062
Part Time	.015	.107	.025	.077	.007	.057	.016	.062
Seeking Work	.003	.036	.010	.011	.003	.011	.006	.011
Not Seeking Work	.005	.018	.000	.019	.003	.016	.002	.016
n	14213	56	25783	362	22368	1415	62364	1833
Mathematical Sciences	*Men*	*Women*	*Men*	*Women*	*Men*	*Women*	*Men*	*Women*
Full Time in Science	.899	.754	.917	.809	.929	.812	.917	.804
Full Time out of Science	.078	.119	.070	.078	.059	.069	.068	.078
Part Time	.018	.077	.007	.071	.010	.079	.011	.076
Seeking Work	.003	.021	.003	.007	.002	.009	.003	.010
Not Seeking Work	.002	.028	.002	.034	.000	.032	.001	.032
n	4923	285	8846	970	7197	1270	20966	2525
Physical Sciences	*Men*	*Women*	*Men*	*Women*	*Men*	*Women*	*Men*	*Women*
Full Time in Science	.896	.746	.895	.782	.939	.832	.910	.807
Full Time out of Science	.076	.099	.085	.086	.041	.049	.068	.066
Part Time	.025	.088	.012	.082	.007	.054	.014	.067
Seeking Work	.001	.010	.005	.014	.010	.026	.005	.020
Not Seeking Work	.002	.057	.003	.036	.002	.039	.002	.040
n	21906	879	32027	2420	25329	4528	79262	7827

Life Sciences	*Men*	*Women*	*Men*	*Women*	*Men*	*Women*	*Men*	*Women*
Full Time in Science	.909	.705	.901	.779	.940	.838	.918	.808
Full Time out of Science	.073	.108	.075	.087	.037	.047	.060	.065
Part Time	.013	.145	.010	.087	.014	.063	.012	.078
Seeking Work	.002	.010	.011	.014	.005	.018	.007	.016
Not Seeking Work	.003	.033	.002	.033	.004	.034	.003	.034
n	16330	2111	34684	8078	31891	15359	82905	25548
Social/Behavioral Sciences	*Men*	*Women*	*Men*	*Women*	*Men*	*Women*	*Men*	*Women*
Full Time in Science	.801	.696	.823	.661	.818	.698	.817	.686
Full Time out of Science	.156	.143	.145	.150	.142	.105	.145	.122
Part Time	.035	.128	.024	.131	.027	.158	.027	.147
Seeking Work	.005	.011	.007	.017	.013	.021	.009	.019
Not Seeking Work	.003	.021	.002	.041	.000	.019	.002	.027
n	15764	2553	38771	12921	32248	23054	86783	38528

TABLE B-7 1995 Labor Force Participation Status, by Sex, Field, and Cohort

	1970 Ph.D.s		1980 Ph.D.s		1990 Ph.D.s		Total	
Engineering	*Men*	*Women*	*Men*	*Women*	*Men*	*Women*	*Men*	*Women*
Full Time in Science	.874	.864	.929	.803	.952	.811	.918	.813
Full Time out of Science	.069	.000	.042	.041	.025	.050	.046	.043
Part Time	.031	.089	.012	.065	.010	.064	.018	.066
Seeking Work	.011	.047	.015	.059	.010	.027	.012	.040
Not Seeking Work	.015	.000	.003	.032	.002	.047	.007	.038
n	21947	361	23688	1480	19655	2553	65290	4394
Mathematical Sciences	*Men*	*Women*	*Men*	*Women*	*Men*	*Women*	*Men*	*Women*
Full Time in Science	.900	.794	.927	.698	.909	.911	.911	.801
Full Time out of Science	.053	.031	.028	.093	.052	.024	.044	.052
Part Time	.034	.096	.021	.176	.021	.045	.026	.107
Seeking Work	.004	.026	.009	.000	.015	.000	.009	.006
Not Seeking Work	.009	.054	.015	.034	.004	.020	.010	.033
n	8396	897	7508	1416	6179	1389	22083	3702
Physical Sciences	*Men*	*Women*	*Men*	*Women*	*Men*	*Women*	*Men*	*Women*
Full Time in Science	.875	.702	.917	.769	.894	.830	.895	.780
Full Time out of Science	.076	.150	.044	.089	.052	.051	.059	.087
Part Time	.025	.049	.013	.051	.030	.052	.022	.051
Seeking Work	.011	.015	.013	.011	.016	.034	.013	.021
Not Seeking Work	.013	.083	.013	.079	.009	.033	.012	.062
n	30327	2267	25962	4753	15716	4474	72005	11494

Life Sciences	*Men*	*Women*	*Men*	*Women*	*Men*	*Women*	*Men*	*Women*
Full Time in Science	.848	.733	.886	.75	.892	.792	.873	.762
Full Time out of Science	.104	.114	.09	.116	.076	.105	.092	.112
Part Time	.019	.089	.007	.067	.015	.046	.013	.064
Seeking Work	.012	.011	.010	.014	.014	.016	.012	.014
Not Seeking Work	.016	.053	.006	.053	.003	.040	.009	.048
n	32398	7809	32230	15867	18892	13797	83520	37473
Social/Behavioral Sciences	*Men*	*Women*	*Men*	*Women*	*Men*	*Women*	*Men*	*Women*
Full Time in Science	.808	.671	.814	.703	.813	.705	.811	.696
Full Time out of Science	.140	.125	.133	.098	.134	.091	.136	.102
Part Time	.041	.158	.039	.156	.039	.162	.039	.158
Seeking Work	.003	.007	.009	.005	.011	.009	.007	.007
Not Seeking Work	.009	.039	.006	.040	.003	.033	.007	.037
n	33058	11125	29532	21113	13966	15578	76556	47816

TABLE B-8 Reasons for Part-Time Employment, by Sex and Year of Survey

1989	No Job Available	No Need to Work	Family Obligations	*n*
Men	.296	.527	.047	7917
Women	.187	.319	.470	8573

1995	No Job Available	No Need to Work	Family Obligations	*n*
Men	.246	.316	.042	15377
Women	.188	.416	.518	11992

TABLE B-9 Reasons for Part-Time Employment, by Cohort, Sex, and Year of Survey

	1989	Older	Middle	Younger
Men	*No Job*	.312	.375	.470
	No Need	.519	.455	.300
	Family	.075	.055	.043
	N	1561	2232	1694
Women	*No Job*	.212	.179	.189
	No Need	.488	.348	.257
	Family	.203	.466	.539
	N	730	2656	4887

	1995	Older	Middle	Younger
Men	*No Job*	.308	.475	.577
	No Need	.282	.221	.212
	Family	.060	.112	.023
	N	3655	2137	1630
Women	*No Job*	.198	.160	.236
	No Need	.462	.432	.354
	Family	.388	.629	.549
	N	2678	4948	3614

TABLE B-10 Reasons for Part-Time Employment, Field, Sex, and Year of Survey

			Engineering	Mathematical Sciences	Physical Sciences	Life Sciences	Social/Behavioral Sciences
1989	**Men**	*No Job*	.285	.102	.355	.371	.257
		No Need	.515	.625	.475	.454	.581
		Family	.042	.050	.058	.037	.048
		N	1345	323	1729	1362	3158
	Women	*No Job*	.181	.193	.222	.239	.164
		No Need	.060	.278	.258	.259	.354
		Family	.724	.503	.508	.456	.465
		N	116	187	563	2032	5675
1995	**Men**	*No Job*	.302	.197	.324	.162	.225
		No Need	.328	.432	.291	.281	.335
		Family	.042	.028	.023	.043	.057
		N	2193	773	3822	3226	5363
	Women	*No Job*	.366	.362	.202	.229	.157
		No Need	.414	.298	.331	.430	.425
		Family	.493	.431	.432	.487	.540
		N	292	420	673	2591	8016

TABLE B-11 Reasons for Part-Time Employment, by Field, Cohort, Sex, and Year of Survey

			Older		Middle		Younger	
			Men	*Women*	*Men*	*Women*	*Men*	*Women*
1989	**Engineering**	*No Job*	.248	.833	.352	.000	.503	.175
		No Need	.371	.000	.486	.179	.252	.025
		Family	.190	.167	.000	.821	.112	.750
		N	210	6	640	28	143	80
	Mathematics	*No Job*	.182	.200	.000	.215	.246	.174
		No Need	.477	.350	.552	.369	.261	.163
		Family	.000	.450	.448	.415	.043	.609
		N	88	20	29	65	69	92
	Physical Sciences	*No Job*	.517	.338	.499	.161	.538	.230
		No Need	.383	.442	.298	.327	.321	.071
		Family	.083	.182	.100	.528	.011	.690
		N	540	77	379	199	184	239
	Life Sciences	*No Job*	.173	.225	.356	.240	.713	.242
		No Need	.631	.376	.413	.247	.226	.191
		Family	.000	.281	.054	.479	.041	.544
		N	214	306	315	691	442	937
	Social/ Behavioral Sciences	*No Job*	.202	.159	.358	.158	.343	.172
		No Need	.684	.623	.512	.393	.345	.295
		Family	.063	.118	.063	.449	.040	.520
		N	509	321	869	1673	856	3539
1995	**Engineering**	*No Job*	.308	.375	.633	.281	.610	.415
		No Need	.375	.125	.076	.500	.346	.421
		Family	.104	.625	.080	.677	.000	.360
		N	672	32	275	96	205	164
	Mathematics	*No Job*	.256	.302	.076	.378	.515	.516
		No Need	.463	.465	.335	.341	.400	.000
		Family	.060	.221	.000	.586	.038	.161
		N	285	86	158	249	130	62
	Physical Sciences	*No Job*	.509	.196	.762	.128	.741	.343
		No Need	.196	.723	.053	.370	.211	.197
		Family	.066	.438	.062	.716	.000	.292
		N	745	112	341	243	464	233
	Life Sciences	*No Job*	.291	.266	.619	.182	.469	.327
		No Need	.180	.405	.164	.476	.197	.385
		Family	.029	.350	.044	.627	.114	.512
		N	611	692	226	1071	290	633
	Social/ Behavioral Sciences	*No Job*	.214	.162	.378	.136	.495	.185
		No Need	.291	.473	.303	.428	.126	.365
		Family	.050	.404	.164	.625	.000	.603
		N	1342	1756	1137	3289	541	2522

TABLE B-12 Predicted Probabilities of Working, by Familial Status and Year of Survey. Based on Multinomial Logit Analyses of Labor Force Participation Status

			Full Time in Science	Full Time Outside Science	Part Time	Seeking Work	Not Seeking Work
Men	**1979**	*Single*	.894	.053	.029	.017	.008
		Married	.920	.057	.016	.005	.002
		Older Children	.927	.058	.010	.004	.001
		Younger Children	.921	.060	.015	.003	.001
	1989	*Single*	.888	.075	.019	.012	.006
		Married	.911	.070	.012	.005	.002
		Older Children	.920	.069	.006	.004	.001
		Younger Children	.925	.061	.010	.003	.001
	1995	*Single*	.854	.085	.024	.023	.014
		Married	.907	.064	.015	.009	.006
		Older Children	.916	.061	.011	.008	.004
		Younger Children	.914	.061	.011	.010	.005

			Full Time in Science	Full Time Outside Science	Part Time	Seeking Work	Not Seeking Work
Women	**1979**	*Single*	.837	.083	.054	.016	.011
		Married	.770	.065	.100	.030	.035
		Older Children	.674	.058	.169	.027	.071
		Younger Children	.559	.051	.198	.044	.148
	1989	*Single*	.860	.088	.034	.011	.008
		Married	.804	.081	.077	.017	.021
		Older Children	.697	.074	.152	.017	.061
		Younger Children	.642	.061	.192	.019	.087
	1995	*Single*	.822	.115	.037	.013	.013
		Married	.789	.096	.067	.011	.037
		Older Children	.714	.089	.124	.010	.062
		Younger Children	.646	.068	.167	.013	.106

TABLE B-13 1979 Mean Work Experience. by Sex, Year of Ph.D., and Marital Status

Ph.D. Year.	Men								Women							
	Total		*Single*		*Married without Children*		*Children at Home*		*Total*		*Single*		*Married without Children*		*Cat Home hildren*	
	Mean	*n*	*Mean*	*n*	*Mean*	*n*	*Mean*	*n*	*Mean*	*n*	*Mean*	*n*	*Mean*	*n*	*Mean*	*n*
57	21.9	2704	21.7	293	21.9	1352	21.9	1059	20.7	199	21.8	91	20.9	68	17.6	40
58	20.6	4115	20.4	428	20.7	1330	20.7	2357	18.8	268	20.6	122	18.7	58	16.3	88
59	19.7	4144	18.7	496	19.9	1352	19.7	2296	17.6	273	19.6	98	18.2	58	15.6	117
60	18.8	4439	18.6	485	18.9	1055	18.8	2899	16.9	300	17.9	164	17.6	59	14.2	77
61	17.7	5304	17.8	607	17.6	1296	17.8	3401	16.1	326	17.5	161	17.6	75	12.3	90
62	16.4	5282	16.0	544	16.9	1201	16.3	3537	15.2	391	16.9	155	16.7	81	12.6	155
63	15.6	5886	14.9	453	15.7	1044	15.6	4389	13.6	563	14.7	215	15.4	100	12.0	248
64	14.6	6951	14.7	746	14.3	1123	14.7	5082	13.2	557	14.3	195	13.0	115	12.3	247
65	13.7	7657	13.6	770	13.8	1223	13.6	5664	12.3	699	13.4	261	13.1	129	10.9	309
66	12.8	9343	12.8	1335	12.9	1544	12.7	6464	11.2	863	12.4	288	12.1	156	10.0	419
67	11.8	9417	11.7	880	11.9	1302	11.8	7235	10.2	1022	11.5	343	11.6	147	8.9	532
68	10.7	10146	10.9	1410	10.8	1033	10.7	7703	9.4	1044	10.2	388	10.6	194	8.3	462
69	9.6	11793	9.4	1829	9.6	1370	9.7	8594	8.6	1246	9.0	421	9.0	302	7.9	523
70	8.7	12846	8.5	2188	8.8	1543	8.7	9115	7.9	1339	8.4	508	8.4	273	7.2	558
71	7.7	14044	7.5	1904	7.6	2017	7.8	10123	7.3	1674	7.6	503	7.7	439	6.8	732
72	6.7	13066	6.5	1907	6.7	2006	6.8	9153	6.2	2022	6.3	709	6.3	529	6.0	784
73	5.6	11630	5.4	1725	5.4	1789	5.7	8116	5.4	1937	5.7	647	5.4	448	5.2	842
74	4.8	11892	4.7	2318	4.7	2334	4.9	7240	4.5	2216	4.7	927	4.5	505	4.3	784
75	3.8	11037	3.8	2689	3.8	2134	3.8	6214	3.6	2509	3.7	913	3.5	782	3.5	814
76	2.8	10003	2.8	2461	2.6	2223	2.9	5319	2.8	2379	2.8	1054	2.8	544	2.7	781
77	1.9	10808	1.8	2872	1.9	3446	1.9	4490	1.9	2514	1.9	995	1.9	615	1.9	904
78	1.0	6862	0.9	1876	1.0	1852	1.0	3134	0.9	1804	1.0	667	0.9	552	0.9	585

TABLE B-14 1989 Mean Work Experience. by Sex, Year of Ph.D., and Marital Status

	Men								Women							
	Total		*Single*		*Married without Children*		*Children at Home*		*Total*		*Single*		*Married without Children*		*Cat Home hildren*	
Ph.D. Year.	*Mean*	*n*	*Mean*	*n*	*Mean*	*n*	*Mean*	*n*	*Mean*	*n*	*Mean*	*n*	*Mean*	*n*	*Mean*	*n*
67	21.4	10083	21.0	1326	21.6	5870	21.0	2887	18.2	1002	20.3	336	18.0	472	15.3	194
68	20.3	12044	20.2	1334	20.3	6902	20.4	3808	17.5	1071	18.6	370	17.9	422	15.2	279
69	19.4	13321	19.1	1056	19.4	7146	19.5	5119	17.4	1265	18.4	424	17.0	488	16.9	353
70	18.2	14773	17.6	1888	18.3	6891	18.4	5994	16.4	1469	17.8	562	15.6	550	15.5	357
71	17.5	15462	17.5	1491	17.4	7215	17.7	6756	15.9	1946	16.3	622	16.3	816	15.0	508
72	16.4	14738	16.1	1807	16.5	6694	16.2	6237	15.1	2180	16.0	669	15.3	906	13.8	605
73	15.3	13656	14.8	1823	15.6	5004	15.3	6829	14.0	2387	14.5	731	13.9	872	13.6	784
74	14.4	14637	14.0	1810	14.4	5793	14.4	7034	13.5	2495	13.7	782	14.1	848	12.6	865
75	13.5	12904	12.9	1561	13.6	4081	13.6	7262	12.0	2830	13.2	829	11.6	991	11.4	1010
76	12.4	11995	11.6	1964	12.4	3539	12.5	6492	11.5	3009	11.9	918	11.6	936	11.1	1155
77	11.3	13865	10.7	1781	11.5	4499	11.4	7585	10.5	3024	11.0	843	11.1	1007	9.7	1174
78	10.4	12763	10.1	1806	10.4	3497	10.5	7460	9.3	3601	9.6	1022	9.6	1092	8.9	1487
79	9.5	12094	9.1	1871	9.6	3472	9.6	6751	8.8	3703	9.2	1217	9.0	1202	8.4	1284
80	8.5	12823	8.2	1850	8.5	3681	8.5	7292	8.0	4085	8.4	1305	7.9	1081	7.8	1699
81	7.6	12190	7.5	1830	7.6	2941	7.7	7419	7.1	4172	7.6	1393	7.2	1133	6.5	1646
82	6.6	12244	6.4	2424	6.4	3257	6.7	6563	6.1	4524	6.2	1182	6.2	1498	5.9	1844
83	5.4	12311	5.2	2543	5.3	3281	5.6	6487	5.0	4799	5.4	1340	5.2	1421	4.7	2038
84	4.6	11580	4.4	2865	4.8	2916	4.6	5799	4.3	4578	4.5	1502	4.5	1350	3.8	1726
85	3.7	11810	3.6	3075	3.6	3436	3.8	5299	3.5	4906	3.7	1916	3.4	1333	3.4	1657
86	2.7	11740	2.7	3379	2.7	3523	2.8	4838	2.6	5249	2.7	1656	2.6	2122	2.4	1471
87	1.8	12700	1.8	4224	1.9	3763	1.8	4713	1.7	5519	1.8	2117	1.8	2031	1.6	1371
88	1.1	7062	1.0	2371	1.1	2418	1.1	2273	1.0	3011	1.0	1155	1.0	1134	0.9	722

Appendix C

Tables

TABLE C-1 Percent Working Full Time in Each Sector, by Sex and Year of Survey

		1973		1979		1989		1995	
		Men	*Women*	*Men*	*Women*	*Men*	*Women*	*Men*	*Women*
Colleges and Universities	*N*	104,553	8,970	134,911	16,878	167,638	35,370	163,145	47,252
	%	56.0	67.8	52.2	61.4	48.7	54.0	45.0	51.38
Government	*N*	21,318	1,312	27,941	2,362	33,264	5,287	37,236	9,208
	%	11.4	9.9	10.8	8.6	9.7	8.1	10.3	10.0
Industry	*N*	47,829	960	72,286	3,470	116,528	15,174	135,486	24,121
	%	25.6	7.3	28.0	12.6	33.9	23.2	37.3	26.2
Private Nonprofit and Hospitals	*N*	9,973	1,275	16,614	3,138	18,889	6,655	16,057	5,796
	%	5.3	9.6	6.4	11.4	5.5	10.2	4.4	6.3
Other	*N*	2,884	653	4,208	1,224	5,904	2,381	8,141	4,338
	%	1.5	4.9	1.6	4.5	1.7	3.6	2.2	4.7
Missing Data	*N*	314	68	2,387	399	1,911	583	2,894	1,254
	%	0.17	0.5	0.9	1.5	0.6	0.9	0.8	1.4
Total	*N*	186,871	13,238	258,347	27,471	344,134	65,450	362,959	91,969
	%	100.0	100.0	100.0	100.0	100.0	100.0	100.0	100.0

Note: Counts are weighted. *Other* is primarily education at below the level of a two-year college. *Missing Data* indicates that respondent did not respond to the questions or their response was unusable.

TABLE C-2 Percent Working Full Time in Various Work Activities, by Sex and Year of Survey

		1973		1979		1989		1995	
		Men	*Women*	*Men*	*Women*	*Men*	*Women*	*Men*	*Women*
Teaching	*N*	66,743	6,008	73,784	9,276	83,539	17,388	76,136	22,575
	%	35.7	45.4	28.6	33.8	24.3	26.6	21.0	24.6
Basic Research	*N*	27,994	2,883	38,634	5,610	52,131	12,016	50,429	14,331
	%	15.0	21.8	15.0	20.4	15.2	18.4	13.9	15.6
Applied Research	*N*	26,094	840	32,538	2,072	64,790	9,181	77,288	16,519
	%	14.0	6.4	12.6	7.5	18.8	14.0	21.3	18.0
Production	*N*	13,001	340	26,845	1,241	40,707	3,792	45,140	5,878
	%	7.0	2.6	10.4	4.5	11.8	5.8	12.4	6.4
Management	*N*	41,175	1,565	62,425	4,437	59,816	9,116	46,953	9,102
	%	22.0	11.8	24.2	16.2	17.4	13.9	12.9	9.9
Professional Services	*N*	4,584	1,003	12,181	3,092	20,926	9,463	36,910	17,713
	%	2.5	7.6	4.7	11.3	6.1	14.5	10.2	19.3
Other Work Activities	*N*	4,391	397	8,564	1,042	19,223	3,568	29,254	5,112
	%	2.4	3.0	3.3	3.8	5.6	5.5	8.1	5.6
Missing Data	*N*	2,889	202	3,376	701	3,002	926	849	739
	%	1.6	1.5	1.3	2.6	0.9	1.4	0.2	0.8
Total	*N*	186,871	13,238	258,347	27,471	344,134	65,450	362,959	91,969
	%	100.0	100.0	100.0	100.0	100.0	100.0	100.0	100.0

Note: Counts are weighted.

TABLE C-3 Percent Working Full Time in Each Sector, by Sex, Field and Year of Survey

	Women				Men			
	1973	*1979*	*1989*	*1995*	*1973*	*1979*	*1989*	*1995*
Engineering								
Academia	47.1	43.1	41.3	42.2	38.7	36.0	36.1	32.2
Industry	35.6	44.7	46.1	46.2	46.2	49.8	53.5	57.0
Government	9.2	9.0	8.0	8.3	10.4	9.6	7.2	7.0
PNP/Hospitals	5.8	2.7	3.8	2.1	4.0	4.0	3.0	2.8
Other Education	2.3	0.5	0.8	1.2	0.8	0.7	0.2	1.0
N	87	367	1,671	3,778	31,717	45,315	63,212	72,496
Mathematics								
Academia	88.0	73.1	67.7	60.6	81.7	72.4	66.1	60.9
Industry	3.4	14.5	23.1	21.9	10.1	17.0	25.5	29.6
Government	3.5	3.4	3.6	5.9	5.3	5.8	4.3	4.2
PNP/Hospitals	1.9	4.5	2.3	3.2	2.1	2.5	2.4	3.0
Other Education	3.2	4.6	3.3	8.5	0.8	2.2	1.8	2.3
N	627	1,132	2,270	3,290	10,925	15,241	21,570	24,827
Physical Sciences								
Academia	60.6	48.0	39.4	39.8	42.0	40.1	38.5	37.6
Industry	17.7	28.9	40.8	43.5	39.9	42.2	46.3	45.7
Government	10.0	9.7	10.0	8.0	11.7	10.6	9.8	10.1
PNP/Hospitals	6.5	7.2	5.3	3.2	4.6	4.8	3.9	4.1
Other Education	5.2	6.3	4.5	5.6	1.9	2.3	1.5	2.5
N	1,814	3,239	7,095	10,543	55,990	70,367	84,777	87,228

Life Sciences								
Academia	70.2	68.0	62.1	59.5	65.4	62.2	56.3	53.1
Industry	5.7	7.7	17.4	19.9	13.2	15.2	23.1	27.3
Government	10.7	9.5	9.0	10.4	14.6	13.8	12.5	12.2
PNP/Hospitals	8.9	10.0	8.4	5.4	5.2	6.3	5.7	4.3
Other Education	4.5	4.8	3.2	4.9	1.6	2.5	2.4	3.0
N	4,893	9,078	22,754	34,263	45,874	63,157	86,440	94,175
Social/Behavioral								
Academia	66.0	59.8	51.2	47.6	70.5	62.3	55.9	49.7
Industry	5.3	11.0	22.2	25.6	8.8	12.2	20.5	25.2
Government	9.9	8.2	7.3	10.7	9.9	10.2	9.8	12.8
PNP/Hospitals	12.2	14.2	13.4	8.5	8.3	11.1	9.4	6.6
Other Education	6.6	6.8	5.8	7.5	2.5	4.3	4.5	5.6
N	5,817	13,655	31,660	40,095	42,365	64,267	88,135	84,233

TABLE C-4 Number Working Full Time in Each Sector, by Sex, Field and Year of Survey

	Women				Men			
	1973	*1979*	*1989*	*1995*	*1973*	*1979*	*1989*	*1995*
Engineering								
Academia	41	158	690	1,593	12,271	16,310	22,816	23,332
Industry	31	164	771	1,746	14,638	22,569	33,819	41,306
Government	8	33	133	314	3,282	4,333	4,558	5,075
PNP/Hospitals	5	10	63	79	1,277	1,790	1,878	2,051
Other Education	1	2	7	13	190	81	40	425
N	86	367	1,664	3,745	31,658	45,083	63,111	72,189
Mathematics								
Academia	552	827	1,537	1,993	8,929	11,040	14,252	15,121
Industry	21	164	524	720	1,102	2,596	5,505	7,344
Government	22	38	82	193	578	887	921	1,051
PNP/Hospitals	12	51	52	105	231	386	512	743
Other Education	19	47	64	247	85	254	343	456
N	626	1,127	2,259	3,258	10,925	15,163	21,533	24,715
Physical Sciences								
Academia	1,100	1,555	2,798	4,193	23,494	28,241	32,640	32,808
Industry	321	935	2,893	4,583	22,312	29,683	39,220	39,850
Government	181	313	711	844	6,541	7,459	8,325	8,796
PNP/Hospitals	118	233	376	334	2,559	3,359	3,338	3,613
Other Education	90	170	235	529	1,025	1,113	1,069	1,770
N	1,810	3,206	7,013	10,483	55,931	69,855	84,592	86,837

Life Sciences								
Academia	3,436	6,175	14,124	20,373	30,002	39,282	48,683	50,023
Industry	279	700	3,953	6,803	6,068	9,621	19,947	25,728
Government	523	860	2,045	3,551	6,711	8,702	10,835	11,503
PNP/Hospitals	433	911	1,909	1,852	2,384	3,960	4,885	4,084
Other Education	206	254	514	1,158	588	1,067	1,435	2,103
N	4,877	8,900	22,545	33,737	45,753	62,632	85,785	93,441
Social/Behavioral								
Academia	3,841	8,163	16,221	19,100	29,857	40,038	49,247	41,861
Industry	308	1,507	7,033	10,269	3,709	7,817	18,037	21,258
Government	578	1,118	2,316	4,306	4,206	6,560	8,625	10,811
PNP/Hospitals	707	1,933	4,255	3,426	3,522	7,119	8,276	5,566
Other Education	337	751	1,561	2,391	996	1,693	3,017	3,387
N	5,771	13,472	31,386	39,492	42,290	63,227	87,202	82,883

TABLE C-5 Percent in Each Work Activity in Academia, by Sex, Field and Year of Survey

	Women				Men			
	1973	*1979*	*1989*	*1995*	*1973*	*1979*	*1989*	*1995*
Engineering								
Teaching	65.9	54.8	47.9	49.0	68.0	54.8	51.4	48.2
Basic Research	4.9	19.8	21.1	10.4	7.1	7.8	10.1	11.9
Applied Research	19.5	14.0	25.6	28.6	10.5	15.7	21.8	26.2
Production	0.0	3.8	1.6	1.1	1.3	1.2	1.5	3.9
Administration	9.8	7.6	3.4	10.4	13.1	20.5	14.9	8.6
Professional Services	0.0	0.0	0.4	0.5	0.1	0.0	0.3	1.4
N	41	157	677	1,542	12,016	16,198	22,456	22,668
Mathematics								
Teaching	86.1	74.5	69.6	65.0	76.7	69.6	61.3	65.5
Basic Research	8.2	13.1	16.1	19.4	14.6	14.9	23.6	18.2
Applied Research	1.9	3.8	6.7	10.6	1.5	2.7	5.4	7.3
Production	1.1	2.9	0.5	1.7	0.6	0.9	1.2	1.1
Administration	2.8	5.4	7.0	3.4	6.7	11.8	8.4	6.2
Professional Services	0.0	0.3	0.0	0.0	0.0	0.2	0.1	1.6
N	538	815	1,485	1,916	8,804	10,873	14,028	14,607
Physical Sciences								
Teaching	59.6	44.0	41.9	45.2	62.9	49.7	44.6	38.8
Basic Research	29.2	38.5	38.8	31.8	24.0	25.9	31.8	33.2
Applied Research	3.3	4.9	9.8	13.6	3.4	6.5	12.0	15.2
Production	0.7	1.3	1.1	2.1	1.0	2.5	1.5	2.7
Administration	5.9	10.6	7.3	5.4	8.8	15.2	9.4	8.3
Professional Services	1.5	0.7	1.2	2.0	0.0	0.3	0.8	1.9
N	1,076	1,506	2,705	3,958	22,993	27,775	32,033	31,451

Life Sciences								
Teaching	48.3	39.8	32.5	31.9	48.6	37.7	30.3	27.8
Basic Research	39.0	42.2	43.9	37.7	27.2	33.6	38.9	37.1
Applied Research	4.7	5.0	11.7	15.9	10.9	10.4	16.4	18.0
Production	0.2	0.5	0.5	1.5	0.8	0.8	0.6	1.5
Administration	7.1	11.0	8.0	6.6	11.5	14.8	9.8	8.3
Professional Services	0.8	1.5	3.3	6.4	1.0	2.7	4.0	7.3
N	3,351	5,971	13,794	20,056	28,873	38,141	46,979	48,880
Social/Behavioral								
Teaching	75.1	62.6	57.7	52.4	71.4	66.3	62.6	58.7
Basic Research	7.8	12.4	14.5	13.0	8.8	8.4	12.7	12.8
Applied Research	2.5	6.0	9.2	14.2	5.1	5.8	7.5	12.5
Production	1.5	0.8	0.4	1.1	0.6	0.9	0.8	1.4
Administration	9.4	14.5	12.6	9.4	12.5	16.2	13.5	9.3
Professional Services	3.7	3.8	5.6	10.0	1.5	2.4	3.0	5.3
N	3,723	7,791	15,716	18,697	28,904	38,742	47,771	41,052

TABLE C-6 Percent in Each Work Activity in Industry, by Sex, Field and Year of Survey

	Women				Men			
	1973	*1979*	*1989*	*1995*	*1973*	*1979*	*1989*	*1995*
Engineering								
Teaching	0.0	0.0	0.4	0.0	0.0	0.3	0.6	0.4
Basic Research	7.1	3.2	5.5	1.2	1.8	3.6	2.7	1.4
Applied Research	21.4	32.3	37.1	33.1	26.8	17.0	28.2	25.6
Production	46.4	41.3	35.7	40.3	34.7	40.7	42.4	45.9
Administration	25.0	21.9	20.7	17.0	36.4	37.0	25.1	21.7
Professional Services	0.0	1.3	0.6	8.5	0.3	1.5	1.1	4.9
N	28	155	704	1,428	14,100	21,783	31,509	35,091
Mathematics								
Teaching	0.0	0.0	0.8	0.0	0.6	0.6	1.5	0.7
Basic Research	20.0	8.0	7.2	0.9	4.4	3.2	6.6	5.3
Applied Research	53.3	17.9	20.9	59.0	31.4	17.1	23.8	34.2
Production	26.7	53.0	39.7	23.3	29.8	44.8	43.5	33.0
Administration	0.0	19.9	30.4	9.5	31.1	31.5	24.1	20.1
Professional Services	0.0	1.3	1.0	7.4	2.7	2.8	0.6	6.8
N	15	151	388	473	1,080	2,436	4,421	4,354
Physical Sciences								
Teaching	0.0	0.2	0.3	0.7	0.1	0.1	0.2	0.3
Basic Research	19.6	16.5	6.8	2.8	10.4	9.8	4.2	4.5
Applied Research	44.1	28.0	48.1	47.8	30.4	22.6	39.4	37.3
Production	14.6	20.0	25.8	30.6	16.5	24.6	29.6	31.8
Administration	19.9	31.9	17.9	10.0	41.7	41.7	26.0	19.9
Professional Services	1.8	3.5	1.1	8.2	0.8	1.3	0.6	6.3
N	281	869	2,626	4,071	21,294	28,192	36,342	35,157

Life Sciences								
Teaching	0.0	0.0	0.8	1.1	0.2	0.4	0.4	0.9
Basic Research	30.8	16.0	6.8	6.6	8.2	5.9	4.1	4.9
Applied Research	23.5	22.4	37.0	36.9	17.8	15.5	33.4	35.4
Production	16.2	16.7	24.9	23.2	17.0	28.7	28.1	23.9
Administration	25.2	32.4	23.3	14.0	51.3	41.9	27.5	18.1
Professional Services	4.3	12.6	7.2	18.3	5.6	7.7	6.5	16.9
N	234	652	3,441	6,241	5,783	8,849	18,039	24,031
Social/Behavioral								
Teaching	1.6	0.4	0.3	1.9	1.3	0.0	0.8	0.7
Basic Research	1.2	0.9	0.6	0.7	3.1	1.5	0.4	0.4
Applied Research	10.6	8.5	8.2	8.5	13.4	14.2	8.2	14.2
Production	12.1	11.6	16.0	8.5	22.7	23.9	27.3	13.8
Administration	18.8	8.3	8.4	6.4	31.3	18.7	12.8	10.2
Professional Services	55.9	70.2	66.5	74.0	28.1	41.7	50.6	60.6
N	256	1,383	6,368	9,891	3,379	7,362	15,532	19,294

TABLE C-7 Percent in Each Work Activity in Government, by Sex, Field and Year of Survey

	Women				Men			
	1973	*1979*	*1989*	*1995*	*1973*	*1979*	*1989*	*1995*
Engineering								
Teaching	0.0	0.0	0.0	0.0	4.5	2.6	1.0	0.1
Basic Research	28.6	0.0	17.0	14.1	7.5	9.1	7.9	7.9
Applied Research	14.3	26.9	44.3	43.4	32.2	23.4	34.1	46.5
Production	57.1	23.1	4.7	7.2	9.3	10.4	19.1	12.6
Administration	0.0	46.2	34.0	22.8	46.3	54.2	38.0	27.8
Professional Services	0.0	3.9	0.0	12.6	0.2	0.4	0.0	5.0
N	7	26	106	263	3,063	3,974	4,271	4,524
Mathematics								
Teaching	0.0	0.0	0.0	0.0	4.4	0.0	0.0	0.0
Basic Research	5.0	0.0	12.1	11.3	12.9	6.1	6.5	16.4
Applied Research	25.0	6.3	24.1	12.0	38.5	39.9	46.2	47.7
Production	15.0	50.0	15.5	18.7	12.3	22.0	11.9	13.0
Administration	55.0	43.8	48.3	52.0	30.9	29.6	35.4	17.1
Professional Services	0.0	0.0	0.0	6.0	1.1	2.4	0.0	5.9
N	20	32	58	150	551	874	613	709
Physical Sciences								
Teaching	0.6	0.0	0.5	0.0	1.7	1.1	0.9	0.4
Basic Research	45.9	37.9	32.7	36.9	34.5	28.3	23.8	20.0
Applied Research	29.4	12.8	29.8	47.6	24.1	24.5	33.9	42.9
Production	0.6	13.8	11.0	4.1	6.0	12.1	7.7	8.8
Administration	17.7	34.1	24.3	10.5	33.4	32.5	32.9	22.7
Professional Services	5.9	1.4	1.7	0.9	0.3	1.5	0.8	5.2
N	170	290	584	555	6,195	6,882	7,646	7,553

Life Sciences								
Teaching	1.6	2.1	1.5	0.2	1.2	0.4	0.9	0.6
Basic Research	52.6	45.8	32.5	22.7	30.2	31.4	25.7	23.5
Applied Research	18.6	11.9	25.6	30.6	28.5	25.4	34.4	39.1
Production	3.9	10.6	6.2	8.4	2.7	5.0	4.0	5.3
Administration	22.1	25.3	31.3	22.2	35.5	35.2	32.4	22.1
Professional Services	1.2	4.3	3.0	15.9	1.9	2.7	2.7	9.5
N	489	771	1,793	3,098	6,385	8,064	9,496	10,181
Social/Behavioral								
Teaching	5.4	0.0	1.1	0.6	2.8	1.1	4.8	0.8
Basic Research	7.4	7.1	3.8	3.1	7.8	5.6	2.8	3.9
Applied Research	11.5	17.5	26.0	21.7	16.0	21.7	26.1	23.5
Production	2.4	11.5	6.9	3.8	3.9	8.8	7.2	8.8
Administration	37.3	45.7	44.0	20.7	55.3	47.2	43.9	23.9
Professional Services	36.0	18.3	18.3	50.1	14.2	15.6	15.3	39.2
N	539	991	2,025	3,708	3,781	5,449	6,718	9,272

Appendix D

Tables

TABLE D-1 Percent Working Full Time in Academia of All Ph.D.s and All Ph.D.s Who Are Working Full Time, by Sex, Field and Year of Survey

		1973		1979		1989		1995	
		Men	*Women*	*Men*	*Women*	*Men*	*Women*	*Men*	*Women*
Engineering	*% of Ph.D.s*	36.7	32.3	34.5	37.4	33.3	37.3	28.5	35.8
	n	33442	127	47329	422	68482	1852	82512	4447
	% of FT	38.7	47.1	36	43.1	36.1	41.3	32.4	42.2
	n	31717	87	45315	367	63212	1671	72496	3778
Mathematics	*% of Ph.D.s*	76.2	63.5	68.2	59.2	62.1	57.8	54.9	50
	n	11719	869	16180	1397	22966	2659	27727	4008
	% of FT	81.7	88	72.4	73.1	66.1	67.7	61.3	60.9
	n	10925	627	15241	1132	21570	2270	24827	3290
Physical Science	*% of PhDs*	38.3	38.4	37.2	36.7	34.2	32.8	31.7	32.9
	n	61358	2864	75878	4235	95396	8540	104500	12860
	% of FT	42	60.6	40.1	48	38.5	39.4	38	40.1
	n	55990	1814	70367	3239	84777	7095	87228	10543
Life Sciences	*% of Ph.D.s*	59.5	48.3	57.7	52.5	50.3	51.4	46	50.4
	n	50438	7119	68133	11773	96767	27498	109811	40987
	% of FT	65.4	70.2	62.2	68	56.3	62.1	53.6	60.3
	n	45874	4893	63157	9078	86440	22754	94175	34263

Social and Behavioral Sciences	*% of Ph.D.s*	63.1	45.7	57.4	46.8	49.4	39.8	43	37.2
	n	47296	8407	69802	17458	99780	40768	99024	51986
	% of FT	70.5	66	62.3	59.8	55.9	51.2	50.5	48.2
	n	42365	5817	64267	13655	88135	31660	84233	40095
Combined Fields	*% of Ph.D.s*	51.2	46.3	48.6	47.8	43.7	43.5	38.9	41.8
	n	204253	19386	277322	35285	383391	81317	423574	114288
	% of FT	55.9	67.8	52.2	61.4	48.7	54	45.4	52
	n	186871	13238	258347	27471	344134	65450	362959	91969

TABLE D-2 Percent and Number of Full-Time Academic Labor Force Who Are Women, by Field and Year of Survey

		1973	1979	1989	1995
Engineering	*% Women*	0.3	1.0	2.9	6.3
	n Women	41	158	690	1593
	n Total	12,312	16,468	23,506	25,117
Mathematics	*% Women*	5.8	7.0	9.7	11.6
	n Women	552	827	1537	2003
	n Total	9,481	11,867	15,789	17,214
Physical Science	*% Women*	4.5	5.2	7.9	11.3
	n Women	1100	1555	2798	4229
	n Total	24,594	29,796	35,438	37,369
Life Sciences	*% Women*	10.3	13.6	22.5	29.0
	n Women	3436	6175	14124	20663
	n Total	33,438	45,457	62,807	71,150
Social and Behavioral Sciences	*% Women*	11.4	16.9	24.8	31.2
	n Women	3841	8163	16221	19341
	n Total	33,698	48,201	65,468	61,899
Combined Fields	*% Women*	7.9	11.1	17.4	22.5
	n Women	8970	16878	35370	47829
	n Total	113,523	151,789	203,008	212,749

TABLE D-3 Number of Full-Time Scientists Working in Academia by Carnegie Type of Institution, Sex, Field and Year of Survey

		1973		1979		1989		1995	
		Men	*Women*	*Men*	*Women*	*Men*	*Women*	*Men*	*Women*
Engineering	*Research I*	6675	17	8121	78	11714	399	11303	663
	Research II	1632	2	2219	8	2997	50	2476	123
	Doctoral	1901	9	2092	23	3052	58	3430	258
	Master's	998	6	1169	12	1915	102	2532	198
	Baccalaureate	172	0	156	2	306	15	340	52
	Medical	121	0	370	9	602	28	874	96
	Engineering	159	0	182	0	401	4	305	28
	Other	169	2	127	2	458	0	321	19
	Missing	444	5	1874	24	1371	34	1943	156
	Total	12271	41	16310	158	22816	690	23524	1593
Mathematics	*Research I*	3705	146	4533	271	5515	441	5142	576
	Research II	956	37	974	55	1308	98	1337	191
	Doctoral	1187	61	1428	95	1950	206	2041	242
	Master's	1909	186	2318	227	3502	497	4287	474
	Baccalaureate	828	96	981	102	1225	192	1392	276
	Medical	19	2	144	19	103	47	241	95
	Engineering	66	0	43	0	120	5	105	57
	Other	68	1	72	12	118	14	232	0
	Missing	191	23	547	46	411	37	434	92
	Total	8929	552	11040	827	14252	1537	15211	2003

continued

TABLE D-3 Continued

		1973		1979		1989		1995	
		Men	*Women*	*Men*	*Women*	*Men*	*Women*	*Men*	*Women*
Physical Sciences	*Research I*	9857	376	10549	514	12473	1171	12773	1587
	Research II	2174	56	1965	115	2278	181	2208	272
	Doctoral	2807	99	2961	120	3105	235	3788	293
	Master's	4252	253	4328	259	5467	438	5288	800
	Baccalaureate	2273	165	2827	209	3313	335	3012	425
	Medical	520	64	1053	181	1598	202	1723	290
	Engineering	214	0	225	2	125	8	232	15
	Other	139	9	266	8	183	14	355	87
	Missing	1258	78	4067	147	4098	214	3761	460
	Total	23494	1100	28241	1555	32640	2798	33140	4229
Life Sciences	*Research I*	14375	1287	15375	2147	19102	5249	18384	6574
	Research II	2819	198	3219	232	4475	834	4340	1231
	Doctoral	2527	236	2399	446	3593	1070	3304	1602
	Master's	3785	550	4486	798	5295	1596	5789	2774
	Baccalaureate	1547	266	1896	445	2014	648	2274	1040
	Medical	3847	734	9659	1773	13112	4454	14156	6429
	Engineering	24	0	66	5	88	0	107	22
	Other	65	11	63	7	148	34	211	129
	Missing	1013	154	2119	322	856	239	1922	862
	Total	30002	3436	39282	6175	48683	14124	50487	20663

Social and Behavioral Sciences	*Research I*	11838	1264	13873	2868	16260	5524	12481	6243
	Research II	3213	243	3668	532	4121	1358	3615	1368
	Doctoral	4016	480	5801	1081	6761	1732	6042	2240
	Master's	6556	1146	9449	1775	13184	3569	11280	4346
	Baccalaureate	2711	428	3447	836	5185	1810	4566	2114
	Medical	601	147	1746	718	2446	1711	2384	2330
	Engineering	0	3	74	0	95	0	42	0
	Other	232	17	221	103	581	265	526	215
	Missing	690	113	1759	250	614	252	1622	485
	Total	29857	3841	40038	8163	49247	16221	42558	19341
Combined Fields	*Research I*	46450	3090	52451	5878	65064	12784	60083	15643
	Research II	10794	536	12045	942	15179	2521	13976	3185
	Doctoral	12438	885	14681	1765	18461	3301	18605	4635
	Master's	17500	2141	21750	3071	29363	6202	29176	8592
	Baccalaureate	7531	955	9307	1594	12043	3000	11584	3907
	Medical	5108	947	12972	2700	17861	6442	19378	9240
	Engineering	463	3	590	7	829	17	791	122
	Other	673	40	749	132	1488	327	1645	450
	Missing	3596	373	10366	789	7350	776	9682	2055
	Total	104553	8970	134911	16878	167638	35370	164920	47829

TABLE D-4 Number of Full-Time Scientists With and Without Tenure-Track Positions by Carnegie Type of Institution, Sex, Field, and Year of Survey

		1979		1989		1995	
		Men	*Women*	*Men*	*Women*	*Men*	*Women*
Engineering							
Research I	*Off-track*	1277	24	984	65	1726	85
	On-track	6628	50	9447	271	8850	431
Research II	*Off-track*	50	4	150	2	274	0
	On-track	2118	4	2717	48	2137	111
Doctoral	*Off-track*	209	10	176	4	450	43
	On-track	1883	11	2715	51	2914	202
Master's	*Off-track*	211	0	302	4	262	0
	On-track	958	12	1492	96	2246	198
Baccalaureate	*Off-track*	0	0	42	1	29	26
	On-track	140	2	247	14	311	26
Medical	*Off-track*	146	5	146	7	454	60
	On-track	143	2	367	16	305	6
Engineering	*Off-track*	75	0	52	0	70	16
	On-track	107	0	315	4	235	12
Total		13945	124	19152	583	20263	1216
Mathematics							
Research I	*Off-track*	519	78	563	74	734	166
	On-track	3916	185	4305	321	4223	294
Research II	*Off-track*	77	17	48	8	16	18
	On-Track	895	38	1147	82	1244	173
Doctoral	*Off-track*	85	23	50	20	84	32
	On-track	1328	72	1797	179	1903	210

Master's	*Off-track*	126	27	158	12	106	43
	On-track	2177	200	3097	456	4164	415
Baccalaureate	*Off-track*	164	23	39	14	156	18
	On-track	817	79	1142	168	1218	258
Medical	*Off-track*	39	6	37	18	84	32
	On-track	62	11	62	20	125	43
Engineering	*Off-track*	0	0	2	0	0	8
	On-track	43	0	118	5	105	49
Total		10248	759	12565	1377	14162	1759
Physical Sciences							
Research I	*Off-track*	1977	193	2147	346	3154	492
	On-track	7167	174	7652	433	7006	575
Research II	*Off-track*	216	46	297	32	292	98
	On-track	1637	41	1649	89	1575	151
Doctoral	*Off-track*	406	21	243	41	499	112
	On-track	2409	76	2645	160	2998	181
Master's	*Off-track*	323	46	340	52	413	143
	On-track	3970	208	4786	338	4741	657
Baccalaureate	*Off-track*	359	62	434	37	509	138
	On-track	2390	145	2729	289	2500	287
Medical	*Off-track*	255	82	441	79	634	157
	On-track	719	38	792	67	835	16
Engineering	*Off-track*	92	0	9	0	42	0
	On-track	119	2	116	4	175	15
Total		22039	1134	24280	1967	25373	3022

continued

TABLE D-4 Continued

		1979		1989		1995	
		Men	*Women*	*Men*	*Women*	*Men*	*Women*
Life Sciences							
Research I	*Off-track*	2519	641	2644	1359	3592	1896
	On-track	11122	893	12411	2436	11972	3065
Research II	*Off-track*	280	59	387	168	569	195
	On-track	2801	130	3631	507	3404	818
Doctoral	*Off-track*	216	79	358	201	387	329
	On-track	2100	340	2796	806	2753	1167
Master's	*Off-track*	488	117	396	166	752	350
	On-track	3946	668	4541	1356	4960	2402
Baccalaureate	*Off-track*	219	88	130	78	399	175
	On-track	1670	342	1766	526	1875	809
Medical	*Off-track*	1970	612	3043	1595	4316	2374
	On-track	5922	676	7431	1658	7986	2526
Engineering	*Off-track*	7	0	0	0	37	0
	On-track	52	5	88	0	70	22
Total		33312	4650	39622	10856	43072	16128
Social and Behavioral Sciences							
Research I	*Off-track*	1587	555	1900	1303	2189	1898
	On-track	11860	2103	13185	3710	9947	3893
Research II	*Off-track*	523	107	303	273	539	360
	On-track	3091	423	3328	968	3023	988
Doctoral	*Off-track*	778	221	429	281	724	567
	On-track	4985	839	5841	1322	5296	1643

Master's	*Off-track*	965	200	797	470	860	573
	On-Track	8451	1565	11667	2869	10368	3773
Baccalaureate	*Off-track*	345	211	659	413	647	486
	On-Track	3084	602	4176	1263	3919	1628
Medical	*Off-track*	560	274	915	680	1015	1394
	On-Track	1026	268	1123	626	1254	599
Engineering	*Off-track*	29	0	40	0	22	0
	On-Track	45	0	55	0	20	0
Total		37329	7368	44418	14178	39823	17802
Combined Fields							
Research I	*Off-track*	7879	1491	8238	3147	11395	4537
	On-Track	40693	3405	47000	7171	41998	8258
Research II	*Off-track*	1146	233	1185	483	1690	671
	On-Track	10542	636	12472	1694	11383	2241
Doctoral	*Off-track*	1694	354	1256	547	2144	1083
	On-Track	12705	1338	15794	2518	15864	3403
Master's	*Off-track*	2113	390	1993	704	2393	1109
	On-Track	19502	2653	25583	5115	26479	7445
Baccalaureate	*Off-track*	1087	384	1304	543	1740	843
	On-Track	8101	1170	10060	2260	9823	3008
Medical	*Off-track*	2970	979	4582	2379	6503	4017
	On-Track	7872	995	9775	2387	10505	3190
Engineering	*Off-track*	203	0	103	0	171	24
	On-Track	366	7	692	13	605	98
Total		116873	14035	140037	28961	142693	39927

TABLE D-5 Logit Analysis on Whether a Scientist Has a Tenure-Track Position by Sex and Year of Survey. *b* Indicates Regression Coefficient; *z* Indicates Value of *z*-test.

		1979		1989		1995	
Variable		*Women*	*Men*	*Women*	*Mmen*	*Women*	*Men*
Married	*b*	–0.212	0.223	–0.163	0.344	–0.053	0.119
	z	2.09	2.02	2.04	3.72	0.58	1.43
Children <6 at Home	*b*	–0.105	0.086	0.087	–0.040	0.021	0.308
	z	0.78	0.96	0.83	0.45	0.18	3.99
Not a US Citizen	*b*	–0.457	–0.495	–0.159	–0.279	–0.377	–0.218
	z	2.33	3.41	1.05	2.14	2.33	2.17
Career Year	*b*	0.118	0.281	0.125	0.099	0.115	0.144
	z	6.10	18.85	8.70	6.81	7.17	13.40
Career Year2	*b*	–0.002	–0.005	–0.002	–0.001	–0.002	–0.002
	z	2.76	11.65	5.20	1.52	5.02	8.19
Engineering vs.	*b*	–0.092	–0.160	0.961	0.588	0.992	0.250
Social/Behavioral Sciences	*z*	0.32	0.83	4.84	3.97	4.02	2.32
Math vs.	*b*	0.001	0.281	0.701	0.570	0.684	0.771
Social/Behavioral Sciences	*z*	0.01	1.84	4.65	3.70	3.51	5.33
Physical Sciences vs.	*b*	–0.948	–0.584	–0.537	–0.525	–0.399	–0.624
Social/Behavioral Sciences	*z*	7.31	4.62	4.78	4.53	2.51	6.19
Life Sciences vs.	*b*	–0.274	–0.315	–0.296	–0.104	0.031	–0.260
Social/Behavioral Sciences	*z*	2.12	2.70	2.73	0.92	0.32	2.93
Medical vs. Research I	*b*	–0.546	–0.391	–0.556	–0.515	–0.582	–0.485
	z	3.95	3.77	5.46	5.46	5.23	6.09
Research II vs. Research I	*b*	0.221	0.536	0.820	0.810	0.695	0.736
	z	1.16	3.41	5.09	5.45	3.78	6.00
Doctoral vs. Research I	*b*	0.763	0.397	0.939	0.992	0.753	0.966
	z	4.72	2.93	6.82	7.01	5.13	8.59

Master's vs. Research I	*b*	1.192	0.731	1.407	1.230	1.314	1.365
	z	8.32	5.95	11.41	9.57	9.83	12.86
Baccalaureate vs. Research I	*b*	0.826	0.885	1.450	0.971	1.029	0.985
	z	4.87	5.01	9.13	6.17	6.07	7.32
Private vs. Research I	*b*	–0.582	–0.508	–0.632	–0.631	–0.405	–0.624
	z	5.88	5.97	7.94	8.40	4.55	9.71
Ph.D. Prestige	*b*	0.071	0.043	0.191	0.280	0.246	0.291
	z	1.28	0.84	3.94	5.84	4.40	7.33
Time from Baccalaureate to Ph.D. > 10 Years	*b*	0.251	0.093	0.041	–0.288	0.117	–0.415
	z	2.09	0.81	0.44	2.91	1.22	5.14
Missing Data on Having Young Children	*b*	–0.089	0.297	0.235	–0.102		
	z	0.49	1.83	1.81	0.90		
Missing Data on Prestige of Ph.D.	*b*	–0.116	–0.023	0.342	–0.029		
	z	1.02	0.27	3.67	0.37		
Constant	*b*	0.201	–0.560	–0.549	–0.573	–0.978	–1.086
	z	0.82	2.40	2.55	2.55	4.01	5.56
Unweighted Observations		10,078	7,168	4,912	7,801	3,279	8,853

TABLE D-6 Number of Full-Time Scientists on Tenure Track With and Without Tenure by Carnegie Type of Institution, Sex, Field, and Year of Survey

		1979		1989		1995	
		Men	*Women*	*Men*	*Women*	*Men*	*Women*
Engineering							
Research I	*Untenured*	1063	32	2198	166	1961	310
	Tenured	5565	18	7249	105	6889	121
Research II	*Untenured*	464	2	659	28	293	45
	Tenured	1654	2	2058	20	1844	66
Doctoral	*Untenured*	442	5	789	23	760	107
	Tenured	1441	6	1926	28	2154	95
Master's	*Untenured*	276	0	390	60	660	92
	Tenured	682	12	1102	36	1586	106
Baccalaureate	*Untenured*	0	2	92	8	102	13
	Tenured	140	0	155	6	209	13
Medical	*Untenured*	76	2	118	14	134	6
	Tenured	67	0	249	2	171	0
Engineering	*Untenured*	0	0	89	2	28	12
	Tenured	107	0	226	2	207	0
Total		11977	81	17300	500	16998	986
Mathematics							
Research I	*Untenured*	755	97	837	109	830	129
	Tenured	3161	88	3468	212	3393	165
Research II	*Untenured*	133	11	235	28	182	108
	Tenured	762	27	912	54	1062	65
Doctoral	*Untenured*	322	26	492	83	291	96
	Tenured	1006	46	1305	96	1612	114

Master's	*Untenured*	339	55	764	126	930	153
	Tenured	1838	145	2333	330	3234	262
Baccalaureate	*Untenured*	212	20	299	65	357	136
	Tenured	605	59	843	103	861	122
Medical	*Untenured*	13	11	5	2	73	0
	Tenured	49	0	57	18	52	43
Engineering	*Untenured*	0	0	0	0	37	0
	Tenured	43	0	118	5	68	49
Total		9238	585	11668	1231	12982	1442
Physical Sciences							
Research I	*Untenured*	1121	54	1261	174	1202	231
	Tenured	6046	120	6391	259	5804	344
Research II	*Untenured*	269	6	240	29	128	44
	Tenured	1368	35	1409	60	1447	107
Doctoral	*Untenured*	389	21	485	66	455	73
	Tenured	2020	55	2160	94	2543	108
Master's	*Untenured*	499	39	470	109	713	340
	Tenured	3471	169	4316	229	4028	317
Baccalaureate	*Untenured*	614	52	512	149	490	126
	Tenured	1776	93	2217	140	2010	161
Medical	*Untenured*	246	11	327	37	329	16
	Tenured	473	27	465	30	506	0
Engineering	*Untenured*	32	2	0	4	3	15
	Tenured	87	0	116	0	172	0
Total		18411	684	20369	1380	19830	1882

continued

TABLE D-6 Continued

		1979		1989		1995	
		Men	*Women*	*Men*	*Women*	*Men*	*Women*
Life Sciences		*Men*	*Women*	*Men*	*Women*	*Men*	*Women*
Research I	*Untenured*	2436	453	2560	1181	2047	1254
	Tenured	8686	440	9851	1255	9925	1811
Research II	*Untenured*	488	54	568	168	634	289
	Tenured	2313	76	3063	339	2770	529
Doctoral	*Untenured*	657	181	542	327	558	500
	Tenured	1443	159	2254	479	2195	667
Master's	*Untenured*	609	243	704	395	1076	886
	Tenured	3337	425	3837	961	3884	1516
Baccalaureate	*Untenured*	294	175	157	142	442	292
	Tenured	1376	167	1609	384	1433	517
Medical	*Untenured*	1725	345	2048	843	2634	1320
	Tenured	4197	331	5383	815	5352	1206
Engineering	*Untenured*	0	0	29	0	9	0
	Tenured	52	5	59	0	61	22
Total		27613	3054	32664	7289	33020	10809
Scial and Behavioral Sciences							
Research I	*Untenured*	2247	1116	2363	1343	1754	1405
	Tenured	9613	987	10822	2367	8193	2488
Research II	*Untenured*	640	141	338	381	276	410
	Tenured	2451	282	2990	587	2747	578
Doctoral	*Untenured*	1297	399	840	467	1181	761
	Tenured	3688	440	5001	855	4115	882
Master's	*Untenured*	1731	521	1872	1010	1994	1175
	Tenured	6720	1044	9795	1859	8374	2598

Baccalaureate	*Untenured*	673	314	1286	387	701	525
	Tenured	2411	288	2890	876	3218	1103
Medical	*Untenured*	420	146	374	228	384	251
	Tenured	606	122	749	398	870	348
Engineering	*Untenured*	0	0	0	0	0	0
	Tenured	45	0	55	0	20	0
Total		32542	5800	39375	10758	33827	12524
Combined Fields							
Research I	*Untenured*	7622	1752	9219	2973	7794	3329
	Tenured	33071	1653	37781	4198	34204	4929
Research II	*Untenured*	1994	214	2040	634	1513	896
	Tenured	8548	422	10432	1060	9870	1345
Doctoral	*Untenured*	3107	632	3148	966	3245	1537
	Tenured	9598	706	12646	1552	12619	1866
Master's	*Untenured*	3454	858	4200	1700	5373	2646
	Tenured	16048	1795	21383	3415	21106	4799
Baccalaureate	*Untenured*	1793	563	2346	751	2092	1092
	Tenured	6308	607	7714	1509	7731	1916
Medical	*Untenured*	2480	515	2872	1124	3554	1593
	Tenured	5392	480	6903	1263	6951	1597
Engineering	*Untenured*	32	2	118	6	77	27
	Tenured	334	5	574	7	528	71
Total		99781	10204	121376	21158	116657	27643

TABLE D-7 Logit Analysis on Whether a Scientist in a Tenure-Track Position Has Tenure by Sex and Year of Survey. *b* Indicates Regression Coefficient; *z* Indicates Value of *z*-test.

Variable		1979		1989		1995	
		Women	*Men*	*Women*	*Women*	*Men*	*Men*
Married	*b*	–0.297	0.131	–0.026	0.297	0.154	0.386
	z	2.13	0.86	0.24	2.28	1.17	3.15
Children <6 at Home	*b*	0.023	–0.109	0.039	0.042	–0.098	–0.078
	z	0.12	1.01	0.29	0.37	0.64	0.81
Not a US Citizen	*b*	0.279	0.11	–0.427	–0.331	–0.256	–0.219
	z	0.92	0.51	1.89	1.69	0.96	1.59
Career Year	*b*	0.569	0.731	0.562	0.638	0.487	0.62
	z	18.5	27.44	21.06	24.65	15.76	26.9
Career Year2	*b*	–0.011	–0.013	–0.009	–0.01	–0.008	–0.01
	z	12.14	17.66	10.73	13.15	7.83	15.91
Engineering vs. Social/Behavioral Sciences	*b*	–0.46	–0.503	0.163	–0.26	0.307	0.422
	z	1	1.99	0.74	1.39	1.11	2.97
Math vs. Social/Behavioral Sciences	*b*	–0.31	0.026	0.328	0.011	0.462	0.56
	z	1.61	0.15	1.95	0.06	1.99	3.28
Physical Sciences vs. Social/Behavioral Sciences	*b*	–0.347	–0.601	–0.383	–0.504	0.04	–0.265
	z	1.75	3.56	2.32	3.13	0.16	1.65
Life Sciences vs. Social/Behavioral Sciences	*b*	–0.86	–0.814	–0.255	–0.45	–0.217	–0.734
	z	4.86	5.49	1.71	2.98	1.55	5.44
Medical vs. Research I	*b*	–0.365	–0.546	–0.922	–1.166	–0.729	–1.207
	z	1.56	3.68	5.44	7.9	3.82	8.64
Research II vs. Research I	*b*	0.551	0.203	0.42	0.248	0.086	0.347
	z	1.91	1.09	2.16	1.41	0.36	2.13
Doctoral vs. Research I	*b*	0.283	–0.099	0.11	0.029	–0.043	0.015
	z	1.38	0.59	0.65	0.18	0.21	0.11

Master's vs. Research I	*b*	0.765	0.727	0.405	0.255	0.42	–0.121
	z	4.54	4.96	2.93	1.76	2.57	0.96
Baccalaureate vs. Research I	*b*	0.318	0.665	0.483	0.301	0.557	0.405
	z	1.34	3.2	2.53	1.51	2.43	2.03
Private vs. Research I	*b*	–0.51	–0.709	–0.482	–0.536	–0.512	–0.733
	z	3.56	6	4.23	4.95	3.84	7.41
Ph.D. Prestige	*b*	–0.104	0.014	0.029	0.062	–0.187	–0.047
	z	1.4	0.22	0.43	0.98	2.32	0.83
Time from Baccalaureate	*b*	1.219	1.423	0.973	0.619	0.861	0.397
to Ph.D. > 10 Years	*z*	7.4	8.87	7.54	4.3	6.21	3.14
Missing Data on Having Young Children	*b*	–0.046	–0.219	–0.105	0.154		
	z	0.18	1.04	0.65	0.97		
Missing Data on Prestige of Ph.D.	*b*	0.459	0.393	0.361	0.199		
	z	2.79	3.54	2.86	1.86		
Constant	*b*	–3.082	–4.066	–4.383	–4.834	–3.365	–4.456
	z	8.94	12.55	13.11	14.41	8.75	14.31
Observations		8242	6113	3773	6664	2296	7105

TABLE D-8 Number of Full-Time Scientists on Tenure Track by Rank, Carnegie Type of Institution, Sex, Field, and Year of Survey

		1979		1989		1995	
		Men	*Women*	*Men*	*Women*	*Men*	*Women*
Engineering		**1**					
Research I	*Instructor*	16	0	16	0	27	0
	Asst. Prof.	807	31	1785	164	1647	295
	Assoc. Prof.	1833	16	2263	55	2426	103
	Full Prof.	3972	3	5383	52	4738	33
Research II	*Instructor*	15	0	0	0	0	0
	Asst. Prof.	251	2	597	32	286	45
	Assoc. Prof.	629	0	619	16	617	37
	Full Prof.	1223	2	1501	0	1234	29
Doctoral	*Instructor*	34	0	9	0	0	0
	Asst. Prof.	325	5	548	20	647	93
	Assoc. Prof.	435	4	528	26	1128	82
	Full Prof.	1089	2	1630	5	1139	27
Master's	*Instructor*	16	0	17	0	0	0
	Asst. Prof.	87	1	250	54	408	97
	Assoc. Prof.	484	2	533	24	819	45
	Full Prof.	371	9	692	18	1019	56
Baccalaureate	*Instructor*	0	0	0	0	0	0
	Asst. Prof.	0	0	92	8	68	13
	Assoc. Prof.	42	2	49	5	144	13
	Full Prof.	98	0	106	1	99	0
Medical	*Instructor*	0	0	0	5	0	0
	Asst. Prof.	76	2	24	9	93	6
	Assoc. Prof.	0	0	130	2	63	0
	Full Prof.	67	0	213	0	149	0
Engineering	*Instructor*	76	0	46	0	30	0
	Asst. Prof.	0	0	35	2	23	12
	Assoc. Prof.	0	0	132	2	125	0
	Full Prof.	31	0	102	0	57	0
Total		11977	81	17300	500	16986	986

TABLE D-8 Continued

		1979		1989		1995	
		Men	*Women*	*Men*	*Women*	*Men*	*Women*
Mathematics							
Research I	*Instructor*	29	5	0	2	59	0
	Asst. Prof.	762	90	834	98	794	120
	Assoc. Prof.	1243	62	1017	136	1068	107
	Full Prof.	1882	28	2454	85	2302	67
Research II	*Instructor*	0	0	0	0	0	0
	Asst. Prof.	142	13	174	29	164	111
	Assoc. Prof.	265	15	338	31	514	58
	Full Prof.	488	10	635	22	566	4
Doctoral	*Instructor*	8	0	0	2	0	0
	Asst. Prof.	342	26	457	83	286	76
	Assoc. Prof.	481	33	588	52	897	102
	Full Prof.	497	13	752	42	720	32
Master's	*Instructor*	36	2	0	2	17	0
	Asst. Prof.	466	69	761	131	838	127
	Assoc. Prof.	875	74	1093	174	1481	126
	Full Prof.	787	55	1243	149	1828	162
Baccalaureate	*Instructor*	0	0	17	0	0	0
	Asst. Prof.	188	22	267	61	343	115
	Assoc. Prof.	377	22	311	54	368	53
	Full Prof.	252	35	547	53	507	90
Medical	*Instructor*	0	0	0	0	0	0
	Asst. Prof.	28	9	5	4	57	0
	Assoc. Prof.	0	2	17	9	52	10
	Full Prof.	26	0	40	7	16	33
Engineering	*Instructor*	0	0	0	0	0	0
	Asst. Prof.	0	0	0	0	37	0
	Assoc. Prof.	15	0	50	5	0	32
	Full Prof.	28	0	68	0	68	17
Total		9217	585	11668	1231	12982	1442

continued

TABLE D-8 Continued

		1979		1989		1995	
		Men	*Women*	*Men*	*Women*	*Men*	*Women*
Physical Sciences							
Research I	*Instructor*	56	5	180	23	38	39
	Asst. Prof.	883	51	1013	144	1041	216
	Assoc. Prof.	1773	70	1332	145	1583	155
	Full Prof.	4423	48	5127	121	4240	148
Research II	*Instructor*	0	0	0	1	0	3
	Asst. Prof.	269	7	214	26	129	44
	Assoc. Prof.	291	9	277	38	326	10
	Full Prof.	1077	25	1158	24	1104	94
Doctoral	*Instructor*	12	0	31	0	19	0
	Asst. Prof.	285	23	348	66	401	70
	Assoc. Prof.	986	34	732	47	690	94
	Full Prof.	1126	19	1534	47	1888	17
Master's	*Instructor*	36	3	34	3	55	0
	Asst. Prof.	460	36	428	112	655	357
	Assoc. Prof.	1548	103	1325	86	1309	176
	Full Prof.	1917	66	2999	137	2722	124
Baccalaureate	*Instructor*	14	3	37	2	0	0
	Asst. Prof.	437	39	473	142	468	136
	Assoc. Prof.	798	42	527	56	565	81
	Full Prof.	1138	61	1692	89	1448	70
Medical	*Instructor*	0	0	0	0	0	0
	Asst. Prof.	157	16	161	23	244	7
	Assoc. Prof.	319	18	256	28	94	9
	Full Prof.	224	4	375	16	497	0
Engineering	*Instructor*	0	0	10	0	30	0
	Asst. Prof.	32	2	0	4	0	15
	Assoc. Prof.	8	0	41	0	60	0
	Full Prof.	79	0	65	0	82	0
Total		18348	684	20369	1380	19688	1865

TABLE D-8 Continued

		1979		1989		1995	
		Men	*Women*	*Men*	*Women*	*Men*	*Women*
Life Sciences							
Research I	*Instructor*	173	13	144	57	63	9
	Asst. Prof.	2030	389	2339	1110	1731	1115
	Assoc. Prof.	3142	279	3094	762	3169	1075
	Full Prof.	5753	201	6834	505	6892	838
Research II	*Instructor*	67	2	0	4	0	3
	Asst. Prof.	501	46	500	159	595	310
	Assoc. Prof.	765	45	1054	245	795	298
	Full Prof.	1455	37	2077	99	1999	207
Doctoral	*Instructor*	0	2	17	0	8	18
	Asst. Prof.	584	141	511	272	484	452
	Assoc. Prof.	756	130	1029	385	881	426
	Full Prof.	760	67	1239	149	1380	271
Master's	*Instructor*	39	10	0	0	0	27
	Asst. Prof.	512	219	541	391	828	747
	Assoc. Prof.	1347	215	1016	437	1231	824
	Full Prof.	2048	219	2984	526	2901	786
Baccalaureate	*Instructor*	44	11	8	0	0	0
	Asst. Prof.	208	166	166	163	379	265
	Assoc. Prof.	706	96	386	208	294	296
	Full Prof.	712	69	1163	155	1150	248
Medical	*Instructor*	48	12	0	12	56	9
	Asst. Prof.	1412	353	1616	658	2221	1103
	Assoc. Prof.	1947	211	2399	644	2075	857
	Full Prof.	2494	98	3394	344	3634	553
Engineering	*Instructor*	0	0	0	0	0	0
	Asst. Prof.	0	5	29	0	9	0
	Assoc. Prof.	52	0	0	0	0	0
	Full Prof.	0	0	59	0	61	22
Total		27555	3036	32599	7285	32836	10759

continued

TABLE D-8 Continued

		1979		1989		1995	
		Men	*Women*	*Men*	*Women*	*Men*	*Women*
Social/Behavioral Sciences							
Research I	*Instructor*	149	9	82	43	77	100
	Asst. Prof.	2302	1117	2246	1215	1556	1268
	Assoc. Prof.	2648	585	3444	1394	2800	1113
	Full Prof.	6758	375	7413	1058	5514	1390
Research II	*Instructor*	0	16	0	31	0	0
	Asst. Prof.	610	178	383	390	276	410
	Assoc. Prof.	921	122	1143	380	941	370
	Full Prof.	1560	107	1802	167	1806	208
Doctoral	*Instructor*	136	4	5	0	0	0
	Asst. Prof.	1088	388	791	448	1164	659
	Assoc. Prof.	2068	255	2423	543	1482	521
	Full Prof.	1652	191	2590	331	2633	463
Master's	*Instructor*	59	26	27	45	0	22
	Asst. Prof.	1701	581	1545	1024	1555	1184
	Assoc. Prof.	2872	602	3481	873	2655	1592
	Full Prof.	3711	348	6614	927	6061	917
Baccalaureate	*Instructor*	111	16	53	4	0	3
	Asst. Prof.	796	287	774	355	625	559
	Assoc. Prof.	748	187	1318	524	1070	653
	Full Prof.	1429	107	2031	380	2172	413
Medical	*Instructor*	41	17	0	2	5	37
	Asst. Prof.	385	131	247	219	300	130
	Assoc. Prof.	248	59	262	215	418	201
	Full Prof.	352	61	614	190	508	231
Engineering	*Instructor*	0	0	0	0	0	0
	Asst. Prof.	0	0	0	0	0	0
	Assoc. Prof.	45	0	55	0	20	0
	Full Prof.	0	0	0	0	0	0
Total		32390	5769	39343	10758	33638	12444

continued

TABLE D-8 Continued

		1979		1989		1995	
		Men	*Women*	*Men*	*Women*	*Men*	*Women*
Combined Fields							
Research I	*Instructor*	423	32	422	125	264	148
	Asst. Prof.	6784	1678	8217	2731	6769	3014
	Assoc. Prof.	10639	1012	11150	2492	11046	2553
	Full Prof.	22788	655	27211	1821	23686	2476
Research II	*Instructor*	82	18	0	36	0	6
	Asst. Prof.	1773	246	1868	636	1450	920
	Assoc. Prof.	2871	191	3431	710	3193	773
	Full Prof.	5803	181	7173	312	6709	542
Doctoral	*Instructor*	190	6	62	2	27	18
	Asst. Prof.	2624	583	2655	889	2982	1350
	Assoc. Prof.	4726	456	5300	1053	5078	1225
	Full Prof.	5124	292	7745	574	7760	810
Master's	*Instructor*	186	41	78	50	72	49
	Asst. Prof.	3226	906	3525	1712	4284	2512
	Assoc. Prof.	7126	996	7448	1594	7495	2763
	Full Prof.	8834	697	14532	1757	14531	2045
Baccalaureate	*Instructor*	169	30	115	6	0	3
	Asst. Prof.	1629	514	1772	729	1883	1088
	Assoc. Prof.	2671	349	2591	847	2441	1096
	Full Prof.	3629	272	5539	678	5376	821
Medical	*Instructor*	89	29	0	19	61	46
	Asst. Prof.	2058	511	2053	913	2915	1246
	Assoc. Prof.	2514	290	3064	898	2702	1077
	Full Prof.	3163	163	4636	557	4804	817
Engineering	*Instructor*	76	0	56	0	60	0
	Asst. Prof.	32	7	64	6	69	27
	Assoc. Prof.	120	0	278	7	205	32
	Full Prof.	138	0	294	0	268	39
Total		99487	10155	121279	21154	116130	27496

TABLE D-9 Percent With a Given Rank by Sex, Field, and Year of Survey

		Men			Women			Difference		
		1979	*1989*	*1995*	*1979*	*1989*	*1995*	*1979*	*1989*	*1995*
Engineering	*Asst. Prof.*	14.0	19.4	19.0	51.2	58.8	56.9	−37.2	−39.4	−37.9
	Assoc. Prof.	28.7	24.7	31.3	30.0	26.0	28.4	−1.3	−1.3	2.9
	Full Prof.	57.3	55.9	49.7	18.8	15.2	14.7	38.5	40.7	35.0
	n	11,907	17,228	16,986	80	500	986			
Mathematics	*Asst. Prof.*	21.9	21.6	20.0	40.3	33.5	38.1	−18.4	−11.9	−18.1
	Assoc. Prof.	35.5	29.3	33.7	35.6	37.4	33.8	−0.1	−8.1	−0.1
	Full Prof.	42.6	49.1	46.3	24.1	29.1	28.1	18.5	20.0	18.2
	n	9,125	11,648	12,982	585	1,231	1,442			
Physical Sciences	*Asst. Prof.*	14.4	14.4	15.6	27.0	39.6	47.6	−12.6	−25.2	−32.0
	Assoc. Prof.	31.3	21.9	23.5	40.4	29.0	28.2	−9.1	−7.1	−4.7
	Full Prof.	54.3	63.8	60.9	32.6	31.4	24.3	21.7	32.4	36.6
	n	18,277	20,245	19,688	684	1,380	1,865			
Life Sciences	*Asst. Prof.*	20.5	18.0	19.4	45.1	38.8	37.7	−24.6	−20.8	−18.3
	Assoc. Prof.	31.6	27.6	25.7	32.2	36.7	35.1	−0.6	−9.1	−9.4
	Full Prof.	48.0	54.5	54.9	22.8	24.4	27.2	25.2	30.1	27.7
	n	27,392	32,577	32,836	3,035	7,274	10,759			

Social and Behavioral Sciences	*Asst. Prof.*	22.8	15.6	16.5	48.2	35.1	35.1	–25.4	–19.5	–18.6
	Assoc. Prof.	29.4	30.8	27.9	31.2	36.5	35.8	–1.8	–5.7	–7.9
	Full Prof.	47.8	53.6	55.6	20.6	28.4	29.1	27.2	25.2	26.5
	n	32,310	39,274	33,638	5,743	10,756	12,444			
Combined Fields	*Asst. Prof.*	19.5	17.2	17.9	45.4	37.1	37.9	–25.9	–19.9	–20.0
	Assoc. Prof.	30.8	27.4	27.7	32.4	35.9	34.6	–1.6	–8.5	–6.9
	Full Prof.	49.7	55.4	54.4	22.2	27.0	27.5	27.5	28.4	26.9
	n	99,011	120,972	116,130	10,127	21,141	27,496			

TABLE D-10 Percent With a Given Rank by Sex, Carnegie Type, and Year of Survey

		Men			Women			Difference		
		1979	*1989*	*1995*	*1979*	*1989*	*1995*	*1979*	*1989*	*1995*
Research I	*Asst. Prof.*	17.9	18.4	16.9	50.7	39.8	38.5	–32.8	–21.4	–21.6
	Assoc. Prof.	26.3	23.9	26.6	29.9	34.8	31.2	–3.6	–10.9	–4.6
	Full Prof.	55.8	57.7	56.5	19.4	25.4	30.3	36.4	32.3	26.2
	n	40790	47578	42367	3384	7180	8289			
Medical	*Asst. Prof.*	27.6	21.0	28.4	54.3	39.0	40.6	–26.7	–18.0	–12.2
	Assoc. Prof.	32.2	31.4	25.8	29.2	37.6	33.8	3.0	–6.2	–8.0
	Full Prof.	40.2	47.6	45.8	16.4	23.3	25.6	23.8	24.3	20.2
	n	7757	9748	10482	992	2387	3186			
Research II	*Asst. Prof.*	17.3	15.0	12.8	41.5	39.7	41.3	–24.2	–24.7	–28.5
	Assoc. Prof.	27.3	27.5	28.1	30.0	41.9	34.5	–2.7	–14.4	–6.4
	Full Prof.	55.3	57.5	59.1	28.5	18.4	24.2	26.8	39.1	34.9
	n	10441	12469	11352	636	1694	2241			
Doctoral	*Asst. Prof.*	22.3	17.0	19.0	44.1	35.4	40.2	–21.8	–18.4	–21.2
	Assoc. Prof.	37.0	33.7	32.0	34.1	41.8	36.0	2.9	–8.1	–4.0
	Full Prof.	40.6	49.4	49.0	21.8	22.8	23.8	18.8	26.6	25.2
	n	12607	15684	15847	1336	2514	3403			
Master's	*Asst. Prof.*	17.6	14.1	16.5	35.9	34.5	34.8	–18.3	–20.4	–18.3
	Assoc. Prof.	36.9	29.0	28.4	37.6	31.1	37.5	–0.7	–2.1	–9.1
	Full Prof.	45.6	56.9	55.1	26.5	34.4	27.8	19.1	22.5	27.3
	n	19318	25497	26382	2631	5106	7369			

Baccalaureate	*Asst. Prof.*	22.2	18.7	19.4	47.4	32.5	36.3	–25.2	–13.8	–16.9
	Assoc. Prof.	33.0	25.9	25.2	29.4	37.5	36.4	3.6	–11.6	–11.2
	Full Prof.	44.8	55.4	55.4	23.2	30.0	27.3	21.6	25.4	28.1
	n	8098	9996	9700	1148	2260	3008			
All Types	*Asst. Prof.*	19.5	17.2	17.9	45.4	37.1	37.9	–25.9	–19.9	–20.0
	Assoc. Prof.	30.8	27.4	27.7	32.4	35.9	34.6	–1.6	–8.5	–6.9
	Full Prof.	49.7	55.4	54.4	22.2	27.0	27.5	27.5	28.4	26.9
	n	99011	120972	116130	10127	21141	27496			

TABLE D-11 Percent of Scientists in Given Types of Positions Who are Female by Field and Year of Survey.

		Engineering		Mathematics		Physical Sciences		Life Sciences		Social/Behavioral Sciences	
		Percent Women	*Deviation from % Full Time*	*Percent Women*	*Deviation from % Full Time*	*Percent Women*	*Deviation from % Full Time*	*Percent Women*	*Deviation from % Full Time*	*Percent Women*	*Deviation from % Full Time*
Full Time	*1979*	0.9		6.9		5.0		12.3		16.5	
	1989	2.9		9.8		7.5		21.3		24.1	
	1995	5.7		11.0		10.6		27.2		30.9	
Off-Track	*1979*	2.1	1.2	14.7	7.8	11.0	6.0	21.9	9.6	24.7	8.2
	1989	4.3	1.4	14.0	4.2	13.1	5.6	33.9	12.6	40.4	16.3
	1995	6.6	0.9	21.2	10.2	17.1	6.5	34.6	7.4	46.8	15.9
On-Track	*1979*	0.7	–0.2	6.0	–0.9	3.6	–1.4	10.0	–2.3	15.1	–1.4
	1989	2.8	–0.1	9.5	–0.3	6.3	–1.2	18.2	–3.1	21.5	–2.6
	1995	5.5	–0.2	10.0	–1.0	8.7	–1.9	24.7	–2.5	27.0	–3.9
Untenured	*1979*	1.8	0.9	11.0	4.1	5.5	0.5	18.9	6.6	27.3	10.8
	1989	6.5	3.6	13.6	3.8	14.7	7.2	31.6	10.3	35.0	10.9
	1995	12.9	7.2	18.7	7.7	20.3	9.7	38.0	10.8	41.9	11.0
Tenured	*1979*	0.4	–0.5	4.7	–2.2	3.2	–1.8	7.0	–5.3	11.0	–5.5
	1989	1.5	–1.4	8.3	–1.5	4.5	–3.0	14.0	–7.3	17.7	–6.4
	1995	3.0	–2.7	7.4	–3.6	5.9	–4.7	19.7	–7.5	22.5	–8.4

Assistant Professor	*1979*	2.6	1.7	10.6	3.7	6.5	1.5	20.1	7.8	28.0	11.5
	1989	8.0	5.1	14.0	4.2	16.4	8.9	32.6	11.3	37.9	13.8
	1995	15.0	9.3	17.9	6.9	22.3	11.7	39.0	11.8	43.5	12.6
Associate Professor	*1979*	0.7	–0.2	6.0	–0.9	4.6	–0.4	10.1	–2.2	15.9	–0.6
	1989	3.0	0.1	11.9	2.1	8.2	0.7	23.0	1.7	24.5	0.4
	1995	5.0	–0.7	10.0	–1.0	10.2	–0.4	30.9	3.7	32.2	1.3
Full Professor	*1979*	0.2	–0.7	3.4	–3.5	2.2	–2.8	5.0	–7.3	7.1	–9.4
	1989	0.8	–2.1	5.9	–3.9	3.2	–4.3	9.1	–12.2	12.7	–11.4
	1995	1.7	–4.0	6.3	–4.7	3.6	–7.0	14.0	–13.2	16.2	–14.7

NOTE: Deviation from percent full time is the difference between the percent women in a given category and the percent women working full time in that field. Positive values indicate proportionally more women in that category than the representation of women in that field.

TABLE D-12 Multinomial Logit Analysis on Academic Rank, by Sex and Year of Survey. *b* Indicates Regression Coefficient; *z* Indicates Value of *z*-test

Variable		1979		1989		1995	
		Women	*Men*	*Women*	*Men*	*Women*	*Men*
Married	*b*	–0.297	0.131	–0.026	0.297	0.154	0.386
	z	2.13	0.86	0.24	2.28	1.17	3.15
Children <6 at Home	*b*	0.023	–0.109	0.039	0.042	–0.098	–0.078
	z	0.12	1.01	0.29	0.37	0.64	0.81
Not a US Citizen	*b*	0.279	0.11	–0.427	–0.331	–0.256	–0.219
	z	0.92	0.51	1.89	1.69	0.96	1.59
Career Year	*b*	0.569	0.731	0.562	0.638	0.487	0.62
	z	18.5	27.44	21.06	24.65	15.76	26.9
Career Year2	*b*	–0.011	–0.013	–0.009	–0.01	–0.008	–0.01
	z	12.14	17.66	10.73	13.15	7.83	15.91
Engineering vs. Social/Behavioral Sciences	*b*	–0.46	–0.503	0.163	–0.26	0.307	0.422
	z	1	1.99	0.74	1.39	1.11	2.97
Math vs. Social/Behavioral Sciences	*b*	–0.31	0.026	0.328	0.011	0.462	0.56
	z	1.61	0.15	1.95	0.06	1.99	3.28
Physical Sciences vs. Social/Behavioral Sciences	*b*	–0.347	–0.601	–0.383	–0.504	0.04	–0.265
	z	1.75	3.56	2.32	3.13	0.16	1.65
Life Sciences vs. Social/Behavioral Sciences	*b*	–0.86	–0.814	–0.255	–0.45	–0.217	–0.734
	z	4.86	5.49	1.71	2.98	1.55	5.44
Medical vs. Research I	*b*	–0.365	–0.546	–0.922	–1.166	–0.729	–1.207
	z	1.56	3.68	5.44	7.9	3.82	8.64
Research II vs. Research I	*b*	0.551	0.203	0.42	0.248	0.086	0.347
	z	1.91	1.09	2.16	1.41	0.36	2.13
Doctoral vs. Research I	*b*	0.283	–0.099	0.11	0.029	–0.043	0.015
	z	1.38	0.59	0.65	0.18	0.21	0.11

Master's vs. Research I	*b*	0.765	0.727	0.405	0.255	0.42	–0.121
	z	4.54	4.96	2.93	1.76	2.57	0.96
Baccalaureate vs. Research I	*b*	0.318	0.665	0.483	0.301	0.557	0.405
	z	1.34	3.2	2.53	1.51	2.43	2.03
Private vs. Research I	*b*	–0.51	–0.709	–0.482	–0.536	–0.512	–0.733
	z	3.56	6	4.23	4.95	3.84	7.41
Ph.D. Prestige	*b*	–0.104	0.014	0.029	0.062	–0.187	–0.047
	z	1.4	0.22	0.43	0.98	2.32	0.83
Time from Baccalaureate	*b*	1.219	1.423	0.973	0.619	0.861	0.397
to Ph.D. > 10 Years	*z*	7.4	8.87	7.54	4.3	6.21	3.14
Missing Data on Having Young Children	*b*	–0.046	–0.219	–0.105	0.154		
	z	0.18	1.04	0.65	0.97		
Missing Data on Prestige of Ph.D.	*b*	0.459	0.393	0.361	0.199		
	z	2.79	3.54	2.86	1.86		
Constant	*b*	–3.082	–4.066	–4.383	–4.834	–3.365	–4.456
	z	8.94	12.55	13.11	14.41	8.75	14.31
Observations		8242	6113	3773	6664	2296	7105

TABLE D-13 Multinomial Logit Analysis on Academic Rank, by Sex and Year of Survey. *b* Indicates Regression Coefficient; *z* Indicates Value of *z*-test

Panel A: 1979

	Women		Men	
	Asst. Prof. vs Full Prof.	Assoc. Prof. vs Full Prof	Asst. Prof. vs Full Prof	Assoc. Prof. vs Full Prof
Career Yr.	–0.841	–0.363	–1.015	–0.404
	20.33	10.22	33.83	16.02
Career Yr Squared	0.016	0.006	0.019	0.005
	15.41	6.52	27.25	7.69
Engineering[1]	0.171	0.011	–0.434	–0.202
	0.27	0.02	1.53	1.13
Mathematics[1]	0.537	0.211	0.502	0.385
	2.31	1.14	2.61	2.88
Physical Sciences[1]	0.818	0.602	0.498	0.431
	3.49	3.38	2.66	3.44
Biological Sciences[1]	0.392	0.095	0.629	0.447
	2.00	0.59	4.07	4.22
Medical School[2]	1.273	0.638	0.851	0.574
	4.09	2.36	5.05	4.81
Research II[2]	–0.785	–0.592	–0.355	–0.310
	2.37	2.35	1.75	2.24
Doctoral[2]	–0.542	–0.141	0.494	0.536
	2.17	0.72	2.66	4.31
Master's[2]	–0.996	–0.412	–0.796	–0.173
	4.95	2.62	5.02	1.62
Baccalaureate[2]	–0.748	–0.617	–0.193	0.114
	2.83	2.85	0.87	0.74
Constant	7.109	4.094	7.176	3.791
	19.32	12.09	27.12	16.55
Observations	2129	2129	6113	6113

NOTE: 1-Comparison is to Social/Behavioral Sciences. 2-Comparison is to Research I University. Absolute value of *z*-statistics in parentheses.

continued

TABLE D-13 Continued

Panel B: 1989

	Women		Men	
	Asst. Prof. vs Full Prof.	Assoc. Prof. vs Full Prof	Asst. Prof. vs Full Prof	Assoc. Prof. vs Full Prof
Career Yr.	–0.846	–0.349	–1.032	–0.384
	24.37	11.10	32.94	14.83
Career Yr Squared	0.015	0.005	0.018	0.005
	16.90	6.18	25.10	7.54
Engineering[1]	–0.559	–0.342	–0.506	–0.454
	1.77	1.21	2.25	2.87
Mathematics[1]	–0.020	0.165	0.066	0.100
	0.10	1.17	0.33	0.82
Physical Sciences[1]	0.581	0.177	0.434	–0.026
	3.07	1.25	2.37	0.22
Biological Sciences[1]	–0.197	0.052	0.360	0.024
	1.26	0.45	2.22	0.24
Medical School[2]	0.741	0.354	1.077	0.545
	3.51	2.09	6.42	4.82
Research II[2]	0.027	0.400	–0.364	–0.036
	0.11	2.08	1.82	0.28
Doctoral[2]	–0.133	0.285	0.088	0.474
	0.65	1.88	0.47	4.12
Master's[2]	–0.867	–0.428	–0.597	–0.051
	5.38	3.60	3.71	0.52
Baccalaureate[2]	–0.757	–0.436	–0.245	–0.137
	3.54	2.70	1.12	0.95
Constant	8.101	4.361	8.850	4.512
	23.35	13.53	28.79	17.05
Observations	3779	3779	6681	6681

NOTE: 1-Comparison is to Social/Behavioral Sciences. 2-Comparison is to Research I University. Absolute value of z-statistics in parentheses

continued

TABLE D-13 Continued

Panel C: 1995

	Women		Men	
	Asst. Prof. vs Full Prof.	Assoc. Prof. vs Full Prof	Asst. Prof. vs Full Prof	Assoc. Prof. vs Full Prof
Career Yr.	–0.827	–0.345	–1.013	–0.391
	18.05	8.56	35.53	17.01
Career Yr Squared	0.014	0.005	0.017	0.005
	11.42	4.78	27.01	9.00
Engineering[1]	–0.892	–0.709	–0.660	–0.069
	2.20	1.93	3.67	0.55
Mathematics[1]	–0.674	–0.052	–0.008	0.264
	2.17	0.22	0.04	2.13
Physical Sciences[1]	0.044	–0.160	0.355	–0.006
	0.13	0.59	1.91	0.05
Biological Sciences[1]	–0.108	–0.051	0.628	0.035
	0.59	0.36	3.96	0.36
Medical School[2]	0.717	0.302	1.678	0.595
	2.83	1.45	10.20	5.17
Research II[2]	0.221	0.278	–0.144	0.034
	0.67	1.04	0.74	0.26
Doctoral[2]	–0.158	0.282	0.407	0.502
	0.59	1.32	2.44	4.46
Master's[2]	–0.708	–0.076	–0.217	0.072
	3.37	0.46	1.47	0.75
Baccalaureate[2]	–0.164	0.225	–0.131	–0.058
	0.57	0.99	0.58	0.40
Constant	8.387	4.493	9.133	4.863
	18.91	10.99	31.12	19.50
Observations	2300	2300	7114	7114

NOTE: 1-Comparison is to Social/Behavioral Sciences. 2-Comparison is to Research I University. Absolute value of *z*-statistics in parentheses.

Appendix E

Table

TABLE E-1 Regression Estimates of Log of Salary by Years for Tenure-Track Faculty at Research Universities, by Sex and Year of Survey

Variable		1979		1989		1995	
		Men	*Women*	*Men*	*Women*	*Men*	*Women*
Years since Ph.D.	*b*	0.012	0.014	0.009	0.015	0.009	0.014
: in years	*t*	24.58	10.33	15.37	13.18	15.03	11.62
Years squared.	*b*	–8.1E-05	–0.00014	–0.000082	–0.00024	–8.3E-05	–0.00016
: in years squared	*t*	7.06	3.58	6.15	8.11	6.25	5.56
Is Assistant Professor?	*b*	–0.344	–0.348	–0.344	–0.346	–0.338	–0.331
: binary	*t*	88.29	34.94	77.86	41.57	63.86	36.41
Is Associate Professor?	*b*	–0.212	–0.192	–0.244	–0.208	–0.261	–0.255
:binary	*t*	86.66	24.83	91.38	35.55	83.7	39.14
Missing data on Ph.D. quality?	*b*	–0.002	–0.012	0.039	0.032	0.103	0.153
:binary	*t*	0.52	0.84	7.94	2.83	16.02	10.93
Ph.D. quality.	*b*	0.004	–0.01	0.013	0.01	0.018	0.039
: 1-5	*t*	3.63	2.83	10.91	3.64	10.98	11.08
Ph.D. in engineering?	*b*	0.08	0.096	0.201	0.254	0.08	0.086
: binary	*t*	30.43	4.56	72.43	22.85	25.28	7.99
Ph.D. in mathematics?	b	0.027	0.034	0.1	0.099	–0.021	0.004
: binary	*t*	8.35	2.88	27.97	10.63	5.34	0.33
Ph.D. in physical sciences?	*b*	0.018	0.001	0.039	0.011	–0.035	–0.125
: binary	*t*	6.29	0.11	12.65	1.2	9.83	12.17
Ph.D. in social/behavioral science?	*b*	0.055	0.025	0.059	0.015	–0.038	–0.067
: binary	*t*	21.03	3.42	21.77	2.69	12.32	11.94
Elapsed time to Ph.D. > 10?	*b*	0.034	0.027	0.025	0.04	0.025	0.021
: binary	*t*	10.78	4.16	7.46	7.81	6.3	3.65
Data on elapsed time is missing?	*b*	0.036	–0.017	0.063	0.063	0.029	0.005
: binary	*t*	11.98	1.65	17.66	7.29	7.23	0.64

Job in private university?	*b*	0.001	–0.003	0.087	0.037	0.112	0.071
: binary	*t*	0.25	0.52	36.72	8.03	40.82	13.25
Job in Research I School?	*b*	0.023	0.017	0.061	0.008	0.08	0.064
: binary	*t*	12.41	2.85	28.12	1.69	28.98	11.28
Prestige of employing department.	*b*	0.004	0.015	0.008	0.026	0.006	0
: 1-5	*t*	2.57	3.4	5.35	7.24	6.67	0.05
Prestige is missing?	*b*	0.039	0.056	0.027	0.123	0	0
: binary	*t*	8.68	3.91	5.52	10.44	.	.
Number of publications.	*b*	0.002	0.002	0.005	0.004	0.003	0.004
	t	20.77	4.58	46.8	12.19	32.13	18.36
Constant	*b*	3.987	3.972	4.04	3.967	3.956	3.827
	t	510.86	174.48	445.44	201.32	378.69	194.97
Observations		39238	3005	50612	7580	52749	10187
R-squared		0.64	0.68	0.54	0.56	0.43	0.47

NOTE:: b = unstandardized regression coefficient; t = absolute value of t-statistics.

Glossary

- **CEEWISE**: The Committee on the Education and Employment of Women in Science and Education of the National Research Council.
- **CWSE**: The Committee on Women in Science and Engineering of the National Research Council.
- **DRF**: Doctorate Records File which combines information for all years of the SDR.
- **ISI**: Institute for Scientific Information.
- **NRC**: The National Research Council.
- **NSF**: The National Science Foundation.
- **OSEP**: The Office of Scientific and Engineering Personnel of the National Research Council.
- **R&D**: Research and development.
- **RA**: Research assistantship.
- **S&E**: Science and engineering.
- **SED**: The Survey of Earned Doctorates.
- **SDR**: The Survey of Doctorate Recipients.
- **TA**: Teaching assistantship.

- *Labor Force* is defined as Ph.D.s in S&E fields who are living in the United States and are under the age of 75. The labor force includes both part time workers and those who are unemployed, including the small number of scientists and engineers who are not looking for work. Retired scientists are not counted in the labor force.
- *Full-time labor force* is defined as members of the labor force who are working full time in some area of science or engineering.
- *Employed Outside of S&E* includes doctoral scientists and engineers who are working full time in occupations that are not directly related to S&E as defined by the *Survey of Doctorate Recipients*.
- *Unemployed* includes those without jobs who are seeking work.
- *Out of the Labor Force* are those who are not working and not seeking work.
- *Underemployment* includes part-time workers and the unemployed.